The Noumenal Republic

The Noumenal Republic
Critical Constructivism After Kant

Rainer Forst

polity

First published in German as *Die noumenale Republik* by Suhrkamp © Rainer Forst 2021

This English edition © Rainer Forst 2024

The right of Rainer Forst to be identified as Author of this Work has been asserted in accordance with the UK Copyright, Designs and Patents Act 1988.

First published in 2024 by Polity Press

Polity Press
65 Bridge Street
Cambridge CB2 1UR, UK

Polity Press
111 River Street
Hoboken, NJ 07030, USA

All rights reserved. Except for the quotation of short passages for the purpose of criticism and review, no part of this publication may be reproduced, stored in a retrieval system or transmitted, in any form or by any means, electronic, mechanical, photocopying, recording or otherwise, without the prior permission of the publisher.

ISBN-13: 978-1-5095-6225-1 <hardback>
ISBN-13: 978-1-5095-6226-8 <paperback>

A catalogue record for this book is available from the British Library.

Library of Congress Control Number: 2023945920

Typeset in 10.5 on 12pt Sabon
by Fakenham Prepress Solutions, Fakenham, Norfolk NR21 8NL
Printed and bound in Great Britain by TJ Books Ltd, Padstow, Cornwall

The publisher has used its best endeavors to ensure that the URLs for external websites referred to in this book are correct and active at the time of going to press. However, the publisher has no responsibility for the websites and can make no guarantee that a site will remain live or that the content is or will remain appropriate.

Every effort has been made to trace all copyright holders, but if any have been overlooked the publisher will be pleased to include any necessary credits in any subsequent reprint or edition.

For further information on Polity, visit our website: politybooks.com

CONTENTS

Preface vii
Sources x

Introduction: Between Two Worlds: Critical Constructivism After Kant — 1

I. Autonomy, Progress and Solidarity: Basic Questions of Social Philosophy — 23
1. Noumenal Alienation: Rousseau, Kant and Marx on the Dialectics of Self-Determination — 25
2. The Justification of Progress and the Progress of Justification — 54
3. The Rule of Unreason: Analyzing (Anti-)Democratic Regression — 73
4. Solidarity: Concept, Conceptions and Contexts — 85
5. Social Cohesion: On the Analysis of a Difficult Concept — 101

II. Justice, Rights and Non-Domination in a New Key: Critical Political Theory — 115
6. Normativity and Reality: Toward a Critical and Realistic Theory of Politics — 117
7. The Point and Ground of Human Rights: A Kantian Constructivist View — 132
8. A Critical Theory of Transnational (In-)Justice: Realistic in the Right Way — 153
9. Structural Injustice with a Name, Structural Domination without a Face? — 178

10. Kantian Republicanism versus the Neo-Republican
    Machine: The Meaning and Practice of Political Autonomy 194

III. Debates: Political Liberalism, Luck Egalitarianism,
    Contractualism and Discourse Ethics   213
11. Political Liberalism: A Kantian View   215
12. The Point of Justice: On the Paradigmatic Incompatibility
    Between Rawlsian "Justice as Fairness" and Luck
    Egalitarianism   240
13. Justification Fundamentalism: A Discourse-Theoretical
    Interpretation of Scanlon's Contractualism   255
14. The Autonomy of Autonomy: On Jürgen Habermas's
    Auch eine Geschichte der Philosophie   267

Bibliography   281
Index   300

PREFACE

Human beings have the ability to transcend their reality. In the normal course of their lives and actions, they question whether this course can be improved and whether it is generally going in the right direction. The same is true of the orders to which they belong. Wherever people seek orientation, engage in criticism or strive for progress, the counterfactual appears in the factual, what ought to be in what is. In this book I try to explain how this transcending power should be understood. Taking Kant as my starting point, I argue that, as rational, justifying beings, we can go beyond the habitual normativity of the spaces of justification in which we operate by appeal to a critical normativity whose radical core points to the principle of self-legislation, in the individual and the collective sense. A critical-constructivist theory with a practical intent, as I develop it in the following, must answer the question of how we can actually become what we already are in a "noumenal" sense, namely autonomous authorities with respect to the norms that claim to be valid for us.

No one thinks for him- or herself alone, certainly not a theorist of justification. So, at this point I must express my gratitude for the many stimuli I have received through talks, lectures, conferences and feedback (not least through the privilege of numerous workshops devoted to my theory). To try to name everyone who deserves consideration in this regard would lead to an interminable list. Here, therefore, I will mention the most important institutions and individuals who provide the framework for my work; others will be acknowledged in the introduction and at the beginning of the relevant chapters. In the first place, I would like to thank the members of my research colloquium, which has existed since 2004 and which for several years I have been running with Darrel Moellendorf.

PREFACE

The discussions conducted in the colloquium with internationally established as well as with younger colleagues are a constant source of learning. For many years, the context for the colloquium has been provided by the interdisciplinary Research Center "Normative Orders," the Centre for Advanced Studies "Justitia Amplificata" (and the successor program "Justitia") and the Leibniz Award research group "Transnational Justice," as well as by more recent networks such as the "Research Institute Social Cohesion" and the initiative "ConTrust – Trust in Conflict." For this, I would like to thank not only the funding institutions – the German Research Foundation, the Alfons und Gertrud Kassel-Stiftung, the Federal Ministry of Education and Research, the State of Hesse and Goethe University Frankfurt – but also the colleagues with whom I currently lead, or in the past led, these major undertakings, Nicole Deitelhoff, Klaus Günther and Stefan Gosepath.

In addition, I benefited from numerous discussions at the Berlin Social Science Center, where I hold a research professorship; in this context, I owe special thanks to Michael Zürn. In the fall of 2019, I had the honor of being part of the University of Michigan Law School as a Thomas E. Sunderland Faculty Fellow and Visiting Professor, where I had many productive encounters; for that, my special thanks go to Daniel Halberstam. The same holds for short-term visiting professorships at Rice University in Houston and at the University of Washington in Seattle, for which I am grateful to Christian Emden and the late Bill Talbott.

In preparing the manuscript, Sonja Sickert provided as always major assistance, and I would not have been able to accomplish it without the excellent work of Aline Fehr, Felix Kämper, Greta Kolbe, Carlos Morado, Jan Paul Reimann, and Amadeus Ulrich. I would also like to thank Ian Malcolm from Polity for his trusting collaboration and also Ellen MacDonald-Kramer, Rachel Moore and Susan Beer for their help in publishing this book. As always, Ciaran Cronin's translation skills were of great value in clarifying my ideas.

When expressing my gratitude for the happy moments of cooperation that sustain my efforts, I am particularly concerned to mention three colleagues who are no longer with us and whose absence I feel acutely. The untimely deaths of two longtime friends and outstanding colleagues, Glen Newey (1961–2017) and Rainer Schmalz-Bruns (1954–2020), with whom I often engaged in passionate debates, opened up an irreparable breach in the networks of discourse that are important for me. With Karl-Otto Apel (1922–2017), one of my revered teachers from early student days onward has passed away. I remember him with immense gratitude for how he embodied and communicated his enthusiasm for the "ultimate" questions of philosophy.

As always, the greatest debt of gratitude is to my family, Mechthild, Sophie and Jonathan, for inspiration, support and much besides.

SOURCES

Chapter 1: "Noumenal Alienation: Rousseau, Kant and Marx on the Dialectics of Self-Determination." *Kantian Review* 22:4, 2017: 523–551.

Chapter 2: "The Justification of Progress and the Progress of Justification." In A. Allen and E. Mendieta (eds.), *Justification and Emancipation: The Critical Theory of Rainer Forst*. University Park: The Pennsylvania State University Press, 2019, pp. 17–37.

Chapter 3: "The Rule of Unreason: Analyzing (Anti-)Democratic Regression." *Constellations* 30:3, 2023: 217–224.

Chapter 4: "Solidarity: Concept, Conceptions and Contexts." In A. Sangiovanni and J. Viehoff (eds.), *The Virtue of Solidarity*. Oxford: Oxford University Press, forthcoming.

Chapter 5: Social Cohesion: On the Analysis of a Difficult Concept. Unpublished in English.

Chapter 6: "Normativity and Reality: Toward a Critical and Realistic Theory of Politics." In S. Eich, A. Jurkevics, N. Nathwani and N. Siegel (eds.), *Another Universalism: Seyla Benhabib and the Future of Critical Theory*. New York: Columbia University Press, 2023, pp. 36–50.

Chapter 7: "The Point and Ground of Human Rights: A Kantian Constructivist View." In D. Held and P. Maffettone (eds.), *Global Political Theory*. Cambridge: Polity, 2016, pp. 22–39.

SOURCES

Chapter 8: "A Critical Theory of Transnational (In-)Justice: Realistic in the Right Way." In T. Brooks (ed.), *The Oxford Handbook of Global Justice*. Oxford: Oxford University Press, 2020, pp. 451–472.

Chapter 9: Structural Injustice with a Name, Structural Domination without a Face? Unpublished in English.

Chapter 10: "Kantian Republicanism versus the Neo-Republican Machine: The Meaning and Practice of Political Autonomy." In J. Christ, K. Lepold, D. Loick and T. Stahl (eds.), *Debating Critical Theory: Engagements with Axel Honneth*. Lanham: Rowman & Littlefield, 2020, pp. 17–34.

Chapter 11: "Political Liberalism: A Kantian View." *Ethics* 128:1, 2017: 123–144.

Chapter 12: "The Point of Justice: On the Paradigmatic Incompatibility between Rawlsian 'Justice as Fairness' and Luck Egalitarianism." In J. Mandle and S. Roberts-Cady (eds.), *John Rawls: Debating the Major Questions*. New York: Oxford University Press, 2020, pp. 148–160.

Chapter 13: "Justification Fundamentalism: A Discourse-Theoretical Interpretation of Scanlon's Contractualism." In M. Stepanians and M. Frauchiger (eds.), *Reason, Justification, and Contractualism: Themes from Scanlon*. Berlin: De Gruyter, 2021, pp. 45–58.

Chapter 14: "The Autonomy of Autonomy: On Jürgen Habermas's *Auch eine Geschichte der Philosophie*." *Constellations* 28:1, 2021: 17–24.

The articles have been slightly edited for the present volume. Permission to reprint these texts is gratefully acknowledged.

INTRODUCTION
Between Two Worlds: Critical Constructivism After Kant

Reason thus refers every maxim of the will as universally legislating to every other will [...], and it does so not for the sake of any other practical motivating ground or future advantage, but from the idea of the *dignity* of a rational being that obeys no law other than that which at the same time it itself gives.[1]

Now in this way a world of rational beings (*mundus intelligibilis*) as a kingdom of ends is possible, and possible through their own legislation of all persons as members.[2]

The idea of a constitution in harmony with the natural right of human beings, one namely in which the citizens obedient to the law, besides being united, ought also to be legislative, lies at the basis of all political forms; and the body politic which, conceived in conformity to it by virtue of pure concepts of reason, signifies a Platonic ideal (*respublica noumenon*), is not an empty figment of the brain, but rather the eternal norm for all civil organization in general, and averts all war.[3]

1 The idea of Kantian constructivism

Kant's words seem to lead us into the depths (or shallows) of his metaphysics of two worlds – the one intellectual–noumenal,

---

[1] Kant, *Groundwork of the Metaphysics of Morals*, IV:434 (emphasis in original). References to Kant's writings give the volume and page numbers of the Royal Prussian Academy of Sciences edition (*Kants gesammelte Schriften*), which are included in the margins of the translations. The *Critique of Pure Reason* utilizes the customary format of "A" and "B" to refer to the first and second edition. Pages of the English translations are only given where editions do not contain the Academy pagination.
[2] Ibid., IV:438.
[3] Kant, *The Conflict of the Faculties*, VII:90f.

the other empirical – and thus to land us in all of the problems associated with this dualism. Far from wishing to trivialize these problems, I want to propose a different perspective on these questions *after Kant*, or rather two such perspectives: according to the first, there is a sense in which we cannot escape such dualisms in our moral and political practice; according to the second, this dualism loses the appearance of an aporetic metaphysical problem once we understand the world we live in in the correct pragmatist sense, that is, reasonably.

Let me begin with the first of these perspectives. Anyone who takes seriously the statements to be found in human rights declarations to the effect that "All human beings are born free and equal in dignity and rights" (Article 1 of the Universal Declaration of Human Rights of 1948) and that this dignity is "inviolable" (Article 1[1] of the German Basic Law of 1949), rather than dismissing them as ideological or utopian platitudes, must be able to explain the sense in which these propositions are true. They do not describe the empirical reality, since it is simply not true that all people are born in equal, inviolable dignity and with equal rights – rather, many of them grow up in conditions of extreme inequality, dependency and ignominy, from which they can hardly escape. This analysis is factually true. But can both truths hold simultaneously – that of the normative statement and that of the social reality? They must, for otherwise we could not adopt a justified critical stance on reality – and we might even be betraying those whose human rights are trampled underfoot.

The philosophical discussion about how such counterfactual normative statements can be justified is indeed interminable; but that they require a justification seems indisputable. This provides the point of departure for my interpretation and further development of Kant. When we raise the question of a justification for the normative status of dignity, it may be helpful to reflect on ourselves as the beings who pose this question and who owe each other an answer. For we not only ask for reasons, but also use, evaluate and justify reasons. And, where we must acknowledge that there are no good reasons for denying others equal respect, we show ourselves and them respect as justifying beings, as equal normative authorities who owe each other good reasons for how they treat one another and for the normative order to which they are subject. Then the status of equal dignity is not justified based on an empirical proof or a divine norm, which would in any case be impossible, but through rational recognition of ourselves and others as justifying beings, as authorities in the space

INTRODUCTION

of justifications who form a community of justification.[4] In Kant's terms, this implies the mutual respect of persons as self-determined purposive ends in themselves, as legislating members in the "kingdom of ends," a status that constitutes their "worthiness" (*Würdigkeit*).[5] Is there any better justification of this dignity than being an *autonomous* member of the "law-giving" community regarding the norms that should apply to all?[6] That this reflection, specifically in virtue of the emphasis it places on the equal status of being a lawmaking member in the space of justifications, is unavoidably a form of moral reflection Kant explains by the fact that, as justifying beings who ask the practical question "What should I do?," we are already operating as *responsible* subjects in the space of *practical* reason. Here there is no escape, for our world *is* the world of justifications. However, we are not simply subject to it, but should understand ourselves in it – and this is Kant's revolutionary insight – in a *counterfactual* sense as legislative authorities.[7]

Turning now to the second perspective: What kind of world is this, the world of justifications? Let us assume in a realistic, pragmatic spirit that our world of action is indeed a world of justifications that guide our thought and action. Then these are, first of all, *de facto* valid justifications that can be quite diverse in nature: conventional, instrumental, religious, legal, well or poorly considered, blinded by ideology, and so on. This is in fact the empirical–noumenal substance, so to speak, from which we draw the justificatory material for our action; the normative orders within which we operate are, in this factual sense, "orders of justification." But, if we understand ourselves as beings endowed with practical reason, it is not only a matter of acting *rationally* and prudently in these already established justificatory spaces. We can also ask whether they are *reasonable*, and this includes asking whether they are morally reasonable – that is, *justifiable* on moral grounds. In every human practice, however congealed it may be with ideology (where "ideology" means justifying the unjustifiable), one always has the possibility, even if only slight, of asking: Are these norms, customs and traditions, these laws and ordinances, this ruling order as a whole, justified? In accordance with which criteria should this be evaluated?

---

[4] On such a conception of authority, see Darwall, *The Second-Person Standpoint*. O'Neill, *Constructing Authorities*, stresses the discursive authority of reason.
[5] Kant, *Groundwork of the Metaphysics of Morals*, IV:439.
[6] "*Autonomy* is thus the ground of the dignity of human and of every rational nature." Kant, *Groundwork of the Metaphysics of Morals*, IV:436 (emphasis in original).
[7] See Schneewind, *The Invention of Autonomy*.

INTRODUCTION

Where this critical question arises, it may be stifled *de facto* in the space of *noumenal power*. However, it can be raised over and over again, and morally speaking it *must* be raised for the sake of the justifiability of our actions and of the structures that guide and bind us. To rise above the existing space of justifications, perhaps initially to a limited and subsequently a greater extent, is part of the human practice of justification when this is not completely obstructed, which means that humans, as participants in this practice, are potentially *noumenal beings* who *transcend* the reality they encounter. Kant's reflection on humans as legislating beings who enjoy equal status in the realm of ends, and are obliged to offer each other reasons that are uniformly generalizable, is in my view the appropriate reflection on our situation as justifying, transcending beings in this sense. We belong to the factual world of justifications, but we are also members of a realm of critical problematization and of mutual respect that binds us here and now and *places a duty on us to offer justifications* in moral or political contexts. The kingdom of ends – properly understood – is *of this world*. We must not succumb to the misconception that we are members of two strictly separate worlds, nor to ontological or metaphysical dualism, but must recognize that we would not be able to orient ourselves reasonably in this one world if we could not question and transcend the given justifications. In other words, the *counterfactual* question concerning better justifications is part of the *facticity* of our normative world of justification. The worlds in question, the noumenal and the empirical, are therefore not really two separate worlds, but two different *perspectives* on ourselves as subjects of justification. Thus, the counterfactual, transcending-noumenal normativity of self-determined legislation appears within the *de facto* normativity of our empirical–noumenal spaces of justification – as a prefiguration of genuine individual and collective autonomy.

What does asking for reasons in this transcending sense involve and what kind of validity can the corresponding answers claim? This is where what I call "critical constructivism after Kant" comes into play and, since I discuss this in previous works[8] and in the chapters in this volume, I will confine myself here to the main lines of argument. If we formulate the question concerning the reason-giving transcending of given justifications in *transcendental* terms, then it

---

[8] See in particular the following sections from my books: *Contexts of Justice*, chs. 4 and 5; *The Right to Justification*, chs. 1–4; *Justification and Critique*, chs. 1, 2 and 4, and *Normativity and Power*, chs. 1–3.

concerns the conditions of the possibility of justifying valid norms of responsible action (or of political rule). Evidently, this transcendental reflection does not detach itself from human practice so much that it loses its connection to the latter; rather, the question of justification is as much an imminent as a transcending one. It refers to the faculty that is the sole faculty of critical justification – namely, reason. In practical contexts, this means practical reason, which on a Kantian understanding is not just a faculty with knowledge of *how* moral norms can be justified, but one which also knows and recognizes *that* responsible individuals in moral contexts must justify themselves by appeal to appropriate reasons. In moral contexts, therefore, there is an *imperative* to justify that is recognized by practical reason, and I express this in terms of a moral *duty* or a moral *right* to justification in contexts involving generally and reciprocally binding norms.

In order to determine what constitutes an appropriate justification of such norms, we reconstruct the validity claims they raise and ask what it would mean to redeem them.[9] In moral contexts, norms claim to be reciprocally and generally valid in the strict sense. This means that they must be redeemable in justificatory discourses in which the criteria of reciprocity and generality hold sway regarding the *procedure* itself (who may participate? how are the criteria of validity to be applied?) and the *quality* of the justified norms (are they reciprocally and generally rejectable?). In political contexts in which, for example, basic norms of justice are at stake, the same criteria apply, although we must distinguish between a core moral content and a specific form of organization of an order of justification, as well as between basic norms of justice and further norms legitimated on this basis. In both the moral context and that of political–social justice, the distinction between factual and counterfactual discourses must be taken into account and, at the same time, their immanent, dialectical connection must be recognized: While the counterfactual question of whether a norm is really (reciprocally and generally) justified must always remain present in both contexts, both are also concerned with conducting real discourses of justification. The reason for this, in moral contexts, is that respect for others as equal normative authorities requires taking their perspective seriously and, in political contexts, that the practice of reciprocal–general justification is *the* practice of justice. All other relevant normative notions of freedom,

---

[9] This is what constitutes the discourse-ethical core of my approach. I connect this with the constructivist approaches of Onora O'Neill and John Rawls, which I have explained elsewhere; see fn. 8.

equality, democracy or human rights must be justified on this basis, as I try to show in the chapters comprising Part II of this book.

Why do I speak of "constructivism" in this context? Here we should extricate ourselves from some overhasty metaethical and metaphysical assumptions. The idea that valid norms are the result of a justification procedure that heeds certain criteria of reason, so that norms are "constructed," should not be understood in the sense of *metaphysical* constructivism; what is meant is rather *practical* constructivism, according to which values and normative reasons do not belong to a higher-order reality but are instead constructed practically, and thus are brought into being for us. Whether such moral norms and the reasons for them are *discovered* or *created* together in reciprocal–general justification procedures is a philosophically interesting question,[10] but a secondary one when it comes to the validity of the procedure. More important is *who* constructs *what* in the process, and *on what basis*, and how the *validity* of these norms is justified – namely, in the constructivist sense, through the procedure *alone*.[11] The idea underlying Kantian constructivism can be expressed as follows: Those norms are valid that emerge from a justificatory construction procedure that contains the decisive normative conditions of norm generation in an appropriate way.[12]

This formulation clarifies what is often overlooked in theories and in critiques of constructivism.[13] For even the discursive–factual, and not just the counterfactual–hypothetical, generation of norms can only succeed if the authoritative, fundamental normativity is already contained in the procedure that is supposed to lend validity to the constructed norms. The relevant principle here I call the principle of the *conservation and production of normativity*; it says that a procedure can only generate binding normativity if there is a basic

---

[10] See recently Larmore, *Morality and Metaphysics*.
[11] See the depiction of the construction plan of reason in O'Neill, *Towards Justice and Virtue*, pp. 59–61. See also her *Constructing Authorities*, esp. chs. 4 and 5.
[12] Here I leave to one side the genealogy of constructivism in moral philosophy with regard to Kant. It should be noted, however, that while Rawls's 1980 Dewey Lectures on "Kantian Constructivism in Moral Theory" initiated the debate in the Anglo-American world, this had already been discussed in German philosophy in the context of the Erlangen and Constance schools (see, for example, Lorenzen, *Normative Logic and Ethics*), which played an important role in the development of discourse ethics beginning in the 1960s. On this, see in particular Apel, "The Apriori of the Communication Community and the Foundations of Ethics," pp. 256–285.
[13] Andrea Sangiovanni's critique in his "Scottish Constructivism and The Right to Justification" brought home to me the importance of this point. See my response in "Justifying Justification," pp. 170–177.

normativity that grounds the procedure and is operative in it.[14] It follows that any construction of norms must rest on a basis that cannot be constructed in the same way as the constructed norms, because the process must ensure that the latter have been constructed in the right way. This is why, in Kant, there is a categorical imperative of practical reason that serves to justify categorically valid moral imperatives and why, in discourse ethics, there are principles from which the formal features of discourse are derived or, in Rawls, an "original position" in which principles of justice are constructed. In my approach, constructivism means that the *principle of justification*, which specifies, depending on context, which norms are to be constructively justified in which way, must not only be normatively *binding* (as in Kant, and in discourse ethics, albeit in an ambivalent sense),[15] but also that it cannot itself be constructed, but has a *reconstructive* character. The underlying normativity of this principle grounds the normativity of the (justified) norms constructed on this basis.

Rawls expressed this with exemplary clarity in his pioneering interpretation of Kantian constructivism. According to Rawls, Kant's categorical imperative is not constructed but "*laid out*" as a procedure[16] based on a reflection of practical reason as it appears in moral deliberation and judgment. This is why Kant refuses to deduce the principle of morality itself from another principle; according to Kant, it "itself has no need of justifying grounds,"[17] but it does require a reflection on reason as a justificatory, responsibility bearing faculty. Moreover, according to Rawls, underlying the Kantian approach is a particular notion of persons as being able to use practical reasons specifically in community with others, a notion that is neither constructed nor set forth, but is instead "elicited" – in my terms, reconstructed – from our moral reflection.[18] Rawls expresses this point, both with reference to Kant and to his own "non-metaphysical" version of "political" constructivism, by saying that the construction process is based on "principles of practical

---

[14] See also Chapter 7, section 7.3, in this volume.
[15] While Jürgen Habermas rejects the morally binding character of the discourse principle, Karl-Otto Apel ascribes normativity to it in too emphatic a sense, arguing on transcendental-pragmatic grounds that all general discursive claims to validity, and not only moral validity claims, entail the duty to engage in argumentation. On Habermas, see Chapter 14 in this volume; on Apel, see my discussion in *The Right to Justification*, pp. 55–57, and in my essay "Letzte Gründe."
[16] Rawls, "Themes in Kant's Moral Philosophy," p. 99.
[17] Kant, *Critique of Practical Reason*, V:47.
[18] Rawls, "Themes in Kant's Moral Philosophy," p. 99.

reason in union with conceptions of society and person," which are themselves "ideas of practical reason."[19]

My own conception accordingly assumes the following order of argumentation. First, the general principle of justification must be reconstructed as a *principle of practical reason*. It states that norms must "earn" their validity in a way that corresponds to their claim to validity – that is, moral norms that claim to be valid in a strictly reciprocal and general way must be justified in discourses of justification that reflect the criteria of reciprocity and generality procedurally and as regards their content. They are *criteria of practical reason*. Reciprocity in this context means that nobody may make claims that are denied to others (reciprocity of content) and that nobody may simply impute their own values, interests or needs to others, even in a well-meaning sense, but must seek a language of justification that can be shared in a normative sense (reciprocity of reasons). Generality means that no one may be excluded from the community of equal subjects of justification for whom the respective norms claim to be equally valid. Discourses of justification that are guided by these criteria – both on the factual and the counterfactual understanding – are *procedures of practical reason*.

It follows from the foregoing that the authorities of this constructive justification are the persons who have a duty to respond to each other in this way and thus to take responsibility for their actions (or their normative order). This conception of persons as the highest normative authorities who know and recognize that they have a *duty of and a right to justification* is a *conception of practical reason*. All of these notions are the product of a consistent, recursive[20] reflection on what it means to be a morally or politically responsible subject of justification. There is no secret metaphysics at work here, but instead a fundamental reflection on what it means to "stand" in the space of normative justifications, that is, to enjoy the status of author and addressee of norms.[21]

---

[19] Rawls, *Political Liberalism*, p. 90. On the similarities and differences between Rawls and Kant, see most recently my "Political Liberalism: A Kantian View," Chapter 11 in this volume.

[20] See O'Neill, *Constructions of Reason*, ch. 1, albeit in a sense that is not criterially determined in this way.

[21] Conversely, however – contrary to the fear expressed by Cohen, *Rescuing Justice and Equality*, chs. 6 and 7 – this does not mean that constructivism incorporates social facts in a way that detracts from the "purity" of moral principles or the idea of justice. A Kantian conception is not guided by facts but by principles of reason that take facts into account in the right, justifiable way.

To allude briefly to some wide-ranging discussions in moral philosophy, this conception differs from a form of "constitutivism" that anchors the duty of categorical moral justification in the conditions of autonomous agency itself,[22] in that it is concerned with the conditions of morally *responsible* action, not of self-determined action as such. For persons who are not morally autonomous also act, and they act deliberately, possibly on the basis of ethical or religious reasons that are not generalizable. But they do not act in a morally responsible way unless they seek reciprocal–general reasons in moral contexts.[23]

One of the distinctive features of the approach based on a theory of justification is that it situates the duty to justify in the social world in such a way that the individual is viewed from the outset as a communal being, so that moral reflection is not understood as a subjectivist or monological form of generalizing thinking. The moral person is always a member of a *community of justification*. In the moral context, this community includes all moral persons in general, but at the same time it emphasizes responsibility toward and for concrete individuals.[24] The objectivity of constructivist morality is achieved *intersubjectively*, through discourses of justification within a community of responsibility, in relation to which moral persons understand themselves. The bond of practical reason is a moral bond, and individual moral authority can only be exercised together with *all* others.[25]

As already emphasized, the version of constructivism I advocate does not assume that there are no values other than those constructed in this way. There are various sources of normativity, some of which are specific (particular communities of shared values), some general (a universalistic religion, for example). And in the sphere of morality as well, it is not necessary to dispute the reality of certain values or reasons in principle.[26] My approach remains agnostic regarding these questions. The crucial point is that, in *the context of morality* (not in that of the good in general), the principles and criteria of practical reason are understood as transcendentally and pragmatically

---

[22] As argued in Korsgaard, *Self-Constitution*. For a critique, see Enoch, "Agency, Shmagency."
[23] On the various conceptions of autonomy, see Forst, *The Right to Justification*, ch. 5.
[24] See Wingert, *Gemeinsinn und Moral*, and Benhabib, *Situating the Self*.
[25] On this basic idea of discourse ethics, see Habermas, "Discourse Ethics"; in a different vein, also Herman, *The Practice of Moral Judgment*.
[26] See Scanlon, *Being Realistic about Reasons*, and Larmore, *Morality and Metaphysics*, versus Korsgaard, *The Sources of Normativity*, p. 35, who advocates a procedural as opposed to a substantive version of moral realism.

reconstructed principles and criteria that are valid *without exception* for practically rational beings, unless they arrive at better reconstructions of these basic concepts with the help of that same reason. There is no reflexive faculty of value cognition that could transcend or trump the reflection of reason. It generates moral truth "for us"; it remains an open (metaphysical) question whether further dimensions of truth or reality are opened up by reasons.

The criteria of reciprocity and generality enable us to determine the reasons that are, in Scanlon's formulation, "reasonably rejectable" in a *substantive* way, lending specific content to his abstract formulation.[27] This has two advantages over a consensus theory: first, given existing, real dissension, we can specify in greater detail which norms are reciprocally and generally rejectable and which are not; and second, in real cases of consensus, it can be shown that they may not be well founded or may go far beyond what would be reciprocally and generally required (in the sense of being supererogatory, something which Scanlon had in mind when he proposed the negative formulation). These points are indispensable for a critical theory of justification.[28]

It follows from what has been said that we must distinguish different levels of normativity within Kantian constructivism. The basic level is the binding power of the *principle of justification* as a principle of practical, justifying reason. It states not only how reciprocal–general norms could be justified in morally relevant practical contexts, but that there is a duty and a corresponding right to such justification. This *right to justification*, which follows from the principle of justification itself, is the morally fundamental right and, in political contexts, it is the only, as one might say with Kant, "innate" right, just as he speaks of an "original" human right to freedom from the arbitrariness of others in a legal condition in which general laws hold sway.[29]

A second level of normativity is that of moral norms that are generated by a strictly reciprocal–general justification – a procedure of *moral constructivism*. In this context, as already noted, forms of factual justification are to be combined with forms of counterfactual

---

[27] See Scanlon, "Contractualism and Utilitarianism," and *What We Owe to Each Other*; on this, see my "Justification Fundamentalism," Chapter 13 in the present volume, and Scanlon, "Responses to Forst, Mantel, Nagel, Olsaretti, Parfit and Stemplowska," pp. 131–134.
[28] I use the criteria of reciprocal and general rejectability in the substantive sense especially in my theory of toleration in Forst, *Toleration in Conflict*.
[29] Kant, *The Metaphysics of Morals*, VI:237.

justification, thus the greatest possible discursivity toward those affected in combination with reflection on justifiability in a comprehensive moral community of all human beings who belong to the moral community of justification.

At the political–legal level of *political constructivism* (within a political community of justification), further normativities must be distinguished. At a fundamental level, human rights and basic principles of justice must be grounded in such a way that they form a basic structure of justification in which those who are subject to a normative order become part of the general authority that governs this order – and who at the same time are protected as legally, politically and socially non-dominated equals, for example, by basic rights.[30] Moreover, with regard to human rights, one must distinguish between the justification of a general list as opposed to concrete forms of these rights. Beyond the level of basic rights and principles, political–legal norms must be justified that spring from a basic structure of justification and are legitimized by its procedures. Especially when norms originate in majority opinions, however, their fundamental justifiability remains open to question – here, those whose reciprocally and generally non-rejectable claims have been overruled have a discursive veto right.

Factual and counterfactual justification are also intertwined at the level of political constructivism. As important as it is to install democratic and rights-securing justification practices within a basic structure of justification (or what I call "*fundamental justice*"), it remains indispensable to question the justifiability of these procedures, as well as their results, and to enable and even to institutionalize this scrutiny in a critical, Kantian "reasoning" public sphere – for example, through certain formats such as minority rights to object or deliberative forums, in addition to forms of judicial review. These are important steps leading to a justified basic structure (what I call "*full justice*"), which is a regulative idea in the Kantian sense. Normative orders, speaking in ideal terms, are orders that seek to realize the ideal of the *noumenal republic* of which Kant speaks by continually improving the position of the subjected, who are at the same time supposed to be law-givers. This constitutes political and moral progress.

This ideal, which Kant calls "Platonic," must not be confused with a fixed, substantial ideal such as the one developed in Plato's

---

[30] On this, see, in addition to the chapters in Part II of the present volume, Forst, "The Justification of Basic Rights."

Republic. It is only a formal ideal based on principles, whose real shape, according to the Kantian point, must be developed *autonomously*. Here there is no "ideal theory" that would only need to be "applied," but principles of autonomy that must be realized and developed autonomously. This development is part of creative collective self-determination.

The practice of justification, whether moral or political, is thus always situated between the worlds – the world of what is factually justified and that of what is justifiable, which is always open to further scrutiny. Hypothetical and real justification form a dialectical unity that demands progressively better realizations of the practice of reciprocal–general justification, but scrutinizes every such realization regarding its procedures and its results in terms of the same criteria. Within a normative order, which is and should be an order of justification as a practice, institutions must be created that provide for such scrutiny and make genuine authorship possible.

Kantian constructivism, thus understood, takes seriously the demand for autonomous legislation in the context of morality, as well as in that of politics. In this respect, it is a form of *critical constructivism* that is itself based on the critical principle of reason of not recognizing any authorities in the space of reciprocal–general norms other than the discursive community of all in common, bound solely by the principle of justification. Thus, autonomy is a property of each individual and also of all individuals together, and practical reason is exercised individually and collectively – in reciprocal giving and asking for reasons. The answer to the question of the justification of norms lies in the reflection on ourselves as justifying beings. In this way, autonomy becomes possible and the insight that normativity cannot be grounded on non-normative facts or on unquestioned values becomes guiding. An empirical notion of well-being, for instance, would only become part of a moral justification if it entailed reciprocal–general reasons for promoting or taking into account such well-being; and speaking in terms of "absolute" values would only acquire its moral meaning if what normatively followed from those values could be justified in reciprocal and general terms. However, this points to the fact that the status of individuals and of all as equal normative authorities of justification is *categorically* valid on the correct understanding of what it means to be part of the practice of justification. To understand this is to recognize that, in moral contexts in which we unavoidably find ourselves, practical reason commits us to a certain form of justification.

INTRODUCTION

As Kant and many others have argued,[31] one cannot properly enter the space of morality through non-moral considerations, neither when it comes to grounding the duty of justification nor to explaining moral motivation. Someone who tries to justify morality based on non-moral "interests," for instance, will not arrive at it; and those who observe morality from non-moral motives act in conformity with morality, but do not act morally. Moral autonomy corresponds to the autonomy of morality. But this does not open up a separate realm of reasons or ends that constitutes the "true reality" in some sense; rather, it follows from a reflection on what we are as practical beings, namely that we are *responsible to each other*. In the case of the good life, the form that practically responsible answers take is up to us in many respects. But when it comes to what we owe to others in a moral sense, we are not free regarding this form, because autonomously accepting responsibility is bound up with the ability to provide answers in accordance with practical reason.

The task of morality as a whole, as well as of justice as the chief virtue of political and social institutions, is to banish the rule of arbitrariness from human relations so far that it rules out any violation of basic respect or any form of social and political domination (by which is meant the submission to an order without justification). Autonomous action stands against arbitrary, heteronomous action; just orders obviate the arbitrary rule of some over others, where arbitrariness means acting or ruling without justifying reasons. The contrasting concept to arbitrariness is that of dignity; it is a bulwark against the arbitrariness of wrongfulness and injustice. The status of dignity in this context is not a reified status of social "worthiness"; rather, it materializes wherever people enjoy or struggle for a right to justification. In the ideal case of a noumenal republic, the entire normative order would be an order of autonomy and of the realization of the right to justification; in reality, if things go well, we take steps toward it. This does not mean that, within a justified framework of law, people cannot act as they wish – but they can do so specifically *within* this framework, which they co-determine as part of the legislative apparatus.

Kantian constructivism is an expression of a critical theory of normativity that emphasizes the autonomy of individuals in common with others, and it cannot be used to justify orders of value or rule that restrict that autonomy. Everything that is valid between persons must *merit* this validity – here what Kant says about pure reason

---

[31] For example, Prichard, "Does Moral Philosophy Rest on a Mistake?"

holds true, namely that it must "subject itself to critique in all its undertakings" and that it may not "restrict the freedom of critique through any prohibition without damaging itself."[32] Reason has "no dictatorial authority," but its "claim is never anything more than the agreement of free citizens, each of whom must be able to express his reservations, indeed even his *veto*, without holding back."[33]

An essential part of such a critical theory of normativity is that it must scrutinize itself self-critically regarding its own limitations. As for Kant's theory itself, it serves to expose and repudiate the morally arbitrary and discriminatory gradations and exclusions to be found in his work with regard to political participation based on gender and economic status, or the (greater or lesser) value of particular cultures and "races."[34] Moreover, recalling the noumenal and counterfactual conception of the equal worthiness of all human beings as members of the moral community of responsibility, it serves to repudiate the morally arbitrary restriction of this membership to beings who are currently in full possession of their mental powers.[35] This restriction confuses a moral–noumenal determination of rational human nature with an empirical determination of entities who are able to actively exercise the faculty of reason.[36] In a Kantian conception, the claim to *act* in a morally responsible way is addressed to the latter – but this imperative is valid also and especially *toward* those who do not yet or no longer have such reason, for example due to age or illness or contingencies of birth. To define them out of the moral community is in the highest degree morally arbitrary, and it confuses the two questions of moral agency and of moral standing.

The idea underlying Kantian constructivism is as simple as it is complex: in moral and political contexts, we should understand ourselves as noumenal, moral equals who constitute the authority of legislation together in accordance with practical reason as the faculty of responsible justification. And that we should really *become* the authorities that we always already *are* in the normative sense, is the imperative of critical Kantian constructivism.

---

[32] Kant, *Critique of Pure Reason*, A738/B766.
[33] Ibid., A738f./B766f.
[34] On the latter, see especially Flikschuh and Ypi, *Kant and Colonialism*, and the comprehensive discussion in Eberl, *Naturzustand und Barbarei*, pp. 316–361.
[35] See the important study of Schidel, *Die Relationalität der Menschenwürde*.
[36] An example of this is Sangiovanni, *Humanity without Dignity*, who searches in vain (also in my approach) for the "natural property" (p. 73) with reference to which human dignity could be established and therefore abandons the concept; on this, see also Forst, "Justifying Justification," pp. 170–177.

INTRODUCTION

2 Discussion contexts and outline of the argument

The following chapters can be read – this at least is my hope – as steps in an argument leading to a comprehensive philosophy of justification that systematically takes up and connects topics in moral, social and political philosophy. At the same time, however, each chapter is the fruit of specific contexts of discussion which, even when they address classical questions, assume the form of a current discourse in which I intervene. This is the principle underlying philosophical and basic theoretical research, and thus at this point I would like to express my general thanks to the many colleagues who are mentioned individually in the relevant chapters. Thinking is a dialogical activity, and each text is a conversation with specific others and an invitation to many unknown others to participate. This is not only true of a philosophy of justification.

The fact that I divide the first two parts of the book into discussions of "Basic Questions of Social Philosophy" and of "Critical Political Theory," respectively, does not mean that I subscribe to the distinction between social philosophy and political philosophy, according to which the former deals with social questions of the "successful life" and the latter primarily with questions of justice within a political order.[37] The distinction between questions of the good and the just is important, but the moral-philosophical orientations from which I start have a lot to say about classical questions in social philosophy, such as the meaning of self-determination as a social practice, *without* having to appeal to notions of the good.

I argue for this in Chapter 1 in an exemplary way, where, following Rousseau, Kant and Marx, I reconstruct an important tradition of critical theories of *alienation* that understand it not as a failure to live a good life, but as a fractured relationship to others and to oneself as beings who are "actually" but not "really" equal normative authorities in the domain of morality and of political and social life. I analyze the lack of recognition by and of others as moral or political equals as first-order alienation, whereas an extreme form of second-order alienation consists in not being aware of oneself as a normative authority. Autonomy as Kant understands it provides the key to analyzing and overcoming such forms of alienation.

---

[37] For example, Celikates and Jaeggi, *Sozialphilosophie*, p. 11; see also Honneth, "Pathologies of the Social."

INTRODUCTION

The postcolonial age has witnessed an intensification of criticism of the traditional Enlightenment *concept of progress* and, as a result, the criteria of social and moral progress are in need of reconsideration. This is the topic of Chapter 2. The question of the justification of progress calls for reflection on the progress of justification, that is, on the processes through which individuals (and collectives) achieve self-determination as normative authorities, in social and in political life. Where this is successful, progress is discernible, in accord with central claims of the Enlightenment *and* of postcolonial criticism. This also shows that the opposition between immanent and transcending critique, or between historical and universalistic justifications of normativity, must be overcome. The question of justification arises in concrete historical contexts and at the same time points beyond them.

The concepts of progress, regress and, more specifically, of *regression* form a unity. Contemporary analyses of the crisis of democracy often connect the rise of authoritarian populism with the concept of democratic – or better: anti-democratic – regression. Understanding regression broadly as the rule of unreason, Chapter 3 discusses the normative presuppositions of such uses of the concept with a view to identifying and avoiding several important mistakes in the ongoing discourse. The discussion notably aims to prevent an unjustified fixation on the *status quo ante*, an inappropriate diminution of the concept of democracy, and a false categorization of democracy critique. Finally, the chapter develops its own analysis of the causes of democratic regression and of the paradoxes of our time.

The concept of *solidarity* belongs to the inventory of normative basic concepts of social and political thought, but is notoriously controversial. In Chapter 4, I try to explain why this is so. I count solidarity among the "normatively dependent" concepts whose core meaning only crystallizes in combination with other normative sources in particular contexts into particular conceptions of solidarity. Then the controversy over the "correct" definition of solidarity becomes more transparent, because it is a dispute over differently situated normative views of social and political life that can collide, as, for example, the solidary commitment to emancipatory justice can collide with a nationalistic understanding of solidarity.

Something similar holds for the multifaceted concept of *social cohesion* discussed in Chapter 5. Here it is also important not to commit oneself prematurely to a particular normative understanding of this concept, but first to analyze the relevant dimensions descriptively as a prelude to clarifying possible normative uses. The task of elaborating a critical understanding of cohesion can then be taken up, addressing the problem that social exclusions are sometimes justified as measures for strengthening "cohesion." This becomes an object of ideology critique.

The chapters in the second part of the book begin with a programmatic text on the understanding of reality shaped by a theory of justification, as already mentioned. Chapter 6 takes as its starting point the opposition between a Platonic conception of the world of values and an understanding of *realism* that is widespread in the social sciences, but also increasingly in political theory, which leaves little room for normative questions and considerations, let alone for the autonomy of morality. I try to show, on the one hand, that the empirical analysis of the orders of justification in which we actually move provides the key to a realistic, but *noumenal* understanding of power – and that, on the other hand, such analysis cannot ignore the question of justification as a normative question. As observers of normative orders, we are always also participants in them and, especially in our role as participants, we cannot avoid the question of justification as a political–moral request and demand. The empirical program thus gives rise to a program of critical theory as a critique of relations of justification.

Chapter 7 documents an intervention in the diverse debates about moral, legal and political understandings of *human rights* in which I recall their historical development and their purpose of securing for people a status as non-dominated equals who are not only protected by the law, but can also contribute to shaping it as politically autonomous subjects. From there, I develop a Kantian constructivist theory of human rights and their various normative dimensions based on the right to justification. This right is the basis of human rights.

In Chapter 8, I continue the discussion of questions of *transnational justice* in which I have participated for some time (in addition to that on human rights) from the perspective of contemporary Frankfurt School critical theory in confrontation with alternative theoretical approaches. I argue that we must overcome false oppositions between "idealist" and "realist" approaches and show how a critical social-scientific examination of multiple contexts of domination must be combined with reflection on principles of justification and non-domination. A discussion of "practice-dependent" and alternative, non-relational approaches opens up space for a third position, which starts from a critical understanding of political and social practice and avoids distorted accounts of the structural injustice characteristic of transnational contexts.

INTRODUCTION

Continuing my work on the notion of "noumenal power" and responding to some critiques, I turn in Chapter 9 to the puzzle of how the fact that many analyses depict *structural domination* as anonymous and "faceless" can cohere with the fact that at the same time it is criticized as an *injustice* bound up with certain responsibilities of social actors. As a solution to this puzzle, I propose an understanding of structural power and domination that views structures as empowering or disempowering groups and actors, ones that must be analyzed as structures of injustice, so that responsibilities can be named without reducing the complexity of these structures. Otherwise, the question of emancipation would be left in a void.

In recent neo-republican political theory, Quentin Skinner and Philip Pettit in particular have defended an understanding of *non-domination* as protection against possible arbitrariness by others. In Chapter 10, I draw on Kant (and on central ideas of German idealism, also to be found in Axel Honneth's theory of recognition) to develop an alternative republican understanding of non-domination that emphasizes the importance of political autonomy over the protection of personal freedom of choice. Using the thought experiment of a neo-republican machine that calculates secure spaces of individual freedom without allowing for political autonomy, I show why a Kantian understanding of authorship within a normative order is indispensable for political republicanism.

In the chapters comprising Part III, I engage in discussions with approaches that are close to my own and yet are different in relevant ways: John Rawls's theory of justice, Thomas Scanlon's contractualism and Jürgen Habermas's discourse ethics.

In Chapter 11, I suggest a Kantian reading of Rawls's political liberalism. As much as Rawls distanced himself from a comprehensive Kantian doctrine, we ought to read his account as a non-comprehensive Kantian moral–political theory. According to this reading, the liberal conception of justice is compatible with a plurality of comprehensive ethical doctrines as long as they share the independently grounded, "freestanding" principles of justice which define the "reasonable."

Following this, in Chapter 12 I ask whether a Kantian understanding of justice such as Rawls's is compatible with the consequentialist theory of luck egalitarianism. Drawing on Rawls, but also based on fundamental considerations of justice, I argue that the respective approaches rest on radically different paradigms – not least because luck egalitarianism, which emphasizes the distinction between imputable choices and circumstances for which no one is responsible,

INTRODUCTION

ends up in the contradictory attempt to use a morally highly arbitrary distinction to overcome social moral arbitrariness.

In the following chapter, I develop a discourse-theoretical reading of Scanlon's contractualism with respect to moral and political justification. In my view, Scanlon's moral theory is best reconstructed as exhibiting "justification fundamentalism" rather than "reasons fundamentalism" (as he calls his account). This means that the duty of justification toward moral equals is a basic demand of practical reason, and it implies the constructivist priority of criteria and procedures of justification (or non-rejectability) for any valid normative reason.[38]

In Chapter 14, I continue a philosophical dialogue with Jürgen Habermas, who has accompanied and shaped my thinking for decades. The question I pursue in the form of an interpretation of his three-volume work *Also a History of Philosophy* goes back – how could it be otherwise? – to Kant and to Habermas's interpretation of Kant. It concerns the relationship between history and normativity and the *autonomy of morality* as compared to *sittliche* or ethical and religious justifications and motivations. My question essentially is: Does this autonomy remain intact in light of Habermas's genealogy of modernity? In what way can and must the discourse-theoretical understanding of communicative reason differ from a Kantian understanding of practical reason?[39]

I have emphasized the dialogical structure of thought, at least of my own. This includes other important discussions that I have not included here for reasons of space, such as a critical engagement with Arthur Ripstein's recent interpretation of Kant,[40] my contributions to *Festschriften* for Nancy Fraser[41] and Christoph Menke,[42] or my discussion of Allen Buchanan's political philosophy[43] or of Andrea Sangiovanni's conception of solidarity.[44] The aforementioned and many more were and are indispensable discussion partners. This is how thought advances – assuming things go well. In contrast to Part

---

[38] For Scanlon's reply, see his "Responses to Forst, Mantel, Nagel, Olsaretti, Parfit, and Stemplowska."
[39] For Habermas's response to my critique, see Habermas, "Reply," pp. 68–71. For another round of our exchange, see my "Die Welten der Rechtfertigung" and his reply "Antworten."
[40] Forst, "Might and Right." See also Ripstein's reply: "From Constitutionalism to War – and Back Again," pp. 240–248.
[41] Forst, "What's Critical About a Critical Theory of Justice?"
[42] Forst, "Das Recht der Negativität."
[43] Forst, "The Grounds of Institutional Moral Theory."
[44] Forst, "The Meaning(s) of Solidarity." See also his response in Sangiovanni, "Response to Critics."

INTRODUCTION

III of the German edition of this book, I decided not to reprint the political essays on the current crisis of democracy contained there. This is not because I no longer consider them to be valid, quite the contrary, but I am planning to publish them in a separate volume.[45]

Since the publication of *Normativity and Power* I have had the immense privilege of being able to reflect on and respond to a number of critical essays on my work by highly esteemed colleagues.[46] These contributions have appeared together in journal symposia or in separately published essay collections.[47] I have not included my respective replies in the present volume, but they represent important milestones for the clarification and further development of my thinking. In my response to Simone Chambers, Lea Ypi and Stephen White, I present key aspects of a critical theory of politics as I understand it.[48] In responding to Seyla Benhabib, Jeff Flynn and Matthias Fritsch, I specifically address the questions of the historicity of the grounding of the right to justification and various democratic-theoretical and moral-philosophical aspects of my approach.[49] In the replies to critiques of a text on basic rights containing an extensive discussion of various theories of rights, including that of Habermas,[50] I explain and develop my conception of rights in dialogue with Laura Valentini, Glen Newey, Marcus Düwell and Stefan Rummens.[51]

The theory of noumenal power has also attracted a number of detailed and challenging critiques by, among others, Albena Azmanova, Clarissa Hayward, Steven Lukes, Simon Susen, Pablo Gilabert, Mark Haugaard and Matthias Kettner, to which I have responded in a reflection on the possibilities and limitations of this theory.[52] Some of these thoughts have found their way into Chapter

---

[45] See, for example, Forst, "Two Bad Halves Don't Make a Whole," or Forst, "The Neglect of Democracy."
[46] To this context also belong my replies to criticisms of Andrea Sangiovanni, Amy Allen, Kevin Olson, Anthony Simon Laden, Eva Erman and Simon Caney in Forst, "Justifying Justification," all to be found in Forst, *Justice, Democracy and the Right to Justification*.
[47] The symposia contributions were published in *Philosophy and Social Criticism* (41:3, 2015); *Political Theory* (43:6, 2015); *Netherlands Journal of Legal Philosophy* (45:3, 2016); and *Journal of Political Power* (11:1–3, 2018). The essay collections in question are Haugaard and Kettner, *Theorising Noumenal Power* (containing the contributions from the *Journal of Political Power*); Allen and Mendieta, *Justification and Emancipation*; Herlin-Karnell and Klatt, *Constitutionalism Justified*; and Forst, *Toleration, Power and the Right to Justification*.
[48] Forst, "A Critical Theory of Politics: Grounds, Method and Aims."
[49] Forst, "The Right to Justification: Moral and Political, Transcendental and Historical."
[50] Forst, "The Justification of Basic Rights."
[51] Forst, "What Does it Mean to Justify Basic Rights?"
[52] Forst, "Noumenal Power Revisited."

9. In addition to my understandings of justification, respect, alienation and injustice, my conception of power has been the subject of critiques by Amy Allen, Sarah Clark Miller, Melissa Yates, Catherine Lu, John McCormick, Mattias Iser and John Christman, which also prompted me to write a comprehensive reply.[53]

Basic questions of the right to justification at the intersection of legal philosophy and constitutional law, as well as questions of power, played an important role in the critiques of Arthur Ripstein, Andrea Sangiovanni, Claudio Corradetti, Christian Hiebaum, Bernhard Schlink, Sameer Bajaj and Enzo Rossi, Lois McNay, Matthias Klatt, Eoin Daly, Alon Harel, Christian Rostbøll and Ester Herlin-Karnell, which I addressed in a more wide-ranging response.[54] Finally, Teresa Bejan, Chandran Kukathas, John Horton, Daniel Weinstock, Melissa Williams, Patchen Markell and David Owen challenged my theories of tolerance, justification and power so pointedly with their texts that I was compelled to respond with a detailed rejoinder.[55]

If any progress is discernible in these replies and in the reflections gathered here, it is due to such outstanding colleagues who forced me to produce better arguments. I owe a great debt of gratitude to them and to future critics.

---

[53] Forst, "Navigating a World of Conflict and Power."
[54] Forst, "The Constitution of Justification."
[55] Forst, "The Dialectics of Toleration and the Power of Reason(s)."

Part I

AUTONOMY, PROGRESS AND SOLIDARITY
Basic Questions of Social Philosophy

— 1 —

NOUMENAL ALIENATION
Rousseau, Kant and Marx on the Dialectics of Self-Determination*

But one who makes himself a worm cannot complain afterwards if people step on him.[1]

1.1 Alienation and the inalienable

In the following, I argue that alienation should be understood as a particular form of individual and social heteronomy that can only be overcome by a dialectical combination of individual and collective autonomy, recovering a deontological sense of normative authority. I discuss alienation in the sense of the German *Entfremdung*, not in the sense of *Veräußerung* or *Entäußerung*. Kant, Hegel and Marx use these latter terms for the transfer of property or for the objectification of one's labor as a form of property, that is, for certain forms of what we can call externalization. As these philosophers, following Rousseau, emphasize, some of these forms of externalization lead to alienation as *Entfremdung* because they contribute to modern forms of slavery, which is a (or maybe *the*) paradigm case of social alienation. This points toward my main thesis, which concerns alienation as a loss or denial of autonomy, thus not relying, as is usually the case in alienation theory, on a particular notion of authenticity.

---

* Many thanks to Lea Ypi and Howard Williams for their excellent written comments on an earlier draft – and to the participants of the workshop on Kant and Marx in London in May 2017 for a discussion I benefited from. The same applies to Hartmut Rosa's colloquium, where I discussed these thoughts in December 2020. I am also grateful to Nate Adams and Paul Kindermann for their great help in preparing this text.
[1] Kant, *The Metaphysics of Morals*, VI:437.

Alienation as *Entfremdung* has been one of the central concepts of Hegelian and Marxist social criticism,[2] and their debt to Rousseau is often acknowledged. However, the importance of Kant is largely ignored, leading to a particularly one-sided alienation theory that is in danger of neglecting its moral and political point.[3] Detached from its deontological moral and political elements, alienation is primarily understood as self-estrangement coupled with social estrangement or, to use the words of Rahel Jaeggi, as a form of non-relatedness (*Beziehungslosigkeit*) to oneself and others, as a failure to "appropriate" one's self and one's surrounding world.[4] The focus is on certain qualitative aspects of authentic self-identification and ways of relating to others – and on the "loss of self" or "loss of meaning" within them and the lack of social "resonance," as one could say with Hartmut Rosa.[5] The relevant social "pathologies," to use Axel Honneth's term, are analyzed in ethical terms as lack of self-identification or self-realization and ultimately as a loss of certain necessary conditions for the good life. According to Honneth, social philosophy, which begins with Rousseau's question of alienation, does not primarily ask the question of political and social justice but inquires into the "limitations that this new form of life imposed on human's self-realization."[6]

In this tradition of thought, providing a philosophical account of what it means to live a non-alienated life requires an anthropologically grounded notion of the authentic and good life as truly realizing one's self. But, before we follow this path and attempt to articulate substantive notions of the good – or ethical notions of non-alienated personal identity[7] – in order to provide normative grounds for analyses of social alienation, it is useful to reconsider Kant's role in the development of the notion of alienation. Even though he did not make use of the term *Entfremdung*, Kant's moral and political philosophy teaches us something very important for any critical social analysis of alienation and something highly relevant for understanding Marx as well.

---

[2] It has not been center stage in so-called "analytic Marxism," as Ripstein, "Rationality and Alienation," notes, which he explains by the conception of human agency and rationality used in these approaches.
[3] See, for example, the Hegelian accounts in Honneth, *Disrespect*, ch. 1, or Jaeggi, *Alienation*.
[4] See Jaeggi, *Alienation*.
[5] Rosa, *Resonance*.
[6] Honneth, *Disrespect*, p. 5.
[7] See Frankfurt, *The Importance of What We Care About*; Schroeder and Arpaly, "Alienation and Externality"; Ferrara, *Reflective Authenticity*.

If we think about alienation in Kantian terms, the main source of alienation is a denial of standing or, in the extreme, losing a sense of oneself as a rational normative authority equal to all others. I call the former kind of alienation, where others deny you equal standing as a normative authority in moral or political terms, *first-order noumenal alienation*, as there is no proper mutual cognition and recognition of each other in that social context. I call the latter kind of alienation, where a subject does not consider themselves an equal normative authority – or an "end in oneself" – *second-order noumenal alienation* (again, in a moral and a political form). As many after Rousseau and Hegel have shown, the first kind of alienation can lead to the second. However, in this tradition mainly influenced by Hegel and following Kojève's and Sartre's influential theory,[8] many have assumed that social alienation leads to self-alienation and a loss of self-respect.[9] But there is no necessary causal connection here, for otherwise the struggle for recognition would not get off the ground.[10]

From a Kantian point of view, moral and political forms of noumenal alienation have to be analyzed as forms of heteronomy: to live an alienated way of life is to lack a certain standing as a moral and political normative authority equal to others, meaning that you lack this standing *vis-à-vis* others as well as (possibly) yourself. To criticize and overcome such forms of alienation politically and morally presupposes certain ideas and practices of individual and collective self-determination – of exercising normative *authority* and *authorship*. This includes qualitative aspects of relating to yourself and others that I analyze under the rubric of *authorization*, but they need not be based on ethical ideas of the good life. Rather, they are based on a reflection of what it means to be an autonomous agent of reason and an active subject of justification: an equal normative authority in the space of reasons and the social realm. Noumenal alienation results from a lack of being recognized or a lack of recognizing yourself as an agent of justification equal to others, as having an equal right to justification.[11] In this sense, alienation violates the *dignity of humans as moral and political law-givers* – a dignity seen by Rousseau, Kant and Marx as *inalienable*: it can be denied or violated, but it cannot be lost.

[8] See Kojève, *Introduction to the Reading of Hegel*; Sartre, *Anti-Semite and Jew*.
[9] See Honneth, *The Struggle for Recognition*, ch. 6.
[10] See Forst, *Contexts of Justice*, ch. 5.3, and Forst, *Justification and Critique*, ch. 6; Iser, *Empörung und Fortschritt*.
[11] See Forst, *The Right to Justification*, and Forst, *Justification and Critique*.

With this analysis I think we can capture moral and political aspects of social and political life where "alienation" does important critical work without making reference to reasonably contestable ideals of what it means to "truly" realize yourself or to achieve a good or authentic life. In addition, the analysis I suggest highlights the political connection between individual and collective autonomy, introducing democracy as a major practice of overcoming alienation – a dimension often overlooked by ethical theories focusing on self-realization. And for this purpose we must start with Rousseau.

1.2 Rousseau: Overcoming individual alienation through political *aliénation totale*

Rousseau had a keen sense for the social forms of alienation that modern life brings with it. Yet the most important point for my purposes is that he suggests a *political* solution to the modern problem of individual alienation.

In his first *Discourse*, Rousseau took aim at the alienating herd character of modern societies in his critique of modern civilization: "One no longer dares to appear what one is; and under this perpetual constraint, the men who make up the herd that is called society will, when placed in similar circumstances, all act in similar ways unless more powerful motives incline them differently."[12] Conformity leads to other-directedness, and the "refinement" of knowledge and morals is only the flattening and loss of true emotions and a sense of communal life.[13] Already here, one must note that Rousseau connects this critique of the loss of self-direction, individuality and true moral and communal life with a critique of social stratification, hierarchies and domination: "Without men's injustices, what would be the use of Jurisprudence? What would become of History if there were neither Tyrants, nor Wars, nor Conspirators?"[14]

This connection is developed further in the *Discourse on Inequality*, where we find the full analysis of alienation. Arguing against Hobbes's thesis of the "natural" human drive to compete with others and to

---

[12] Rousseau, "Discourse on the Sciences and Arts *or* First Discourse," p. 8.
[13] "We have Physicists, Geometricians, Chemists, Astronomers, Poets, Musicians, Painters; we no longer have citizens; or if we still have some left, dispersed in our abandoned rural areas, they waste away indigent and despised. Such is the condition to which those who give us bread and our children milk are reduced, and such are the sentiments they get from us." Ibid., p. 24.
[14] Ibid., p. 16.

achieve a power advantage, Rousseau argues for the simplicity and peacefulness of human nature based on the natural interest in one's well-being and the capacity for empathy and compassion. It is only in the development of more complex forms of social life that hierarchy and an ill-fated and pathological desire for recognition and superiority arise, based on *amour-propre*, a particular form of selfishness. It leads to a constant desire to compete and compare, and it turns into an alienating form of other-directedness even in those who are more successful in this competition:

> To be and to appear became two entirely different things, and from this distinction arose ostentatious display, deceitful cunning, and all the vices that follow in their wake. Looked at in another way, man, who had previously been free and independent, is now so to speak subjugated by a multitude of new needs to the whole of Nature, and especially to those of his kind, whose slave he in a sense becomes even by becoming their master; rich, he needs their services; poor, he needs their help.[15]

The slave metaphor serves a double function in this discourse: as signaling the other-directedness and loss of individual autonomy over one's judgments and actions, driven by an exaggerated desire for recognition and success, and as being subjected to a normative order of hierarchies and structural constraints beyond one's control, even if one does well within that order. That kind of socialization makes a human being "a Slave, and he becomes weak, timorous, grovelling."[16] These aspects of alienation need to be combined, as Rousseau places the critique of *conformity* in a context of social *domination*, given that the desire for recognition is also a desire to rule – and sometimes even a desire to be ruled over (what Kant will particularly emphasize). Loss of autonomy in judgment and loss of social self-determination go together.

Fred Neuhouser rightly stresses that Rousseau's critique of "sociable man, always outside himself"[17] can be called a critique of alienation. In being completely dependent on the arbitrary judgments of others and existing "*always* outside oneself,"[18] they lose an internal sense of "self-affirmation" and autonomous self-worth.[19] In my reading of alienation, this kind of dependence on the arbitrary evaluation of

---

[15] Rousseau, "Discourse on the Origin and Foundations of Inequality among Men *or* Second Discourse," p. 170.
[16] Ibid., p. 138.
[17] Neuhouser, *Rousseau's Theodicy of Self-Love*, p. 187.
[18] Ibid., p. 84 (emphasis in original).
[19] See also Ferrara, *Modernity and Authenticity*.

others is an important part of alienation because it makes subjects not only vulnerable to the judgment of others without resort to any possibility of self-affirmation but also makes them vulnerable to forms of social domination and submission – what Rousseau calls slavery. Slavery as extreme alienation for Rousseau thus is not just total dependence on others' recognition but also subjection to domination and accepting certain terms of social hierarchy. Thus, this is not a mere "ethical" question of self-realization or self-affirmation, but also one of social self-determination and non-domination.

This becomes obvious where Rousseau introduces the story of the rich and powerful imposing a false social contract in order to preserve their privileges by securing them politically and legally.[20] Here social alienation leads to political and legal alienation, that is, new forms of slavery: "All ran toward their chains in the belief they were securing their freedom."[21] For Rousseau, the resulting political state of affairs is one of institutionalized arbitrary rule, that is, *domination*, the main evil in social life: "[I]n the relations between man and man the worst that can happen to one is to find himself at the other's discretion."[22] Accordingly, the "conversion of legitimate into arbitrary power"[23] is the highest form of human inequality and, I want to add, alienation, because it truly deprives human beings of their powers of self-determination and turns them into slaves.

Thus, for Rousseau, alienation primarily has a moral–political meaning: it refers to subjection to a normative order, where (a) an *artificial hierarchical world* of social relations has been set up that the powerless cannot control; (b) this order shields itself from critical scrutiny by *appearing to be justified*, or in any case unavoidable for furthering social goods like justice and welfare, and so is accepted even by the "slaves"; (c) the powerless are ruled by the powerful *arbitrarily*, that is, are dominated (within the limits the normative order allows for such rule); (d) those subjected, including the powerful, are driven by *external motives* of economic and social competition and the desire for success and recognition, thus leading estranged lives. In sum, it is an estranged world of slaves – and masters – who deem themselves to be free. Both kinds of noumenal

---

[20] This is how Rousseau describes the ideological ruse of the rich: "Let us institute rules of Justice and peace to which all are obliged to conform, which favor no one, and which in a way make up for the vagaries of fortune by subjecting the powerful and the weak alike to mutual duties." Rousseau, "Discourse on the Origin and Foundations of Inequality among Men *or* Second Discourse," p. 173.
[21] Ibid.
[22] Ibid., p. 176.
[23] Ibid., p. 182.

alienation I articulated above are present here: those dominated are not respected as normative authorities and, in accepting that domination, they do not recognize their own authority.

Such a comprehensive analysis of alienation can explain the solution that Rousseau puts forth in his *Contrat Social*. For, if alienation were mainly a problem of gaining access to self-guided sources of authentic self-realization, a political revolution would not do because it would not guarantee a society of non-conformity. So, the solution is not to be sought by looking inward, by gaining access to some "true self" waiting to be realized, but rather in a radical move to overcome the chains of social and political slavery: morally and politically establishing persons as *equal normative authorities* within their society, in both noumenal respects (first- and second-order) of recognizing others and oneself. But Rousseau does not distinguish between moral and political autonomy, as Kant later would (and to some extent Marx also would not; more about that later). Rather, for Rousseau the political establishment of the new and non-dominated social contract overcoming the false one is a moral act; "the moral act as such," as Habermas calls it.[24]

To break the "chains" human beings find themselves in everywhere – and to overcome the mentality of slavery, as "slaves lose everything in their chains, even the desire to be rid of them"[25] – requires a moral–political revolution, a new grounding of a normative order. For the complete form of alienation is (in the above mentioned sense of externalizing or selling oneself)[26] alienating one's liberty and accepting slavery as justified, which, according to Rousseau's deontological argument, one cannot morally do: "These words *slavery* and *right* are contradictory; they are mutually exclusive."[27] The right to one's freedom as a self-determining being is thus *inalienable* for Rousseau, for "to renounce one's freedom is to renounce one's quality as man, the rights of humanity, and even its duties."[28] It would be an immoral act, as one would no longer regard oneself as an agent and would thus no longer take responsibility for oneself. Further, it is conceptually impossible to successfully authorize another to have complete dominating power over one because on a deontological account such authorization is contradictory: no authorization of another can nullify or destroy the moral authority of the authorizing agent.

---

[24] Habermas, *Theory and Practice*, p. 106.
[25] Rousseau, "Of the Social Contract," p. 43.
[26] See ibid., pp. 44f.
[27] Ibid., p. 48 (emphasis in original).
[28] Ibid., p. 45.

That would be a perfect form of moral alienation, and the right social contract is exactly its opposite through an alternative form of alienation: the *aliénation totale* of all with all, establishing a new sovereign over their wills that is the collective expression of their own will, if guided by the *volonté générale* furthering the common good.

The formation of the new order, in which no one reserves a privilege for themselves, establishes a form of complete self-determination, where the individuals unite with all without reservation but still "obey only [themselves] and remain as free as before."[29] The "as before" is misleading, for the new form of self-determination is of a moral and political quality that did not exist before; still, what Rousseau stresses is that the "natural" non-domination is translated and preserved in this new civil state. The major clause of the contract thus is one of "the total alienation of each associate with all of his rights to the whole community."[30] The general will is (by definition) purely general and reciprocal, as it only regulates what concerns all and what is in the common interest.

I will not go into the details of how Rousseau thought to socially and politically guarantee such reciprocity and generality. But the proto-Kantian character of the solution to the problem of alienation is obvious: obeying and being free is the same thing if guided by reciprocally and generally justifiable laws, and these laws express and secure the freedom of all equally and as equals. Non-alienation is established by the status of being an equal law-giver, following one's own will as the general will. Being free and being bound by such law is the same, and only such law can establish *non-alienation as non-domination* because you follow no other will than yours. In the *Contrat Social*, Rousseau also modifies his earlier critique of rationality, favoring "natural" inclinations, and stresses that transitioning into the civil state achieves a "remarkable change in man by substituting justice for instinct," where "the voice of duty succeeds physical impulsion" and where a citizen is willing "to consult his reason before listening to his inclinations."[31] In sum, and anticipating Kant, Rousseau affirms that "obedience to the law one has prescribed to oneself is freedom."[32] Overcoming alienation in the aspects articulated above means establishing a form of moral–political autonomy that overcomes social and political heteronomy and

---

[29] Ibid., pp. 49f. See Neuhouser, "Rousseau," and the interpretation by Cohen, *Rousseau*.
[30] Rousseau, "Of the Social Contract," p. 50.
[31] Ibid., p. 53.
[32] Ibid., p. 54. For an interpretation of Kant's political philosophy along these lines, see Maus, *Zur Aufklärung der Demokratietheorie*, and also Shell, *The Rights of Reason*.

other-directedness by establishing the rule of collective reason – or better, by establishing the status of persons as justificatory equals who determine themselves individually and collectively as autonomous normative authorities. Alienation is the lack of such authority. And with that, we are already on Kantian ground.

1.3 Kantian alienation: On (not) being a normative authority

Kant takes over Rousseau's conception of autonomy for the political sphere but grounds it in a conception of moral, noumenal freedom. I focus first on this moral conception of autonomy and highlight the relevant aspects of noumenal moral alienation before turning to the political.

According to Kant, it is characteristic of human nature that human beings regard themselves as members of two worlds, the noumenal and the phenomenal. As beings guided by principles of reason, they consider themselves non-determined by empirical inclinations and interests and as morally free (and responsible). Their moral freedom is a "practical idea"[33] that has its practical implications by following the moral law of the categorical imperative, which alone enables them to act autonomously, that is, on the basis of universally valid reasons. Thus, human beings express their "proper self"[34] (*eigentliches Selbst*) by willing freely and rationally according to the categorical imperative. They are not their true or proper self – that is, are alienated – when they are guided heteronomously, though they might believe that they are most themselves in doing so, following their desires and personal choices. In short, they are most alienated when they think they are at home with themselves. Why is that? According to Kant, heteronomous action is a kind of action that the agent did not rationally *authorize*; more precisely, where the agent is not the real *author* of the action and where agents are not fully expressing themselves as an *authority* of reason. This needs to be unpacked.

In the *Groundwork*, Kant explains the *inalienable* moral status of human beings as normative authorities in terms that resonate strongly with every reflection on the moral evil of instrumentalizing others as "mere means." Such reflections are as influential for Marx's analysis of exploitation and alienation as is Rousseau's social

---

[33] Kant, *Critique of Pure Reason*, A808/B836.
[34] Kant, *Groundwork of the Metaphysics of Morals*, IV:457 (tr. altered).

criticism – mediated by the importance of Hegel for Marx. According to Kant, the rational will wills an end, and the only end that does not serve as a means for another end and is thus truly universal (and rationally justified) is the end of the human being itself, as someone rationally determining his or her ends. This is a reflexive truth: if you confer a status of an end on something by rationally willing it, the very agent of such willing is an end it itself.[35] All other ends serve this very end, as only through rational willing do they become ends. Thus, human nature as rational nature is an end in itself, and the "absolute worth"[36] of human beings as self-determining beings of such a nature means that one should respect every person – including oneself – *"always at the same time as an end, never merely as a means."*[37] This is the categorical imperative of non-instrumentalization, and with respect to the topic of alienation, it means the following: moral alienation as first-order noumenal alienation exists where persons treat others as a mere means, as an object they can control, use or destroy. They do not respect them as a moral person or as an equal; in the extreme, they treat them as a "thing" (*Sache*).[38] The noumenal aspect in them doing so is that they have a morally mistaken belief about others and violate their noumenal freedom and capacity as well as their own, as they do not understand what it means to be an end like and among others. For you, as the addressee of their action, the alienation is of a noumenal and practical nature because you experience this as a form of disrespect and instrumentalization, as an insult. Second-order noumenal alienation appears where you do not even have such an experience but where you disregard your own worth as an end and normative equal to others. Kant discusses this aspect mainly in the context of duties to oneself (which I leave aside here for the moment); he clearly sees disregarding one's own dignity, and becoming a "worm," as he says in the *Metaphysics of Morals*,[39] as a failure to respect one's own standing as an end in oneself.

The idea of "dignity" does important work in this context. By this Kant means the basic moral status of persons as law-givers who are at the same time subjects to that very law: as autonomous rational beings. Those who are such law-givers belong to what Kant calls the "kingdom of ends," that is, the "systematic union of several

---

[35] See the argument made by Korsgaard, *The Sources of Normativity*.
[36] Kant, *Groundwork of the Metaphysics of Morals*, IV:428.
[37] Ibid., IV:429 (emphasis in original).
[38] Ibid.
[39] Kant, *The Metaphysics of Morals*, VI:437.

rational beings through common laws."[40] As sovereign (*Oberhaupt*) in such a kingdom, the human being has an inviolable and inalienable dignity as a being "that obeys no law other than that which at the same time it itself gives."[41] Such dignitaries have no price, which is a relative value based on use value or esteem, what Kant calls market price (*Marktpreis*) or fancy price (*Affektionspreis*, in the sense of sentimental value);[42] rather, they have inner worth or *Würde*. This distinction, in its deontological form, remains central for any further Hegelian or Marxist social criticism.

The idea of "dignity" also refers to a particular exercise of agency for Kant, a form of action based on one's self-respect as someone with dignity. Acting out of a sense of duty presupposes that one recognizes one's own dignity and the equal dignity of others in "just this capability, to be universally legislating, if with the proviso of also being itself subject to precisely this legislation."[43] Acting out of a sense of duty thus includes the avoidance of causing first-order noumenal alienation, that is, disrespect for others whom one does not properly regard as an end and thus is alienated from, and it presupposes the absence of second-order noumenal alienation, as failure to respect oneself and one's own dignity. Both kinds of noumenal alienation are alienation from one's nature as a member of the kingdom of ends.

Respecting oneself and others as members of the kingdom of ends, one does not bow before a feudal nobleman, but only before someone of supreme moral character.[44] It is the attitude of the upright gait, of an equal among equals in moral terms, whatever the particular social standing is. It is, as Kant says near the end of the *Critique of Practical Reason*, "*respect for ourselves* in the consciousness of our freedom."[45] In an important reflection on "servility" (*Kriecherei*) as a lack of virtue, Kant affirms that the moral demand of respecting one's own dignity, that is, of "moral self-esteem" (*moralische Selbstschätzung*),[46] requires human beings to avoid a "servile spirit" of disavowing one's dignity: "Waiving any claim to moral worth in oneself, in the belief that one will thereby acquire a borrowed worth, is morally false *servility*."[47] The value of dignity is beyond any price.[48]

---

[40] Kant, *Groundwork of the Metaphysics of Morals*, IV:433.
[41] Ibid., IV:434.
[42] Ibid., IV:435.
[43] Ibid., IV:440.
[44] Kant, *Critique of Practical Reason*, V:76f.
[45] Ibid., V:161 (emphasis in original).
[46] Kant, *The Metaphysics of Morals*, VI:435.
[47] Ibid. (emphasis in original).
[48] Ibid., VI:462.

Marx will add important complexity to our understanding of the dynamics of moral alienation and the rise of "false consciousness" in the form of such servility. Here it is important to note that the concept of alienation best captures the two forms of lack and loss of moral authority that Kant analyzes: the lack or loss of respect for others and the lack or loss of respect for oneself as a moral authority equal to others in the kingdom of ends. Both are forms of being alienated from that kingdom, in one dimension the lack of respect for or by others, in another the lack of self-respect. Both are intertwined in complex ways; first-order noumenal alienation is already a form of self-denial (as an equal to others one thinks to be of lesser value), and a loss of self-respect (second-order alienation) can also lead to moral disaster and self-destruction. Analytically, however, it is important to keep the two apart, as not every experience of disrespect leads to a loss of self-respect. As Honneth explains in his interpretation of the struggle for recognition, being disrespected can lead to a loss of self-respect.[49] But here we need to distinguish between disrespect that *denies* and *insults* the dignity and self-respect of another and disrespect that *damages* and *destroys* the self-respect of the other. First-order alienation implies the former but not the latter, which is second-order alienation. The struggle for equal recognition – moral or legal, political or social – *presupposes* that the latter has been overcome to some extent.[50]

In his discussion of virtues and vices, Kant offers important interpretations of first-order alienation that connect Rousseau and Marx.[51] In the *Anthropology*, Kant discusses social passions that arise as a reflection of hierarchical social orders and which aim to dominate others by different means, such as honor, force or money. They are outer-directed vices to make use of the outer-directed vices of others, namely to gain in honor, dominion or wealth by succumbing to your power. Thus, those who use these powers humiliate themselves as well as others, as both let their passions rule over them and thus fail to be "ends for themselves."[52] Dominating others is also a case of self-domination, as one conveys one's "slavish disposition" (*Sklavensinn*)[53] by that kind of competition for power

---

[49] Honneth, *The Struggle for Recognition*, p. 138.
[50] Honneth is aware of this problem for his strong thesis about the damage of self-respect through misrecognition and tries to account for it in saying that the negative feelings accompanying disrespect harbor necessarily (*unverbrüchlich*) moral and cognitive insights motivating a struggle against injustice. See ibid.
[51] See also Wood, *Kant's Ethical Thought*, pp. 259–265.
[52] Kant, "Anthropology From a Pragmatic Point of View," VII:271.
[53] Ibid., VII:272. In the context of Kant's condemnation of the enslavement of either

and influence. Ambition (*Ehrsucht*),[54] tyranny (*Herrschsucht*)[55] and greed (*Habsucht*)[56] are its main expressions. Like Rousseau and Marx, Kant thought that modern societies especially produce such forms of slavish mindsets of people deeming themselves masters over others.[57]

It is important to note at this point what the deontological conception of noumenal non-alienation can and cannot provide for us. First and foremost, it explains a moral sense of self-respect and self-worth: a sense of one's "inalienable" dignity as an equal moral authority who co-authorizes moral norms through reciprocal and general justification. In that sense, a morally autonomous person is the co-author of such norms and authorizes them – they take themselves to be a moral authority for themselves and for others (in a "kingdom of ends").[58] Second, as remarked above, there is a notion of the non-alienated, "true" (*eigentlich*) self here but not in the ethical sense of the term relating to the good or "authentic" life. Noumenal moral authority as autonomy reflects on and reasonably *endorses* and thus *authorizes* (based on the criteria of reciprocal and general justification) one's motives for action, morally speaking, and, in this sense, the morally autonomous person "owns" these motives. But, in so reflecting on one's desires, inclinations and commitments as morally acceptable, one does not necessarily overcome alienation in the sense that one no longer considers those desires or commitments that do not conform to morality as one's own, as the person one is. That would be too strong a notion of authorship and authorization, as if only our moral self were our "true" self and everything else was "alien" because it was heteronomous.[59]

The most promising explanation of the "wholehearted" identification with one's desires – of the sort that Harry Frankfurt sees as a condition for freedom of the will and self-determination – is

---

yourself or others, I want to point out that the discussion about Kant's explicit degradation of non-white "races" and about the ambivalent stance of the early as compared to the later Kant with regard to colonialism and slavery is very important. A clear position on this can be found in Kleingeld, "Kant's Second Thoughts on Race," and Kleingeld, "Kant's Second Thoughts on Colonialism."

[54] Ibid.
[55] Ibid., VII:273.
[56] Ibid., VII:274.
[57] This stands in a long tradition of moralistic critiques of social vices; Montaigne was a master of this genre.
[58] On the notion of moral authority here see especially Darwall, *The Second-Person Standpoint*, pt. IV.
[59] This is a tendency in Korsgaard, *The Sources of Normativity*, as well as Korsgaard, *Self-Constitution*.

as a reflective process of authorization[60] rather than as a process of uncovering basic "volitional necessities"[61] of one's character. But such processes of authorization, reason-responsive as they are, neither turn one into the autonomous sole "author" of one's life nor resolve questions of ethical identity (what I "really want" or "really am") with exclusively moral answers. Moral autonomy, that is, being the moral authority over one's actions, morally authorizes these actions and their motives, but that seems neither a necessary nor a sufficient condition for the good life or for ethical autonomy.[62] Whether exercising moral authority over our ethical commitments (for example, partial commitments of love) and ideals (which may run counter to moral norms) is seen as liberating or constraining, that is, as overcoming alienation or rather as alienating in a different way, depends very much on our personal identity in a qualitative, biographical sense. Overcoming moral noumenal alienation is a moral duty toward others and thus also for oneself, as far as one is under a duty to respond to others as equals and as an equal, but it is not a necessary component of the good life. As Kant says, happiness (*Glückseligkeit*) is a thoroughly empirical and indeterminate concept, not one of reason.[63] And heteronomy may play a big part in it. From the perspective of morality, such heteronomy leads to alienation; from the perspective of the good and happy life, morality can be alienating. Moral autonomy is different from ethical authenticity or happiness, and the two notions of non-alienation they refer to are also conceptually different.

So far, the analysis of Kant has stayed at the level of moral considerations. But, following Rousseau, in his republican theory Kant provides a political interpretation of his notion of autonomy – and, I add, of the account of alienation implicit in this interpretation. The republican account of alienation starts from a critique of a society in need of enlightenment, where moral and political autonomy does not exist: a state of "*self-incurred immaturity.*"[64] In such a state, human beings are alienated from each other and themselves as normative authorities; thus they need to establish themselves as such authorities by using their normative power of reason as a public

---

[60] See especially Moran, *Authority and Estrangement*, and Hinshelwood, "The Relation between Agency, Identification, and Alienation."
[61] Frankfurt, *Necessity, Volition, and Love*.
[62] On different conceptions of autonomy see Forst, *The Right to Justification*, ch. 5.
[63] Kant, *Groundwork of the Metaphysics of Morals*, IV:418.
[64] Kant, "An Answer to the Question: 'What Is Enlightenment?'" VIII:35 (tr. altered; emphasis in original).

power, exercising the "freedom to make *public use* of one's reason in all matters."[65] Kant highlights that there is a complex dialectic of social critique at play here, where overcoming noumenal moral and political alienation is intertwined: in a society in which free spirit and free speech are repressed, human beings may "gladly remain immature for life."[66] Still, courageous and free minds will emerge at a certain point of social development, conflict and internal critique, and they will "disseminate the spirit of a rational valuing of one's own worth and of the calling of all humans to think for themselves."[67] But such an "*avant-garde*"[68] cannot claim the authority of leadership if it is not supported by a public form of enlightenment and the public use of critical reason.[69] Even a political revolution might not suffice to achieve a "true reform in one's way of thinking" if not accompanied by such public freedom.[70] The public use of reason is the essential means for overcoming noumenal alienation in the political realm.[71] Courage and critique are the main virtues of emancipation in this respect – and, like Marx, Kant sees authoritarian forms of religion like authoritarian political rule as a major obstacle on the way toward social emancipation.

The same characteristics appear in Kant's republican conception of alienation as in Rousseau's. To live a politically alienated life is to live in an artificial world that does not stand the test of public reason, a world with unjustified hierarchies and forms of domination, and a world in which those subjected (or at least a part of them) feel comfortable in their state of immaturity and being dominated or "guided." Those subjected live an "externalized" or "estranged" life, following the authority of persons, groups or institutions that should have no authority over them, as their authority is unjustified and contrary to reason.

The corresponding Rousseauian–Kantian republican theory of non-alienation implies that there can be no personal liberty without public liberty as political autonomy, and no political autonomy without the free exercise of public reason and the establishment of citizens as sovereign public authorities. The "touchstone" (*Probierstein*) of

---

[65] Ibid., VIII:36 (emphasis in original).
[66] Ibid., VIII:35 (tr. altered).
[67] Ibid., VIII:36 (tr. altered).
[68] To use the term by Ypi, *Global Justice and Avant-Garde Political Agency*.
[69] See Habermas, *Theory and Practice*, p. 40: "in a process of enlightenment there can only be participants."
[70] Kant, "An Answer to the Question: 'What Is Enlightenment?'" VIII:36.
[71] See Wood, *Kant's Ethical Thought*, pp. 300–309, on the importance of free public reason for political progress in Kant.

the justification of laws binding a people, as Kant remarks in the Enlightenment essay, is "whether a people could possibly impose such a law upon itself."[72] In his fully worked-out political theory, Kant develops this abstract theory of a general will into a concrete theory of legislation that leaves no room for the formation of that will in the hands of a monarch. In "On the Common Saying," Kant takes up the formulation of the touchstone and affirms that the idea of political autonomy (as an idea of reason) must become a practical reality: it is the duty of "every legislator to give his laws in such a way that they *could* have arisen from the united will of a whole people and to regard each subject, insofar as he wants to be a citizen, as if he had joined in voting for such a will."[73] True freedom is only possible if collective freedom as political autonomy producing a general will is a reality; and this can only be the case in a republican state where every citizen[74] can be a "co-legislator" (*Mitgesetzgeber*)[75] with an adequate legislative voice and vote. Generally binding public law is "the act of a public will," where "all decide about all, hence each about himself" – the true form of public justice, as "it is only to oneself that one can never do wrong."[76] This shows, as in Rousseau's case, that it is only through complete political alienation in the form of subjection under the general will that true freedom as self-government and self-legislation becomes possible – and thus the overcoming of a state of alienation and immaturity becomes possible as well. Republican "total alienation" overcomes dominating alienation in a feudal or otherwise oppressive society.

In *The Conflict of the Faculties*, Kant calls this Rousseauian ideal a *respublica noumenon*, a Platonic ideal of a constitution based on the natural right of humans, saying that those "obedient to the law, besides being united, ought also to be legislative."[77] The natural right he refers to is the "innate right" of every human being to "freedom (independence from being constrained by another's choice), insofar as it can coexist with the freedom of every other in accordance with a universal law."[78] Arthur Ripstein correctly interprets this right to independence as grounded on the inalienable status of human beings

---

[72] Kant, "An Answer to the Question: 'What Is Enlightenment?'" VIII:39 (tr. altered).
[73] Kant, "On the Common Saying," VIII:297 (emphasis in original).
[74] Kant qualified the group of active citizens heavily and restricted it to men with a certain economic standing.
[75] Kant, "On the Common Saying," VIII:294.
[76] Ibid., VIII:294f.
[77] Kant, *The Conflict of the Faculties*, VII:90f.
[78] Kant, *The Metaphysics of Morals*, VI:237. More on this in Chapters 7 and 10 in this volume.

as ends in themselves and as the relational right "that no person be the master of another."[79] In my understanding, it is a variation of the right to justification as a right to non-domination and as a right to be the co-author of every norm binding on you, a right that grounds all other rights one may have in a normative order, including rights to personal liberty.[80] It is, so to speak, a noumenally grounded right – the right to be the authority for norms that bind you and to be such an authority together with all bound. That is how freedom and subjection go together – by truly generally and reciprocally justifiable norms governing all equally. This criterion eliminates privileges and unjustifiable hierarchies between moral persons and between citizens, whatever the normative context might be. Being noumenally alienated means to be deprived of such authorship, either socially (first-order alienation) or in your own understanding (second-order).

On the basis of the innate right to independence and non-domination, Kant makes all rightful law dependent on the general will,[81] whether it is in the realm of private or public right. Only the "concurring and united will of all [...] can be legislative,"[82] as only that will applies to all, subjected equally, and is authorized by all equally. Freedom under law means that each person is governed by no laws other "than that to which he has given his consent"[83] as an equal. This is the meaning of the "original contract,"[84] as an idea of reason; that is, the relinquishing of "wild, lawless freedom" for the sake of freedom under one's own law.[85] Kant adds, in line with his deontological view, that overcoming the alienation of the wild form of freedom does not mean that the new form of freedom as self-determination guarantees the "happiness" of the people, "for happiness can perhaps come to them more easily and as they would like it to in a state of nature (as Rousseau asserts) or even under a despotic government."[86]

It might even be the case, as in the above reflection on the possibly ethically alienating power of moral autonomy, that republican non-alienation is perceived as alienating by a collective. This can come in at least two forms. First, if the "liberation" from a non-republican to a republican state is forced upon a people in a colonizing form of liberation. In *Perpetual Peace*, Kant is clear that such forms

---

[79] Ripstein, *Force and Freedom*, p. 36.
[80] See Forst, "The Justification of Basic Rights."
[81] Kant, *The Metaphysics of Morals*, VI:264.
[82] Ibid., VI:314.
[83] Ibid.
[84] Ibid., VI:315.
[85] Ibid., VI:316.
[86] Ibid., VI:318.

of forced liberation cannot be justified and, in his later work, he rejected colonialism, whether liberating or not, thus correcting his earlier positive remarks about colonialization.[87] Autonomy can only be achieved autonomously. But there could be a second form, even where no external force is used but where internal criticism leads to new forms of political order, overcoming traditional, hierarchical forms of political order.[88] Such new forms of republican order might then be experienced by many as alienating, as a strange, non-fitting, inauthentic form of order. This can consist in the persistent power of religious, patriarchal, nationalist or other forms of thought, but it can also be a worry about the dangers of corruption that a new regime might bring with it, a loss of stability and trust. Not all of these reflections need to be oppressive or conservative in a non-emancipatory sense.[89] They express an ethical worry of alienation, about a new form of life that is not seen as authentic but as artificial. Yet, for this critique to be free from the suspicion of harboring veiled forms of domination, it would have to be the subject of free public reason, and the voice of dissent and minorities must not be silenced in such discussions.[90] Likewise, the right to co-determine democratically one's normative order is an inalienable right – yet the form in which this right is exercised is to be determined by the participants alone and need not conform to hegemonic examples. Self-determination goes all the way down and cannot be restricted by "Western" models, for example.[91] But the authority to be a co-author of one's normative order must also not be denied by dominating justification narratives. They must never subject persons to the status of being mere means for dominant "values" or "proven" ways of life. That is where republican non-alienation may come into conflict with communitarian notions of non-alienation.

The Kantian ideal of non-alienation combines a highly individualistic and a highly collectivistic aspect – the full independence of each person as an end in themselves, and the collective exercise of normative authority. The dialectics of self-determination connects the two, as no true personal independence is possible without true commonality in an order of self-government. Alienation is thus

[87] See the texts in Flikschuh and Ypi, *Kant and Colonialism*.
[88] Lu, *Justice and Reconciliation in World Politics*, ch. 6, and Lu, "The Right to Justification and the Good of Nonalienation."
[89] See Lear, *Radical Hope*.
[90] See Ci, *Moral China in the Age of Reform*.
[91] See my work on human rights in Forst, *The Right to Justification*, ch. 9, Forst, *Justification and Critique*, ch. 2, and Chapter 7 in this volume. On the question of progress, see Chapter 2 in this volume.

always a social phenomenon, that is, a lack of respect for one's membership in a normative order as an equal authority, morally and/or politically. And it is a cognitive phenomenon, either by failing to respect others or being disrespected – or, as in second-order alienation, as not respecting oneself as a moral or political equal. The first form of alienation violates the dignity of persons, the second form ignores it. But in a Kantian understanding that dignity can never be normatively destroyed, for even those who give themselves up do not lose their moral right to equal normative authority. No person must ever be reduced to a thing that has a price or lost its value. Their dignity is inalienable, and that notion of inalienability is the ground of the Kantian critique of alienation.

1.4 Marxian alienation: Instrumentalization and lack of control

One might think that Marx's analysis of social alienation as a state of persons being reduced to a thing with a market price has obvious parallels to Kant's thought but that we cannot find an account of moral alienation, especially in its second-order form, in Marx. But that is a mistake. For Marx strongly emphasized the loss of sense of one's own inalienable moral worth – even though, in a similar way to Rousseau, he did not distinguish between the moral and the political–social aspects of overcoming alienation in the way Kant did. Marx is also closer to Rousseau than to Kant in stressing that true freedom requires overcoming class rule. Yet, while Kant and Rousseau thought that true freedom can only exist in a republic, Marx envisioned a liberated and non-alienated society beyond a state-like structure of government.

Especially in his early writings, Marx had a clear sense of second-order noumenal alienation, that is, the loss of a sense of one's own dignity and worth as a normative equal to others. The critique of the slavish state of mind of the proletariat, produced by ideological delusion, is a standard topic in these writings – as is the deformed state of mind of the philistines and the bourgeois class. For example, in a letter to Ruge from May 1843, Marx affirms the distance of the philistine from truly human, intellectual beings, in language reminiscent of Rousseau's and Kant's cultural criticism: "As for human beings, that would imply thinking beings, free men, republicans. The philistines do not want to be either of these. [...] The self-confidence [*Selbstgefühl*] of the human being, freedom, has first of all to be aroused again in the hearts of these people."[92] And, with respect to those who are dominated by such philistines, Marx adds: "On the other hand, people who do not feel that they are human beings become the property of their masters like a breed of slaves or horses."[93] He continues by characterizing the principle of monarchy as "the despised, the despicable [*verächtlich*], *the dehumanised man*,"[94] indicating the connection between social (first-order) and subjective (second-order) alienation. In a further letter (September 1843), he stresses the program of radical critique as "analysing the mystical consciousness that is unintelligible to itself, whether it manifests itself in a religious or a political form."[95] The term "mysticism" is important for Marx's critique of noumenal alienation, both with respect to religion and the belief in private property and its legitimacy. Mysticisms cast a spell over the minds of people and make them accept noumenal alienation.

Critiquing religion was one of the most important ways to dispel noumenal alienation for the sake of intellectual and social emancipation – the work of enlightenment, in Kantian terms.[96] Religious belief is a particular example of an alienated and alienating form of thought because it redirects ideas of individual and communal freedom into an imagined sphere and thus furthers the acceptance of unfreedom and domination in the actual world. Marx often speaks of "religious self-estrangement"[97] which needs to be overcome by materialist critique, as in the Theses on Feuerbach. Likewise, a critique of the system of private property and the economy based on it needs to dispel the alienating isolation of the human being who sees in the other "not the *realisation* of his own freedom, but the *barrier* to it."[98] Both religion and bourgeois ideology constitute a "*Schein*," a mere pretense of freedom that, in its ideological character, veils the true freedom of normative equals and makes humans accept social forms of domination while they deem themselves to be free.[99]

---

[92] Marx, "Letters from the Deutsch-Französische Jahrbücher," pp. 134–137.
[93] Ibid., p. 137.
[94] Ibid., p. 138 (emphasis in original).
[95] Ibid., p. 144.
[96] See Ypi, "From Revelation to Revolution."
[97] Marx, "Theses on Feuerbach," p. 4.
[98] Marx, "On the Jewish Question," p. 163 (emphasis in original).
[99] See Marx, "The Holy Family, or Critique of Critical Criticism," p. 116 (emphasis in original): "Precisely the *slavery of civil society* is *in appearance* the greatest *freedom* because it is in appearance the fully developed *independence* of the individual, who considers as his *own* freedom the uncurbed movement, no longer bound by a common bond or by man, of the estranged elements of his life, such as property, industry, religion, etc., whereas actually this is his fully developed slavery and inhumanity."

NOUMENAL ALIENATION

Thus critique needs to take aim at the *"holy form [Heiligengestalt]* of human self-estrangement."[100] In a nutshell: "The criticism of religion ends with the teaching that *man is the highest being for man*, hence with the *categorical imperative to overthrow all relations* in which man is a debased, enslaved, forsaken, despicable being."[101] Such relations are relations of both first- and second-order noumenal alienation, as human beings are both disrespected (*verachtet*) and disrespect themselves (*verächtlich*) in these social structures and modes of thought. They are under the spell of false beliefs that deny their sense of equal moral and political–social authorship; what Marx calls the "real" or "whole man"[102] – the human being who ought to say: "*I am nothing and I should be everything.*"[103] Their claim is the basic human claim to emancipation, not just that of a particular class but that of the "general rights of society."[104] That universal class does not make use of a particular right, "because no *particular wrong* but *wrong generally* [*Unrecht schlechthin*] is perpetuated against it; which can no longer invoke a *historical* but only a *human* title."[105] Overcoming that kind of basic moral injustice and alienation is "the *complete retrieval* [*Wiedergewinnung*] of the man"[106] who have lost themselves in the course of a history of domination. This is as much Kant as it is Hegel, but the Kantian aspect explains why Marx spoke of a *categorical imperative of emancipation* here: it is the imperative of true moral and social emancipation, based on a deontological right to non-domination and to be an equal normative authority.

The famous analysis of the four aspects of alienation in his *Economic–Philosophical Manuscripts* has to be seen in this light. In whatever form alienation is analyzed – as alienation from the product of one's labor, from the process of production, from one's "species being" as a socially and mentally self-determining (and creative) being,[107] or from one another such that persons only regard

---

[100] Marx, "Contribution to the Critique of Hegel's Philosophy of Law," p. 176 (emphasis in original).
[101] Ibid., p. 182 (emphasis in original).
[102] Ibid.
[103] Ibid., p. 185 (emphasis in original).
[104] Ibid., p. 184.
[105] Ibid., p. 186 (emphasis in original).
[106] Ibid. (tr. altered; emphasis in original).
[107] See Marx, "Economic and Philosophic Manuscripts of 1844," p. 277 (emphasis in original): "Similarly, in degrading spontaneous, free activity to a means, estranged labour makes man's species-life a means to his physical existence [...]. It estranges from man his own body, as well as external nature and his spiritual aspect, his *human* aspect."

each other as means and not as ends in social and economic life[108] – the Kantian moral conception of the equal dignity and inalienable authority of persons is not just obviously at work, but also every form of alienation is noumenal because in every one of these forms humans misrecognize one another and themselves as part of a structured social process of reified agents producing and exchanging "things." The analysis of noumenal alienation shows that every social alienation is also "self-estrangement."[109]

Two aspects of this analysis of alienation need further emphasis. First, the development of an alienated society, which Marx (following Rousseau to some extent) outlines, is connected with a process of growing class domination, as the alien product of proletarian labor becomes at the same time an alienating object, in the way "that someone else is master of this object, someone who is alien, hostile, powerful, and independent of him."[110] Being alienated thus also means to be dominated and exploited as an object yourself, to be under "the coercion and the yoke of another man"[111] – another who, in the right analysis, has to be seen as the representative of a class, not as an evil individual. Thus, the theme of *Entfremdung* in Marx must never be reduced to an ethical issue of being "truly" and authentically oneself, as it first and foremost addresses relations of *Knechtung*, that is, of social domination in the form of economic exploitation and general political and legal oppression.

The second important aspect of alienation leads to its political aspect rather than its moral dimension. As already noticed, Marx often calls the alienated society one of "mysticism," by which he means the ideological veil it casts over structures of domination. Unveiling this mysticism is an important task of overcoming the noumenal power of the capitalist normative order.[112] The most important text of Marx to understand this aspect of first- and second-order noumenal alienation is the analysis of the fetish character of commodities in *Capital*.[113]

In this central chapter of his work, Marx – in line with earlier criticisms – stresses that in an estranged society social relations become reified relations between "things" that have a doubly dominating or

---

[108] See Quante, "Das gegenständliche Gattungswesen."
[109] Marx, "Economic and Philosophic Manuscripts of 1844," p. 275.
[110] Ibid., p. 278.
[111] Ibid., p. 279.
[112] See Forst, *Normativity and Power*, esp. ch. 2, and Forst, "Noumenal Power Revisited," as well as Chapter 9 in this volume.
[113] For the following, see my discussion in "Justice after Marx," including the critique, in Forst, *Normativity and Power*, ch. 7.

oppressive character because (a) they benefit some, while others are exploited, and (b) they are not transparent and therefore cannot be subjected to social criticism or control. Social relations assume the "fantastic [*phantasmagorische*] form of a relation between things,"[114] and the result is an artificial world of asymmetry and exploitation that is not intelligible to those who are part of it, and in this sense it is "alien" even if it seems familiar: it is not really one's own. The emphasis here is not on interpersonal class oppression but on a general and more anonymous form of domination and class rule – an artificial world of things that conceals the real relations between human beings in the process of production and shrouds it in an ideological veil of ignorance: "To them, their own social movement takes the form of the movement of things, and these things, far from being under their control, in fact control them."[115] So, apart from instrumentalization and class domination or exploitation, it is the lack of transparency and control that Marx criticizes here; the foundation of this critique, strongly reminiscent of Rousseau, is a notion of social autonomy as collective autonomy.

In the fetishism chapter, therefore, Marx contrasts his analysis of capitalist alienation with the "association of free men" in which the means of production are socialized, and hence under collective control. Social relations are accordingly "transparent,"[116] a word he often uses to describe the necessary kind of control: "The life-process of society, which is based on the process of material production, does not strip off its mystical veil until it is treated as production by freely associated men, and is consciously regulated by them in accordance with a settled plan."[117] This notion of social autonomy overcoming alienation is in line with earlier texts, where Marx emphasizes that alienated social orders confront the individual as an alien force, which needs to be transformed into something transparent and intelligible that can be brought under control. The injustice to be overcome is not just one that produces palaces for the rich and deprivation and hovels for the workers;[118] capitalist society also deprives workers of the ability and opportunity to determine in an autonomous way the basic structure to which they are subject – and to regard themselves as free agents who can change their society in the first place. Their totality of social relations appears to them as

[114] Marx, *Capital*, vol. 1, p. 83.
[115] Ibid., p. 85 (tr. altered).
[116] Ibid., p. 90.
[117] Ibid.
[118] Marx, "Economic and Philosophic Manuscripts of 1844," p. 273.

part of an "alien power."[119] This shows that it is the loss of collective power and autonomy in particular that is the political key feature of the condition of alienation – namely, that individuals cannot be social beings together with others in a self-determining collective.[120]

Throughout Marx's work, this political idea of overcoming alienation as an obscure power that dominates social relations is central: "Freedom in this sphere can only consist in socialised man, the associated producers, rationally regulating their interchange with Nature, bringing it under their common control, instead of being ruled by it as by the blind forces of Nature."[121] The analysis Marx offered shares the characteristics of the republican account of alienation offered by Rousseau and Kant: human beings find themselves within an artificial order of things that is not transparent to them but veiled by the noumenal power of religious, feudal or capitalist ideologies. These ideologies hide relations of domination and thus seal the normative order off from public scrutiny and criticism.[122] Domination here does not just refer to the unjustified exercise of social and political power but also to the moral issue of instrumentalization, of not being treated as an end but rather as a thing or commodity, of having a "market price," as Kant says.[123] The lack of critique manifests itself in the extreme in the acceptance of an order of domination by those subjected to it, thus leading an outer-directed, non-autonomous life, where they are not just denied a role as equal normative authority but where they do not even consider themselves to be such authorities with a claim to a social and political standing based on this fundamental moral status. First- and second-order noumenal alienation are both present: those subjected to such an order do not recognize each other as justificatory equals and they do not recognize themselves as having such standing.

While Marx's critical analysis of alienation is in line with the republican accounts of Rousseau and Kant, his idea of gaining and exercising collective control differs from their republicanism. Whereas in earlier writings Marx uses republican ideas of political autonomy,[124] as seen above, in his later writings Marx is guided by a notion of *social* rather than *political* autonomy. The difference is

---

[119] Ibid., p. 278.
[120] Ripstein, "Rationality and Alienation," p. 463.
[121] Marx, *Capital*, vol. 3, p. 807.
[122] For a comprehensive social analysis of fetishism critique, see Rasmussen, "The Symbolism of Marx."
[123] See also Buchanan, "Exploitation, Alienation, and Injustice."
[124] See Leipold, "Marx's Social Republic."

that social collective autonomy is not mediated by political institutions (with the exception of a transitional period), which according to Marx would only be necessary in a society in which there are still fundamental conflicts over questions of production and distribution. Marx thought he had discovered the truth about the contradictions inherent in capitalist society and about the crisis that would eventually lead society beyond this historical malaise. He had a conception of injustice and alienation in capitalist societies and a view of a society beyond politically determined justice – that is, a notion of a society of complete human control and order after the breakdown of the capitalist order. Before that great change, political institutions are more part of the problem than of the solution; after it there would not be any need for them because genuine universality and community would prevail in a "true realm of freedom"[125] beyond the realm of necessity. This is why the question of the exercise of political autonomy over economic relations as part of a theory of (socialist republican) political justice is absent from the Marxian program – before the historical turn it is not possible, after it, it is not necessary. Thus, his notion of overcoming alienation is social but also to some extent *apolitical*.[126]

There are many more relevant differences that need discussion in this context, such as the difference between overcoming alienation by revolution, as in Marx (and possibly in Rousseau), and overcoming alienation by the peaceful and piecemeal method of public criticism and political reform, as in Kant (who, despite his argument against the lawfulness of revolutionary change, regarded the French revolution as a major emancipatory step).[127] But the commonalities among their social criticism and critiques of alienation ought not to be overlooked. First, all of them require a deontological argument about the moral equality and independence of human beings who are equal moral authorities to each other. That moral status or, in traditional terms, inalienable "dignity" forbids any social order in which humans become mere things or instruments for others.[128] Second, overcoming first-order noumenal alienation means to respect others and to be respected as an equal

---

[125] Marx, *Capital*, vol. 3, p. 807.
[126] See, among many, the criticisms of this kind of political alienation in Marx by Habermas, *Theory and Practice* and "Towards a Reconstruction of Historical Materialism," as well as Lefort and Gauchet, "Sur la démocratie"; see also Howard, "From Marx to Kant."
[127] Ypi, "On Revolution in Kant and Marx"; Williams, "The Political Philosophies of Kant and Marx."
[128] For an important discussion and defence of Kantian socialist ethics, going back to

moral–political authority within the normative order to which one is subject. And third, to struggle for such a status presupposes a form of self-respect that is lost in second-order noumenal alienation. Therefore the first task is to attack and overcome second-order noumenal alienation – by radical critique, the public use of reason and sober social analysis. The "mysticism" of the dominating and alienating normative order must be dispelled and the sense of one's own worth as a justificatory agent equal to others must be appealed to and furthered.

1.5 Conclusion

The term "noumenal alienation" highlights three central aspects of my analysis. First, it is meant to indicate that the very ground of every critique of alienation as a denial of normative agency is a noumenally ascribed moral status of "being" an equal normative authority, even if that status is denied in practice by others as well as by oneself. The dignity of human beings as equal normative authorities is a moral and – in that sense – noumenal, not an empirical, idea, though it materializes in a number of ways within a normative order in the status of being a non-dominated legal, political and social equal.[129] This deontological notion of moral status is foundational: there can be no moral criticism of alienation without the *inalienable* right to be respected as a normative equal authority and author of binding norms. The moral scandal of alienation as denying equal standing requires a moral ground that no historicist or purely "immanent" form of critique can provide.[130] Marx for one, as shown above, was not a historicist when it came to the "categorical imperative" to overcome "*das Unrecht schlechthin*":[131] absolute injustice.[132] Nor was Rousseau, who believed in an inalienable right to moral and political self-determination – what Kant would later call the "innate" right of human freedom.

Hermann Cohen, see van der Linden, *Kantian Ethics and Socialism*; for a related view, see Gilabert, "Kantian Dignity and Marxian Socialism."

[129] See my view on "fundamental justice" in Forst, *Justification and Critique*, chs. 2 and 5, and Forst, *Normativity and Power*, chs. 7–10.

[130] Forst, *Normativity and Power*, and Forst, "The Justification of Progress and the Progress of Justification," Chapter 2 in this volume.

[131] Marx, "Zur Kritik der Hegelschen Rechtsphilosophie," p. 390 (emphasis in original).

[132] In *Collected Works*, "Unrecht schlechthin" is translated with "wrong generally," which is misleading. See Marx, "Contribution to the Critique of Hegel's Philosophy of Law," p. 186.

NOUMENAL ALIENATION

The second important meaning of "noumenal" points to the essential recognitional and cognitive dimension of alienation. First-order alienation means not to be respected as a normative equal morally and politically and it also means, from a different perspective, not respecting others as such equals. Hence the term, in whatever material forms such disrespect, domination, exclusion and marginalization arise, refers to a cognitive intersubjective relation. Second-order alienation is also a special cognitive relation, namely to oneself as a lack of recognition of oneself as a normative authority.[133] Alienation is much more than a state of mind, as it refers to intersubjective relations, social structures and a whole social order, but it also expresses a cognitive attitude toward others and to oneself. It is of a noumenal nature.

The third aspect is connected to this. We cannot analyze relations of alienation without an understanding of the "noumenal" power complexes that are at work in justifying relations of alienation – with the help of ideological justification narratives[134] that veil the asymmetries and structures of domination in place. That is why struggles for emancipation take place primarily on the noumenal power level; without overcoming first- and second-order alienation, that is, without changing the perceptions of oneself and of others, no social change toward overcoming alienation will be possible. There is a complex dialectical interplay between cognitive and practical emancipation, as the one requires and, ideally, furthers the other. But, as Rousseau, Kant and Marx saw, no process of emancipation can get off the ground without a moral understanding of yourself and your own dignity even if – and especially when – it is materially denied to you. That is why struggles for noumenal power are essential, aiming to change the general social realm of justifications. Such struggles have to take into account a complex intersection of class, gender and race domination, going far beyond the limits of the thought of Rousseau, Kant and Marx, not to mention the transnational character of current forms of domination.[135] But here, too, the noumenal dimension of social criticism remains crucial.

Let me conclude with a conceptual remark. There are a number of concepts in our moral vocabulary that I call "normatively dependent concepts," as they only gain normative substance by being connected

---

[133] For a paradigmatic analysis of the notion of reification along cognitivist lines, though focusing on ethical rather than moral aspects of the relation to self and others, see Honneth, *Reification*.
[134] Forst, *Normativity and Power*, ch. 3.
[135] See Chapter 8 in this volume.

to other normative principles or values. Toleration,[136] solidarity,[137] legitimacy[138] and trust[139] are examples of such concepts. They are often mistakenly seen as values in themselves, but actually they are not; for example, solidarity can be a good or a bad thing depending on the justifications for it. Non-alienation is another such normatively dependent concept. In my analysis, I have used a notion of moral and political autonomy, of moral and political normative authorship, to give it substance. Alienation generally means that a person is disconnected from themselves, others and their social context in a normatively relevant way, but that normative relevance needs to be explained by other concepts. For the reasons explained in this paper, I think it is important to understand, first, that for Rousseau, Kant and Marx the normative concepts that do the work are those of equal moral and political authority and autonomous co-authorship and, second, that the noumenal aspect of alienation sheds light on the two relevant forms of first-order and second-order alienation that we need to distinguish. In this way, the deontological aspects of a critique of alienation come to the fore.

Given the character of normative dependence, one can also use other values to give the term alienation normative substance. Think, for example, of the many criticisms of "alienated" life-forms because of their commercialized, anonymous, mute, technological, routine-based, "herd"-like, monotonous, legalistic, paternalistic, etc. character – criticisms that go back to and combine many strands of critical thought, ranging from Rousseauian romanticism to Marx, Kierkegaard and Nietzsche, and from there to Lukács, Adorno and Horkheimer, and many others. Some of these criticisms, especially those of commercialized reification[140] and of a lack of autonomous "appropriation"[141] of one's social relations, derive their normative power in large part from sharing the noumenal deontological account; but some are also based on other values, like an ethical ideal of self-realization, authenticity or "resonance" with one's environment, including nature.[142] Such analyses can be sociologically and normatively powerful. However, the analysis of noumenal alienation and its basis in a certain notion of the *inalienable* moral

---

[136] Forst, *Toleration in Conflict*, §3.
[137] See Chapter 4 in this volume.
[138] Forst, *Normativity and Power*, ch. 8.
[139] See Forst, "The Justification of Trust in Conflict."
[140] See Honneth, *Reification*; Satz, *Why Some Things Should Not Be for Sale*.
[141] Jaeggi, *Alienation*.
[142] Rosa, *Resonance*.

status of persons reminds us of a categorical difference in the validity claims on which critiques of alienation rest. The critique I reconstructed rests on a deontological moral claim and thus requires – with Rousseau, Kant and Marx – a *categorical imperative* of overcoming the forms of domination that constitute noumenal alienation, while certain ideals of self-realization or social life that do not rest on such moral foundations may still be well founded but cannot claim the same kind of validity. They appeal to the attractiveness of the ethical vision they express but they ground no strong moral duties – think, for example, of the difference between a critique of capitalist commercialization producing "empty" forms of life and a critique of capitalist exploitation as a form of domination. The duties to avoid or overcome relations "in which man is a debased, enslaved, forsaken, despicable being," to use Marx's words,[143] require deontological foundations. They should not be mixed with values of a different normative order and importance.

---

[143] Marx, "Contribution to the Critique of Hegel's Philosophy of Law," p. 182.

— 2 —

THE JUSTIFICATION OF PROGRESS AND THE PROGRESS OF JUSTIFICATION*

2.1 The dialectics of progress

The concept of progress is dialectical in nature. On the one hand, progress is a necessary term for anyone who is interested in human emancipation understood as overcoming social domination (which I call "moral–political progress") or anyone interested in improving people's living conditions by medical means (which I call "progress in life conditions"), for example. On the other hand, some of those who are engaged in struggles for emancipation think that this implies overcoming the very concept of progress, being, as Ashis Nandy[1] says, one of the "dirtiest" words, a word that all too often did – and still does – justify domination across and within societies. It seems to be wedded to a universalist teleological form of thinking, according to which some societies or groups have reached that telos earlier than others and thus have the authority, and maybe even the mission, to pull the less progressed people out of their "self-incurred immaturity," to use Kant's term, into the light of reason and freedom,

---

* I am indebted to the participants of the conference "Justification and Emancipation" at Penn State University in April 2017 for a discussion of this paper from which I have greatly benefited – with special thanks to Amy Allen and Eduardo Mendieta for making this event possible. I am also grateful to the participants in the conference "Normative Orders in Transition" at Goethe University Frankfurt in June 2017, where I presented this paper, and to Lea Ypi for her written comments on an earlier version. My thanks go also to Paul Kindermann and Ciaran Cronin for their help in preparing this text. At the Krupp-Reimers research colloquium about the "Herrschaft des Konkreten" 2018, I was invited to discuss a text that corresponds in principle to the present one; for queries about it, I want to thank all participants in that circle, especially Tim Rojek for his commentary "Fortschrittsbegriffe, ihre Dialektik und die Gefahren einer Herrschaft des Konkreten."
[1] Nandy, "Fortschritt," p. 53.

possibly even overcoming their ignorant or indolent reluctance by force.[2] As Amy Allen emphasizes, the idea of progress is deeply entangled with imperialist universalisms of this kind, "nourished by a philosophical and cultural imaginary that justifies the political subjugation of distant territories and their native populations through claims that such peoples are less advanced, cognitively inferior, and therefore naturally subordinate."[3]

This critique points to the essential aspect of the dialectic implicit in the concept of progress, namely the tension between its normative and its historical meaning, i.e., between the ideal expressed and the reality it stands for. Could it be, as some argue, that the reality of domination weighs so heavily that no ideal content can be saved for that term, so that the said dialectics comes to an end? Or can we, as I believe, and furthermore should we develop a de-reified, non-teleological, non-dominating, emancipatory conception of progress? For, otherwise, how shall we call social developments through which relations of colonial (or neo-colonial) domination are overcome through social struggle? If we can't avoid calling such developments social progress, we must carefully reflect on those standards for progress that do not lead to new forms of domination under the guise of liberation, possibly hidden from sight. Nevertheless, such standards must exist if we do not want to give up the language of progress altogether.

I believe that we are unavoidably caught in the dialectic of progress: If our critique of false notions of progress is situated and not merely abstract and empty, we also argue *for* progress, both in theory and in practice, because *overcoming false progress is true progress*. Being against progress because one is motivated by an account of non-domination or emancipation is also to be for it, and I don't see how we, who understand ourselves as participants and not merely distant observers of history, could (as Allen suggests) say that we should not be committed to any backward-looking claim to progress and yet still hold onto a contextual, forward-looking imperative of progress.[4] That strikes me as a contradictory and ahistorical view which refuses to learn from history, a history containing regress as well as (we hope) progress, whatever criteria of emancipation we use. Especially in our role as critical theorists, the critique of domination

---

[2] On Kant's own complex relation to questions of colonial rule, see Flikschuh and Ypi, *Kant and Colonialism*; McCarthy, *Race, Empire, and the Idea of Human Development*; as well as Valdez, *Transnational Cosmopolitanism*.
[3] Allen, *The End of Progress*, p. 1.
[4] Ibid., p. 127.

in its many forms – economic, racial or sexist (or a combination thereof) – obliges us to think of ourselves as participants in ongoing struggles for emancipation (whether successful or not), struggles that did not begin with us.

2.2 Moral–political progress

A proper understanding of the contemporary discussion about the concept of progress requires us to make a distinction between two major fields of discourse already alluded to.[5] On the one hand, in many societies there is a debate over the appropriate definition of technological progress as qualitative progress in life conditions: How much environmental destruction does unfettered economic growth bring with it? What is our stance on artificially modifying food or on genetically improving human nature? What is permitted in medical research? These are genuine evaluative questions concerning progress in specific areas of science, technology and economics that examine its social costs. In pluralistic societies, it is not unusual that these debates involve clashes between very different value systems, so that the search for shared norms proves to be difficult.

On the other hand, there are debates about progress that also call for a normative language, although one of a different kind. In such cases, resistance to certain conceptions of progress is fueled less by ethical evaluations of a desirable way of life than by an impulse of justice – one that demands what I call "moral–political progress." What is deplored are social or economic structures that are dominating – i.e., that lack sufficient justification among those who are subjected to them – and what is revealed is a desire for emancipation that should not be confused with a general form of skepticism concerning progress. The targets of such criticism are unjustifiable and imposed conceptions of development that "colonize" social lifeworlds, to use Habermas's expression[6] – also in an effort to "develop," "modernize," and sometimes even to "liberate" societies.[7] Whether it is powerful states, associations of states or international organizations (in cooperation with certain groups within a society) that are accused of neo-colonialism does not change the fact that here it is essentially a matter of how social and

---

[5] The following section is adapted from my *Normativity and Power*, ch. 4.
[6] Habermas, *The Theory of Communicative Action*, vol. 2, ch. 8.
[7] See Tully, "On Law, Democracy and Imperialism." See also Gädeke, *Politik der Beherrschung*.

political power is structured and organized – and of how much social self-determination is possible in a globalized society. These conflicts are not simply a matter of being for or against "globalization," however, because many of the global political and economic relations that are criticized as asymmetrical cannot be changed except through global coordination.[8] Such criticism is not just directed against external domination, since it most often also criticizes internal domination, i.e., a lack of justification and of justificatory standing within a given normative order.[9]

Both debates – but especially the latter – show that the discussions about the concept of progress should not be viewed in terms of a simple pro or contra. Instead, we must keep the social dimension of these controversies in mind. Then the question is often not whether a society should "develop" but who determines this process and defines the corresponding goals. The decisive question raised by the concept of moral–political progress remains how the power to define such progress and the paths leading to it is structured.

2.3 Self-determined progress

With this we arrive at an important insight. Although the concept of progress is used in a normative sense in the two fields of debate mentioned, it is not a normative concept in its own right. Technological progress cannot count as social progress in life conditions without social evaluations of what it is good for, who benefits from it, and what costs it generates. Nor can true social progress as moral–political progress exist where the changes in question are enforced and experienced as colonization. Technological progress must be socially accepted, and socially accepted progress is progress that is determined and brought about by the members of the society in question. Democratic political forms and procedures are not primarily to be seen as development *goals* but as essential *conditions* of social advancement such that the goal of democracy ought not to be attained by non-democratic means – and that progress in life conditions achieved, say, by a technocratic, authoritarian regime cannot counterbalance the lack of moral–political progress in political and social justice. Of particular importance in this regard

---

[8] See Hale et al., *Gridlock*, as well as Forst, "Two Bad Halves Don't Make a Whole."
[9] For an evolutionary theory of moral progress that focuses on the question of equal status, see Buchanan and Powell, *The Evolution of Moral Progress*.

are the many "empowerment" initiatives, such as political initiatives in civil society forums and organizations or economic empowerment measures – for example, through microcredits or more comprehensive social policy measures, especially those where underprivileged groups (in many countries, first and foremost, women) win participation rights through social struggles. Increasing the scope of agency for individuals and collectives, as Amartya Sen emphasizes, is the central means and goal of development and progress.[10]

As the example of contemporary China demonstrates, in an age of multiple modernities, there is no universally valid script for the combination of economic, cultural and political modernization in the sense of democratization. But, in the long run, it is doubtful whether the one can succeed without the other. A regime is strengthened by increases in prosperity; but it is simultaneously tested and placed in question by technical capabilities and by new upwardly mobile social groups. Social dynamics lead to political dynamics. However, such processes do not unfold along a single, predictable path. This may be unsettling for those who hope to derive prognostic wisdom from sociological research about modernization, yet, normatively speaking, that is also a good thing because every process that deserves to be called progress should be one that those subjected initiate and control themselves. This is difficult enough. But, once again, it becomes apparent that the evaluative criteria for progress refer to the concepts of non-domination and self-determination – as fundamental requirements of justice understood as an autonomous and collective *practice*, not as a teleologically fixed result.

This seems to give rise to a dilemma. I began by emphasizing the critique of unilateral Western notions of social development and progress; but now a series of normative concepts such as autonomy, democracy and justice, which seem to owe their existence to a Western political and cultural background, come back into play. Have we reverted from criticizing a form of particularism that disguises itself as universalism back to this very particularism? With this fear we must contrast a different perspective, for the critique of the unilateral or imposed, of the dominating and oppressive idea of progress or of the corresponding practice is, to repeat, itself normative, and it calls for nothing less than collectively self-determined forms of social development. This language therefore is the authentic language of progress, and what critics as well as proponents of the idea of progress must recognize is that progress is a *reflexive* concept: every

---

[10] Sen, *Development as Freedom*.

progressive process must be constantly questioned as to whether it is in the justifiable social interest of those who are part of this process.

2.4 Emancipation, reverse orientalism and foundationalism

The true logic of progress is not primarily a social-technical, scientific or technological logic of reaching a certain telos; rather, it is a social logic in the sense that it must be supported and defined by the members of a normative order themselves. There are no predetermined blueprints for this, though there is a reflexive principle of justice as justification, which states that only those who are subjected to such an order may define the steps that constitute its "progress." This is in line with the basic principle of discursive justice as non-domination, which says that no one may be subjected to specific rules or institutions that cannot be adequately justified to him or her as a free and equal normative authority. That is the core meaning of self-determination that is central to social progress. It implies a basic human "right to justification," which is as much a right to the protection of individuals as a right to equal participation in social and political decision-making processes.[11] According to this principle, progress means that a society successfully strives for new levels of justification that ensure not only that political and social relations can be justified in a reciprocal and general way but also that there are institutions for producing such justifications in autonomous discursive practices in the first place.[12] Hence the justification of progress can only be achieved if those who are subjected to the social order that changes are themselves the agents determining this change through processes of justification – and real progress consists in setting up frameworks for justification that overcome domination in the sense of persons or groups not being respected as free and equal authorities of justification. The *justification of progress* lies in the *progress of justification* as a social practice among equals.

I want to argue that the concept of justification is crucial to understanding and evaluating social progress. But we need to conceive of social progress in the right way and avoid reified and dominating ways of thinking about what a structure of justification is or what it means to be respected as a justificatory equal. In short, we must

---

[11] See Forst, *The Right to Justification*, and Forst, *Justification and Critique*.
[12] I trace such a logic of progress with reference to the question of toleration in Forst, *Toleration in Conflict*.

understand progress in non-teleological terms and conceive of it in a *deontological*, process-oriented way: the imperative for progress is, as Allen also says, the imperative of emancipation as "the minimization of relations of domination"[13] – or, as I would add, that of overcoming domination. There is no fixed ideal or telos that would pre-determine what this means, as the participants *themselves* will be the sole agents who justify this in discursive practice, taking their guidance from the criteria of reciprocity and generality. Any theory that calls itself critical needs to stress this, for, to adopt Bernard Williams's rendering of the basic Habermasian insight of discursive non-domination, "the acceptance of a justification does not count if the acceptance itself is produced by the coercive power which is supposedly being justified."[14] This is why true liberation and progress consist in the autonomous creation of conditions of non-domination and mutual justification.

The imperative of progress Allen wants to hold onto is an imperative of "genuine respect and openness to the Other,"[15] taking the agency of others seriously, avoiding any conception of others as "not yet capable of autonomous self-rule,"[16] and, in addition, realizing the central value of freedom.[17] I agree with all of this. But I fail to see how the thoroughly Rortyan "metanormative contextualism"[18] that Allen advocates could serve that purpose. How can standards for evaluating progress in a postcolonial age be reparticularized and reparochialized in the way she suggests – that is, by appealing to "the normative inheritance of modernity, particularly to its notions of freedom, inclusion and equal moral respect"?[19] Was it not precisely *that* inheritance, according to Allen herself, that dominated the allegedly unfree and unreasonable "others"? Of course, she uses this contextualism to remind the moderns of their contingent heritage and to respect other cultures with "humility"[20] about their own standpoint. But that has major disadvantages because it still implies that the West or, even worse, modernity is the true normative

---

[13] Allen, *The End of Progress*, p. xiv. The dialogue with Amy Allen, which reaches back to her earlier critique in "The Power of Justification" and my reply in "Justifying Justification," has also been continued by her in her response to my text in "Progress, Normativity, and Universality" and my further reply in "Navigating a World of Conflict and Power."
[14] Williams, *In the Beginning Was the Deed*, p. 6.
[15] Allen, *The End of Progress*, p. 32.
[16] Ibid., p. 155.
[17] Ibid., p. 195.
[18] Ibid., p. 121.
[19] Ibid., p. 33.
[20] Ibid., p. 75.

source of universal freedom, equality and respect, and that other cultures are not really participating in this history, or if they are, they do so primarily as victims of the oppressive implications of these values historically understood. So it is "we" (Westerners) who have to do better this time. But again, the "others" (non-Westerners) – occasionally referred to as the "subaltern," using Spivak's term (albeit in a much less dialectical way than Spivak herself)[21] – seem to be outside of this normative horizon, only this time, "we" ought to treat them as dialogue partners rather than as objects of domination. But we only do so because "we" are moderns, while they are not. So it seems, according to Allen, that we do not share any normative framework with them – i.e., we still *impose* ours, but this time in a friendly, humble, non-oppressive way.

So, what exactly is the normative standing of these "others" – who are they? Implicitly, I think, Allen's answer is clear: they are our justificatory equals, and we must not impose our normative orders on them. Explicitly, however, she says the opposite: we do not share a normative status with them, since we do not share any normative basis according to Allen's relativistic framework; thus, we regard these "others" as alien but treat them with respect because we as moderns think this is the right thing to do. But that is a unilateral, generous move on our part, as the metanormative contextualist implies. We ought to be open to learning from them about what they think, but there is no common moral language binding us all – for such a language of, say, them having a right to justification would impose an alien and dominating framework upon them. According to Allen, it is to force a notion of reason on "others" that disempowers them and leaves them speechless and justificationless and that presumes a universalism that does not exist. In her view, any framework of Kantian-style practical reason "explicitly or implicitly excludes, represses or dominates all that is associated with the so-called Other of reason, whether that be understood in terms of madness, irrationality, the emotions, the affects, embodiment or the imagination, all of which are symbolically associated with black, queer, female, colonized, and subaltern subjects."[22]

But I believe that the opposite is the case. I think that the right to justification accords the "subaltern" precisely the voice that they can claim as justificatory equals, including the voice that criticizes

---

[21] Ibid., p. 152. For Spivak's dialectical critique of Kant, see Spivak, *A Critique of Postcolonial Reason*, ch. 1. For an interpretation, see Dübgen, *Was ist gerecht?*
[22] Allen, *The End of Progress*, p. 137.

dominant discourses of justification. In virtue of its reflexive and critical character, the right to justification is the right to question any reification of justification and the noumenal power structures that deny a voice to certain groups who are deemed "unreasonable."[23] So to deny others such standing as justificatory equals in the name of particularism about justification is the wrong way to go; it just reproduces the dominating image of "us" as moderns and of others as non-modern, non-reasonable "others" who are completely different from us – a form of alienating others that I call *reverse orientalism*. This critique is in line with Edward Said's powerful reflections on orientalism, a particular form of "othering" the other in an imperialist, racist and ethnocentric mode, denying these others a voice and a sense of justice.[24] In a powerful afterword from 1995, Said criticizes romanticizing and essentializing readings of his critique that celebrate the "other" and combine postmodern and postcolonial thought in the wrong way by no longer criticizing the perversions of the "grand narratives of emancipation and enlightenment" but giving up the general imperative of emancipation.[25] With Said, I want to uphold this imperative, and with him I want to affirm that "the subaltern *can* speak, as the history of liberation movements in the twentieth century eloquently attests."[26]

To be sure, Allen thoroughly reflects on this issue, since it goes to the heart of her enterprise. As moderns, on a first level of normativity, we are, according to her, committed to modern values such as freedom and equality, but on a reflexive second level, we know that these commitments are parochial, contextual and historical, and thus we will not impose them. They are not context-transcendent.[27] But, here we need to ask: What does the metanormative level ask us to do? If it requires us to treat others with equal respect and engage in an "open-ended dialogue"[28] with them, as Allen wants us to do, what is the metanormative framework for that kind of discursive respect? It is the right to justification, expressing a context-transcending imperative – what else could it be? To deny this and still hold onto the imperative of equal respect is flatly contradictory.

---

[23] If, for example, the subaltern "define themselves as subjects on patriarchal terms or they allow themselves to be constituted as objects of imperialism" (ibid., p. 153), they are subjected to exactly the kinds of noumenal power structures this concept is meant to capture. See my *Normativity and Power*, ch. 2, and Chapter 9 in this volume.
[24] See Said, *Orientalism*, pp. 201 and 281.
[25] Ibid., pp. 351f.
[26] Ibid., p. 335 (emphasis in original).
[27] Allen, *The End of Progress*, p. 211.
[28] Ibid., p. 210.

Otherwise, to repeat, we leave the others in a normative void. Whereas some might generously interpret "the normative horizon of Enlightenment modernity" as taking "openness to criticism and reflexivity as normative goals," being willing "to unlearn,"[29] others are simply happy parochialists, i.e., neo-colonial, imperialist modern fascists who want to make an empire great again and interpret Enlightenment modernity as licensing that. What do we say to them – that they got modernity wrong? But we just learned from Allen that modernity harbors a lot of imperialist racism and fascism. So modernistic contextualism is a no-go unless it is countered by the universalism of justificatory equality, according to which each person has a justified claim to the same status of being a normative authority. In short, if false universalism based on parochialism is the problem, enlightened particularism is not the solution. The only solution is enlightened, self-critical universalism, since it is the only one that equips the excluded with a right to justification and critique.

We – as critics arguing and fighting for emancipation – express our *No* to the dominating parochialists, whether they argue in a particularist ("this is how we live around here") or false universalist way ("we live the true way of life" or "we belong to the master race"), and we take our stance against racism, sexism, economic exploitation and cultural and social humiliation to be as foundational as it can be – as did and do those who argued against slavery, torture or political or sexual oppression. Such foundationalism is not a stance of authoritarianism, as Allen claims in her critique of my approach,[30] but exactly the opposite, because it emphasizes the necessary authority to *resist* authoritarianism, whether contextualist or universalist. If you want to resist oppression, your stance better be as strong as it can be. And if you resist fascism, you do not "invite" the fascist to see things your way in a non-foundationalist exchange; rather, you are convinced that he is wrong, and that is how you act and why you act. In other words, we do not have the liberty in this world to be the contextualists Allen wants us to be. We have to take a stance, and for that we need the authority to say *No* to domination. The *No* to false foundations is foundational.

People in other societies have the same right, and parochial contextualism does not serve these critics well either. We disenfranchise them from their own societies by looking at them through the lens of reverse orientalism, as if freedom and equality were Western,

[29] Ibid., p. 218.
[30] Ibid., p. 221.

modern values that we can use but they cannot. In my view – and this is where Allen and I are truly at odds – contextualism speaks the voice of the powerful because it relativizes the oppositional claim, silences critics and tells them that they are out of tune with their society. Contextualism is the theory of the dominant who claim the interpretive privilege to define their culture and society and deny others their right to justification. But the *No* to racism, sexism or other forms of domination is never non-foundationalist, and it is never misplaced in *any* cultural context; it is just the voice of radical critique. The subaltern speak even where they are not heard, and they have the *right* to a voice wherever they are dominated and turned into the "subaltern" in an essentialist and dominating way.[31]

As Uma Narayan argues with respect to the rejection of gender as well as cultural essentialism, one needs to avoid both forms of identity and norm imposition:

> Postcolonial feminists have good reason to oppose many of the legacies of colonialism, as well as ongoing forms of economic exploitation and political domination by Western nations at the international level. However, I do not think that such an agenda is well served either by uncritically denigrating values and practices that appear to be in some sense 'Western' or by indiscriminately valorizing values and practices that appear 'Non-Western.' Political rhetoric that polarizes 'Western' and 'Non-Western' values risks obscuring the degree to which economic and political agendas, carried out in collaboration between particular Western and Third World elites, work to erode the rights and quality of life for many citizens in both Western and Third World Contexts.[32]

Narayan not only points to the reality of multiple domination that needs to be captured in ways that avoid one-sided social analyses; she also shows why false universalism that imposes a notion of "sameness" on others, and thus leads to the imposition of Western normative orders on other societies in order to dominate them, has to be rejected. The same applies to false notions of "difference" that essentialize and unify other societies, and thus silence critical voices within them, as if to call for the respect for women's rights were an "alien" and alienating claim in a non-Western society, "leaving feminists susceptible to attacks as 'Westernized cultural traitors' who suffer from a lack of appreciation for 'their traditions' and respect for 'their culture.'"[33] This is a form of what Foucault once called "enlight-

---

[31] See Dübgen, *Was ist gerecht?* See also Iser, *Empörung und Fortschritt.*
[32] Narayan, "Essence of Culture and a Sense of History," p. 99.
[33] Ibid., p. 102.

enment blackmail,"[34] which we should resist, regardless of whether it comes from a reified form of Enlightenment thought or from a reified form of anti-Enlightenment thought. We need to recognize (with Said and Narayan) that it can equally be an orientalist, postcolonial form of blackmail: either to be uncritically for "enlightened" forms of modern political and social life, while ignoring their dominating aspects, or to be against them and thus ignore the dominating effects of "authentic" non-Western forms of life, celebrating them as the "other" of modernity, thus essentializing them.

2.5 Subaltern reason and the critique of historicism

I think that the *No* to domination, insofar as it appeals to the right to justification, is the voice of subaltern reason, since reason is the critical faculty of justification and domination is the denial of justification and of justificatory standing to persons, restricting the justification community in an arbitrary way when it comes to matters of moral concern, as Rorty did, for example, by questioning the idea of a universal moral language.[35] Yet, since morality is a set of universal norms that claim to be reciprocally and generally justifiable, restricting morality to a justification community in an arbitrary, culturally biased way is unjustifiable and irrational.[36] This is why we cannot be radical contextualists about reason when it comes to epistemic and moral truth claims.[37] Rejecting radical contextualism means that we can, of course, be wrong in thinking that we found the best justification for a claim to truth (so far), but it also implies that there are general criteria for such a debate.[38] To criticize reified notions of rationality for excluding some as "other" – as mad, for example – of course implies that these others are rational, according to a non-reified notion of reason, not that they are really an "other" of reason. Only reason itself can criticize its reified forms in a justifiable way.

A theory cannot claim to be "critical" unless it seeks explicit reassurance about its concept of reason and subjects it to criticism,[39] for no matter how much critical theory opposes the "pathologies of

---

[34] Foucault, "What Is Enlightenment?," p. 42.
[35] Rorty, *Contingency, Irony, and Solidarity*.
[36] Cf. Habermas, *Truth and Justification*.
[37] Cf. Gethmann, "Universelle praktische Geltungsansprüche."
[38] In the following, I use arguments from my Introduction to *Normativity and Power*.
[39] On this, see in general Habermas, *The Theory of Communicative Action*.

reason" in modernity, nevertheless, as Axel Honneth emphasizes, it always subjects "universality – which should, at the same time, be both embodied by and realized through social cooperation – to the standards of rational justification."[40] Hence, I conclude (*pace* Honneth), that no other concepts – for example, concepts of the "good" – can take the place of the imperative and the criteria of rational justification. A historical *a priori* claiming priority over the imperative of reciprocal and general justification, such that it could determine what counts as genuine progress and what does not, is therefore not possible. The kind of "normative reconstruction" of the "promise of freedom"[41] of modern societies undertaken by Honneth presupposes that the "moral rationality"[42] that is supposed to become effective in realizing individual freedom points beyond the established institutions. But then the reflexive and justificatory pressure exerted by individuals and groups on social institutions is not bound to a "pre-given" ethical life or promise, and the critique of injustice is not only able to look, as Honneth claims following Hegel, "just beyond the horizon of existing ethical life."[43] On the contrary, it can see as far as reciprocal–general justification permits or demands. Therefore, normatively speaking, it is not the case that "social and historical conditions [...] [are] needed to determine what can be considered 'justified' in each case."[44] This cannot be fixed by any social facts or any institution, but must be determined in collective discursive practice. The conditions that make social educational processes possible cannot limit them from the perspective of a theory of validity.[45] That would invert the relationship between genesis and validity, and thus the *enabling* of freedom would turn into the *limitation* of freedom. To paraphrase Heidegger, the normative possibility of freedom has a higher status than its normative reality.[46]

The only form of progressive critique that merits the name is one oriented to rational standards of justifiability in a socially situated way. That critique is always "immanent" in the sense that it takes the status quo as its starting point is trivial; what is not obvious, however, is the demand that it should orient itself to "settled," "pre-given,"

---

[40] Honneth, *Pathologies of Reason*, p. 28.
[41] Honneth, *Freedom's Right*, p. vii.
[42] Ibid., p. 2.
[43] Ibid., p. 8. (In German: "knapp über den Horizont der existierenden Sittlichkeit.")
[44] Honneth, *Freedom's Right*, p. 338.
[45] As says Honneth, *Freedom's Right*, pp. 57 and 62.
[46] Heidegger, *Being and Time*, p. 63 (emphasis in original): "Higher than actuality stands *possibility*."

"accepted" or "inherent" norms.[47] There are forms of criticism of which this is true because they reveal the explicit or implicit contradictions within an order of justification in an immanent way – and with good reasons. But that the reasons in question are good does *not* follow from the fact that one appeals to accepted or inherent norms. Libertarians who criticize capitalism for not adhering consistently enough to the market principle and thus becoming mired in contradictions also argue in an immanent way that appeals to systemic features of capitalism. But they cannot justify their criticism toward those who, qua free and equal persons, should be the authorities who determine which economic system can be politically justified, insofar as market processes undermine this very authority (as must be shown in a justice-based analysis).[48] Hence, the fact that a critique is immanent is neither a reason for nor a hallmark of its legitimacy. A radical critique that rejects an entire historically developed understanding of the market, by contrast, may have much more going for it. And a critique that seeks to transform a liberal understanding of the market into a socialist one will hardly be able to justify this in a purely "immanent" way – nor will it have to. Radical criticism may be immanent *or* transcending such that it is no longer clear where the one form of criticism ends and the other begins – as, for example, when Luther described the Pope as the true "Antichrist," the Levellers declared the King "by the grace of God" to be the servant of the people or Marx saw bourgeois society as a context of modern slavery. Settled ethical life is the *object* of criticism, not its *ground* or *limit*. To recall the words of Adorno: "The limit of immanent critique is that the law of the immanent context is ultimately one with the delusion that has to be overcome."[49]

These remarks bear on a further problem – namely, that of the *historicity* of the normative foundations of progressive criticism. Should we consider the criteria of reason or normativity as "historically contingent," as Seyla Benhabib, for example, argues when she describes the right to justification as "a contingent legacy of struggles against slavery, oppression, inequality, degradation, and humiliation over centuries" and accordingly as a historical "achievement"?[50]

---

[47] The two latter provisions can be found in Jaeggi, *Critique of Forms of Life*, pp. 205 and 199.
[48] See Forst, *The Right to Justification*, ch. 8.
[49] Adorno, *Negative Dialectics*, p. 182.
[50] Benhabib, "The Uses and Abuses of Kantian Rigorism," p. 784. In what follows, I draw on my reply in "The Right to Justification." These questions concerning justification are also the focus of my discussion with White, "Does Critical Theory Need Strong Foundations?," and my reply in my "A Critical Theory of Politics." See also Allen,

As I tried to show in my historical analysis of the development of the practice of toleration in its many different forms and justifications, we do in fact have to understand such concepts against the background of concrete historical processes of which we ourselves are part. This enables us to see how the demand for reciprocal and general justifications gave rise and continues to give rise to a historical dynamic that forces existing conceptions and justifications to go beyond themselves – always in a dialectical process, involving new attempts to bring this dynamic to a close.[51] If we want to distinguish in a historically situated, dialectical way between emancipatory and non-emancipatory struggles and developments and to view certain developments as "achievements" or "learning processes," we cannot assume that our assessment of them is merely "contingent", i.e., the arbitrary product of these very developments. Think of Williams's critical theory principle mentioned above – an evaluation produced by what is evaluated is not sufficiently justified. This rules out historicism about the standards of critique.

Of course, we cannot claim that certain developments are "necessary" either, for want of an equivalent of Hegel's absolute spirit. Finite reason does not have access to a "worldless" standpoint from which it can regard its own norms from a distance as "merely contingent" or to a divine standpoint of the *Weltgeist* from which it could recognize historical necessity. From a finite rational perspective that understands itself as practical, the principle of justification is *the* principle of reason and the right to justification is its moral implication – no more, but no less either. There is no transcendent perspective from which its contingency *or* necessity could be ascertained, but we have no need of such a perspective either. The only perspective to which we have access is that of a participant, not one of a transhistorical observer.

Consistency demands that we recognize that the pioneers of emancipation developed their positions in societies in which they were regarded as immoral or crazy judged by the dominant standards of justification – for example, the aforementioned radical Levellers or Pierre Bayle, who defended the thesis, which was frowned upon at the time, that even atheists are capable of being moral and that reason is a faculty of justification independent of religion.[52] Should

---

"The Power of Justification"; Sangiovanni, "Scottish Constructivism and the Right to Justification"; Laden, "The Practice of Equality"; and my reply in my "Justifying Justification."

[51] See Forst, *Toleration in Conflict*.
[52] On this, see Forst, *Normativity and Power*, ch. 5.

we follow the historicist in saying that what first made these positions true was that they *won out* over time and hence that they were *not justified* when these radical thinkers were alive? Should we join with those who condemned Bayle and others in crying "heresy" because this corresponded to the order of justification valid at the time? Could we ever understand and valorize emancipatory and radical criticism on this basis – the criticism of those who in their own day spoke a language in which they called slavery a crime and not a form of benevolence, in which they called tyranny by its name and not divine right, and in which intolerance no longer counted as service to God but instead as brutal violence? If we view these languages as "achievements," then we cannot regard them either as contingent or necessary but only as *moral progress*, as progress in our moral self-understanding through *morally justified* innovation but not through historical "success." The latter would represent a form of moral Darwinism, in which the winners decide what constitutes moral truth. But this would have nothing to do with critical theory. "Prevailing" historically cannot define the criteria for what counts as success in evaluative terms; only critical reason can.

But reason does not elevate itself to a superhistorical power in this regard either. It is only convinced here and now of what counted and counts as reasonable. The twofold analysis of orders of justification as historically occurring social facts and as orders with a claim to justification that opens them up to criticism enables us to say that, even though certain criticisms were considered to be unjustified in their time, they were nevertheless justified from a superior normative point of view because they brought the principle of justification itself to bear – even if, as is most often the case, they did not win out in history.[53]

The perspective outlined enables us to define a conception of progress that cannot be suspected of disguising ethnocentrisms. Only those processes can count as moral–political progress that breaks open orders of justification in ways that make new forms of reciprocal and general justification possible, so that those affected can determine *themselves* in which direction their society should develop. In this way the notion of progress can be prevented from becoming an instrument through which social and political autonomy is lost – for example, by other economically or politically powerful societies or institutions dictating to a society how it should develop. Genuine progress occurs where new levels of justification are made accessible

---

[53] On this, see my interpretation of Bayle, ibid.

or are achieved through struggles that turn subjects into justificatory authorities in the first place. Comprehensive progress involves more than just the existence of better-justified social relations (for example, ones involving a higher standard of living). It occurs when the justification conditions within a society are such that a basic structure of justification exists or begins to develop. Discursive autonomy is realized only in internal processes and procedures, not in conditions imposed from the outside. A critical theory cannot dispense with such a concept of progress.

2.6 The right to reason

In his treatise on *African Philosophy Through Ubuntu*, Mogobe Ramose, one of the great African philosophers, defends the "African's inalienable right to reason" as a means toward "the authentic liberation of Africa."[54] This right to reason independently from the concepts and noumenal powers of the colonizers, past and present, means, on the one hand, criticizing the "will to dominate," which "currently manifests itself in the name of 'democratization', 'globalization' and 'human rights.'"[55] On the other hand, it means developing a critical reconsideration of what democracy, globalization and human rights mean from an African perspective. On the basis of an ontology of belonging together historically and morally called "Ubuntu," Ramose claims that the search for an emancipatory politics is a search for democracy based on African traditions of consensus-seeking, not following Western models of party rivalry, for example.[56] And, with respect to economic globalization, Ramose argues that we need to overcome a global system of exploitation that "translates the questionable metaphysics of the dogma of thou shalt kill in pursuit of individual survival into practice"[57] and should start to take human rights for Africans, such as the right to life, seriously. I wholeheartedly agree with Allen that we need to enter into a dialogue with thinkers like Ramose and many others – but what we learn from them is not just something about cultural difference; rather, we learn something about the real problems of our world, the brutalities of the various forms of domination that exist, including, not least, economic domination. That is what critical theory is about, and that

[54] Ramose, *African Philosophy Through Ubuntu*, p. 4.
[55] Ibid., p. 6.
[56] Ibid., p. 101.
[57] Ibid., p. 147.

is what we learn from a dialogue with others who are not simply "others" in a global world. For critical theory, the main problem is not reason but the destruction of reason (to use Lukács's term) that goes on in many parts of the world in a systematic way.

Otherwise, if we cut ourselves off from the struggles of others and ontologize cultural differences, we will not be able to do what Spivak asks us to do – namely to develop a "transnational literacy"[58] that allows us to criticize transnational forms of domination and to engage in transnational struggles for justice. Such a conception of justice cannot be imposed on multiple social contexts but must be developed discursively – but for that to happen, a common normative framework of moral equality and claims to discursive autonomy must exist. If such a framework is missing, any transnational moral–political language, including a critical one, is an imposition.

In a similar spirit, Achille Mbembe argues for a critical theory that provides the social-analytic tools to identify "transnational networks of repression" that combine "[f]oreign corporations, powerful nations, and local dominant classes"[59] into what I call situations of "multiple domination." In my view, a critical theory of transnational justice must start from such forms of domination.[60] This includes analyzing the power structures of religious, economic and political domination that deny the development of an autonomous form of political thinking in African societies, as Mbembe points out.[61] The first task is to reclaim what I call "noumenal power,"[62] which Mbembe links to life itself: "To have power is therefore to know how to give and to receive forms. But it is also to know how to escape existing forms, how to change everything while remaining the same, to marry new forms of life and constantly enter into new relationships with destruction, loss, and death."[63] The struggle against destructive and for autonomous creative power is of both a local and a transnational nature:

> Whatever the location, epoch, or context in which they take place, the horizon of such struggles remains the same: how to belong fully in this world that is common to all of us, how to pass from the status of the excluded to the status of the right-holder, how to participate in the construction and the distribution of the world. [...] The path is clear:

---

[58] Spivak, *A Critique of Postcolonial Reason*, p. 399.
[59] Mbembe, *Critique of Black Reason*, p. 5.
[60] See Forst, *The Right to Justification*, p. 257.
[61] Mbembe, *Critique of Black Reason*, pp. 87f.
[62] Forst, *Normativity and Power*, ch. 2.
[63] Mbembe, *Critique of Black Reason*, p. 132.

on the basis of a critique of the past, we must create a future that is inseparable from the notions of justice, dignity, and the *in-common*.[64]

If the language of human rights, self-determination and transnational justice – properly defined and reappropriated – is the language of progress, as Ramose and Mbembe argue, then this is not primarily a historical or a sociological insight or demand. Rather, it follows as a moral imperative from the critique of false ideas of progress as well as from the critique of the prevention of social progress, for emancipation from a situation of oppression and exploitation is a human right, now and at all times. We are therefore bound to adhere to this concept of progress as long as forms of human domination exist and as long as there is a moral imperative to overcome them. The struggle for emancipation requires a universal moral language that relativism betrays.

---

[64] Ibid., pp. 176f. (emphasis in original).

— 3 —

THE RULE OF UNREASON
Analyzing (Anti-)Democratic Regression*

3.1 The crisis of democracy and the concept of regression

In contemporary debates about the crisis of democracy, it is often said that we are living in a time of an anti-democratic regression and, insofar as it is a phenomenon that develops within democratic systems, this is also called "democratic regression," as Armin Schäfer and Michael Zürn do.[1] I think this addresses a crucial dimension of the critical analysis of our present, but I also see the need for further conceptual reflection and clarification. For "regression" is a complex concept with many connotations, and its usage must be considered carefully, in particular because it is important to avoid several fallacies in the discussion about it, of which I discuss three – that of the status quo ante fixation (section 3.2), that of the reduction of the concept of democracy (section 3.3), and that of the misclassification of critiques of democracy (section 3.4). These considerations lead to my own assessment of the causes of democratic regression (section 3.5).

I begin with some remarks on the concepts of crisis and regression. A crisis is the moment in which the fate of a person or a society is decided, when there is no more going back and not yet a way

---

* I thank Peter Niesen for the invitation to the workshop "Zur Diagnose demokratischer Regression" in Hamburg in November 2021. The discussion of my (first) thoughts there has helped me a lot. I owe further important insights to the discussion of my keynotes at the Philosophy and Social Sciences conference in Dublin in May 2022 and the annual conference of the Research Institute Social Cohesion in Bremen in July 2022. Special thanks go to Greta Kolbe, Felix Kämper, Carlos Morado and (especially) Amadeus Ulrich for their help in preparing the text.
[1] Schäfer and Zürn, *Die demokratische Regression*. Cf. also Geiselberger, *Die große Regression*; King and Sutterlüty, "Destruktivität und Regression im Rechtspopulismus."

forward. It marks, as Schleiermacher says, the "border between two different orders of things" ("*Grenze* [...] *zwischen zwei verschiedenen Ordnungen der Dinge*").[2] The old is dying, and the new cannot be born, as Gramsci puts it.[3] One should, therefore, be cautious about talking of a crisis *of* democracy (in distinction from a crisis *within* democracy, or a crisis with which democracy has to cope), because this is the situation where it seriously teeters on the brink as to whether it will last.

With regard to socio-political orders, I distinguish between two types of crisis.[4] A *structural crisis* occurs when the order is structurally no longer able to fulfill its tasks. We ascertain a *crisis of justification* when the self-understanding of an order shifts so that it loses its very own concept. Then, authoritarian political visions can emerge under the guise of democratic rhetoric, for example in movements that proclaim "We are the people" but really mean "Foreigners out." If such movements are understood as democratic, we experience a crisis of justification that can lead to regression.

Regression is a weighty concept when applied to societies, not only, but especially since the *Dialectic of Enlightenment*, which states that the "curse of irresistible progress is irresistible regression."[5] Drawing on psychoanalysis,[6] Horkheimer and Adorno do not merely mean the "impoverishment of thought no less than of experience,"[7] but also a regression behind forms of civilization to the point of "barbarism," into a world in which ideological delusion leads to irrational inversions of all kinds, including the willingness to annihilate others collectively. Habermas, in turn, employs the notion of a "self-inflicted regression" (*selbst verantwortete Regression*) to oppose construing this as an atavistic "relapse into barbarism," but rather as "the absolutely new and from now on *always present* possibility of the moral disintegration of an entire nation that had considered itself 'civilized' according to the standards of the time."[8] This is what the talk of a "civilizational rupture" (*Zivilisationsbruch*) implies.

---

[2] Schleiermacher, "Über die Religion," p. 325.
[3] Gramsci, *Prison Notebooks*, vol. 2, p. 33.
[4] Cf. Forst, "Two Bad Halves Don't Make a Whole."
[5] Horkheimer and Adorno, *Dialectic of Enlightenment*, p. 28.
[6] Enlightening on this is King, "Psyche and Society in Critical Theory and Contemporary Social Research," and especially King, "Autoritarismus als Regression." See also Brown, "Neoliberalism's Frankenstein."
[7] Horkheimer and Adorno, *Dialectic of Enlightenment*, p. 28.
[8] Habermas, *Auch eine Geschichte der Philosophie*, vol. 1, p. 174 (translation R.F. and emphasis in original).

I propose to locate the talk of "democratic regression" on a spectrum that ranges from this extreme form of civilizational rupture to phenomena of social and political regression of a particular quality. By regression we mean, if we retain the two dimensions of structure and justification (or of social and political relations and of self-understandings), not only the one or the other kind of regress, but a comprehensive, collective undercutting of standards that must not be put into question – and, indeed, must not be questioned at the price of *reason*. Regression is, in classical Frankfurt terms, a victory of unreason: reason alone, in a comprehensive, practical and theoretical sense (to be defined in more detail), should be the standard for the usage of such a demanding concept. Hence the real dimension of regression is the noumenal one, and thus the space of justifications,[9] because epistemic or moral standards of what cannot be rejected with good reasons are not merely moved away from a bit, but are either forgotten, misinterpreted or, worse, explicitly rejected. A regression of this kind does not simply represent a step backward, but sustainably prevents possible moral–political progress. This is especially true when it affects not only individual groups but large sections of society.

3.2 Status quo (ante) fallacy

A democratic regression, as Schäfer and Zürn understand it, is not characterized merely by a structural lack of collective self-determination, but by the citizens "turning away" from democracy.[10] They call this a "double alienation" – of the practice from the democratic ideal and of citizens from democracy as an institutional form.

Both use the word "ideal," which should help to avoid a mistake often made when using the term regression: the *fallacy of a status quo (ante) bias* as a normative fixation on this state of affairs.[11] For it is all too easy[12] for formulations similar to "the departure from already achieved democratic standards" to creep in when regression

---

[9] Forst, *Normativity and Power*.
[10] Schäfer and Zürn, *Die demokratische Regression*, p. 11.
[11] Svenja Ahlhaus and Peter Niesen, "Regressionen des Mitgliedschaftsrechts," pp. 613f., point this out. However, they do not choose the path of a moral–political rational determination of the standards of progress or regression, but rather propose a standard of progressive cosmopolitanism, introduced as relative, that calls for further development rather than restoration.
[12] Also in Schäfer and Zürn, *Die demokratische Regression*, pp. 12, 49–56.

is deplored, and suddenly a phase of autocratic populism appears like the sinful apostasy from the paradise of democratic conditions, which, by implication, seems to have existed before. There is, however, a *non sequitur* involved here: Structurally, there can be a regression with respect to certain democratic achievements without implying that the *whole* system previously conformed to truly democratic ideals. And, in the self-understanding, there can be a push toward an *explicit*, say xenophobic, celebration of the authoritarian, which merely brings to light the xenophobia that was already *implicit*.[13] The fallacy of the status quo (ante) bias then also obstructs the analysis of the (structural and cultural) causes and tendencies that led to regression; they were inherent in the previous state or were produced by it.[14] Even more, the paradox arises that the problematic condition that led to the crisis in the first place is elevated to an ideal.

In addition, there is also an (anti-)democratic regression where there was *no* democracy at all in a sophisticated sense, but now the way to it is *even more* blocked than before. For the regression is, as I said, not only a step backward, but a lasting obstruction of the possibility for moral–political progress. I emphasize here this dimension of progress, understood as the improvement of social and political relations of justification (a point to which I will return),[15] because, as Horkheimer and Adorno highlight, technological progress can go hand-in-hand with moral–political regression.

Consequently, the "ideal" spoken of must (and here I go beyond Schäfer and Zürn) be an ideal of *reason* – "ideal," however, not in the sense of a utopian vision of the perfect world, but in the sense of principles that are rationally valid and that accordingly cannot be rejected with good reasons. Classically said: principles of reason, because a different kind of normativity cannot carry the fundamental critique of irrationality expressed in the concept of regression. If one fails to see this, one falls prey to a conventionalism that can only assess regression based on already achieved and institutionalized standards or socially accepted ideals. That not only entails the aforementioned danger of ideological nostalgism (the keyword here is: "defense of democracy"), but also that one can no longer explain why this ideal should be *valid* at all – what the source of its normative force is. Otherwise, there could be a fascist regression, a patriarchal regression, etc., on the same level – that is, a departure

---

[13] Peter Gordon, "The Authoritarian Personality Revisited," is very clear on this.
[14] Cf. my analysis of Thomas Mann's notion of a "neglect" (*Verwahrlosung*) of democracy in Forst, "The Neglect of Democracy."
[15] Cf. Forst, *Normativity and Power*, ch. 4, and Chapter 2 in this volume.

from fascist or patriarchal standards once achieved or recognized, which is taken to be regrettable. That something has once been established or recognized does *not*, considered properly, provide a good reason why it should be valid and rescued. The reasons must come from some other, clearer source. Otherwise, we obstruct the way to look critically at what existed before and at the regressive tendencies of the present *at the same time*. However, that is what we should be able to do from a standpoint of reason that can prove itself critically and discursively and allows us to speak of stagnation, progress or regression in a differentiated manner. Regression is a *negative concept of reason*, so to speak, because it marks out *real unreason*. Only from a rationally justifiable normative standpoint can we speak about regression in social-analytical terms; historicist conventionalism is not a suitable candidate for this.[16] This is not to say that judgments about regression do not, in social-diagnostic terms, refer to temporal processes; they usually do, even if a single condition can also be called "regressive." Importantly, however, temporal process statements about regression, where they compare two states of affairs, appeal to a superior normative standard that is *not* temporally grounded, though it is related to those states of affairs. The social-scientific and the normative perspective must be recognized in their different logics.

The distance from conventionalism can be explained by recourse to the concept of progress that I argued for in critical discussions with, in particular, Amy Allen.[17] In order to avoid conceptions of progress that contain ethnocentric notions of "developed" societies or veil structures of domination that envision teleological ideals that could also be paternalistically realized by external actors, I advocate a reflexive and emancipatory, non-teleological conception of progress that locates it where those subjected to a normative order increasingly become normative authors of that order, as (ideally speaking) moral and political equals. The justification of progress lies in the progress of justification, as a progressive process of producing structures of autonomous justification that replace structures of domination (as a denial of justification). Progress exists where the right to justification[18]

---

[16] The need to specify normative criteria of rationality for progress or regression also becomes clear where the former is determined pragmatically as successful problem solving and the latter as a blockage in this respect, as Rahel Jaeggi, "Vorne," for example, does. Otherwise, the definition would remain formal or empty; regressive movements also claim to solve problems and thereby gain many supporters.

[17] Cf. Allen, *The End of Progress*, and Allen, "Progress, Normativity, and Universality"; for my responses, see Chapter 2 in this volume and Forst, "Navigating a World of Conflict and Power."

[18] Forst, *The Right to Justification*.

is incrementally realized by persons in an autonomous manner, that is, determined by the affected persons themselves.

Regression, therefore, does not just mean any kind of regress or setback with respect to such processes of emancipation, but developments that radically question and deny the foundations of progress, so that the understanding and possibilities of progress are chipped away. Regressive developments do not just indicate that there is a relevant lack of justificatory quality in social and political institutions; rather, regression implies that there is a serious defect in the understanding of oneself and others as equal subjects of justification. Entire social groups are excluded as irrelevant from the space of justification, and it is closed off and distorted by false, ideological justifications that justify the unjustifiable (which is, in short, the definition of ideology I use here). In the extreme, they twist an aggressive, bellicose attack into an act of anti-fascist liberation, transform migrants into threats, make economic structures of domination appear to be based on individual freedom, turn an electoral defeat into a victory and, ultimately, democracy into a tool of domination that violates basic rights. In the end, such regressions exhibit what I analyze as first- and second-order *alienation* – the denial to others of the status of being equal justificatory authorities, and in the extreme, even the disrespect of oneself as such an authority.[19] Here, the aforementioned crisis of justification reaches its climax. Regressive movements not only deny rights and practices of reciprocal–general justification; they aim to destroy them – and with them reason, too. Eventually, not only does the rhetoric turn violent, but the actions as well.

3.3 The conceptual reduction of democracy

The relevant kind of democratic regression lies within the space of reasons – where one is willing to give up the concept of democracy as a form of rational rule, grounded in the collective search for good, reciprocal–general justifying reasons among equals, completely or in part – and nonetheless considers this a democratic act.[20] Therefore, the meaning of democracy has to be grasped with precision. Otherwise, all empirical cats will turn gray in, as it were, a night of conceptlessness. Then the person who enjoys the liberal–democratic status

---

[19] See Chapter 1 in this volume.
[20] See Forst, *Die noumenale Republik*, pt. III.

quo because it secures his stock profits would be a good democrat, whereas the person who criticizes the respective economic system as undemocratic and thus rejects the current form of democracy appears to be an anti-democrat. And yet it is the former, not the latter, who suffers from a deficient conception of democracy. Here everything depends on clear terminology.

This requires, however, that the concept of democracy is not interpreted in a truncated manner. And there lies a second mistake, which can be encountered in everyday rhetoric as well as in scientific discourses – a mistake of *conceptual reduction*. If we look at it from a historical–normative point of view, the idea of democracy entered the modern political era as a normative order to overcome forms of arbitrary social and political rule (*domination*). First in the resistance against feudal rule, later in the struggle against economic exploitation in the capitalist–industrial age, in the protest against political authoritarianism, the oppression of women or against state-bureaucratic and oppressive forms of socialism – and today against late-capitalist, neo-feudal (national or global) socio-economic structures and authoritarianism in its many variations, and also against contemporary forms of racism and discrimination based on origin, religion and gender. Modern democracy did not arise as a beautiful and abstract idea of deliberative community building but as a battle cry against oppression, exploitation and exclusion of different sorts. It is not simply some prudent way of governing but the political *practice of justice*, and its primary task is to establish structures of fair and effective public–general justification in which those who are subjected to arbitrary rule and domination can become subjects of justification who can co-determine the normative order to which they belong as equals. The demand for democracy is a demand for justice, that is, for no longer being treated as a "normative nothing," but instead attaining the status of being an equal normative authority – for becoming politically what one always already morally *is* (but is hardly allowed to be in reality). This morally grounded claim to justice is at the same time a demand of reason to be respected as an equal justificatory authority for the norms that claim general validity.[21]

This is why moral–political respect among equals is normatively inscribed in democracy. And that is also why a conception of democracy is regressive that puts political power in the hands of a few or privileged groups or assumes that majorities may use the

---

[21] For a more elaborate view, see the chapters in Part II of this volume.

power of democracy to dominate minorities, that is, to deprive them of social resources, cultural rights or opportunities for participation that have to be guaranteed among equals. It is equally problematic to allow talk of "illiberal democracy" and merely to add critically that the "liberal" is important as a supplement, as if it did not belong immanently to democracy[22] – which, however, does not mean that democracy includes the claim to have unlimited property rights.[23] For it is equally mistaken to declare an economic order that undermines or ignores the principles of democracy as a component of democracy. An economic–libertarian, capitalist (at best) partial democracy that forces people into economic dependency and marginalization is not sufficiently democratically justifiable.

The normative conception of democracy I rely on realizes the *right to justification* as a general, morally grounded right in the form of individual basic rights[24] as well as of reflexive, if it goes well: self-improving political and social institutions that are exposed to public criticism and provide for institutional ways of autonomous change and self-correction.[25] There is no concrete blueprint set up by an "ideal" theory of democracy to be realized, but there is a first principle: that every form of political rule and social organization that lays a claim to democratic justification must be judged by whether the right to justification is realized in the best possible way (or at least better than before), namely in a politically autonomous way. Wherever that is not the case, there is *democratic stagnation* or *regress*. And, where this principle is not even understood or openly rejected, there is *noumenal, anti-democratic regression*.

3.4 Misclassified critiques of democracy

The relation between the levels of structure and self-understanding is also of importance in another respect. For it is surely possible that a neo-fascist or right-wing populist movement, in its critique of democracy, identifies real problems, such as those of the lack of representation of certain strata or groups, and thereby gains support. But that does not turn it into a *democratic* movement. Here we

---

[22] See Mounk, *The People vs. Democracy*. For the opposite view, see Müller, *Democracy Rules*.
[23] Rawls, *Justice as Fairness*.
[24] See Forst, "The Justification of Basic Rights."
[25] See also Forst, *Contexts of Justice*, ch. 3, and Chapter 2 in this volume; Lafont, *Democracy without Shortcuts*.

have another error, that of the *causal–normative fallacy*: Deficient structures of representation and political will-formation or of social exclusion can, much like the negative economic effects of the global market, lead to the alienation of certain groups from the social and political system in which they live – they may then explicitly bid democracy adieu or think that true democracy means that an authoritarian "leader" like Trump calls the shots. That, and the fact that they may see migrants as the root of evil and commit themselves to an aggressive "hatred of the non-identical," to use Adorno's term, has nothing to do with a democratic impulse or a democratic "breaking up of exclusion" (*Aufbrechen eines Ausschlusses*),[26] as Philip Manow writes – it merely calls for "democracy" as a means of illegitimately overpowering others. Therein lies no "return" of the repressed demos.[27] To be sure, criticisms that the excluded raise of exclusions that are ideologically hidden behind the label of "democratic representation" are, here Manow is right, necessary as a demand for the democratization of democracy. In this regard, the rhetoric may also be brute, because the quality of the justification of a claim is not measured by the elegance of the language used; that does not make those who revolt in such a manner a "mob" (*Pöbel*).[28] However, a right-wing populist authoritarian criticism of supposedly undemocratic mechanisms of contemporary societies, which claims to represent the "true people" who are "finally" making themselves heard via Trump or the German AfD, does *not* make such criticism democratic, because in doing so a problematic, criticized kind of "representation" is replaced by one that is essentially anti-democratic.[29] To speak of *democratic* criticism in that case is a fallacy – such as the one that overlooks the fact that many of those who complained about democratic deficits after the German refugee situation in 2015 would have been delighted if "non-majoritarian institutions"[30] had closed the borders. Not all those who cry loudly for "participation" are democrats, neither in terms of the preferred political form of rule nor in terms of content. Not all critiques of existing democracies, even if to some extent justified, are of a democratic nature.

[26] Manow, *(Ent-)Demokratisierung der Demokratie*, p. 50.
[27] See ibid., p. 51, with reference to Priester, *Rechter und linker Populismus*.
[28] For a different view, see Koschorke, "Twitter, Trump und die (Ent-)Demokratisierung der Demokratie," with reference to Manow *(Ent-)Demokratisierung der Demokratie*.
[29] See especially Urbinati, *Me the People*; Arato and Cohen 2021, *Populism and Civil Society*.
[30] Cf. the problem diagnosis of Schäfer and Zürn, *Demokratische Regression*, ch. 4, which I do not follow here.

A non-regressive democracy is based on the principle that there is only one supreme *normative authority* in the space of norms that apply to all, and that is the justificatory community of all *as equals*. To realize this status of equality (or of *non-domination*, understood in that way)[31] legally, politically and socially is the (never-ending) task of democracy and human rights; they form a normative unity. For, like the political order of democracy, human rights express the irreducible right to justification; that is why the claim to collective self-determination is a human right, and so there can be no legitimate form of democracy that restricts human rights. Against this background, the criticism of one-sided or repressive systems of representation is justified.

3.5 Crises and the paradox of democratic regression

Crises are opportunities for progressive as well as regressive thinking because they invite narratives of crisis causation that may be closer to or further away from the truth. A crisis is the time of unreason or, if things go well, of learning. Contemporary democracies are in a precarious position in that respect. During the Financial Crisis of 2008 and onwards it became clear that nation-states can not only be negatively affected by the global interconnectedness of the financial system, but also that they hardly have enough power to intervene and control that system in a regulatory way at the national level. Some respond to this with calls for national isolation (Brexit, for example), others with calls for transnational regulation. Both invoke the name of democracy. Here we find the core of the enduring social crisis that shapes our time. The belief in effective democratic politics presupposes that the problems that arise can be overcome by collective political power. However, when this confidence fades, the quest for democratic power often turns irrational, into the delusion of nationalist self-empowerment, which produces not real political power but aggression that is often directed against the worst off groups.[32] In the doubt as to whether democratic power, which continues to be primarily conceived of in terms of the nation-state, can still be reality changing, lies the root of a deep insecurity that haunts democratic

---

[31] On the difference between my view and that of neo-republicanism, see Chapter 10 in this volume.
[32] Similarly, already Adorno, *Aspects of the New Right-Wing Extremism*, a lecture at the University of Vienna on right-wing radicalism and the dialectic of powerlessness in 1967.

societies worldwide. The authoritarian populism of "take back control" (or "make great again") is a consequence of this, fueled by the skepticism about whether the ruling classes are willing and capable of bringing about change, and, paradoxically, this not rarely leads to some of the members of those classes being chosen as the ones who could do things differently in "unorthodox" ways.

The ecological crisis also reveals the limits of the national power to act, but also of the will to act as collectives, not least of democratic states. Here, transnationally coordinated democratic responses and, above all, institutions have to be found; the European Union should take a pioneering role in this. But doubts are growing as the crisis worsens. The same is true with regard to the scandalous realities of global poverty and economic dependence.

In the crisis of global migration, some call for closing borders to preserve the democratic infrastructure of societies, while others insist on respect for human rights and rightly stress that no democratic majority has the authority to let others fall into destitution and rightlessness. Here, too, we see how quickly the call for democracy can become an instrument of oppression – and how necessary a non-regressive understanding of democracy is.

Regressions stood out even more strongly in the Covid-19 pandemic, which had to do with the fact that we were dealing with immediate existential threats and corresponding fears. Then, the impulse of isolating oneself against "foreign" threats becomes just as virulent as that of solidarity, which must be examined reflexively, however, for it not to turn into a limited, nationalistically defined "cohesion."[33] We find a particular democratic regression where people in democratic societies put themselves into the role of subjects who either want to be ruled harshly by a Leviathan or think that this is already the case and revolt against "vaccination Nazis."[34] In both cases, this understanding of freedom is unworthy of a democracy. For democratic freedom means deciding responsibly to refrain from risking lives in ways that are avoidable. No one has the freedom to endanger others in ways that cannot be justified, and this is a democratic insight.

We live in a time of the *paradox of democratic regression*: All serious political challenges – whether it is a pandemic, climate change, financial crises, global poverty or the question of war and peace – are of a *transnational* nature, and yet the political impulses of

---

[33] See Chapters 4 and 5 in this volume.
[34] Cf. Forst, *Die noumenale Republik*, ch. 16; Forst, "Freiheiten, Risiken und Rechtfertigungen."

the reaction to them go more and more in a *national* or nationalistic direction, up to the aggressive desire for demarcation and exclusion. As if one could thereby leave the global problems out of the equation, which have been caused, after all, by one's own politics (if we think of Western societies in particular), one thinks in terms of borders – even to the point of denying the realities of the ecological danger, the coronavirus, etc. In such denial of reality as a form of profound irrationality, regression is just as evident as in the celebration of power that the powerless have when they cheer for authoritarian populists who delude them into believing in a different reality.[35] This is a clear sign of political alienation and the rule of unreason.

The most serious form of alienation that democracy has to fear I call *noumenal alienation*.[36] It begins at a first-order level, where persons do not recognize each other as equal normative authorities, and it may lead to an extreme, second-order level, where people no longer respect themselves as such an authority. The existing orders, which we call democracies, produce this kind of alienation in many ways (not to mention non-democratic ones). Social groups are forced into relations in which it becomes difficult for them to regard themselves as normative authorities, and it is not unusual that other groups that also do not exactly have a privileged social status relegate the former to the margins of society and tell them they do not belong. The neglect of democracy, which expresses itself wherever persons are denied their status as equal justificatory authorities, sometimes clothed in the false invocation of democracy, has many causes, structural and mental ones. But it is one of the negative dialectical truths of critical analysis that many rebellions against democratic regression (such as the rule of elites) are themselves regressive. The regressive core consists in denying and fighting the right to justification among equals.

---

[35] On this cf. King, "Autoritarismus als Regression."
[36] See Chapter 1 in this volume.

— 4 —

SOLIDARITY
Concept, Conceptions and Contexts*

4.1 A contested and elusive concept

Solidarity is an elusive and contested concept, and debates about it abound:[1] Is it a moral value or a virtue, or can it also be found in groups of criminals, and can the solidarity of some violate the rights and standing of – and the solidarity with – others? Is solidarity a feeling, or can it be motivated by rational considerations of self-interest or moral reflection? Is solidarity necessarily of a particular communal nature, or can it also have universalist forms? Is it based on social relations and expectations of reciprocity, or does it have its place in relations of asymmetry, one-sided dependence and non-shared vulnerability? Can solidarity be combined with or even be based on demands of justice, or is it the "other" of justice, going beyond it in altruistic or supererogatory ways? Can it be institutionalized by law, or does it presuppose intrinsic motives and voluntary action to which one cannot be coerced? In short, the very nature of solidarity – its grounds, motives, content, scope and form – is the subject of numerous disagreements, not just in light of the different

---

* Many thanks to the participants of the Florence Workshop "Solidarity: Its Nature and Value" at the European University Institute in May 2019 for helpful comments and questions, especially to the organizers of the conference and editors of this volume, Andrea Sangiovanni and Juri Viehoff, and to Margaret Kohn and Tommie Shelby for their commentaries. Thanks also to Ciaran Cronin, Felix Kämper and Amadeus Ulrich for their valuable suggestions and help in preparing this text.

[1] See, for example, the various contributions to Bayertz, *Solidarity*, and to Banting and Kymlicka, *The Strains of Commitment*; also the important works by May, *The Socially Responsive Self*; Kolers, *A Moral Theory of Solidarity*; Scholz, *Political Solidarity*; Stjernø, *Solidarity in Europe*; Brunkhorst, *Solidarity*; Shelby, *We Who Are Dark*; Derpmann, *Gründe der Solidarität*; and Sangiovanni, "Solidarity as Joint Action."

histories and trajectories of the concept, but also in light of the different uses we make of it in our normative vocabulary.[2]

If we want to make some headway in understanding the concept and overcome its elusiveness, we should avoid certain dead ends of analysis. It seems inappropriate to argue that there are different "concepts" of solidarity in play, since we would then no longer be able to explain what is supposed to qualify all of them as concepts of *solidarity*.[3] Similarly, we should avoid being "held captive"[4] by a particular picture of solidarity, say the one associated with the socialist tradition or with social activism, and declare it to be the "true" or "authentic" form of solidarity.[5]

I suggest instead that we use the distinction developed by John Rawls between a "concept" and various "conceptions"[6] – the concept contains the essential features of a term, whereas conceptions are thicker interpretations of these features – and situate the different conceptions of solidarity in the social and normative contexts where they play a special role. Following this methodological approach, however, requires particular care. For neither can one start from a quasi-Platonic, conceptual *eidos* and derive the criteria for every legitimate usage of the term from it, nor can one inductively examine all semantic usages of the word for common features, which would then constitute the core concept. The former approach is dogmatic, the latter uncritical and in any case unrealistic. Rather, we should aim to achieve a "reflective equilibrium" (to use another Rawlsian term, although in a different sense than he did) by going back and forth between paradigmatic examples of forms of solidarity in certain contexts, historical and contemporary, on the one hand, and a determination of basic features they share, on the other. This process is in principle an open-ended one, as one can always go back and re-enter the hermeneutical–analytical circle: Was the concept defined too narrowly or broadly? Are the different conceptions appropriately determined? The general aim is to provide the definition of a concept that reveals meaningful distinctions between different conceptions of solidarity. In that way, we might be able to

---

[2] For an illuminating analysis of the different trajectories of the concept, see Sangiovanni, *Solidarity*, and my comments in "The Meaning(s) of Solidarity." With respect to the dominant usages of the concept, Bayertz, "Four Uses of 'Solidarity,'" is very useful.

[3] For an argument against employing different "concepts" with regard to liberty (commenting on Isaiah Berlin), see my "Political Liberty" in Forst, *The Right to Justification*, ch. 5, and also, with respect to toleration, Forst, *Toleration in Conflict*, §1.

[4] Wittgenstein, *Philosophical Investigations*, §115, p. 48.

[5] See, for example, Jaeggi, "Solidarity and Indifference."

[6] Rawls, *A Theory of Justice*, p. 5.

answer some of the questions outlined above and, most of all, avoid declaring a particular conception of solidarity as the general concept – a mistake occasionally made in corresponding debates, especially when it comes to politically charged concepts such as solidarity (or toleration, justice, liberty, and so on).

4.2 The concept of solidarity

The general concept of solidarity refers to a special *practical attitude* of a person toward others. It involves a form of "standing by"[7] each other (from the Latin *solidus*)[8] based on a *particular normative bond* with others constituted by a *common cause* or *shared identity*. The two latter notions are not mutually exclusive, because a shared identity can be correlated with a common cause. Still, sometimes, such as in the case of working-class solidarity, the common cause determines the commonality more than a particular social situation or identity marker (for example, you do not need to be a worker to be solidary with the cause of the working class).

Solidarity expresses a willingness to act with and for the sake of others based on the motive of affirming the collective bond, that is, of furthering the common cause or the shared identity (or both), when this is required. Solidarity as a practical attitude exists as long as this bond is perceived to be important and binding, and it materializes when corresponding action is felt to be required, especially in the face of threats or particular challenges.[9] Solidarity is not generally, on the basic conceptual level, a fighting creed, but it is required as a practice when "needed," i.e., when called for to affirm or defend the common project. Solidary action is voluntary and based on inner conviction because it springs from the motive of the common bond as felt and perceived by those who act (which does not exclude motivational forces that, in their view, leaves them with no alternative other than to be solidary, especially if connected with strong social expectations to act loyally).[10]

---

[7] In German: *füreinander einstehen*.

[8] In the tradition of Roman law, the term referred to a particular kind of collective liability of a group for the costs generated by one member and vice versa. That meaning is still preserved in the term today. The history of the concept is reconstructed by Wildt, "Solidarity."

[9] This is stressed by Sangiovanni, "Solidarity as Joint Action," pp. 343ff. It seems to me, however, that solidarity as a practical attitude, as a willingness to act if required, is essential, independent of whether it finds expression in action or not.

[10] The point of loyalty is stressed by Shelby, *We Who Are Dark*, pp. 69f.

It is important to note that solidary action is expected of members of the collective precisely when it is costly, also when narrow self-interest might actually deem it to be too costly. This is when reasons rooted in the "deeper" bond come into play as justifying and motivating forces. As far as the basic concept of solidarity is concerned, however, it is not justified to add to its defining features that its demands are always supererogatory,[11] since costly actions can also be demanded by duties of reciprocal, symmetrical solidarity. At the general conceptual level, it is difficult to determine the point at which the call for particular actions by some members overstrains the bonds of solidarity uniting the collective, especially given that people usually belong to various overlapping, but also possibly conflicting, contexts of solidarity (family, nation and class, for example – which is, in other words, the classic material of drama). The general concept of solidarity entails no particular metric of what solidarity requires in concrete contexts. That is determined by the various conceptions of the collective bond that grounds particular contextual instances of solidarity.

There is some reciprocity involved, since *each* member of a solidary communal context is expected to act in solidarity if they have the opportunity; however, this is far from a straightforward economic form of reciprocity in which one (ideally) receives an equivalent for one's contribution or in which contributions have to be roughly equal. *Solidary reciprocity* rather means: One's own contribution serves the general, common cause, and those who can contribute more or something special do it to further that cause, so that when they act in such ways, they feel neither superior nor exploited (and those who contribute less do not feel like second-class members). Such solidarity can reach so far that one feels bound to save the body or execute the last will of a deceased comrade or friend, assuming that he or she *would* have done the same. Solidary reciprocity can take imagined and yet real, highly asymmetrical forms. This also includes solidary support for people struggling in a certain way for a cause (such as human rights) that I feel committed to, even though I may not know them personally or they may be in a position where they could not possibly reciprocate what I do (and vice versa). Nevertheless, there is a common cause between us, for which we work together, each doing their share.[12]

---

[11] As Wildt, "Solidarity," p. 213, does.

[12] This notion of imagined reciprocity exceeds the notion of reciprocity and joint action that Sangiovanni, "Solidarity as Joint Action," p. 350, thinks defines solidary action. For

It is often said that solidarity is owed most to the weakest member of a collective, but this is only half of the truth: It is *owed* to the collective and its general cause and common good, but it may *materialize* in the shape of a particular concern for those who are weakest, depending on the specific nature of the common bond. There are many historical layers that have been stored in the term and that need to be distinguished here, ranging from Catholic social doctrine to the communist movement or to forms of nationalism.

So, these are, to summarize, the components of the general concept of solidarity, abstracted from concrete contexts and conceptions: a *practical attitude* that takes the form of a willingness to act based on a *common bond* that implies a common *cause* or shared *identity* that ought to be furthered. The bond *itself* is the motivating force, and it can call for particular actions *beyond* narrow self-interest. The *reciprocity* involved can take many forms, including asymmetrical ones, as long as the bond justifies what it means to do one's share. If these features appear in a certain practical context, we encounter a form of solidarity.

4.3 Normative dependency

So far, solidarity sounds like a virtue, and, with respect to its character of overcoming one's narrow self-interest to further a common cause, it surely is. But that does not make it a *moral* virtue or something intrinsically good, since a Mafia family may also depend quite a lot on the solidarity of its members. And nationalist movements have historically used the language of solidarity effectively for many purposes, including aggressive ones.[13] Hence, solidarity is a morally neutral virtue that can be used for good or bad concerns and goals; in this respect, it is similar to courage, for example.

The concept itself is, therefore, a *normatively dependent* one, which means that normative conceptions of solidarity are in need of interpretive supplementation by other normative principles (such as justice) or values (such as national welfare or serving God's honor). The concept of solidarity is contextually and normatively promiscuous – it can serve many ends and does not contain any particular ends in itself, neither moral nor political ones. Such ends must be

---

an argument about transnational solidarity, see Gould, "Transnational Solidarities." I hesitate to call that kind of solidarity less "robust," as Taylor, "Solidarity," does.

[13] See Schmitz-Berning, *Vokabular des Nationalsozialismus*, pp. 602f., on the use of the term "national solidarity" during National Socialism.

connected with the idea of solidarity – i.e., of standing in for others based on a particular shared bond and common cause – and the bond or cause in question must be spelled out independently as something worth caring about. Here the relevant justifying reasons can be specific and relative to particular social contexts, but they can also be of a universalist nature. Religious forms of solidarity often combine particularistic and universalistic claims because they are rooted in a particular faith, but may (and often do) regard the truths and imperatives of that faith as being universally valid.

This means that reasons of solidarity are *not* reasons of a normative kind categorically distinct from reasons of morality, justice, religion, friendship, etc.[14] They are of a particular nature, however, insofar as reasons of political solidarity, for example, are reasons to promote the *particular* political cause of a concrete collective one feels bound to and identifies with, even though there may be other political collectives that are of a similar in nature. Still, the bond that justifies solidary actions is not binding in virtue of the mere fact of membership.[15] Rather, it is binding for a person because she values the cause or identity of the collective for particular normative reasons. She sees certain values *embodied* in a particular way by this community with which she identifies and not by others (though this may change). Reasons of solidarity thus combine *independent* evaluative considerations with a special attachment and bond to a *concrete* collective with which one identifies. This bipolar nature of solidarity can create a dynamic of critique of one's collective in light of the relevant evaluations and possibly of changing solidarities between collectives. At the level of basic conceptual analysis, it is not possible to define the proper ratio between particular combinations of the fact and history of membership and identification, on the one hand, and independent evaluative components, on the other, as these vary with contexts and conceptions of solidarity.

Once again, it should be emphasized that this conceptual analysis does not imply that the reasons for valuing the bond through which solidarity arises are good moral reasons; a one-sided and nationalist, perhaps even chauvinistic affirmation of a national identity can be just as much a basis for solidarity as a post-conventional anti-nationalist solidarity with marginalized groups. A religiously based form of solidarity can lead to a solidarity with the exploited in foreign parts

---

[14] The opposite view is defended by Derpmann, *Gründe der Solidarität*.
[15] A view held by Rorty, *Contingency, Irony, and Solidarity*, ch. 9.

of the world or to a hostile isolation against "foreign infiltration" by other religious groups of one's own country.

Our normative vocabulary contains other, similar terms, such as toleration or legitimacy, which only express a personal or institutional moral virtue if they are accompanied by independently grounded good reasons and justifications.[16] Unlike justice, for example, they do not stand for intrinsically justified virtues.[17] To be sure, a particular interpretation of justice may not be well founded, but it can be criticized in terms of the core concept of justice *itself* as a matter of overcoming arbitrariness in social relations (which is the core meaning of justice), whereas such a reflexive critique is not possible in the case of solidarity or toleration (although it has often been tried). One can criticize a particular act of solidarity for not being sufficiently solidary, but that does not tell us anything about the value of the cause that shall be furthered. Whether an act or attitude of solidarity is well founded depends on such additional values.

The idea of normatively dependent concepts is different from that of "essentially contested concepts,"[18] because the normative conceptions, but not the concept itself, are contested and conflict with each other. In fact, I doubt whether there really are any essentially contested concepts all the way down. For if there were, as argued above, it would not be clear whether a contest between normative interpretations of a concept really was a contest about the *same* concept. If it is, there is a non-contested core concept that unites the contending positions.

4.4 Normative contexts and conceptions of solidarity

One can distinguish various *conceptions* of solidarity depending on the values or principles that lend normative substance to the bond of solidarity in certain *practical contexts*. That renders my account contextualist in a certain conceptual, non-relativistic way and takes seriously the multiplicity of what could be meant by a "common bond," "shared identity," or "common cause." As we saw above, it has to express something of value to all members of the solidary

---

[16] See the discussions of toleration and legitimacy as normatively dependent concepts in Forst, *Toleration in Conflict*, §3, and Forst, *Normativity and Power*, ch. 8, respectively.
[17] See my argument in Forst, "Justice."
[18] Gallie, "Essentially Contested Concepts."

community; but what that value is and what exactly it entails depends on the respective context.

So "context" here is a complex notion involving the following aspects: It specifies the *normative nature* (or the point) of the solidary bond and demarcates the *community* of solidarity. It is not just a context of action but a normative context of self-understanding, both individually and collectively. Most notably, it is a *context of justification* that determines the relevant reasons for solidary action. At the same time, it is a context of normatively binding social relations of *mutual recognition*.[19] Which actions in particular are required depends on a further step of contextual specification; for example, there is a conception of solidarity among friends, but what exactly a concrete friendship requires friends to do or not depends on the history and particular nature of their relation. The context of justification has to be spelled out at various levels, i.e., that of a general conception and that of a particular case.

4.4.1 Ethical contexts

In *ethical* contexts of family and intimate partnerships, friendships or other forms of community, solidarity is based on particular communal bonds centered on a notion of the shared and mutually enjoyed good. These bonds ground concretely what it means to be solidary or to lack solidarity. I call such contexts "ethical" because the communally affirmed notion of the good relevant here is (at least in part) constitutive of one's ethical–personal identity, one's form of life or *ethos*. When you act in solidarity with others in this context, you affirm your own identity, you recognize who and what you are, and the common project is part of yourself – and that motivates you to do what is required. The personal investment in this form of solidarity can be very high, depending on the level of identity involvement.

The nature of the commitment and of the actions that are required and justifiable, as well as the scope of the community of solidarity, depend on these particular identity contexts. In this realm, one usually is a member of multiple ethical contexts, which may lead to priority issues or conflicts, for example between loyalty to and solidarity with your family and to your religious community or to a friend who is in

---

[19] See my distinction between contexts of recognition and of justification in Forst, *Contexts of Justice*, ch. 5.

need of support. None of these contexts of solidarity is self-justifying or takes natural precedence; it is all a question of ethical justification, where the question of who you are and what you owe to others with whom you share a strong communal bond is essential. Such a practice of justification, searching for what you "really care about,"[20] will also determine what exactly acting in solidarity means, including whether it requires you to sacrifice something important or to take risks. The main "currency" of justification here is the "ethical identity investment" (as we may call it) you share with concrete others.[21]

4.4.2 Legal contexts

It may sound surprising to list the legal domain as a context of solidarity, since this does not seem to cohere with the notions of "common bond" or "solidary reciprocity" and the idea that solidarity is a voluntary, non-coerced act. And, indeed, many people think that solidarity must be located outside the bonds of legal duties and obligations or, for that matter, of what justice demands.[22] However, as we know since Hegel and Durkheim, modern social systems presuppose certain forms of institutionally mediated solidarity, where one contributes one's share without expecting a narrow *quid pro quo*.[23] Social insurance schemes are an example of such systems, which is why in German they are called *Solidargemeinschaften*, that is, communities of solidarity.[24] Leibniz can be seen as a pioneer of such solidary schemes of "institutionalized solidarity,"[25] because he argued for an insurance scheme (in cases of fire and flooding) – *assecurazione contra casus fortuitos* – in which society as a whole should stand in for those affected by such disasters.[26] He compared society to a ship whose welfare is the responsibility of all, so that we have to help each other in case of need for the sake of the general context of cooperation – adding that the need in question should not be the result of one's own blameworthy behavior.

---

[20] Frankfurt, *The Importance of What We Care About*.
[21] Cf. Taylor, "Solidarity" (although not in these terms).
[22] Wildt, "Solidarity," and Denninger, "Constitutional Law and Solidarity."
[23] Durkheim, *The Division of Labour in Society*, and Honneth, *The Struggle for Recognition*.
[24] Metz, "Solidarity and History," and Preuß, "National, Supranational, and International Solidarity."
[25] Nullmeier, "Eigenverantwortung, Gerechtigkeit und Solidarität," and Esping-Andersen, *Social Foundations of Postindustrial Economies*.
[26] Leibniz, "Öffentliche Assekuranzen." See also Zwierlein, *Prometheus Tamed*.

Many social insurance schemes are built on such ideas, including social welfare and health-care schemes, and it remained a matter of dispute whether carelessness and other vices disqualify one from the scheme of solidarity or not. These are issues that are still relevant today, in practice as well as in theory, if you think, for example, of luck egalitarianism and its (too) strict distinction between individual responsibility and the circumstances for which one cannot be held responsible.[27] In any case, whether it is a private insurance scheme (for instance a car or home insurance) to which one contributes without ever necessarily receiving an equivalent in return, while others are bailed out from emergency situations resulting from bad behavior or bad luck, or whether it is a socially obligatory scheme (say of general public health insurance), some form of solidary reciprocity is always involved, since it is generally accepted that those in need will receive more benefits than those who are not. Although free riding is not explicitly accepted, it is for the most part tacitly tolerated for the sake of maintaining the overall integrity of the scheme.

The legal form does not preclude solidarity, properly speaking, even in a mandatory scheme. For, as Durkheim argued, its members are asked to accept the system not only and not primarily because of its sanctioning force but because of its justification, its *raison d'être*, and the way it functions – which means they should not exploit it, even if they could, nor long for changing it politically for their own benefit, even if they could do so with the support of a majority. Both as subjects of the law who could cheat but do not do so and, more importantly, as law-givers in a democratic legal state, its members accept the solidary scheme as justified and as an expression of a common civic bond. Otherwise, we would run into the paradox that the social struggles of solidary workers and others for such social insurance schemes throughout the nineteenth and twentieth centuries were really struggles to overcome "true" solidarity based on voluntary action by institutionalizing social rights. This institutionalization, however, is not beyond solidarity but retains it as a claim to recognize and accept the social, solidary sense of such systems.[28]

It is true that those libertarians, for example, who would rather abolish such schemes are, as members of these systems, legally obliged to act in accordance with norms of solidarity without really being in solidarity, and here we should recognize that certain

---

[27] See Chapter 12 in this volume.
[28] Cf. Marshall, *Citizenship and Social Class*; Brunkhorst, *Solidarität unter Fremden*.

external actions conforming to solidarity can be enforced, although the internal attitude cannot be. Yet one cannot infer from the fact that the law is coercive that all those who are subject to it follow it *because* it is coercive. Some do, some don't. It is always difficult to infer the nature of motivating reasons from actions. One cannot, for example, assume that acts of solidarity in ethical contexts were in fact motivated by the right reasons; maybe group pressure was the driving force. As far as legal contexts are concerned, if the laws were only followed out of fear of being caught when violating them, functioning legal states would have to take the form of repressive police states. And, from a political perspective, the assumption that "the state" as a separate agent installs legal systems of obligations independently of the political will of citizens and forces its subjects to comply with them is a remnant of a pre-democratic notion of law. The institutionalization of a system of social solidarity can and should be a political act of solidarity, as well as its maintenance and improvement; and its neoliberal dismantling can rightly be criticized with good reasons as an act of de-solidarization.[29]

4.4.3 Political contexts

In *political* contexts, we encounter various forms or conceptions of solidarity:

An *ethical–political* form of solidarity refers to national bonds and a shared history, or perhaps even an ethnic–historical identity interpreted as a political identity and as a project to be pursued and continued, for example, through national independence. The fact that such communities, their histories and meanings are often "imagined"[30] or fabricated does not mean that the motivating force of such ideas or communities is any less powerful. Nationalism, whether it assumes more benign or more malicious forms, remains a major normative source of solidary practical motivation.

A *political–social* form of solidarity exists where there is less ethical investment in a particular communal identity that is regarded as valuable, but where a common cause and project motivates people to act in solidarity, such as the creation of a new form of life or a new society. In most cases these are fighting creeds, as in the struggles for class liberation, democracy or ecological transformation. The nature

---

[29] Brown, *Undoing the Demos*.
[30] Anderson, *Imagined Communities*.

of the project can be seen as moral or self-serving; interpretations of class struggle, for example, can come in Hegelian–Marxist or in Nietzschean guises.

Political–social solidarity often aims at establishing a *just* society, as in movements for gender and racial equality or for overcoming class and caste exploitation as grave forms of injustice – "*Unrecht schlechthin*" (absolute injustice), in Marx's words.[31] Such movements may share certain elements with ethical–political collectives, involving a positive valuation of marginalized or exploited forms of life; yet the thrust of these communal struggles is to establish a new, more just society or a transnational order of justice. That is what calls for solidarity; it is grounded in justice as a *general* principle to be realized in a *particular* social context. Justice-based conceptions of solidarity come in two forms: those that demand solidarity in order to *establish* a just political and social order, and those that require solidarity in order to *preserve* it – where preserving justice also implies promoting and improving it.

It is important to distinguish the forms of solidarity involved in struggles for justice from more institutionalized forms of solidarity, which presuppose that a certain level of justice has already been established (as rare as this may be the case). For the former, solidarity is required to combat injustice, and it is difficult to determine to what extent that struggle should itself be bound by principles of justice (as I think it should). The second form of solidarity is clearly guided by principles of justice, for example, when it is a question of realizing a demanding form of social justice, say one that accords with Rawls's difference principle. This necessitates an ethos of justice that gives people reasons not to act or vote on their short-term self-interests, an ethos that cannot be fully realized in the form of legal duties.[32] It implies a form of solidary reciprocity which is based on the conviction that social justice involves a balance between contributions and benefits that does not serve the optimization of one's self-interest in the narrower sense.[33]

In contemporary societies, solidarity is often required in a way that combines the motives of establishing and preserving justice, because the existing institutions realize justice at best partially while

---

[31] Marx, "Zur Kritik der Hegelschen Rechtsphilosophie," p. 390 (emphasis in original). Cf. Forst, "Noumenal Alienation," Chapter 1 in this volume.
[32] G. A. Cohen, Jürgen Habermas and John Rawls agree on this point. See, for example, Rawls, *A Theory of Justice*, §79; Cohen, *Why Not Socialism?*; and Habermas, *Im Sog der Technokratie*, ch. 5.
[33] See also Sangiovanni, "Solidarity as Joint Action."

undermining it at the same time. Justice in its true sense – a notion on which I cannot elaborate here[34] – means using existing institutions (such as nation-states) to overcome the obstacles to establishing transnational institutions of democratic justice, given existing transnational realities of global injustice. The community of solidarity with respect to social and political justice must be broader than the nation-state because states are part of transnational schemes of cooperation and, most importantly, of enforced and asymmetrical "cooperation," which include relations of political, social and economic exploitation which ought to be overcome by institutions of transnational justice. From a comprehensive perspective of justice, we recognize that national solidarity must not be realized at the price of a lack of solidarity with others who are exploited and dominated.[35]

In this context, the reasons for drawing the line around a justification community or a community of solidarity are different from those in ethical contexts. There, the basis for solidarity is the ethical investment in a communal context; in the case of justice, the basis is a moral–political conception of what one owes to others as members of a shared normative order, which may transcend national ones.[36] This implies a normative (and graduated) notion of solidarity that is grounded in the principle that no one ought to be subjected to a normative order (including the global economy) of which they cannot be a co-author with equal standing. Bound by claims of justice, we owe solidarity to those who are denied such standing and should not accord our fellow nationals normative priority in a way that is detrimental to this duty.

Solidarity in contexts of (in-)justice is a duty based on the basic right of persons to be respected as equal normative authorities in all those normative orders to which they are subjected. In cases where we share such orders with them – whether it is a state or an encompassing, global economic scheme – we have duties of justice as participants in such orders which are, at the same time, duties of solidarity defined by justice. In those (unlikely) cases where we are not implicated (however indirectly) in such orders in which persons are being denied equal standing as justificatory agents, we nevertheless have a "natural duty"[37] of justice (and solidarity) to help

---

[34] See especially my work on transnational justice in Forst, *The Right to Justification*, pt. III; Forst, *Normativity and Power*, pt. V; and Chapter 8 in this volume.
[35] Lessenich, "Doppelmoral hält besser."
[36] See Habermas, *Im Sog der Technokratie*, pp. 102–111.
[37] Rawls, *A Theory of Justice*, §19.

them overcome that injustice. In both cases, existing injustice and shared projects of justice ground duties of solidarity, but in different ways depending on the context.

A special case of duties of solidarity based on considerations of justice is to ensure that refugees are treated respectfully in the normative orders they reach.[38] They are fellow human beings who are fleeing from injustice or from living conditions that are intolerable, especially given the existing global possibilities for the redistribution of resources, and members of better-off countries owe them a standing as agents of justice who have claims upon them as cosmopolitan compatriots and participants in a transnational normative order of resource distribution. Here, as elsewhere, it is important to be clear about whether we are talking about general moral, legal or moral–political duties of solidarity. All of these categories are involved in this case.

4.4.4 Moral contexts

In *moral* contexts, finally, solidarity is based on our common humanity and calls for actions ranging from morally obligatory assistance in cases of need to supererogatory actions beyond any assumption of reciprocity – except, perhaps, for the hope that, should we ever find ourselves in a similar situation, others would do something similar for us. Solidarity covers all of these cases, from "ordinary" help to extremely costly forms of assistance, although supererogatory action is an especially praiseworthy service of solidarity. The realm of solidarity thus allows for an additional space for extremely solidary and laudable actions and efforts; and I should add that this is generally the case, also in other contexts.

Moral solidarity, traditionally called *Brüderlichkeit* (brotherhood)[39] by idealists like Schiller or Beethoven (either ignoring women or including them as "brothers"), is not the "other" of morality in the sense of an opposite, even when morality is understood along Kantian lines;[40] rather, it is an *aspect* of morality that recognizes others as vulnerable beings for whom one must "stand in," given their finitude and frailty and the fact that we all share a human form of life. Morality, after all, is a form of caring for and about

---

[38] Owen, *What Do We Owe to Refugees?*
[39] Munoz-Dardé, "Fraternity and Justice."
[40] Habermas, "Justice and Solidarity." He retracts this in favor of a political understanding of solidarity in Habermas, *Im Sog der Technokratie*, p. 104, fn. 23.

others, even if one does not share a more particular form of life or identity with them. Respecting the uniqueness and vulnerability of the "concrete other,"[41] while also respecting and treating them as an equal is precisely what morality demands.[42] Acts of solidarity are always concrete acts, but that does not mean that the reason for performing them cannot be universalistic in nature. From the moral point of view, we have no good justifying reason not to show solidarity with others in need.

4.5 Conclusion

The foregoing analysis intends to contribute not only to illuminating the various meanings of the term "solidarity" (and the different normative conceptions of solidarity) but also to avoiding some of its pitfalls. The latter stem especially from mistaking a particular conception of solidarity for the whole concept; for example, by assuming that solidarity must always be ethical or political in nature, that it is categorically different from justice, or that it is always supererogatory. Solidarity comes in many forms and with many justifications and grounds. One must not reduce this plurality, but instead describe it properly.

As indicated, this opens up the possibility of conflicts between the contexts and dimensions of solidarity mentioned – among friends, comrades, citizens or all those suffering from injustice. My main point in this regard is that the normatively dependent concept of solidarity does not tell us to which form we ought to accord priority. This is where we reach bedrock in a dispute between, for example, a Humean and a Kantian view. Drawing on Hume, one might argue that the forms in which the identity investment is greatest, thus possibly the ethical ones, should take precedence.[43] Or one might develop a moral theory of the worst evils to be avoided, thereby according priority to the moral aspect (depending, however, on the ethical identification with such priorities).[44] Kantians understand the emotional and social appeal of ethical forms of solidarity, but believe that those forms of solidarity based on the categorical imperative of equal respect should have greater normative weight.[45]

[41] Benhabib, *The Rights of Others*.
[42] Wingert, *Gemeinsinn und Moral*.
[43] Rorty, *Contingency, Irony, and Solidarity*.
[44] Sangiovanni, *Humanity without Dignity*.
[45] Herman, *Moral Literacy*; Forst, *The Right to Justification*, pt. I.

The reason for this is that, in a Kantian framework, solidarity is a virtue only if founded on practical reason, based on the best justification among equal human beings. Seen in this light, the question of solidarity points to larger questions about who we are as moral beings.

— 5 —

SOCIAL COHESION
On the Analysis of a Difficult Concept[*]

5.1 Booms of cohesion

The problematization of the concept of social integration has a long tradition in modern societies, going back to Hegel, Tocqueville and Durkheim, up to communitarianism[1] or the sociological studies of Robert Putnam in *Bowling Alone*.[2] The concept of "social cohesion," however, while not entirely new,[3] has only recently moved to the center of scholarly and, increasingly, political debates, especially in Germany.[4] Initially criticized as a reactionary polemical term, it has now made it into the programs of many parties, which, however, understand it in different ways – from the conservative concept of the homeland (*Heimat*) to social democratic solidarity to multicultural cooperation. The term seems to have become an empty signifier, or as one might also put it: a chameleon.

---

[*] For helpful discussions of these reflections, I would like to thank the colleagues in Konstanz who invited me to give a lecture in April 2019, especially Albrecht Koschorke and Daniel Thym, as well as the colleagues in Frankfurt with whom I had intensive discussions of our contribution to the Research Institute Social Cohesion, especially Nicole Deitelhoff, Klaus Günther and Cord Schmelzle. I owe valuable insights to the many conversations with members of RISC as well as to the feedback on a related lecture in a discussion group on social cohesion (April 2019) convened by Prime Minister Winfried Kretschmann; here I am particularly grateful to Armin Nassehi for valuable exchanges. I am also indebted to Ciaran Cronin, Felix Kämper and Amadeus Ulrich for important suggestions for improving the text.
[1] Cf. Forst, *Contexts of Justice*.
[2] Putnam, *Bowling Alone*; see also Schimank, *Differenzierung und Integration der modernen Gesellschaft*.
[3] See Teufel, *Was hält die moderne Gesellschaft zusammen?*, and Hartmann and Offe, *Vertrauen*. For an illuminating perspective on the international discussion, see Chan et al., "Reconsidering Social Cohesion."
[4] See Dragolov et al., *Radar gesellschaftlicher Zusammenhalt*.

During the Covid-19 pandemic, however, it acquired a more specific meaning and was often used as an appeal, not least in large-scale advertisements by companies or also by governments. Broadcasters even used it as a logo. There, it stood for the generally demanded, widely accepted and, at the same time, prescribed behavior centered on the common good that was supposed to help contain the spread of the virus. For a brief moment, the term seemed to acquire clearer contours. But is it only relevant in times of crisis, and does it presuppose a threat against which one seeks to protect or defend oneself, even if it is a viral one?

With "cohesion," as with other difficult terms, the closer you examine it, the more multifaceted and unwieldy it becomes. In the following, I will shed light on some of these facets in the hope of contributing to a clarification. I will argue:

(1) that we should distinguish between a concept and different conceptions of cohesion;
(2) that the concept contains different levels, of which the one of a particular attitude or stance is the most important;
(3) that this attitude should be located between related concepts such as tolerance and solidarity;
(4) that the concept of cohesion, much like these other notions, can only be extended to generate specific conceptions of cohesion by enriching it with other, additional normative assumptions; and
(5) that, finally, the question of social cohesion must be situated in historical–social contexts, and that societies bring about forms of cohesion especially when they define overarching social and political projects. In this context, I return to the question of crisis and threat.

5.2 A neutral core definition

The chameleon-like nature of cohesion is already made apparent by the question of whether it is a descriptive or a normative term. For the most part, the term is used in a normative sense, and yet it does not represent a value, because cohesion within the Mafia, for instance, or cohesion based on nationalistic fervor is not something of value. The fact that "too much" cohesion, or better: the wrong kind of it, can have something confining and even (in other respects) threatening cohesion is also indicated by the Bertelsmann Foundation's

2012 "cohesion radar," which conducted pioneering research on the notion.[5] This suggests that the concept has no intrinsic normative core, so that when the authors see, for example, "acceptance of diversity"[6] as one of its components, this amounts to positing a norm – thereby moving, analytically, beyond a determination of the *concept* (core meaning of the term) to a specific *conception* (particular understanding of the term). This analytical distinction was proposed by John Rawls in the context of his theory of justice, although he conceived of the core concept of justice aptly as a normative one.[7] In the case of cohesion, by contrast, it is appropriate to start with a *normatively neutral* core concept and proceed to distinguish it from normative conceptions. So, I agree with Joseph Chan, Ho-Pong To and Elaine Chan that one should aim for a minimal definition of the concept; but I go one step further than them in that I do not regard cohesion as a good or value.[8]

The definition found in the Bertelsmann study emphasizes three core spheres, namely social relationships, a sense of connectedness and an orientation toward the common good.[9] Accordingly, the definition reads: "A cohesive society is marked by close social relationships, deep emotional attachment and a pronounced orientation toward the common good."[10] Chan et al. suggest the following definition, which is more careful in the normative language it uses: "Social cohesion is a state of affairs concerning both the vertical and the horizontal interactions among members of society as characterized by a set of attitudes and norms that includes trust, a sense of belonging and the willingness to participate and help, as well as their behavioral manifestations."[11]

In dialogue with and to a certain extent in contrast to these definitions, the definition favored by the German Research Institute Social Cohesion (RISC), which I have suggested, assumes that the concept involves five levels. Moreover, as I said, this definition is normatively more modest and does not presuppose, for example, an "intense emotional attachment." What needs to be investigated is instead which kind of sense of connectedness is conceptually necessary and empirically possible in complex, modern societies.

---

[5] Schiefer et al., *Kohäsionsradar*, pp. 24f. (translation R.F.).
[6] Ibid., p. 23 (translation R.F.).
[7] Rawls, *A Theory of Justice*, p. 5.
[8] See Chan et al., "Reconsidering Social Cohesion," p. 280.
[9] Schiefer et al., *Kohäsionsradar*, p. 23 (translation R.F.).
[10] Ibid., p. 21 (translation R.F.). See also the further development of the concept in Arant et al., *Radar gesellschaftlicher Zusammenhalt*, pp. 24–40.
[11] Chan et al., "Reconsidering Social Cohesion," p. 290.

The five levels that need to be distinguished analytically with regard to social cohesion are (1) individual or collective stances or *attitudes* toward oneself and others, (2) individual and collective *actions* and practices, (3) the intensity and scope of social *relationships* and networks, (4) systemic, *institutional contexts* of cooperation and integration and finally (5) the social *discourses* in a society about its cohesiveness. For societies are self-reflective entities, and self-reflection is part of the overall complex of cohesion. A comprehensive concept of social cohesion must encompass these five aspects, render them analytically accessible and relate them to one another.

The term, therefore, refers to societies whose members have certain positive attitudes toward each other and toward their overall social context, in which they are involved as agents in practices and relationships that contribute to the social order (to be defined in more detail), and which fit into complex institutional processes of cooperation and integration that are discursively thematized and evaluated. Cohesion exists where these levels have a certain quality and sufficiently coincide – in the *attitudes, actions, relationships, institutions* and *discourses* of a society.

This definition of the concept is normatively neutral and does not determine *a priori* the quality of, say, communal cohesion, connectedness and integration. It neither implies that cohesion is characterized by shared traditions or social homogeneity, nor does it conceptually presuppose the acceptance of diversity or democratic contestation. The concept of cohesion itself is thus, as I have put it elsewhere, "normatively dependent,"[12] for it does not contain the normative resources to ground particular conceptions of cohesion that emphasize homogeneity or heterogeneity, or that are collectivist, democratic or authoritarian. Such conceptions require other resources, such as a communitarian "ideal" of an integrated or solidary society, or a particular conception of democracy, which would have to be grounded and justified in a specific way.

On the descriptive level, the notion of social cohesion should encompass all five aspects. However, its focus should be on the attitudinal aspect, indicated by the fact that (in German) "sticking together" (*Zusammenhalten*) is its origin. This sticking together is, however, not that of a flock of sheep under the watchful gaze of the shepherd, but that of those who see themselves as connected or committed to one another. Let us preserve this as a defining characteristic: Cohesion presupposes a sense of being connected

---

[12] Forst, *Normativity and Power*, ch. 8, and Forst, *Toleration in Conflict*, §3.

to a collective and the willingness to take actions that follow from this connectedness and are intended to keep the whole in view and promote it.

Hence, the term also raises the question of whether complex, systemically and culturally differentiated modern societies still form communities that "cohere" at all in the sense of actively supporting social unity – that is, whether they form communities in which the members identify with the collective, even and especially across differences, and stand up for one another.[13] In order to do justice to the reality of modern societies, cohesion should be conceptualized as a form of integration that reflects the plurality of individual group memberships and of forms of systemic differentiation[14] and provides for social as well as political processes of cooperation that involve conflicts. Then the main question concerns the general framework that makes this possible – and (as already mentioned) not primarily an institutional framework, but a "noumenal" framework of attitudes and orientations. This brings us to related attitudinal concepts such as tolerance, trust and solidarity, but also democratic respect, with which we are already on the way to specific conceptions of cohesion.

5.3 Tolerance, solidarity and cohesion

Let us therefore take a closer look at some of these concepts, such as tolerance and solidarity, which seem to occupy different ends of the spectrum of attitudes oriented toward the common good – tolerance seemingly where the greatest possible plurality exists, solidarity where unity prevails. But this impression may be deceptive, because tolerance also requires, and perhaps promotes, cohesion, whereas solidarity may have to cope with diversity and unfamiliarity.

Firstly, concerning tolerance, it denotes an attitude that, from an analytical point of view, consists of three components. In spelling them out, we can already avoid a number of misunderstandings – for example, the misconception that tolerance has something to do with non-judgmental indifference or, as Nietzsche put it, the "inability to say yes and no."[15] Let us consider what we mean when we say that we "tolerate" something, such as someone's opinion, the smell of a dish, or the way in which a group acts. We say this only if something

---

[13] Cf. Habermas, "On Social Identity."
[14] Cf. Nassehi, "Inklusion, Exklusion, Zusammenhalt."
[15] Nietzsche, *Nachgelassene Fragmente 1885–1887*, p. 432.

bothers us about that opinion, smell or action. And, in fact, the first component of tolerance is that of *objection*.[16] The beliefs or practices that we tolerate are ones to which we object as wrong or bad. Otherwise, there would only be indifference or affirmation, but not tolerance.

However, to this must be added a second component, namely that of *acceptance*. It provides reasons why what is wrong or bad should nevertheless be tolerated. Here a balance is struck between negative and positive considerations, because the reasons for acceptance do not suspend the reasons for objection, they merely stand alongside them and tip the balance in the case of tolerance. The objection remains.

Finally, there is a third component to consider – that of *rejection*, so again negative reasons. These mark the limits of toleration. Obviously, these negative reasons must be more serious than the first-mentioned reasons for objecting, because they cannot be trumped by considerations of acceptance. They justify why, from a, let us say, higher point of view, limits have to be drawn – and how.

It is the task of toleration to bring these three components into the right normative order. The respective reasons for objecting, accepting and rejecting can have similar or different origins. All three can have religious sources, such as when one objects to another religion as false, but accepts it in a spirit of peace and fellow humanity until one is compelled to reject it because it leads to blasphemy. But the reasons can also be of different kinds, for example, when a religious objection is confronted with reasons of acceptance and rejection that invoke human rights – the one refers to religious freedom (acceptance) and the other, say, to the right to physical integrity (rejection). Of course, these reasons are not internal to the concept of tolerance itself; it is a virtue that *depends* on other normative resources being brought in in the right way. It is not itself a value (even if this is often asserted). This is a feature it shares with cohesion.

Tolerance also shares this normatively dependent character with the concept of *solidarity*.[17] By this we generally mean a practical attitude of standing by one another, which expresses and presupposes a certain form of common bond. It can be traced back to a common identity or a shared project or at least valued membership in a community. Standing by each other is not based on simple reciprocity, but presupposes that one is willing to contribute more

---

[16] See my analysis in Forst, *Toleration in Conflict*, ch. 1, following King, *Toleration*.
[17] See Chapter 4 in this volume.

than others, if necessary, for the sake of the common cause. However, one expects others to do the same when they are called upon to do their share.

If we want to approach the question of cohesion with the aid of these two concepts, we must make a further differentiation. So let us distinguish between different *conceptions* of tolerance and also of solidarity.

I will limit myself to two conceptions of toleration.[18] The first I call the *permission conception*. We find it in the classical toleration legislations, for instance in the Edict of Nantes (1598), which states:

> [N]ot to leave any occasion of trouble and difference among our Subjects, we have permitted and do permit to those of the Reformed Religion, to live and dwell in all the Cities and places of this our Kingdom and Countreys under our obedience, without being inquired after, vexed, molested or compelled to do any thing in Religion, contrary to their Conscience, nor by reason of the same be searched after in houses or places where they live.[19]

Toleration is thus an attitude and practice of the authoritarian state that gives minorities permission to live in accordance with their beliefs – within the framework that the permitting side *alone* determines. All three components (objection, acceptance and rejection) are in the hands of the authorities; the tolerated are marked and regarded as second-class citizens and are dependent on the protection of the monarch. This is the idea of toleration targeted by the critiques of Goethe ("to tolerate is to offend") and Kant ("arrogant name of *tolerance*"),[20] because here to be tolerated is also to be stigmatized and dominated.

In a long history of democratic revolutions, a "horizontal" conception of toleration emerged in modern times in contrast to the "vertical" conception of permission – namely, the *respect conception*. The essential idea here is that tolerance is an attitude of citizens toward one another, in the knowledge that they disagree on central issues of the good and right life, yet accepting that the institutions they share must be based on norms that all can share as *equals* and do not simply codify the (contestable) values of one group and declare them as the law. The component of objection remains in

---

[18] I discuss four conceptions in Forst, *Toleration in Conflict*, §2.
[19] The Edict of Nantes, quoted from Mousnier, *The Assassination of Henry IV*, pp. 316ff.
[20] Goethe, "Maximen und Reflexionen," p. 507, and Kant, "An Answer to the Question: 'What Is Enlightenment?'" VIII:40 (emphasis in original).

the definitional space of individuals or their communities, but the components of acceptance and rejection are determined in a process of legitimation aimed at norms that can be generally justified. The person of the other is *respected* as politico-legally equal, and their beliefs and ways of acting are *tolerated*.

Thus, it becomes clear that these conceptions of toleration are also associated with different notions of cohesion and, as in earlier eras, discussions of toleration today are always discussions of cohesion as well. According to a "democratically" (better: majoritarian) transformed conception of permission, the "guiding culture" (*Leitkultur*) of a traditional majority determines what counts as the norm (the crucifix in public classrooms or courtrooms, for example) and the extent to which other religious symbols (e.g., headscarf, burqa), practices (e.g., circumcision) or social forms of life (like same-sex marriage) are to be tolerated; yet according to the respect conception, this conventional culture must relinquish its primacy in the face of claims to equality of minorities.[21] Then crucifixes are removed from classrooms and courtrooms, female civil servants are also allowed to wear the headscarf as a religious symbol, the burqa is tolerated (with function-dependent exceptions that must be justified), religious practices are only stopped if they involve clear bodily harm, and same-sex marriage is placed on the same legal level as heterosexual marriage.

From a methodological point of view, this raises the crucial question of cohesion: On which basis is one to decide which of the conceptions is the "right one" – according to fundamental considerations of justice as equal respect or according to how cohesion actually "functions" in a society? If the former, the respect conception is the appropriate one; if the latter, then possibly the permission conception, since here the "cement" of society or its "integrative power" seems not to be overstretched. This is how some argue, but critically, one must ask whether these interpretations of "cement" or "integration" are not themselves exclusionary, for they define cohesion according to what majorities deem appropriate – and minorities have to choose between assimilation or evasion and invisibility. Again, it becomes apparent that specific conceptions of cohesion rest upon normative assumptions that need to be identified and discussed. The fact that what counts as cohesion is defined by established majorities can neither be assumed unquestioningly nor described as "democratic," because democracy (again, to make a normative statement) is not – or

---

[21] See Forst, *Toleration in Conflict*, ch. 12, and Forst, *Normativity and Power*, ch. 6.

should not be – an instrument of domination of minorities and denial of equal rights.

The various conceptions of solidarity constitute a similar case.[22] Depending on the context, solidarity assumes a different normative form. In ethical contexts of family, friendships or even religious communities, there exist very strong assumptions of connectedness, and the circle of solidarity is correspondingly limited. In legal–social contexts, on the other hand, solidarity assumes a more mediated form, such as when it comes to social insurance schemes. But here, too, there are expectations of reciprocity at different stages of life, and the circle of solidarity is again restricted. It is unbounded, however, in moral contexts when it is a question of helping people who are in need. Here the basis of solidarity is our shared humanity.

So, which is the right model for a political community: an ethical–national model that regards the political community as an extended family whose members stand by each other, or rather the legal model that builds on considerations of utility, or the unbounded moral model that presupposes no specific ties? Or a fourth model? Again, the same question arises: Should the guiding principle here be a generally valid, abstract account of justice, or rather the social self-understanding of the majority in a concrete society in which shared nationality still plays a major role, at least for many members of society? The normatively dependent concept of solidarity does *not* help us to answer this question.

But neither does that of cohesion. As we have seen, it is just as normatively dependent. For it receives its normative substance only through other concepts (democracy, justice), while it is also often, not just in political discourse, normatively enriched with the reference to social facts (or what are considered to be social facts). Then, it is said, cohesion gets lost with "too much" toleration, and solidarity dwindles. Others assert the opposite and point out that notions of solidary cohesion that set narrow limits to toleration and allow at best for permissive toleration are exclusionary and not "genuine" forms of cohesion.

Again, it is apparent that there can be no "neutral" conception of cohesion, but that *every* conception that provides orientation in the face of such questions is normatively enriched. And this is also the actual, critical meaning of the term – to force us to reflect on the alternatives between different normative conceptions of cohesion. Such normative conceptions are necessary not only where the question

---

[22] See Chapter 4 in this volume.

is what should hold a society together, but also where assertions are made about what actually holds a society together, relating (or mixing) descriptive and evaluative claims. Here, to put it in terms of classical Frankfurt-style critical theory, there can be no "positivist" perspective of analysis that disregards normative considerations.[23]

5.4 Justification narratives and justice

A comprehensive conception of cohesion in modern, pluralistic societies, as we saw in section 5.2, must take into account the levels of individual attitudes and actions, collective practices, networks and social institutions in their specific normative functions before the question of what "holds" such societies together can be answered. To complete this picture, however, special emphasis must be placed on the fifth level, that is, societal discourses and reflections. For societies interpret themselves, and the hermeneutic reconstruction of this space of self-interpretations is indispensable for any analysis of social cohesion.

But what does it mean to turn to the discursive, the *noumenal* space of a society? The objects of investigation are the frameworks within which values of cooperation are interpreted, institutions are lived and ways of life are evaluated, and these are part of more or less comprehensive *justificatory narratives* that illuminate one's own position within the community and specify who owes what to whom, who has what kinds of advantages or disadvantages, who has certain rights and entitlements.[24] One need only consider the complex justification narratives to which people in the states of the eastern part of Germany appeal when they complain about injustices they have suffered: by the totalitarian state of the GDR, its winding up and takeover by the West, capitalist foreign domination, being overrun by foreigners from different cultures, and so on.[25] In this way, narratives are formed whose quality of cohesion is related to the ideal images of social "cohesion" they contain and how they represent the threats to which it is exposed. Then we see how social and cultural attitudes, including nationalist and possibly xenophobic ones, are

---

[23] See Habermas, *Zur Logik der Sozialwissenschaften*, ch. 2, esp. p. 61.
[24] On the concept of justification narratives, see Forst, *Normativity and Power*, chs. 2 and 3. On political narratives of inclusion and exclusion, see also Koschorke, "Öffnen und Schließen."
[25] See my speech "Demokratie als Lernprozess" on the 30th anniversary of German Reunification in the Paulskirche in Frankfurt: Forst, *Die noumenale Republik*, ch. 15.

mixed and bundled into justificatory narratives that make people at times immune to calls for tolerance and solidarity because, to them, these calls seem hollow and false. Few things corrode social cohesion as much as the solidified impression that one is part of a *system of privilege* that elevates an elite above others and in which these others are excluded and left behind. This is an impression that leads to alienation at both ends of the spectrum, among elites and the excluded. It is of secondary importance whether this impression is justified; what is most relevant is whether it can be discussed, possibly corrected or whether epistemic islands take shape that become inaccessible to each other. The space of justifications that effectively guide people's thought and action is central to the question of cohesion.

Let us define social cohesion with regard to this level accordingly (and provisionally) as follows: a society is "cohesive" in which there is still sufficient overlap between the different justificatory narratives about what kind of society it is, and who has what position and entitlements in it, to ensure that the common institutional system, from kindergarten to parliament, can function. An *overarching narrative of social integration and cooperation* must exist that ascribes and grants relevant belonging to oneself and others, even when others follow different ideas and practices, such as those rooted in different cultural ways of life. But such differences are not seen as threats or barriers to social cooperation. Cohesion, if you will, is a matter of perceiving one's situation in relation to that of others. And this is where the concept of justice comes into play, not as an abstract framework of principles, but as an expectation directed to social institutions and fellow citizens that things will be fair, or at least that efforts will be made to achieve this. Cohesion fades when this expectation is disputed – and even more so when there is not even a basic agreement about what justice means.

Reflexively, one can put the relevant point as follows: Social cohesion exists where the different notions of proper, just social cohesion that exist in group milieus still sufficiently coincide to give rise to a shared normative notion of cohesion, albeit an abstract and multilayered notion. There must be – and here we move to the level of a *democratic conception* of cohesion – sufficient room for difference, tolerance and democratic dispute, but also for an awareness of real togetherness, which must be able to prove and reproduce itself in conflicts.[26] This cohesion breaks down (or does not arise at all) when there is insufficient overlap between the individual (or group) notions

---

[26] See Forst, "The Justification of Trust in Conflict."

of cohesion. Then conflicts turn into combats. Thus, social cohesion exists only where there are sufficiently *shared* justification narratives about the society of which one is a part. This includes the historical aspect of social self-interpretation. Where some see primarily a history of oppression, such as through racism and economic exploitation, while others see a free civil way of life that must be defended, these interpretations diverge too widely, and the appeal to cohesion turns into empty rhetoric.

5.5 Social projects and crises

Despite all historical determination, life, including social life, is lived with an orientation to the future. Shared justification narratives that generate high levels of social cohesion require a social *project* that creates a common bond. Here we come to the issue of the diagnosis of the times at the heart of the question of cohesion. Such projects, which by no means exclude conflicts and disagreements over direction, can assume very different forms – from a historical perspective one could think, for example, of decolonization, the (re)creation of the nation, socialist society, democratization that implements women's rights, the ecological reconstruction of society, and so on. But what is the overarching project of contemporary Western societies? The return to the nation or the opening to multicultural cosmopolitanism?[27] In my view, this question does not yet go to the heart of the matter.

The core question is rather: Do we still believe that the available social and political institutions are even remotely equipped for the major challenges of our time – overcoming the ecological crisis, controlling the global economy, dealing humanely with global migration, overcoming poverty, digitizing our living and working conditions – and, last but not least, securing international peace? What happens within a society that recognizes that this is no longer the case? In what – perhaps pathological – directions do the cries of "take back control" or "make America great again" point? The projects with these slogans on their banners are not only backward-looking; they replace democratic cohesion with division, though they use such cohesion-rhetoric for their aims.

From this perspective, it is not primarily the aforementioned threats that endanger cohesion through the absence of a political–social

---

[27] Cf. de Wilde et al., *The Struggle Over Borders*.

project. What is endangering cohesion is rather the doubt that has been spreading since the 1990s[28] as to whether we even have the political agency to meet these challenges, since they require transnational action but the institutions and the active civic substance that could undertake such action are nowhere to be seen. Without this, however, a politics of democracy and the future lacks a place and orientation. Then political conflicts degenerate into zero-sum games, and everything that is new or "different" is rejected and resisted. Where the way forward seems to be blocked, the "hatred of the non-identical" (Adorno) associated with false nostalgia grows, and people want to go back *somewhere*.[29]

From this perspective, the social and political implications of the Covid-19 pandemic appear ambivalent.[30] For, on the one hand, the truth that cohesion has to prove itself in a crisis was confirmed, and the containment of the virus and the communal management of the diverse costs of these measures constituted, at least briefly, a project that required and also generated solidarity and cohesion. The social space of justification was reconfigured in a powerful way into a single justification (that of containing the virus) in a very short time. On the other hand, the nation-state in an almost classical form bestrode the stage again, demonstrating that it was as capable of action as it was dependent – in the face of a global pandemic and the search for vaccines and possibilities of economic recovery that require action and coordination well beyond the nation-state. The political imagination, however, remained within the national framework, including travel restrictions, ethnic exclusion of allegedly "careless" foreigners who were suspected of causing increased infections, up to lines of conflict within the EU over solidarity and follow-up costs, not to speak of relations between Western and non-Western states and regions.

Hence the question: Is the price for defining an inclusive political project that brings about social cohesion a return to national and, in parts, nationalist thinking? And how exclusionary is this project? Can it promote more than a partial cohesion? Can it be the answer to the aforementioned and other crises that are, at their core, transnational in nature? The question of cohesion is, as a diagnosis of the times suggests, part of the contradictions of our time.

---

[28] See Unseld, *Politik ohne Projekt?*
[29] See my analysis of regression in Chapter 3.
[30] See also Forst, "Freiheiten, Risiken und Rechtfertigungen."

— Part II —

JUSTICE, RIGHTS AND NON-DOMINATION IN A NEW KEY
Critical Political Theory

6

NORMATIVITY AND REALITY
Toward a Critical and Realistic Theory of Politics*

6.1 Plato's paradox

The science of politics is an unusual kind of science. It has one of the longest traditions of all sciences, but it constantly struggles with that tradition. One of the reasons for this is that we have become suspicious of the ethnocentrism of that tradition. But another reason is that the oldest and most important work in Western political thought, Plato's *Republic*, contains a paradox that still haunts us. Plato argues that the central question of those who seek the truth about politics is the nature of the just political order, and he believes that there is only one right answer to that question, an answer based on a metaphysical idea of the good. However, that idea of the good, although it is generally valid, is not accessible to everyone.

As Plato explains in the parable of the cave, those who have left the realm of the shadows that are falsely regarded as reality – fake reality, we might say – and have ascended the path leading to the recognition of the true reality of the good will never be able to return to the cave to explain what they saw, since no one would be able to believe them. Instead, those who had grasped the reality of the good would be killed by those who remain in the cave, ideologically

---

* I presented earlier versions of this text as a keynote at the general conference of the European Consortium for Political Research in Hamburg (August 2018) and at the annual conference of the network Economic Research on Identity, Norms and Narratives in London (June 2019). I thank Peter Niesen and George Akerlof for the respective invitations. Thanks also to Ciaran Cronin for correcting my English. These thoughts were developed in the course of our collective work in Frankfurt on Normative Orders, and I thank Klaus Günther especially for the longtime collaboration. The dialogue with Seyla Benhabib has been an inspiration from early on, when I started to form my thoughts. I dedicate this text to her.

deluded as they are. Thus, the paradox is that the *real* truth about political order is politically uncommunicable, given the *realities* of social life.

So Plato – and the tradition of political thought founded by him – leaves us with a complicated heritage, a confusion as to what kind of reality political science is going to explore: the reality of the cave and its infinite power struggles or the real truth of the ideal political order that we should strive for. This tradition leads to a lot of conceptual problems and rifts, if one thinks, for example, of the ways in which the term "realism" is understood.[1] While for some (social scientists especially), it refers to the cave reality of self-interested rivalry and the normative arbitrariness of social life, for others (philosophers mainly) it refers to the view that certain values, including those guiding political life, are true and real.[2]

6.2 The loss of a shared language in political science

In my view, the Platonic paradox of the political incommunicability of political truth – or, in other words, the incompatibility of two kinds of reality as the object of political science – creates a severe methodological problem within that discipline. The problem goes very deep and ultimately it raises the question of whether political science is a normative or an empirical enterprise. What is the main question of that kind of science – to understand and analyze the political orders we live in or to search for the good or just political order? You may of course say that it is both and try to muddle through somehow. Many say that the scientific part is the domain of social and political analysis – of political behavior and institutional mechanisms – and claim, following Weber and others, that the normative part is not really a scientific one.[3] Others call that position "positivism" and emphasize the importance and

---

[1] This paradoxical problem has led to a number of reactions in the history of political theory, for example, to Hannah Arendt's distinction between philosophical truth and political opinion or to the distinction between a secret doctrine of political philosophy and one that can be communicated publicly by Leo Strauss. See Arendt, "Philosophy and Politics," and Strauss, *Persecution and the Art of Writing*. See also Walzer, "Philosophy and Democracy," and Wolin, *Politics and Vision*. For a more recent discussion of realism, see Sleat, *Politics Recovered*, and Larmore, *What Is Political Philosophy?*
[2] See Nagel, *The View from Nowhere*.
[3] See Weber, *The Vocation Lectures*.

independence of normative political philosophy, trying to stay away from the cave.[4]

As a result, political science is a discipline that allows itself the luxury of a subdiscipline called political theory (or political philosophy) that used to define the enterprise of political science but in the meantime has given way to a new understanding of what science is. The question of the right or just political order is translated into an empirical program of what certain collectives actually recognize as a legitimate order (following Weber), while the original question is seen as being only of historical interest and a matter of (possibly postcolonial–genealogical) critique[5] or one for Platonic idealists. As a consequence, political theory and the other areas of political science have lost touch with one another and developed languages of their own.

This is regrettable, especially at a time of normative crisis, when we are concerned about the future of democracy, the rule of law and multilateral systems of international cooperation, not to speak of social justice – and when we are in need of appropriate conceptual and normative tools to determine, for example, at which point populism transforms democracy into its opposite, into authoritarianism.[6] Can the voices of political scientists or of philosophers still carry weight in the upheavals of our time if empirical and normative analysis rarely meet? Isn't this a time when there is an urgent need to combine the two perspectives and when we have to resist the arbitrariness of definitions of democracy, justice or the rule of law that use the term "democracy" for exclusionary and oppressive forms of politics?

6.3 Justification as a mediating term

The challenge I am formulating here has not gone unnoticed, of course, and I take Seyla Benhabib's work to be exemplary for developing advanced methods of political theory that bridge abstract principles and the realities of social and political life – the apt term "concrete universal" signifies this kind of thinking, as do other terms she uses, such as the combination of the "concrete" and the

---

[4] For example Estlund, *Utopophobia*.
[5] See Allen, *The End of Progress*. See also the debate between Amy Allen and me in Allen and Mendieta, *Justification and Emancipation*, chs. 9 and 10 – and especially Chapter 2 in this volume.
[6] See Forst, "Two Bad Halves Don't Make a Whole."

"generalized" other,[7] or the powerful concept of "democratic iterations," which she coined. The latter refers to "complex processes of public argument, deliberation and learning through which universalist right claims are contested and contextualized, invoked and revoked, throughout legal and political institutions as well as in the public sphere of liberal democracies."[8] In her approach, a particular notion of discourse as containing certain normative principles and as a practice of what Arendt (following Kant) called "enlarged thought"[9] mediates between the ideal and the real and, in this way, she develops Habermas's discourse theory further in important and innovative ways.[10] Still, the notion of discourse used remains primarily a normative one, albeit one that connects practices of morality, law and politics.

In the following remarks, I want to make a different (though not completely unrelated) suggestion as to how to bridge the seeming abyss between the language of normative political theory and the language of empirical analysis – one that I have developed (in dialogue with others) in the interdisciplinary research context of the Normative Orders Centre in Frankfurt.[11] What is essential indeed, in my view, are *mediating terms* that enable us both to analyze political orders and their dynamics descriptively and to develop normative reflections along the very *same* conceptual lines of analysis as in the descriptive work. The mediating term I have in mind is the concept of *justification*.

One might think that this is a typical move by a political philosopher bewitched by Plato, because the realm of justification is basically the realm of values, norms and principles that might be required for normative reflection but is of little use when it comes to understanding real cave life political dynamics of interests, power struggles, institutional mechanisms, path-dependencies, and so on.[12] But this fear is unfounded, for I want to argue for a particular way of understanding the reality of interests, of power and of historical situatedness. In my view, the *real reality* of politics, of the cave as

---

[7] Benhabib, *Situating the Self*, ch. 5.
[8] Benhabib, *The Rights of Others*, p. 19.
[9] Benhabib, *Situating the Self*, p. 139.
[10] For some discussions between us, from which I benefited enormously, see Forst, "Situations of the Self" (with a reply by Benhabib in the same issue: Benhabib, "On Reconciliation and Respect, Justice and the Good Life"), and Benhabib, "The Uses and Abuses of Kantian Rigorism," and my reply in Forst, "The Right to Justification."
[11] See Forst and Günther, *Die Herausbildung normativer Ordnungen*, and Forst and Günther, *Normative Ordnungen*.
[12] See Geuss, *Philosophy and Real Politics*.

well as of a perspective free (or, better, partially free) from the cave, is the *reality of justifications*. We learn to think politically and socially by understanding and using justifications about the foundations and the frameworks of our common life, accepting (often unreflexively), criticizing and occasionally rejecting them, including some rather large and comprehensive narratives. There is no politics outside the realm of justifications. Every single political thought rests on assumptions about how our collective life is and ought to be ordered and, when we think about the "is" – as democratic, productive, one-sided, dysfunctional or what have you – we use and reproduce justifications.

But note that to speak in this way does not mean that I am speaking of *good* justifications from a reflexive or even a Platonic viewpoint; rather, by justifications in an empirical and descriptive sense I refer to what makes people *effectively* think in certain ways and view reality in a certain light. My thesis, in short, is that we do not understand political reality if we do not have the conceptual tools to analyze the multiple – and often contradictory – justifications that constitute political reality as a reality of thought and action. We also do not understand how power works. Let me explain.

6.4 The power of justifications

I begin with a brief reflection on the concept of power, truly an essential concept for political science, for without power there is no collective normative order.[13]

Let us start with a sober definition of power, close to that of Robert Dahl, who suggested that "*A* has power over *B* to the extent that he can get *B* to do something that *B* would not otherwise do."[14] Note that B here is an agent who "does" something that A wants him or her to do – B is not a mere object, like a stone I kick away, but is still an agent with some freedom of action. So, the exercise of power over B requires A to steer B's actions in such a way that they are still the actions of B, but that they now follow the lines intended by A. If B is an agent, the secret of power is to affect his or her agency internally. In other words, A has to "give" B a motivating reason to act in a particular way.

---

[13] See on the following my article "Noumenal Power," originally in the *Journal of Political Philosophy*; also in *Normativity and Power*, ch. 2.
[14] Dahl, "The Concept of Power," pp. 202f.

We can express this by reformulating Dahl's definition of power to say that *power is the capacity of A to motivate B to think or do something that B would otherwise not have thought or done*. Power on this definition is normatively neutral, for we need not take a stance (as many do) at this definitional level on whether what A motivates B to think or do is in B's interest or not – or whether it is justified or not. This is why (contrary to Lukes, for example) I do not think that the concept of power is "essentially contested."[15]

Note that our definition points to the fact that the real site of the resources for and the exercise of power is the cognitive realm, that is, the realm of justifications, since A needs to be able to affect and change the realm of motivational reasons for B. Thus, we define power such that to have and exercise power means being able to influence, use, determine, occupy or even seal off the space of reasons for others. Power in this sense comes in degrees and can be analyzed along a spectrum of intensities.

Our analysis is still normatively neutral, because the means that A uses to influence or colonize the realm of reasons or justifications for B can be a good speech, a sermon, an ideological world description, a lie, a threat, an order or an act of seduction. Those who convince us as teachers or experts exercise power over us, and those who deceive us or who threaten us (credibly) do so, too. But all power is, as I put it, *noumenal* in nature – that is, it takes place in the realm of reasons and justifications. A credible threat (say, with a gun) "gives" you a reason to act in a certain way, as does an ideology. To be the subject of power means that the justifications that make you think or act in a certain way are determined in relevant ways by others: if the determining in question is unintentional, I call that an *effect* of power; if it is intentional, then it is an *exercise* of power.[16]

In this context, I use the terms "reason" or "justification" in a purely *descriptive* sense. Later, I will say something about good justifications and how they can be produced; but here it is important that we remain at a descriptive level. We fail to understand how power is exercised, either individually, collectively or within structures,

---

[15] Compare the countercriticism of Lukes, "Noumenal Power: Concept and Explanation," and my reply in Forst, "Noumenal Power Revisited." The debate (together with other critical exchanges) can also be found in Haugaard and Kettner, *Theorising Noumenal Power*.

[16] On this difficulty, see the critiques by Lukes, "Noumenal Power," Hayward, "On Structural Power," and McCormick, "'A Certain Relation in the Space of Justifications': Intentions, Lateral Effects and Rainer Forst's Concept of Noumenal Power," as well as my replies in Forst, "Noumenal Power Revisited," and Forst, "Navigating a World of Conflict and Power."

if we do not understand the justifications that guide people's actions, as those who have and those who are subject to power. We also do not understand power shifts, or what it means to lose or acquire more power, if we do not understand the justificatory dynamics in the noumenal realm of reasons. To (once again) prevent misunderstanding:[17] these reasons are for the most part not reflected upon or critically tested, but they are nevertheless effective reasons, reasons that "work." The notion of "noumenal" I am using here is an "impure" one, so to speak: it refers to the reasons that motivate us internally, but it does not imply that these are justified reasons based on some standard of reasonableness.

On the basis of such an analysis, we can distinguish more concrete forms of power:

Rule (Herrschaft) is a form of the exercise of power within structured relations based on certain understandings of legitimacy that support such structures – whatever they may rest on.

Domination (Beherrschung) exists where asymmetrical social and political relations backed by hegemonic justifications prevail that limit the space of justification either through ideological force or threats of violence (or both). Political domination exists in two dimensions: that of being ruled by unjustifiable norms and (as a higher-order form of domination) that of the lack of spheres and institutions of justification to discursively question dominant norms and construct alternative ones.

Violence (Gewalt) is an extreme form of the denial of justificatory standing to others, who are thereby reduced to mere physical objects to be moved or destroyed.

Such acts often are meant to have noumenal effects of intimidation or deterrence. But, with respect to those who are its direct objects, the use of violence may be a reflection of A's having lost social power over them, because A no longer tries to move them internally as agents. Think of the kidnapper who kills his or her victim because the latter is not willing to comply, or those who were supposed to pay the ransom refused to do so – which means that the kidnapper's power, as originally intended, fades away, and violence is a reflection of that loss of power. In more political terms, think of the moments at which the tanks in the street lose their power because people overcome their fear or are willing to take the risk of opposing

---

[17] Examples are McNay, "The Limits of Justification," and Bajaj and Rossi, "Noumenal Power, Reasons, and Justification." See my replies in Forst, "The Constitution of Justification." See also Owen, "Power, Justification and Vindication," and my reply in Forst, "The Dialectics of Toleration and the Power of Reason(s)."

them. Their physical power of destruction is the same as before but, because of a shift in the realm of justifications, their social power has been reduced.[18]

6.5 Narratives, structures and reality

Thinking realistically about politics requires that political scientists find ways to analyze and understand the justificatory dynamics that give rise to normative orders and that stabilize or destabilize them. I speak of normative orders as *orders of justification*, since they are based on, produce and reproduce justifications for social and political structures and relations.[19] Normative orders in modern societies rest on complex narratives of justification that support existing power structures and enable individuals or groups to exercise power within such structures, that is, to use their noumenal capital as a power resource.[20] My analysis of power does not suggest that those who hold power can autonomously create a comprehensive social space of reasons for others; rather, they are able to use it in a particular way. Narratives of justification develop historically over long periods of time and form a space of social reasons that provides the justificatory resources for sustaining, changing or rejecting particular normative orders.

Power struggles are struggles to position oneself and one's group within such social realm in a particular way – and to influence the space of reasons for others. This is true for the nationalist who constructs a xenophobic narrative and for the revolutionary who rejects a dominant ideology. If we want to understand the power dynamics within certain normative orders, we need to understand the narratives of justification that dominant groups use and weave together – think of the many strands of discourse within a Trumpian universe, ranging from a Protestant work ethic to racial and racist discourses about who rightly owns a country, giving the term "democracy" an exclusionary meaning. Populists can only be successful if they manage to craft such narratives, combining different normative and historically situated sources and stories into

---

[18] This has been an important insight by Hannah Arendt, though she uses the term *violence* in a broader way. See especially Arendt, "On Violence," and the illuminating discussions in Benhabib, *The Reluctant Modernism of Hannah Arendt*, chs. 3–6.
[19] On this, see Forst, *Justification and Critique*, and Forst, *Normativity and Power*.
[20] See Forst, *Normativity and Power*, ch. 3.

a powerful way of looking at the world, what is wrong with it and how to fix it.[21]

Such narratives of justification, combining national history, religious ideas, economic reflections, social structure, and so on, create social and political reality.[22] Occasionally, this looks like a dark cave reality, as when a certain ideology restricts the realm of justifications; but such realities can also be opened up, as occurs in a liberation struggle. Understanding political reality requires us to find ways to reconstruct dominant social narratives and their rivals. Only then can we understand why, for example, the concept of democracy, when placed in the justificatory realm of different societies, sometimes has the ring of liberation and sometimes that of colonization. As Seyla Benhabib argues in her interventions into debates about social criticism, it is necessary to locate such critique in the narratives that constitute "the horizon of our social lifeworld" and to show how "conflictual and irreconcilable" such narratives are, if we consider past struggles and their success or defeat.[23]

Can such narratives be reduced to social interests? I do not think so, for if we look at how interests get formed and defined, we eventually find: justifications. We can understand neither individual nor collective interests if we do not understand the "strong evaluations"[24] that lie at their basis – some possibly of religious origin, some guided by beliefs in security, material welfare, success, and so on. There is no basic raw empirical fact that determines what interests people have and pursue. We are justificatory beings all the way down and our interests depend on what we consider important and justified. True, we often "rationalize" and fabricate such justifications; but this is not because we do not see a justification for what we want but because we see that it is weak from a public perspective and try to bolster it. If we stick to narrow definitions of self-interest as determining people's behavior, we will never understand, for example, religious motives or the reasons why certain people support certain parties even to the detriment of their "self-interest." They may be victim to ideological justifications (justifying the unjustifiable), but still guided by (bad) reasons.

---

[21] See Müller, *What Is Populism?*, and Mounk, *The People vs. Democracy*.
[22] See Tilly, *Why?*
[23] Benhabib, *Situating the Self*, p. 226.
[24] Taylor, *Human Agency and Language*.

6.6 A realistic normative view

If a realistic conception of political life needs to be sensitive to and analyze the justificatory resources that ground political reality, we can also develop a realistic *normative* perspective from within the cave – and go beyond it.

As I said, no normative order could exist if it was not supported by certain justifications. These have to be structurally reflected and reproduced, regardless of whether the order is a theocracy or a democracy. Following Bernard Williams, we can say that the first political question, that of securing a political order of security, stability and cooperation, is a question of justification, such that there is a "basic legitimation demand" that requires the political order to "offer a justification of its power *to each subject.*"[25] Williams draws some weak normative conclusions from this, namely, that basic political justification entails that those who are subject to rule must be offered good reasons why that is not a form of pure domination. But he also draws stronger conclusions when he argues that a purely self-serving justification cannot count as a justification: "power itself does not justify."[26] That is a normative, not a descriptive statement, since power, of course, does justify itself (all the time) and produces justifications, though often in ideological ways. What Williams does is turn the notion of justification into a *normative* notion, adding criteria for a *good* political justification. And that leads him to a version of what he calls "the Critical Theory Principle," modeled after Habermas's discourse theory, which states that "the acceptance of a justification does not count if the acceptance itself is produced by the coercive power which is supposedly being justified."[27]

Like Williams, I believe that this is a sound principle, but would add that it is a principle of reason. Reason is the faculty of justification, and normative criteria of good justifications – whether in science, politics or art – are rational criteria.[28] We find such criteria not in a Platonic superworld of "real" values, but by reconstructing the criteria of validity immanent in the validity claims we make – and since the validity claim of a political norm is that it is generally and

---

[25] Williams, *In the Beginning Was the Deed*, p. 4 (emphasis in original).
[26] Ibid., p. 5.
[27] Ibid., p. 6.
[28] See Forst, *Normativity and Power*, ch. 1.

reciprocally valid, such norms must be justifiable in reciprocal and general terms.[29]

6.7 A strong normative program

This brief reflection on criteria of justification opens up the possibility of a stronger normative program. I call this a strong program because it operates with heavy normative vocabulary, which, however, is not grounded in a Platonic higher reality but – along Kantian lines – in a constructivist reflection on what it means to understand ourselves as normative justificatory beings.[30] As such beings who use our faculty of reason to produce, test and accept or reject justifications, we face the task of constructing a common world of norms that are binding on and justifiable to all who are subjected to them. As agents of construction, we ought to regard ourselves as equal authorities of the norms that bind us all equally and, as such authorities, we respect each other's *right to justification*.[31] The criteria of justification that hold between us as reasonable and responsible beings do not predetermine the content of our normative constructions, but they do determine the procedure of construction and thus also some content, given the respect we owe each other as constructive normative authorities. As such authorities, we are law-makers and law-takers at the same time, and thus the Kantian notion of *dignity* applies to us as subjects with rights and duties of justification.

Wait a minute, you might now object – how exactly did we get from the descriptive justificatory program to the strong normative one? For surely we never "are" equal normative authorities in the normative orders to which we are subject, and we probably never will be. That may hold true, I would reply, but if you agree with me that it is a serious deficiency of a political order that it does not respect its members as normative authorities who co-determine that order, you will also agree with me that we have to regard ourselves as beings owed recognition of our status as normative agents and equals, thus affirming that, in a normative sense, this is what we *are* – and, I add, what we *really* are.[32] So the thought of two realities comes back, but not, I think, in a paradoxical way – rather, in a dialectical fashion.

---

[29] On the notion of validity claims see Habermas, *Moral Consciousness and Communicative Action*, as well as my analysis in Forst, *The Right to Justification*, pt. I.
[30] See esp. the Introduction to this volume and Chapter 1.
[31] Forst, *The Right to Justification*.
[32] See Chapter 1 in this volume.

Political science is a methodologically grounded reflection on who and what we are as political, justificatory beings, and it reveals to us that we are always members of different worlds – the world of real and effective justifications, and the world of the possibility of better justifications produced by us. This is not the true world of the ideal good, but a world of a better social and political practice than the one we live in. No actuality can eliminate that noumenal possibility completely for us.

Based on the notions of normative authority and the right to justification, which says that no one must be subject to norms, whether of a moral or a political–legal kind, that cannot be properly justified to him or her, other normative notions fall into place. Those *liberties* are justified that reflect the kind of freedom we have as equal normative authorities in the political and legal realm, that is, those liberties that cannot be reciprocally and generally rejected among normative equals. *Equality* means that from a moral point of view we are equals and that we have a basic claim to a secure and equal standing as non-dominated legal, political and social subjects. *Domination* means being subject to a normative order without proper justification and without procedures and institutions of justification being in place; thus, non-domination in a legal, political and social sense means having the *rights* that are required to be secure from such forms of domination and having opportunities to change the normative order one is subject to within adequate structures of collective justification.[33]

Democracy thus does not simply represent one "value" among others. Rather, it appears as the political practice of *justice*, as the institutionalization of a form of non-arbitrary political rule that reflects our standing as equal normative authorities, both in our roles as law-makers and as subjects of the law. Such a normative notion of democracy is surely a regulative notion that can only be attained in piecemeal fashion, but it is not based on an ideal form of the perfect democracy; rather, democracy progresses practically by transforming relations of rule and/or domination into relations of justification, aiming to establish a basic structure of justification that secures our standing as non-dominated, politically autonomous equals. That is how I interpret Benhabib's notion of "democratic iterations." The relevant structure of justification can be a national or a transnational[34] structure, depending on the type of relations that need to be justified; the most important point is that those subject to this order

---

[33] See Forst, "The Justification of Basic Rights."
[34] See Chapter 8 in this volume.

should become its normative authority by way of proper institutions of collective justification.

Such a notion of democracy as the practice of justice as justification enables us to avoid confusing democracy with the domination of minorities by majorities.[35] There is no such thing as illiberal or authoritarian democracy, just as there is no such thing as a democracy that produces structural social injustice; for all of these defects point to and create structures of exclusion that are unjustifiable among normative equals. Such deficiencies transform rule into domination.

6.8 Critical Theory

I apologize for the brevity of this introduction of the strong normative program. Here I could only outline the conceptual map of normative terms and how they fall into place. I have developed the corresponding program elsewhere and will not dwell on it further here. What I hope to have shown is how the choice of a mediating term like *justification* might help to overcome the alienation between the empirical and the normative aspects of our discipline. For if we find ways to analyze the political world of justifications – and especially of rivaling justifications – then we will also find ways to understand the power struggles that mark our present.

At the same time, we ought to shift our self-understanding in such a way that we recognize that we cannot simply observe the justificatory games we (or others) are part of from a view from nowhere.[36] We cannot describe them without some participation, as description requires understanding; we are always socially situated beings, as Benhabib argues. In addition, again following her and Habermas's critical hermeneutics, we have to take a reflexive stance, and that stance is one of evaluation and critical distance. Then we not only ask what the dominant narratives of justification are to which we are subject and how they are reproduced; we also ask whether they are *really* justified, knowing that in any enterprise of justification we are finite, fallible beings who can go wrong, both factually and normatively. But the faculty we call reason is the (finite) faculty to always ask for better justifications. Science is based on us using that faculty in the right way.

---

[35] See Forst, "Two Bad Halves Don't Make a Whole," and Forst, "The Neglect of Democracy."
[36] See Adorno et al., *The Positivist Dispute in German Sociology*.

The synthesis of an empirical and a normative perspective on ourselves as justificatory beings and as members of normative orders that I have in mind is a program of critical theory. Such a theory I call a *critique of relations of justification*, and it involves five cardinal aspects.[37]

First, it calls for a scientific analysis of social and political relations of rule and/or domination that inquires into the structures of justification that reproduce such normative orders. How are justifications produced in such an order, and what are the main sources of justificatory power, ranging from institutions of the public sphere (media, churches, etc.), to economic and cultural power complexes, to institutionalized forms of decision-making and agenda-setting?

Second, it calls for a discourse-theoretical and genealogical reconstruction of the justification narratives that dominate a given space of reasons.[38] How did these narratives come about and what are their – possibly ideological – functions?

Third, we need methodological tools to criticize existing justifications of social and political relations. Are they based on proper empirical grounds and what are their normative premises, implications and potential exclusions?

Fourth, given that a basic structure of justification is a demand of fundamental justice, such a theory must inquire into the possibilities and forces of establishing such a structure, given certain path-dependencies and the reality of rule and/or domination exercised, both within and beyond states.

Fifth, such a theory must be able to account for its own normativity in a self-reflexive, critical way. Ideally, it uses the principle of rational critique as the basis for its own constructive arguments. Thus, for example, it does not use a reified or ethnocentric notion of "false consciousness" or "true interests" when it comes to defining ideology; rather, it calls those justifications ideological that lend reciprocally and generally unjustifiable social relations the appearance of being justified.

6.9 Inside and outside the cave

I do not want to imply that every serious social science should aim at such a synthesis of empirical and normative research in a critical

---

[37] See Forst, *Justification and Critique*, pp. 1–13.
[38] An example for this is the analysis conducted by Boltanski and Thévenot, *On Justification*, in which the term "poleis" is used.

spirit – an endeavor that also calls for a great deal of combined expertise. I propose it as an example for the productive work that a mediating term like justification can perform in combining the two perspectives. Then they no longer look like the antagonistic views of the cave versus that of the moral good; rather, using that mediating term enables us to see how the empirical and the normative are conceptually connected. By using the principle and the right of justification as normative foundations that are both *immanent* to practices and *transcend* them, we can avoid stale distinctions between ideal and realistic theory, while nevertheless gaining the critical distance toward social and political reality that every scientific enterprise requires. Science enables us to model reality in such a way that we can rationally understand it and orient ourselves within it. That is as true of social science (and philosophy) as it is of natural science; all that we need are the right methodological tools. Understanding and evaluating our political world as one of justifications is a way to make good on that promise.

Politics is a power struggle – as a struggle for justification: a struggle for the dominance of some justifications, and a struggle against them becoming dominant. In these power dynamics, the question of justification is often used strategically and ideologically to construct a false reality, a reality of caves. In such a rage against reality, correct news gets called fake news, indigent migrants become enemies of the people, economic exploitation becomes invisible, and so on. This leads to what I call *crises of justification*, meaning not only that we are in danger of losing sight of the criteria for proper justifications, but also that institutions for reflecting on and producing legitimate collective justifications are in danger of becoming eroded and disappearing once people forget what their purpose and ground was.

In such times of crisis, we do not need Platonic sages. But we do need critical theories that uphold the one quest that in social and political life must never rest: the quest for better, real, reciprocal and general justifications. That we have the right to demand such justifications is as important an insight as are the many ways of uncovering how that right is constantly denied through the fabrication of false realities. The critique of such false realities is as much a task of philosophy and social science today as it was in Socrates' time – perhaps even more so. So, Plato was right: Do not cling to your caves.

— 7 —

THE POINT AND GROUND OF HUMAN RIGHTS
A Kantian Constructivist View*

7.1 How to think about human rights

Our thinking about normative concepts is always bound by paradigmatic notions of their primary task in social practice. Human rights are a case in point. Some focus on their moral core as protecting urgent and essential human interests and try to define these; some focus on their being a cross-cultural "lingua franca" and thus look for definitions and justifications that could be approved from within an "overlapping consensus" of all cultures and societies – or at least the "reasonable" ones. Some locate the idea of human rights in international political or legal practice as standards of legitimacy, the violation of which justifies international action or intervention.

Each of these approaches has its advantages as well as its shortcomings, which I will not discuss in detail here.[1] Rather, what I want to argue is that none of them identifies the *political* and *emancipatory* point of human rights properly, the point being that these rights have been (and continue to be) fought for in historical social struggles to establish a legal, political and social status of non-dominated persons within a political normative order – that is, as free and equal persons who are both addressees and authors of the legal, political and social basic structure of their political community. I emphasize that this is the original and primary social context of human rights: the emancipatory struggles and conflicts within particular societies marked by

---

* Many thanks to Nate Adams and Tobias Albrecht for their help in preparing this text and to Pietro Maffettone, David Held and Sarah Dancy for important suggestions to improve it.
[1] For more in-depth discussion of these approaches, see Forst, *Justification and Critique*, ch. 2.

various forms of domination. We only understand the point and ground of human rights if we understand the normative logic of such struggles.

Thus, we ought to free ourselves from some all-too-powerful imaginaries dominating human rights discourse that lead us away from this context. One such misleading imaginary is that of human rights as instruments of the protection of vulnerable persons against threats to their well-being by powerful agents, especially the state.[2] Such ways of thinking about human rights focus on persons as primarily *passive* recipients of certain protections and overlook that the full meaning of these rights from the modern political revolutions onward was to achieve an *active* status of non-domination, such that one is not subject to a legal, political and social normative order that denies you standing as an equal; that is, an order that has not been and cannot be properly justified to you as a free and equal member of society. Domination in my understanding (which differs substantially from neo-republican versions)[3] does not mean being denied equal status in the sense of no longer enjoying freedom of choice from arbitrary interference; rather, and more fundamentally, it means being disrespected in one's basic claim to be a free and equal normative authority within the order to which one is subject, and that implies the basic right to co-determine the structure of that society. This is the *status activus*, to use Jelinek's term,[4] which is a necessary component of human rights: they are not just rights to be protected in one's status as a legally, politically and socially non-dominated person; they are, in a reflexive sense, also basic rights to determine the rights and duties that define that status. Many interpretations of human rights today, even those called "political," pay insufficient attention to this active, political competence.[5]

---

[2] Ignatieff, *Human Rights as Politics and Idolatry*. A more positive variant of this is the idea that human rights are claims to resources required to realize fundamental forms of well-being; this is forcefully argued by Talbott, *Which Rights Should Be Universal?*, and Talbott, *Human Rights and Human Well-Being*.

[3] I discuss the difference between my approach and that of Philip Pettit in Forst, "A Kantian Republican Conception of Justice as Nondomination," and in Chapter 10 of this volume.

[4] Jellinek, *System der subjektiven öffentlichen Rechte*. See also Alexy, *A Theory of Constitutional Rights*, ch. 5.

[5] Even Allen Buchanan, *The Heart of Human Rights*, pp. 28ff., who stresses the status egalitarian function of human rights, partakes in this, as he mainly refers to the quality of being protected by law in this regard, less so to the right to be a political authority; see his discussion of the "status egalitarian function," where democratic rights are missing.

The other imaginary to be avoided is the internationalist–interventionist one already alluded to. This defines human rights as international legal rights and implies that, in the words of Charles Beitz, "the central idea of international human rights is that states are responsible for satisfying certain conditions in their treatment of their own people and that failures or prospective failures to do so may justify some form of remedial or preventive action by the world community."[6] This way of thinking leads to a number of problems. To begin with, the quote shows that the primary context of human rights is not the international order but, rather, the different states, which ought to realize these rights, and that the international context builds on these state contexts and has the task of establishing procedures to legitimately discover, judge and possibly sanction human rights violations. Thus, human rights are a task for states in the first instance and then for the international community; therefore, the human rights that a state has to realize cannot be reduced to those rights the violation of which the international community finds a sufficient reason to intervene over, given the enormous costs and difficulties of an intervention. Such an argument turns the normative order of human rights on its head: first, we need to know which human rights claims are universally justifiable as claims within states, and then we need to think about legitimate cases and, most importantly, procedures and institutions of intervention – which today are still mostly lacking. Otherwise, we would reduce the core of human rights to those rights the violation of which calls for an intervention, and standard – and in my view essential – human rights like those of gender equality or democratic government would no longer be seen as core human rights because – to cite Beitz – "the proper inference from the fact that there are circumstances in which the absence of democratic institutions would not generate [...] reasons for outside agents to act is that the doctrine of human rights should not embrace such a right."[7] This view is remarkably at odds with international human rights documents and human rights practice – such as the social practice of demanding human rights to democracy and gender equality and of actively trying to change regimes that deny these. The "practice-based" internationalist–interventionist paradigm of thinking about human rights, as it is often called, thus focuses on the wrong practice – namely, that of an international regime of

---

[6] Beitz, *The Idea of Human Rights*, p. 13.
[7] Ibid., p. 185. Beitz argues similarly with respect to rights of gender equality (ibid., p. 195).

human rights rather than that of the critique of states which violate these rights as put forth by members of such societies and by outside agents, even though the latter might not have the power or the legitimacy to intervene. Human rights are one thing, the question of an international politics of intervention is another, conditional on many contingent factors. In other words, if the existing system of international legal human rights were considered the "heart" of human rights, as Allen Buchanan argues,[8] we would have to look for the "heart of hearts" to get to the core of human rights and to their justification.[9]

To indicate briefly the further argument I make in this chapter: if I am right about the moral and political *point* of human rights to establish the status of persons within their normative order as legal, political and social equals protected from severe forms of domination, it follows that there is a particular moral *ground* for these rights. Negatively speaking, this is the right not to be subjected to a normative order that denies basic standing as an equal to you and that, reflexively speaking, cannot be justified to you as free and equal; and, positively speaking, it is the right to be an equal normative authority and active agent of justification when it comes to the basic legal, political and social arrangements in your society. This reflexive formulation is necessary, for freedom from domination not just means to be respected as a legally, politically and socially non-dominated equal secured by certain rights; it also means that it is not others who decide without and over you about whether that status is fulfilled or not. Thus, the authority to define non-domination can only lie within a discursive procedure of reciprocal and general justification where all are justificatory equals.

Essentially, the negative and positive formulations used above coincide in the discourse-theoretical, Kantian idea that those subject to a normative order ought to be equal and free *normative authorities* determining that order through procedures and discourses of justification in which all can participate as equals. The main normative concept thus is that of a person as an equal normative authority, having a basic moral claim to be respected in his or her *dignity* to be such an authority – and thus having the basic moral *right to justification*,[10]

---

[8] Buchanan, *The Heart of Human Rights*, p. 274.
[9] I think that Buchanan's constructive justificatory arguments for human rights are to be interpreted in that way; they aim to provide the best philosophical justification for a system of human rights at the center of national and international legal practice, which is different from Beitz's approach.
[10] See Forst, *The Right to Justification*.

which in this context means the basic right to be an equal co-author of the (legal, political and social) norms one is subject to, and which define one's basic standing in society. This implies not just political rights of participation, but all those rights that give you the *normative power* to ward off and overcome various forms of domination – that is, of unjustifiable subjection. Thus, it is a particular view of the point of human rights that leads me to reconstruct its moral core and ground in a certain way and locate it in the basic right to justification. In what follows, I will unpack this argument.

7.2 The point of human rights

An important aspect of the different imaginaries guiding our thinking about human rights is what one considers to be the genealogy of the concept. Those who, like myself, regard them as emancipatory weapons against oppressive regimes and social orders (including feudalism and other forms of economic exploitation – thus the emphasis on *social* non-domination, as I will explain later) locate their origins in the early modern social conflicts in the seventeenth century especially, playing a major role in the revolutions of the eighteenth century and finding their strongest historical expression in the *Déclaration des droits de l'homme et du citoyen* of 1789.[11] Those who emphasize the international legal character of human rights, however, believe that with the Universal Declaration of 1948 a new conception of human rights as internationally secured protections came into being.[12] Whereas the first conception is guided by powerful images of modern revolutions, the second has no less of a powerful image to relate to: namely, the horrors of fascist tyranny and genocide as social evils to be avoided. The first sees human rights as not just constraining, but constituting legitimate political power;[13] the second regards them as bulwarks against extreme forms of oppression and suffering.

Still, as I said above, if one looks at the Universal Declaration of 1948 and other covenants and, last not least, international practice, one must recognize that in the idea, as well as the practice of human

---

[11] See the historical accounts in Bloch, *Natural Law and Human Dignity*; Gauchet, *La Révolution des droits de l'homme*; Hunt, *Inventing Human Rights*.
[12] Beitz, *The Idea of Human Rights*; Moyn, *The Last Utopia*; Ratner, *The Thin Justice of International Law*.
[13] Habermas, *Theory and Practice*, ch. 2; Besson, "Human Rights and Constitutional Law."

rights, states are the main context of their realization (which does not exclude the idea of realizing them in a world state), and the international institutions are only secondary (but of increasing importance) in that regard. Furthermore, it is not just in Article 21 that the Universal Declaration stresses the right to democracy; in its Preamble, it also makes reference to the revolutionary, democratic tradition of human rights by saying that human rights ought to be secured, "if man is not to be compelled to have recourse, as a last resort, to rebellion against tyranny and oppression."[14]

To fix ideas about an active (or activist)[15] political imaginary of human rights as an alternative to the internationalist–interventionist as well as the passive notion of the avoidance of suffering, let me use an image. There is an excellent collection of photographs taken during the "Arab Spring" in 2011 on Tahrir Square, compiled by Karima Khalil.[16] The pictures all show people holding signs asking President Mubarak to leave and to hand over power to a democratic government; some simply say "freedom" or "justice." There is one picture (taken by Hossam el Hamalawy) that shows a man holding a sign that says "Enough Humiliation" (see next page).[17] According to my interpretation, the picture does not just tell us a lot about the notion of dignity grounding human rights (to which I will come back in the next section). It also tells us something important about the point of human rights. For how shall we understand – and now of course I embark on a rational reconstruction and hermeneutic interpretation of my own, though I hope to be true to what the demonstrator meant – the kind of humiliation the activist has had "enough" of?

The picture helps us place the demand and the politics of human rights in the primary political context in which we have to see them: the struggle for basic forms of respect as legal, political and social agents who do not "deserve" to be ruled autocratically by a corrupt and oppressive regime. The humiliation that is decried and for which there is a demand that it end is not just a particular form of being

---

[14] See also Gearty, "Human Rights."
[15] In her book on global justice, Lea Ypi, *Global Justice and Avant-Garde Political Agency*, rightly stresses the importance of political agency in theorizing emancipatory forms of politics, yet leaves the criteria for such progress (as dialectical learning processes facilitated by *avant-garde* political agents) undetermined (though in the discussion of first-order normative principles, Kantian moral equality is usually the reference point – ibid., pp. 54f. and 60).
[16] Khalil, *Messages from Tahrir*. Thanks to Mahmoud Bassiouni for drawing my attention to this collection and for instructive conversations about it.
[17] Ibid., p. 87. Permission to reproduce the picture was kindly granted by the photographer.

denied access to the labor market or to certain social institutions; rather, it is being denied a proper recognition as a legal, political and social authority with certain powers, as someone who "counts" at least to the extent that it is not others who tell him or her what his or her proper place in society is. (There are also many photographs in the book of women holding similar signs and, needless to say – as not just the post-revolutionary developments in Egypt showed – the dialectic of liberation and of oppression has many facets, from the rule of the Muslim Brotherhood to the military rule that followed it.) What is more, the protest sign does not just express the claim to be respected as a person with such powers, usually formulated as rights; it also expresses the claim to be a normative authority when it comes to deciding which rights or duties citizens have. This is the full meaning of an emancipatory claim – it is not just a claim to this or that right or social opportunity, but a right to have a say in the institutional regime to which one is subject. The humiliation to be overcome is, if you will, a comprehensive experience, and the claim to overcome it has a comprehensive character of becoming a rights agent with the full right to determine the structure of rights to which you are subject.

This implies that we must not understand human rights vertically as rights or privileges granted to subjects by a ruler or a government; this is the older tradition of gaining status recognition from a monarch as the feudal lords did when they wrested the Magna Carta from King John in 1215. Rather, the emancipation from political humiliation implies that the rights one has are rights that members of a society mutually recognize and accord *each other*, based on their mutual respect as equal normative authorities within their social order. So, the non-domination aimed at does not just mean having certain important rights, but being the authority to co-determine and secure these rights: a horizontal understanding of human rights.[18] The domination and humiliation to be overcome are twofold: the domination of being denied certain rights that human beings ought to have as legal, political and social equals, and the domination of having no say, no right to justification, within the normative order to which you belong. If you look at the French Declaration, and also at what protesters in human rights struggles demand, this is the full message of those who claim human rights. And that is why the right to democracy is essential to any conception of human rights. For this right expresses the basic right to be a constructive normative agent; and it is only in the discourse among political equals that a justifiable and concrete human rights regime can be determined and realized.[19]

It is not merely Kantian-style political philosophers who describe human rights movements in the thick normative language of dignity or justice; rather, it is the social agents themselves who use such language to express their demands for full respect and human rights – as a fundamental claim of justice among normative equals who are not just takers but also makers of the rights they have, on the assumption that they are free and equal in claiming as well as "constructing" these rights in political discourse. The claims to be respected as rights-bearers and normative authorities are addressed to the regime to which one is subject, to be sure; but what they imply is that it is not up to the regime to deny these claims or to determine their meaning. In a certain sense, they are already part of a process of horizontal justification among those equals who gather in the square (and beyond it, as the community of all subjected). This is why human rights can be formulated (generally and abstractly) in declarations – because among those who respect each other as justificatory equals, there can be no good reason to deny them. This is the normative power by which the protesters are backed when they write

---

[18] Habermas, *Between Facts and Norms*, ch. 3; Günther, "Menschenrechte zwischen Staaten und Dritten." Also Forst, "The Justification of Basic Rights."
[19] See also Tully, "Two Traditions of Human Rights."

such signs. They already "have" these rights, though they are denied their collective political–legal realization.

7.3 The ground of human rights

The consideration of the emancipatory point of human rights shows how a historical and sociological reflection on such rights as emancipatory claims and tools links up with a moral and even a transcendental reflection. For we have to recognize not just the comprehensive character of human rights as realizing a fundamental status as legally, politically and socially non-dominated (and in this sense equal) persons, but also that their normative force implies that, among persons who respect each other morally and who aim to materialize this kind of respect in law, these rights are to be seen as justified horizontally between moral equals. They spell out what it means to be such an equal in the social world – and which rights this implies. So these are rights the possession of which equal justificatory authorities can always claim and can never deny each other – as addressees and authors of such claims and of such rights. The moral ground of these rights is the basic right to justification, or the right to be respected as an equal moral authority, and the substance of these rights comes in when it is determined (in discursive practice) what it means to be recognized as an equal and free normative authority in the legal, political and social realm. I will explain in section 7.4 how such discursive construction is to be conceptualized. But here it is important to understand that these rights, even though they aim at a legal, political and social status and can only be justifiably realized in a democratic regime, have a "ground" that is both moral and, if you will, transcendental: the autonomy of persons with a right to justification as a normative authority equal to all others. Human or basic rights are constructed on that basis, where the agents of construction are autonomous persons, and the principles of construction are principles of justification among equals.[20] Here we arrive at the transcendental, reflexive truth about the ground of human rights: they are rights of and between autonomous equal authorities in the realm of normative reasons, expressing the respect for such autonomy and authority, materialized and justified with respect to the legal, political and social world (and the many dangers of domination). But their ground is the respect for each other as moral equals and as

---

[20] See O'Neill, *Constructions of Reason*; Rawls, *Political Liberalism*, ch. 3.

justifying beings (using practical reason), who are bound to nothing but what they as justificatory equals can claim from each other. They are bound and, at the same time, free as autonomous agents of justification – bound to each other as justificatory equals and to the principle of reason as the principle of general and reciprocal justification for reciprocally and generally valid norms.[21] So the "ultimate" justification of these rights is the principle of justification itself.

It is only in Kant's philosophy that we find the appropriate connection between the prior and "inviolable" moral status of persons that grounds human rights and the activist, constructive aspects of this status as being a law-maker and not a mere law-taker with a claim to protection. Kant's notion of the *dignity* of autonomous persons, with its twofold character of calling for unconditional moral respect as equals and for its operationalization in the mode of discursive justification[22] between legislators in the space of reasons, combines morality, law and politics in the right way to ground human rights.[23] It can explain why the Preamble to the Universal Declaration of 1948 starts with the principle that "recognition of the inherent dignity and of the equal and inalienable rights of all members of the human family is the foundation of freedom, justice and peace in the world," and what the terms "inherent" and "inalienable" are supposed to indicate without making reference to a quasi-religious ground for this status.[24] What it means is that the basis for human rights is the respect for each other person as a moral equal who need not qualify for this status or respect in any other way than by being human. To be respected in that way is, as Kant says, an "innate right" of humans.[25]

The notion of the innate right to independence is Kant's way of bridging the gap between morality and law. In the realm of morality, Kant explains the status of persons as an "end in themselves," that is, as beings whose purposes have to be respected equally (within the bounds of reciprocity) and must not be ignored or instrumentalized by others, with the "idea of the *dignity* of a rational being that obeys

---

[21] Forst, *The Right to Justification*, chs. 1 and 2.
[22] This aspect of Kant's approach is stressed by O'Neill, *Constructions of Reason*, and Habermas's discourse ethics in their respective interpretations.
[23] Habermas, "The Concept of Human Dignity and the Realistic Utopia of Human Rights," p. 469, and Forst, *Justification and Critique*, ch. 4.
[24] For the opposite argument that a Kantian notion of dignity rests on metaphysical foundations comparable to a Catholic one, see Rosen, *Dignity*. For a general discussion of the notion of dignity in the context of human rights, see McCrudden, *Understanding Human Dignity*.
[25] Kant, *The Metaphysics of Morals*, VI:237.

no law other than that which at the same time it itself gives."[26] The beings with such dignity are all equally law-givers in the "kingdom of ends" and thus have to rule over themselves and each other with reciprocally and generally justifiable norms, as the categorical imperative says:

> Our own will, insofar as it would act only under the condition of a possible universal legislation [*allgemeine Gesetzgebung*] through its maxims – this will be possible for us in the idea – is the actual object of respect, and the dignity of humanity consists just in this capability, to be universally legislating, if with the proviso of also being itself subject to precisely this legislation.[27]

To understand why Kant uses the notion of dignity here, it is essential to focus on the "worthiness [*Würdigkeit*] of every rational subject to be a legislating member in the kingdom of ends."[28] By this term, Kant emphasizes the status or rank[29] of persons as moral equals and as active law-givers – that is, as normative authorities subject to no one or no other values than those that can be justified according to the categorical imperative of their own rational will. The imperative asks persons to respect each other as justificatory equals, because being respected as an end in itself means not to be subjected to actions or norms that cannot be justified to each person as an equal. As Kant explains in the *Groundwork*, treating another as a means by making, for example, a false promise, means that the other "cannot possibly agree to my way of proceeding with him and thus himself contain the end of this action."[30] Hence, the moral duty of justification and the right to justification (here duty and right are co-original) express what it means to respect others as ends in themselves and as equal

---

[26] Kant, *Groundwork of the Metaphysics of Morals*, IV:434 (emphasis in original).

[27] Ibid., IV:440. I cannot go into this here but, based on such statements, it is often argued that for Kant only rationally autonomous beings have to be treated with dignity, and thus human beings who are not yet, or no longer, possessing their rational capacities have no such claim to respect. This is a mistake, however. First, this interpretation does not sufficiently distinguish between the dignity of rational agents as acting subjects and the dignity of human beings as objects of actions; and, with regard to the latter, Kant always speaks of human beings as representatives of humanity without any further qualification. Second, and more importantly, this view reads an empirical capacity into a noumenal, non-empirical characteristic of persons, which is contrary to Kant's approach. He affirms that his notion of persons as autonomous ends in themselves is "not borrowed from experience" (ibid., IV:431), thus is a general moral ascription to human beings who do not have to take a rationality test to qualify as ends in themselves.

[28] Ibid., IV:439.

[29] The notion of rank is stressed by Waldron, *Dignity, Rank, and Rights*; see also the discussion in Kateb, *Human Dignity*.

[30] Kant, *Groundwork of the Metaphysics of Morals*, IV:429f.

normative authorities in the realm of justifications or norms. So it is not that dignity is the first "ground" of human rights;[31] rather, it is the term to express the status of every moral person as an equal and autonomous normative authority; as Kant affirms, autonomy "is thus the ground of the dignity of human and of every rational nature."[32] Dignity, equal status and normative authority are all concepts that form a unity based on the idea of the moral autonomy of persons with a basic right to justification (within a reconstruction of the principles and ideas of practical reason as justificatory reason).[33] This basic claim, to be respected in one's dignity as a normative justificatory equal and not be ignored or oppressed in that standing, explains the notion of freedom from "humiliation" that the man in the picture demands. He asserts that no government has a normative authority over him that he cannot share in as free and equal.

For the grounding of human rights, this means that every person has a non-deniable claim to all the rights protections and powers that free and equal persons have to grant and guarantee each other who recognize the need to materialize their standing as equal normative authorities in the world of law and politics. Thus, Beitz's worry that the right to justification as the ground of human rights is too abstract and dissolves into "a generic idea of moral standing"[34] is misplaced, as this ground is necessary but not sufficient for any specification of that standing with respect to the status of being a legally, politically and socially non-dominated person. Human rights secure such status in the legal, political and social world, and thus there is a clear relation between a general moral ground and a more specific context of justifying and theorizing human rights.

In my Kantian view, the right to justification operates between the moral and the legal–political level. Thus, it performs the same function as Kant's "innate" or "original" right of persons. Kant introduces this right as the only "natural" right of persons and as the ground of every justifiable form of law imposed over free and equal members of a kingdom of ends; thus, before explaining the innate right, he stresses the natural legal duty to regard oneself and others as ends in themselves.[35] In this connection, he introduces the innate right thus:

---

[31] See also Waldron, "Is Dignity a Foundation of Human Rights?"
[32] Kant, *Groundwork of the Metaphysics of Morals*, IV:436 (tr. altered).
[33] Forst, *The Right to Justification*, ch. 1.
[34] Beitz, "Human Dignity in the Theory of Human Rights," p. 279.
[35] Kant, *The Metaphysics of Morals*, VI:236.

> Freedom (independence from being constrained by another's choice), insofar as it can coexist with the freedom of every other in accordance with a universal law, is the only original right belonging to every man by virtue of his humanity.[36]

This right to independence under general law has rightly been interpreted by Arthur Ripstein as a right to non-domination,[37] and in this connection one needs to stress *both* aspects discussed by Kant under the headings of private and public right: the right to legally protected independence and the corresponding right to partake in the making of the general law that will bind all. These are the two aspects of the moral right to justification in the realm of law and politics: to be only bound by strictly reciprocally and generally valid laws and to be the co-author of these laws, as Kant stresses in his republican theory.

I cannot go into the details of how Kant constructs a system of legal and political justice – and the rights entailed by that – on this basis. What is most important in this respect is not whether we find an explicit account of human rights in Kant's theory; what is essential is, rather, that in his view the form and justification of all rights or rightful claims has to be strictly reciprocal and general, in accord with the general concept of right, which means "the sum of the conditions under which the choice of one can be united with the choice of another in accordance with a universal law of freedom."[38] The natural right to freedom thus is not a ground for a "derivation" of a list of rights or duties or principles of justice, but entails the moral criteria of justification of any rights or justice claim as well as the principle of the free and equal status of all those who are subjects of the law. This is why the right to freedom – or, in my interpretation, the right to justification – is a foundation for a procedural – and in that sense "non-foundationalist" – construction of basic human rights.[39] Any constructivist view that entails basic moral criteria of the justification of the constructions as well as of the standing of the constructing agents must be based on a reflexive notion of the moral right to justification among equal normative authorities; and the innate right expresses that standing and such criteria. It is thus

---

[36] Ibid., VI:237.
[37] Ripstein, *Force and Freedom*, ch. 2.
[38] Kant, *The Metaphysics of Morals*, VI:230.
[39] Flikschuh, "Human Rights in Kantian Mode," rightly stresses the relational and strictly reciprocal character of any rights claims within Kant's scheme, but finds the innate right incompatible with the "non-foundationalist" and constructivist character of Kant's general approach. That view, however, cannot explain the moral character of Kant's concept of right asking for strict justificatory reciprocity that Flikschuh discusses (ibid., p. 662).

formal and substantive at the same time, a ground of autonomous constructions of right(s) and yet not a basis of their non-discursive derivation.[40] A constructivist view always entails two different kinds of normative argument – or two kinds of normativity. First, the normativity of the principles and ideas of practical reason, to use Rawls's language[41] – that is, in my account, the principle of reciprocal and general justification and the moral notion of free and equal persons as equal normative authorities with a right to justification. And second, the normativity of the norms (or "laws") generated by the constructivist or discursive procedure, be it the categorical imperative or a notion of free and equal discourse. In a Kantian view, it is essential that practical reason, in my understanding justificatory reason, is the basis for the principles and ideas used – but practical reason understood as a rational and, at the same time, moral capacity, that is, of not just knowing how to justify norms, but also knowing that one is under a duty to do so.[42] That is why the duty of and the right to justification are co-original. In other words, the theory I suggest uses the principle of justification itself as the justifying ground for a theory of human rights. That is why I call it a reflexive theory: no other ground is used than the normative principle of justificatory reason.

It is important to see that the normativity of constructed norms depends on the normativity of the principles and the normative standing of the agents of construction. One can only get so much normativity out of a procedure as one invests in it from the start; that is why categorical imperatives presuppose one basic categorical imperative, and that is why the duty and right to justification are basic for any justified norm. For the context of justifying rights, this means that any construction of human rights must rest on a basic

---

[40] Andrea Sangiovanni, "Why There Cannot Be a Truly Kantian Theory of Human Rights," p. 675, argues that there cannot be a Kantian theory of human rights despite the innate right as an appropriate ground, because "it is constitutive of a human right (in my sense) that its violation licenses unilateral action by third parties," which is "straightforwardly denied by Kant's account of the moral obligation to exit the state of nature." This argument is a good example of the hold of the internationalist-interventionist imagination over current human rights thinking. For having a justifiable claim to human rights is one thing, whereas the question of the legitimate institutions or agents to intervene in a state is another. And here a lot is to be said for Kant's skepticism about unilateral interference; yet, that is a point that is irrelevant to the question of which rights persons ought to have within a state.

[41] Rawls, "Kantian Constructivism in Moral Theory"; Rawls, *Political Liberalism*, ch. 3. See also Chapter 11 in this volume.

[42] Here lies an important difference compared to Habermas's version of discourse ethics; see Chapter 14 in this volume.

right itself, as the moral right to justification or the innate right in Kant's theory. We can call this the principle of the *conservation and production of normativity*: human rights can only be grounded on a fundamental notion of a right to have all those rights that free and equal normative authorities cannot reciprocally and generally deny each other if they want to secure and operationalize that status (as the status of discursive authority and non-domination) in the legal, political and social world. If human rights are rights such that free and equal persons cannot with good reasons deny them to each other, then their status as free and equal – and the right to it – is basic; and only such a basis can generate the normativity of such rights. The ground of human rights must not be weaker than their own validity claim; rather, it must contain and transmit its normativity to such rights as rights no one can reasonably reject between moral–political equals.

This is why, to make a long argument short, an interest theory of rights cannot sufficiently ground human rights without adding the normativity generating factor of justification by and through moral equals. An interest theory of rights says, to use Raz's formulation, that a person has a right if an aspect of his "well-being (his interest) is a sufficient reason for holding some other person(s) to be under a duty."[43] This leaves open the criterion for which aspects of well-being, or for which interests, are a sufficient reason to ground a right, and thus attempts are made to narrow down "essential" interests or aspects of well-being to ground rights.[44] Raz himself gives a value-based account of such interests, arguing that "the value of the right to its possessor is its ground."[45] Thus, his approach would better be called a value theory of rights. In order to justify human rights, then, which affirm "the moral worth of all human beings" and distribute "power away from the powerful to everyone,"[46] universalizable essential values of the good life have to be identified. But again, in order for these values to have such normative force, they have not only to reflect the equal moral status of every person, but also express it by being non-rejectable between such persons who seek to establish their status as legally, politically and socially non-dominated (as Raz's characterization of these rights entails) by way of securing human rights. And if this is right, then the normativity of these rights

---

[43] Raz, *The Morality of Freedom*, p. 166.
[44] This unites the very different approaches by Talbott, *Human Rights and Human Well-Being*; Griffin, *On Human Rights*; and Buchanan, *The Heart of Human Rights*.
[45] Raz, "Human Rights in the Emerging World Order," p. 221.
[46] Ibid., p. 226.

does not rest on some prior account of values, but resides in their justifiability between equals who confer their justificatory power to these rights by finding them to be non-rejectable given these persons' moral status as equals and what it requires to secure this status legally, politically and socially. It is the commonly arrived at justification by equal normative authorities that grounds the normativity of human rights. Justificatory equals combine their normative force in and by justifying these rights.

That is why we should see human rights as *congealed and solidified justifications* that can withstand normative doubt (which they need to be able to prove if challenged) and that express the status of moral equals in the legal, political and social world.[47] A number of normative historical experiences and justifications are sedimented when it comes to basic rights to, say, freedom of religion, political participation or access to education. To claim such rights means to use these congealed justifications as normative powers in a contested space of justification and to be able to use them as a package, so to speak, without having to justify these claims anew every time. They provide a safe and secure status or standing in the social world. The basic right to justification gives persons the possibility to own these justifications and use them to ward off illegitimate power claims – but also to contest these justifications if one-sidedness, or narrowness, is feared. So the right to justification, as a "veto right" against false justifications, is always in place, whereas the content of basic human rights is fixed to some extent, but still the possible object of questioning. Yet every such questioning is bound to the criteria of reciprocity and generality as criteria of practical reason. In a moral–political sense, especially within a constitutional regime, human rights thus serve as veto rights against legal or social arrangements that are unjustifiable and violate these rights; but they can only have such normative force by expressing the basic right to justification. This is why declarations and formulations of human or constitutional rights have a higher-order status, yet one that is not immune to questioning or revision. Whether there is a right to personal property and whether it entails a right to own means of production are part of that discourse, as well as what the right to the free exercise of religion entails with respect to the education of one's children, for example. None of their formulations or interpretations is "absolute"; yet the justificatory threshold of criticizing them is high.

---

[47] In my "The Justification of Basic Rights," I discuss two ways to justify particular basic rights on that basis.

To summarize my main grounding argument: respecting persons as equal normative authorities in the realms of morality as well as law and politics is basic, and that respect implies that every person (whether capable of exercising the faculty of justification or not)[48] has a right to justification in the relevant contexts of moral action or political normative orders. This is what it means to respect the dignity of human beings as ends in themselves, to use Kantian language. Since moral and basic legal norms claim to be generally and reciprocally binding for all persons equally, the principle of practical reason says that all those subjected to the norms have to be equal justificatory agents when it comes to their justification heeding the criteria of reciprocity and generality. Reciprocity means that no one may make demands he or she denies to others and no one may impose his or her non-generalizable views, interests or values on others. Generality means that all those over whom norms claim to be valid have to be equally involved.

Human rights are not simply general moral rights but a subset of reciprocally and generally justifiable rights that establish the status of persons as equal normative authorities within a normative order and protect persons from being subject to legal, political or social domination. These rights are based on the basic right to justification, which in this context means to be the co-author of all the justifiable rights and duties that apply to you. This is the equivalent of Kant's innate right to freedom (and rights) under generally justifiable law. But the formulation of the right to justification captures the ideas of equal personhood under law and of being a political co-author of laws, as well as the status of being free from social domination in a more complex way than in Kant's version.

7.4 Constructing human rights

Given what I said so far, I shall define the *concept* of human rights such that they are morally grounded, legally and politically guaranteed rights of free and equal persons who have a basic claim not to be socially or politically dominated or mistreated by states or other agents, and – what is of particular importance – to be the normative authorities of the regime of rights and duties they are

---

[48] In the case of persons who are not yet or no longer capable of exercising the full capacity of justification, justifications of representatives or by justified authorities in light of what could be justified to such persons are required.

subject to.[49] Human rights reflect the insight that the status of being free and equal and not being subjected to the arbitrary power of others needs to be secured by law in a twofold sense: the persons in question must be both the authors and the addressees of the law. Thus, these rights are justified horizontally as those rights that free and equal normative authorities could not deny each other; based on that, they have a vertical justification as rights that no political or social agent or institution may violate and which the state must secure. Their moral core consists in the fact that they confer the status of being a justificatory equal who must not be subjected to others' domination; and their justification lies in identifying those rights that are necessary to secure that egalitarian status in the social world. This implies rights to life, liberty, security, to social and material resources and to the political co-determination of the rights and duties you have.

This approach stresses the moral core of mutual respect essential for human rights, as well as their particular subset function, namely to include only those rights that are required for being secure as a non-dominated, free and equal person in the social and political realm. Classical "liberal" rights protect this status as much as political rights or social rights that provide protection against political or social domination. This view implies non-arbitrary guidelines for the way in which a specific *conception* of human rights has to be constructed, namely by way of a discursive construction in which all those subjected are involved as justificatory agents – in practice as well as in a critical counterfactual dimension. This means that any conception of human rights for a particular context needs to be justified in a discursive manner guided by the criteria of reciprocity and generality, where no one – to repeat these criteria – may make a claim he or she denies to others (reciprocity of content) and where no one may impose his or her interests, needs, perspective or convictions on others who could reasonably reject these (reciprocity of reasons). Finally, no subjected person may be excluded from the relevant justification community (generality).

Several contexts of such constructions of human rights need to be distinguished. The first context in which a conception of human rights is to be justified is the moral–political context of a basic list of general human rights which contains all the rights that, given human experience of various forms of domination thus far, would be

---

[49] The following overlaps with a section of Forst, "Human Rights in Context: A Comment on Sangiovanni."

non-deniable between free and equal persons who share a political and legal order. The reference to historical experience is important, as every concrete conception of human rights is the result of an open-ended learning process; again, there is no deduction or derivation of human rights based on the foundation of the right to justification. The list of human rights is the product of a discursive construction and is necessary as a major reference point for any dispute over whether a certain right is actually a human right. As much as these rights are required in particular, concrete contexts, they must have a moral basis, and if they do, there is a list of such basic rights that substantiate the normative core concept named above. This list is general and vague and needs to be discursively concretized through political–legal constructions; yet, at a universal level, a general moral–political conception of these rights is indispensable. A severe dispute over human rights always goes back to this level.[50] The construction of that basic conception of human rights is and remains a moral–political, reflexive matter; in this form of constructivism, we gather and test the best moral arguments for certain rights to secure the standing of persons who are free from domination and are equal normative political–legal authorities within their normative order.

The second context of constructing a conception of human rights is the political context of a state that has the task of securing basic human rights and also of ensuring that the concrete determination and interpretation of these rights is justifiable to all those subject to it.[51] This does not mean merely to "apply" or to "mirror" a fixed set of morally preconstructed human rights;[52] rather, the political constructions of basic rights on this level determine and interpret what it means in a given political community to have freedom of speech, the right to political participation, to a decent social status, and so on. Human rights are determined by way of discursive political constructivism here, and it is important to note that this is a democratic, moral–political form of justification by the participants themselves. When it comes to basic rights, all must be involved in the determination of these rights as political equals and as critical participants who think reflexively about their own status and that

---

[50] Pace Sangiovanni, "Beyond the Political–Orthodox Divide," and also Benhabib, *Dignity in Adversity*, pp. 126–131, I do not see how we can move directly from the general concept to more particular political conceptions in either the interpretivist way Sangiovanni thinks correct or the discourse-theoretical view that Benhabib proposes with her notion of "democratic iterations."
[51] See my "The Justification of Basic Rights."
[52] This is the worry of Buchanan, *The Heart of Human Rights*, pp. 14–23.

of others, and who may transcend given legal and political forms in order to improve them. So human rights are at the same time the ground for such constructions as they are their result: in abstract form, they are the ground for such constructions because the general moral–political conception provides the justificatory background for any legal–political determination, both in procedure and substance, such that a political community has to determine what it means to realize and secure rights no person can justifiably be denied (which includes the rights of non-members). The result is a concrete conception of human rights for a political community. However, this conception must be in tune with the general moral conception and must be criticizable from that standpoint. Non-deniable core human rights provide something like a discursive veto against unjustifiable constructions of basic rights: persons or groups thus have the normative power to reject a determination of a basic right – say, of gender equality – when a majority in a political community believes that, for example, forced marriage is in line with this general right, or when a political community thinks that it can ban minarets and still respect the human right to religious liberty. In every such political context, non-arbitrary forms of legal interpretation and adjudication of basic rights disputes have to be devised; this is implied by the human right to be protected as a person with equal legal standing.

While there are many such political contexts of discursive construction where participatory equals determine their normative order in a non-arbitrary and constructivist way, being open to reflexive improvement and critique, another moral–political construction is taking place on the international and supranational levels. This is the third context to be analyzed. Here the construction of a conception of human rights is required that is laid down in international declarations, treaties and covenants, where these norms – and possible sanctions for violating them – are understood to be legally binding. In these contexts, the agents of construction are states with particular conceptions of basic rights as well as persons who make particular claims, possibly dissenting from their states' conceptions. The conceptions to be found on this international level therefore may reflect a thinner notion of human rights as compared to the political conceptions within states. Thus, for example, no particular model of democratic organization can be formulated here apart from the general right to democratic participation. Yet, that there is such a right must be stressed within the general moral conception as well as all particular political conceptions and the international conception. Otherwise, the point of human rights – namely, not to be forced to live in a normative order where you are not part of the relevant justification authority as a justificatory equal – would be lost. At this level, a reflection on which rights violations ought to lead to which sanctions, and by which prior procedure and through which agent, needs to be included. Yet it is a mistake to combine this reflection with the basic arguments for human rights on any of the other levels.

I cannot go into further details at this point about such an institutional scheme of international sanctions or into a more detailed discussion of the general list of human rights and how, from that angle, the meaning of such rights changes, given that the persons who claim these rights are seen as active political agents and not just as subjects to be protected or nourished. Just to give one example: the right to social goods such as food, housing and medicine is then no longer primarily a right to certain means of subsistence, but is a right to a social standing as an equal at least to the extent of being a full member of society and not an easy victim of social exploitation.

Above all, the reflexive point of human rights needs to be kept in mind: if human rights are essentially founded on the basic right to be secure in the status of being a normative authority free from political and social domination and co-determining the normative order to which one is subject, then they must be rights constructed by their bearers themselves. This has implications both for the concept and for the various conceptions (and how they are interpreted). It means that human rights protect and express the autonomy of free and equal law-givers and law-addressees. This account is equally true to the historical meaning and function of human rights, to past and contemporary political struggles for human rights and to a moral and transcendental grounding indicated by such terms as "human dignity." That grounding is of a reflexive nature: if we look for a firm basis for reciprocally and generally justified human rights, the very principle of reciprocal and general justification and the right to justification connected to it is the right place to look for such a ground.

8

A CRITICAL THEORY OF TRANSNATIONAL (IN-)JUSTICE
Realistic in the Right Way*

8.1 Critical realism

Recent discussions about justice beyond borders are not just about the scope or the content of justice; in addition, they also concern how the very concept of justice should be understood in the first place, how the injustice existing in the world we live in should be thought of, and what function justice ought to have in this world. In what follows, I will try to shed light on the conceptual, normative and empirical issues at stake in this debate. In doing so, I want to develop further what I call a "critical theory of transnational justice."[1] By this I understand a theory of justice as justification grounded in a constructivist conception of reason which is at the same time "realistic" when it comes to assessing the current world order as one of multiple forms of domination. There is no contradiction in combining abstract reflection in moral philosophy with sociological empirical realism in a single theory; on the contrary, that should be our aim. If we lack

---

* Versions of this chapter were presented at the Association for Social and Political Philosophy Annual Conference at the London School of Economics, a workshop at Durham University, the Frankfurt Global Justice Summer School, the Wissenschaftszentrum Berlin, King's College London, McGill University in Montreal, the Free University in Berlin, the University of Toronto, the University of Manchester, Princeton University, the Society for Applied Philosophy Conference in Cardiff, the University of Michigan and the University of Chicago. I owe particular thanks to Thom Brooks, Julian Culp, Dorothea Gädeke, Stefan Gosepath, David Held, Tamara Jugov, Mattias Kumm, Catherine Lu, Arthur Ripstein, Andrea Sangiovanni, John Tasioulas, Melissa Williams, Lea Ypi and Michael Zürn for their detailed comments. Thanks also to Ciaran Cronin for correcting my English and to Felix Kämper for his help in preparing the manuscript.

[1] Forst, *The Right to Justification*, chs. 11 and 12; Forst, *Normativity and Power*, chs. 9 and 10.

a clear picture of the reality of the injustices surrounding us, our normative thinking is situated in a void or will lead us astray; at the same time, if we do not have a context-transcending normative idea of justice to orient us and enable us achieve distance from the status quo, realism becomes a form of thinking that affirms this status quo.

8.2 Avoiding parochialism and cultural positivism

It is a truism that any notion of justice that applies to transnational contexts needs to be properly universalizable, a requirement that raises the Rawlsian bar for theories based on ethically and culturally particular "comprehensive doctrines" to a higher level than that envisaged by Rawls himself in his reflections on liberal social pluralism in *Political Liberalism*. But we should also aim at more than what Rawls suggests in *The Law of Peoples*,[2] namely at more than a conception of international justice from a liberal standpoint that "tolerates" non-liberal but "decent" peoples and essentially provides the "ideals and principles of the *foreign policy* of a reasonably just *liberal* people."[3] Rather, we should come to develop a non-parochial approach, that is, one that avoids liberal as well as non-liberal one-sidedness and reified culturalist conceptions of "peoples." To be fair to Rawls, it might be better to be aware of one's parochialism than to hide or ignore it; and it is surprising how many tracts on global or international justice leave the question of universalizability and cultural pluralism out of account or marginalize it.[4]

However, criticism of liberal theories often presents the mirror image of that mistake by embracing a certain form of positivism concerning culture, as if the world consisted of separate, identifiable ethical–cultural units – some "Western," some "non-Western" – that need to engage in a conversation about the values they share in order to achieve an overlapping consensus on minimal notions of justice or human rights.[5] In their most problematic versions, such approaches fall prey to the inverse form of thought that Edward Said once called "Orientalism,"[6] that is, a reification of "non-Western"

---

[2] Rawls, *The Law of Peoples*.
[3] Ibid., p. 10 (emphasis in original).
[4] There are exceptions to this, such as Caney, *Justice Beyond Borders*; Nussbaum, *Frontiers of Justice*; Sen, *The Idea of Justice*.
[5] See, for example, Taylor, "Conditions of an Unforced Consensus on Human Rights."
[6] Said, *Orientalism*.

cultural wholes that do not understand or share "Western" values, just adding a positive rather than a negative demeaning evaluation of these cultures.[7] The irony of this is that the justified attempt to "provincialize"[8] the West and criticize false assumptions of the universal validity of its values and institutions ends up by provincializing the "non-West" in a non-dialectical way. Yet if we want to develop a proper notion of transnational justice, we must avoid such cultural positivisms, that is, forms of thought which reify societies and regions into unified and separate systems of order and value, while disregarding the dynamics and tensions within and between different societies. In doing so they position themselves outside of such dynamics and try to provide an "objective" account of normative cultural differences.[9]

8.3 Avoiding practice positivism

Avoiding such forms of cultural positivism calls for a turn toward practice and the development of a critical notion of justice that participants in social struggles in Western or non-Western societies can and do make use of. What is required is reflection on the *practical* meaning of justice when used in different political and social contexts, within and beyond particular normative orders, that is, orders of rule that determine the basic standing of persons and groups (or organized collectives) within a social structural framework. But the practical turn I have in mind differs from many current "practice-dependent" theories that regard legitimate justice claims as claims immanent in already established institutional contexts of social cooperation that are fixed in legal–political terms.[10] Such theories are forms of what I call *practice positivism* in a fourfold sense: first, they refer to complex social relations as forms of "cooperation" – say, within the EU or

---

[7] In a powerful afterword to his *Orientalism*, pp. 329–354, Edward Said criticizes romanticizing and essentializing readings of his argument. According to him, they celebrate the "other" of the West and wrongly combine postmodern and postcolonial thought in such a way that they no longer criticize the perversions of the "grand narratives of emancipation and enlightenment" and renounce the general imperative of emancipation. I expand on this in Forst, "The Justification of Progress and the Progress of Justification," Chapter 2 in this volume.

[8] Chakrabarty, *Provincializing Europe*.

[9] Here I rely on and modify the notion of positivism developed by Jürgen Habermas, "A Positivistically Bisected Rationalism."

[10] See Sangiovanni, "Justice and the Priority of Politics to Morality," and the contributions in Banai et al., *Social Justice, Global Dynamics*. Sangiovanni has reconsidered his approach in "How Practices Matter."

the WTO – and thus run the risk of neglecting the power structures and forms of domination that characterize such institutional settings; second, they aim to reconstruct the animating "idea" or "ideal" of justice immanent in such institutional contexts, as if any such idea or ideal free from social contestation or normative ambivalence could be hermeneutically unearthed;[11] third, they lack a justifying reason why such an immanent notion of justice, even if it could be reconstructed, would have a claim to validity, and thus potentially call might right – or, in other words, lend normative credibility to a status quo that is taken for granted;[12] and finally, fourth, the focus on already established legal–political frameworks obscures the many informal, non-institutionalized modes of power and domination, especially of an economic or cultural nature, that may be part of or exist alongside such institutional forms.

These four aspects are part of what I call practice positivism: giving a positive account of a social setting that should raise our hermeneutic suspicion; assuming that there could be an objective account of its normative idea, neglecting its contestedness from the perspective of social participants – including oneself, who is not an objective observer; granting the status quo a certain normative standing it may not merit; and, finally, providing a one-dimensional account of such a normative order of power relations. To avoid such forms of positivism, we should regard normative orders as contested and contestable orders of justification – where the term "justification" is used both descriptively and normatively, that is, both analyzing the justifications that determine the social space of reasons (and may be bad or ideological) and asking for reciprocally and generally non-rejectable justifications and for an order of justification that could produce such justifications (or at least could be conducive to that aim).[13]

Hence in our initial analysis of the proper location of the concept of justice we need to focus on two forms of practice different from

---

[11] In this, the approach shares a lot with Michael Walzer, *Spheres of Justice*. For a critique, see Forst, *Contexts of Justice*, ch. 4.1.

[12] On this third point, see also Darrel Moellendorf's critique of "justice positivism" in *Cosmopolitan Justice*, pp. 38f. Sangiovanni, "How Practices Matter," p. 163, addresses our critique of his view and responds in a way that a theory based on the right to justification would also suggest, namely that for "a conception of justice to get off the ground, there must be some sense in which the terms of the institution are at least capable of being justified to all persons." Still, Sangiovanni, *Humanity without Dignity*, criticizes the Kantian account of the right to justification and does not follow the path toward a critical theory of justice.

[13] For an account of orders of justification, see Forst, *Normativity and Power*, and Chapter 6 in this volume.

those highlighted by practice-dependent theories, namely, firstly, on the *practice of resisting injustice* and on the meaning of justice in such struggles and, secondly, on the *practices of rule and domination* in which such struggles are located and against which they are directed. If we follow Wittgenstein in trying to determine the meaning and "grammar" of a term by its practical use,[14] we should be aware that the question of justice is not an innocent, purely theoretical question. On the contrary, it is motivated by reflection on the relations and structures of domination characteristic of our time that people in concrete social conflicts and emancipatory struggles strive to overcome. So, a genuine practice-guided view focuses on these practical contexts. Assuming that such a theoretical goal can be achieved, it makes possible a critical theory in the sense in which Marx once spoke of critical philosophy as the "self-clarification of the struggles and wishes of the age."[15]

At the same time, since we do not have a general materialist theory to guide us, we must abstract from these contexts and struggles and reflect on which struggles for justice are emancipatory and which are not. We cannot simply read off from social facts of protest and resistance whether they express *justified* forms of struggle against injustice; that would amount to another form of positivism, namely "resistance positivism." For a critical conception of justice, the question of justification as an independent, albeit contextual, normative question is indispensable. As Habermas argued, understanding the need for reflexive justification of social claims, including one's own, is what distinguishes critical from positivist theory.[16]

8.4 A reflexive and discursive conception of justice

Let us start from a reflection on the grammar of justice, taking our lead from Rawls, who defined the core concept at the center of different conceptions of justice as implying that institutions are just when "no arbitrary distinctions are made between persons in the assigning of basic rights and duties and when the rules determine a proper balance between competing claims to the advantages of social life."[17] The most important qualifiers here are "no arbitrary distinctions" and "proper balance," and Rawls's theory makes a

---

[14] Wittgenstein, *Philosophical Investigations*.
[15] Marx, "Letter to Ruge, September 1843," p. 209.
[16] See Habermas, "A Positivistically Bisected Rationalism," pp. 218f.
[17] Rawls, *A Theory of Justice*, p. 5.

detailed proposal as to how to spell these out. Remaining at the basic conceptual level, I think that the meaning of "proper balance" is that no arbitrary, but only reciprocally and generally justifiable criteria for weighing claims should be used. As a result, the avoidance of arbitrariness and the idea of justifiability come to the fore in our search for a core concept of justice.

According to that concept, justice as a human virtue in a general moral sense implies that humans do not subject others to arbitrary actions and decisions, where "arbitrary" here means "not justifiable with good reasons between the subject and object of action." Hence *political and social justice* refers to the legitimate claim – or the basic right – of each person not to be subjected to a set of institutions, formal or informal, to rules and structures of action in an arbitrary way, such as by the powerful imposing an order on the less powerful, as in Thrasymachus' famous definition of what justice means, realistically speaking.[18] Again, the meaning of arbitrariness is "without good reasons." But, as I said before, what counts as a good reason here is a highly contested matter: Does one accord priority to the most talented, those who are ethically deserving, the needy, the industrious, or to all equally?

At this point, we must take a *reflexive* turn and work our way up from the core concept of justice to a conception of justice as containing a *practice* of public justification, while taking care to avoid arbitrariness. If we want to overcome arbitrary social and political relations and institutions and also exclude arbitrary justifications for such relations and institutions, and if we have no "natural" or objective candidate for what "non-arbitrary" means, then we must take the principle of justification, as a principle of reason (defined as the faculty of justification),[19] as the core of the conception of justice – call it a conception of *justice as justification*. According to the principle of reasonable justification, those justifications for social relations and institutions are free from arbitrariness that can withstand the discursive test of reciprocal and general justification among free and equal persons (as members of a justification community defined in a non-arbitrary way – a problem to which I will return). We arrive at the principle of reciprocal and general justification by a reflexive and recursive[20] consideration of

---

[18] Plato, *The Republic*, book 1.
[19] I develop this view in Forst, *The Right to Justification*, chs. 1 and 2; Forst, *Normativity and Power*, ch. 1.
[20] On the notion of recursive justification, see O'Neill, *Constructions of Reason*.

the validity claim[21] of social and political justice norms that claim to be reciprocally and generally binding on all those who are part of a normative order; that is, an order that determines the basic standing within a social structural framework and is the proper context of claims to justification. Hence a conception of justice as justification relies on just those principles that are implicit in the very claim to justifiability that characterizes justice norms. We can call this reflection a transcendental one, because it reconstructs the conditions of the validity of claims and norms of justice. If we aim at non-arbitrariness as a conceptual core of our notion of justice, such a reflection is what we need to hold onto.

The criteria of reciprocity and generality mean that one may not make a claim on others within a context of justice that one is not willing to grant all others (reciprocity of claims); and they mean, furthermore, that the justification of such claims has to be conducted in a normative language that is open to all and is not determined by just one party (for example, by a religious majority) and that no party may impose its own contestable notion of justified needs or interests on others who could reasonably reject it (reciprocity of reasons). Generality means that no one subject to a normative order must be excluded from participation in the justificatory discourse.

The move from reflection on the core concept of justice to a conception of social and political justice is not yet complete because more needs to be said (and will be said in section 8.8 below) about the principles of a "basic structure of justification" entailed by this conception. But here I need to say a few more words about the issue of grounding. For my last remarks led us onto Kantian terrain, and it may seem that we have lost touch not only with the social struggles of various actors and groups but also with our earlier discussion of cultural pluralism.

However, this is not the case. Just as the outworn distinction between "ideal" and "non-ideal" (or "realist") theory should not irritate us, so too we should not let ourselves be irritated by the dichotomy between a transcendental and a context-immanent mode of theorizing. To begin with the latter: as I argued above, we need to focus on the right practice rather than taking pre-given institutional contexts for granted; and the focus on resistance to injustice is essential in this regard. In a discursive conception of justice, the proper authority for determining what justice means is the subjects

---

[21] The notion of validity claims was developed by Jürgen Habermas and Karl-Otto Apel in their discourse ethics. See Habermas, *Moral Consciousness and Communicative Action*.

who participate in a normative order *themselves* – while empirically speaking, these are not generally equals but find themselves in very different situations of subjection. Thus, struggles for justice within such a scheme aim first and foremost to achieve a higher level of justificatory quality and equality; that is, to secure a better legal, political and social standing for groups who have been marginalized and who struggle to become well-respected subjects of justification.

Given such a context of social and political justice, the question of whether the principle of reciprocal and general justification is a transcendental one – as a principle of practical reason – or is immanent in such contexts does not really constitute an alternative, for it is both simultaneously. And that is how it should be. For how could a principle of *practical* reason not be implicit in practice, at least as a principle to which social agents adhere in their struggles for justification, and how could a principle of practical *reason* not transcend social practice in which the right to justification is all too often violated?

The topic of ideal-based versus realist approaches has attracted a lot of attention in recent debates.[22] But it is a false opposition that haunts philosophical thinking. A critical conception of justice cannot get off the ground without principled argument, although it neither needs to nor ought to design an "ideal" model of the well-ordered society that would only have to be "realized" by intelligent and well-meaning politicians, which is at best a naive, and at worst a technocratic conception.[23] A discursive conception of justice as justification is not compatible with such ideas. But, at the same time, as much as we need critical realism in order to understand and assess our social reality as one involving multiple forms of domination (though also as one that hopefully harbors the potential for critique and emancipation), there is nothing "realistic" about looking at the world as an endless Nietzschean game of Thrasymachean actors, such that every struggle for justice becomes just another struggle for the power to determine social structures your way. From the perspective of a critical theory of justice, there either is what Marx called *Unrecht schlechthin*[24] – absolute injustice – or there is not;[25]

---

[22] See, for example, the discussions in Geuss, *Philosophy and Real Politics*; Larmore, *What Is Political Philosophy?*; Rossi and Sleat, "Realism in Normative Political Theory"; Erman and Möller, *The Practical Turn in Political Theory*.
[23] An example of an approach that calls for an "egalitarian distributor" to realize justice is G. A. Cohen's *On the Currency of Egalitarian Justice*, p. 61.
[24] Marx, "Zur Kritik der Hegelschen Rechtsphilosophie," p. 390.
[25] On Marx's notion of justice, see Forst, *Normativity and Power*, ch. 7.

but if you believe the latter, then normative reflection on justice or emancipation lacks any point. Still, it is important to keep in mind that a conception of political and social justice is not a form of ethical thought that needs to be "applied,"[26] because it is an imperative of political autonomy and justice that those who are subject to a normative order should become its collective authors. The authority of justice is *theirs* – but in the form of a collective project of emancipation bound to principles of justification and equal respect.

The question of authority is important here, since on a truly emancipatory conception of justice the definition of justice is a matter for the participants themselves – but, of course, in a fashion that excludes justificatory arbitrariness, according to the critical theory principle that Williams, following Habermas, expresses adequately when he says that "the acceptance of a justification does not count if the acceptance itself is produced by the coercive power which is supposedly being justified."[27] Hence the need for a basic structure of justification that overcomes the danger that social forces and privileges are merely reproducing themselves within asymmetrical and dominating discursive relations. The authority to define justice rests with those subjected to a normative order; but they need to be, and to respect each other as, equal justificatory authorities if such justification is to be authoritative. Otherwise, it might just be another form of majoritarian domination.

The Kantian groundwork I have been laying down is based on a fundamental moral claim of free and equal persons to be respected as autonomous normative authorities when it comes to the normative orders to which they are subject. This is my version of the Kantian idea of respecting others as "ends in themselves." Their "dignity" means that they *are* such justificatory authorities,[28] and it implies a basic moral *right to justification*. It is a right to justification with respect to all morally relevant actions in moral contexts of interaction, and in contexts of social and political justice it is a right to participate fully in justificatory discourses about the normative order to which you are subject, so that in such contexts it becomes a legal and political right.[29]

---

[26] This is a point of agreement with Geuss, *Philosophy and Real Politics*; Allen, *The End of Progress*, ch. 4, criticizes my view as one of applied ethics, which I think is a misinterpretation.
[27] Williams, *In the Beginning Was the Deed*, p. 6.
[28] See Forst, *Justification and Critique*, ch. 4.
[29] See Forst, "The Justification of Basic Rights."

8.5 Struggles for justice and the problem of universality

Struggles for justice aim at social changes that ensure that those who are subject to a normative order become the social and political authorities who codetermine the essential aspects of that order. As Barrington Moore argued in his historical and cross-cultural study of social resistance, the sense of injustice that motivates people to revolt against a social order always focuses on particular social injustices; but its essential core is what he calls a "pan-human sense of injustice" that leads to moral outrage and anger when persons have the impression that an implicit social contract has been broken by the authorities or powerful groups in society.[30] To affirm their moral and social self-respect, people resist forms of rule that lack proper justification; and, as Moore stresses, what makes people stop complying within a normative order is not so much a certain level of pain or suffering but the moral sense of being dominated or ignored by others. The "iron in the soul" that makes them feel insulted and leads them to resist requires a certain form of moral courage and a sense of self-respect;[31] the language of injustice is directed against man-made situations of domination as violations of basic expectations of reciprocity and social cooperation that individuals "need not, cannot and ought not to endure" as human beings and members of a particular society.[32]

It is important to maintain a firm grasp of the connection between the sense of (in-)justice and the sense of self-respect as an autonomous, non-dominated being.[33] For the essential impulse of resistance based on demands of justice is not the particularistic desire to have more of certain social goods but instead the general desire to be a subject of justification, that is, a normative authority and not a justificatory "nullity" in the order of which one is part. If that sense of being "someone" and of being a justificatory subject in the first place is violated, the result is often rebellion – as an act of self-defense, that is, of the defense of a basic moral and political sense of self. To call this the claim to have one's basic right to justification fulfilled is indeed to use an abstract language; but it is an abstraction that captures the structure of emancipatory demands of justice. They are demands not to be governed "like that," as

---

[30] Moore, *Injustice*, p. 46.
[31] Ibid., p. 90.
[32] Ibid., p. 459.
[33] See Chapter 1 in this volume.

Foucault famously put it,[34] i.e., the demand – in negative terms – not to be subject to normative imposition or – in positive terms – to be a justificatory agent on an equal footing with others when it comes to determining the social structures to which one is subject, be they of a national or transnational nature. The demand in question is one of autonomy, where autonomy is not understood in liberal terms as the freedom and capacity to pursue one's conception of the good, but in a republican, Rousseauian–Kantian fashion as the autonomy to be the co-author of the norms that bind you. It is here that we find the difference from a neo-republican notion of non-domination.[35] So, to put it in a nutshell, if we understand the normative grammar of resistance properly as a struggle for emancipation, then we discover the normative core and grammar of a critical theory of justice.

Again, one might object that it is questionable how a reflection that started from cultural pluralism and deep disagreement about conceptions of justice could have ended up within a discourse-theoretical, Kantian framework.[36] But the worry that hereby controversial normative assumptions about subjective freedom or collective self-determination are being slipped in by the back door is unfounded, because what I am suggesting is in no way an imposition of a selective and partial normative framework but is instead a matter of *countering* normative imposition. It is not based on any values or principles other than that of critique among free and equal persons who are themselves justificatory authorities; therefore, it contains the core of any valid – justifiable – critique of the imposition of norms or values, be it within a state or beyond it. In fact, the normative core of the critique of colonial[37] or neo-colonial[38] impositions as a critique of domination rests on the right to justification, that is, the right not to be subject to a normative order that has not been and cannot be justified to all as equal autonomous subjects. Whether this is expressed in the language of a right or not is not essential here; what is important is the position of not being willing to accept a normative language and order being imposed on you that you cannot share as a justificatory authority.

---

[34] Foucault, *The Politics of Truth*, p. 44.
[35] On this difference, see Forst, "A Kantian Republican Conception of Justice as Non-Domination," and Chapter 10 in this volume; also Gädeke, *Politik der Beherrschung*.
[36] For this worry, see Allen, *The End of Progress*, and my reply in Forst, "The Justification of Progress and the Progress of Justification," Chapter 2 in this volume.
[37] See the classic by Frantz Fanon, *The Wretched of the Earth*, and, for example, Ypi, "What's Wrong with Colonialism?"
[38] See Dübgen, *Was ist gerecht?*; Gädeke, *Politik der Beherrschung*.

As I argued in section 8.2 above, non-Western normative perspectives should neither be "Westernized" nor "Orientalized" in an essentialist way. Liberal parochialism must be avoided as much as other forms of cultural positivism – for example, the unquestioned assumption that certain societies are unified cultural wholes that can be determined by, say, their dominant religious traditions, ignoring the dissent of possibly marginalized groups within such contexts. As Uma Narayan argues with respect to the rejection of gender as well as cultural essentialism, one needs to avoid both forms of identity and norm imposition:

> Postcolonial feminists have good reason to oppose many of the legacies of colonialism, as well as ongoing forms of economic exploitation and political domination by Western nations at the international level. However, I do not think that such an agenda is well served either by uncritically denigrating values and practices that appear to be in some sense "Western" or by indiscriminately valorizing values and practices that appear "Non-Western." Political rhetoric that polarizes "Western" and "Non-Western" values risks obscuring the degree to which economic and political agendas, carried out in collaboration between particular Western and Third World elites, work to erode the rights and quality of life for many citizens in both Western and Third World Contexts.[39]

Narayan not only points to the facts of multiple domination that need to be captured in ways that avoid one-sided social analyses; she also shows why false universalisms that impose a notion of "sameness" on others, and thus lead to the imposition of Western normative orders on other societies in order to dominate them, have to be rejected. The same, however, applies to false notions of "difference" that essentialize and unify other societies and thus silence critical voices within them, as if to call for respect for women's rights were an "alien" and alienating claim in a non-Western society, "leaving feminists susceptible to attacks as 'Westernized cultural traitors' who suffer from a lack of appreciation for 'their traditions' and respect for 'their culture.'"[40] Narayan argues against both what Foucault once called "Enlightenment blackmail" and the reverse,[41] orientalist form of blackmail: either to be uncritically for "enlightened" forms of modern political and social life, while ignoring their dominating

---

[39] Narayan, "Essence of Culture and a Sense of History," p. 99.
[40] Ibid., p. 102.
[41] Foucault, "What Is Enlightenment?," p. 39.

aspects, or to be against them and thus ignore the dominating effects of traditional forms of life.

Reflexive universalism, as I call it, avoids such one-dimensional reductions and essentialist forms of cultural positivism by providing a normative yardstick that consists in the very idea and structure of questioning *any* form of domination or normative imposition. The principle of critique, of challenging normative orders, is at the core of such questioning, and thus any concrete narrative or structure of justification can be made the subject of radical questioning, which asks whether the structure in question is truly reciprocally and generally justifiable. The principle of asking for better justifications and of asking for structures of justification in the first place is as immanent to normative orders, as it transcends their historical and social forms if they are repressive, narrow, exclusionary or in other ways deficient. Since the principle leaves the authority to determine justice with those who participate in discourses among free and equal persons and thus aim to establish such discursive structures in the first place, it never speaks a language of justice that is alien to them. Rather, it locates the power to define that language with the participants and their discursive constructions. Keeping in mind the critical theory principle that Habermas and Williams remind us of, such discourses can only claim to construct justice if they do not structurally reproduce the social asymmetries and forms of power that define a given normative order. Social critique can never do without a counterfactual standard of reciprocal and general justifiability; in other words, the principle of critique that grounds critical theory is never exhausted by the existing social forms of justifiability. Thus, the first task of justice is to establish a basic structure of justification that facilitates a reflexive practice of critique and construction by according roughly equal justificatory power to all those subjected to it.

8.6 Contexts of (in-)justice

The focus on a grammar of justice as expressed by the resistance to injustice provides us with orientation with regard to a number of further distinctions that need to be questioned: relational versus non-relational approaches to justice; the question of the "all affected" versus the "all subjected" principle; and the difference between internationalist and cosmopolitan approaches to the question of the duties and institutions of justice.

If we follow Sangiovanni's view that relational conceptions of distributive justice consider certain social relations – relations of cooperation or institutions of coercion, for example – as the proper "ground" of justice duties,[42] while non-relational conceptions locate the grounds of justice claims in general considerations of human dignity or human needs, the position laid out so far does not clearly fall on either side. The basic right to justification is an unconditional moral claim of respect based on the dignity of human beings as equal normative authorities. In moral, interactional contexts, this means that each person is owed reciprocal and general justifications for any actions that affect him or her in a relevant way, while, in social and political contexts, this means that no one should be subjected to a normative order in which he or she has no standing as a justificatory equal. Thus, the moral grounds of this right are both relational, since moral persons are always regarded as co-authorities of valid norms, and non-relational, since the right to justification does not depend on a particular social context in order to constitute a valid moral claim. Still, only when situated in contexts of justice (i.e., concrete contexts of rule and/or domination) does this general "ground" of justice claims "ground" particular claims to justice, depending on the nature of the rule or domination to which one is subjected.

Normatively speaking, a context of social or political justice is one in which one's *moral* status of being an equal normative authority needs to be transformed into a *social and political* status of being a justificatory agent because one is subjected to a normative order of rule and/or domination in need of reciprocal and general justification. This is a relational view, but not of the positivistic sort criticized earlier, which focuses on (what it sees as) relations of cooperation or positive institutions of (intrastate or superstate) coercion. If we develop a critical theory of justice from the situated perspective of social agents struggling against injustice, we should avoid positivistic restrictions on the kinds of context we focus on, and we should especially avoid calling a context of asymmetrical social relations a context of "cooperation." A social and political status of normative co-authorship and non-domination (understood in that way) is not only required where one is part of a social (economic) and political scheme of reciprocity and cooperation, or where one is subject to state power and coercion, but also more generally where power is exercised over persons as a kind of rule within a certain framework of justification or as a kind of domination lacking a proper scheme

---

[42] Sangiovanni, "Global Justice, Reciprocity, and the State," p. 8.

of justification. These forms of rule or domination can be formal and legally constituted, but they can also be of a rather informal nature, like economic forms of power and domination, where persons or groups are subjected to a general normative order of production and exchange on a global scale, which is not as tightly legally regulated and institutionalized as the market within a state. A normative order is any order of social norms and rules that governs persons and collectives with regard to their social and political status and determines their options as members of a social framework. We live in multiple orders of such a kind, and a theory of transnational justice requires a nuanced view of these different orders of subjection (a point to which I will return).

From a critical perspective, the argument by Nagel, for example, that "justice is something we owe through our shared institutions only to those with whom we stand in a strong political relation" of state power mistakes a conclusion for a premise,[43] because such strong political relations should not be seen as an *a priori* condition, but instead as an *a posteriori* conclusion of justice duties – that is, such political relations are required to overcome certain forms of unregulated and arbitrary rule, whether it be formal or informal.[44] State-like forms of regulation, viewed from a normative point of view, can be demanded by justice when arbitrary rule violates – in a moral perspective pre-political, in a political perspective contextual – the rights to justification of persons not to be subjected to domination (defined as arbitrary rule in its two forms: rule without proper structures of justification being in place and rule that is not properly, i.e., reciprocally and generally, justified). In this way, the right to justification precedes institutional contexts but only gains specific traction and form in being directed against certain forms of domination calling for the establishment of structures of justification necessary to ban arbitrary rule. Such a right to justice has its place in political relations, but the right to have such relations, as a right to non-domination, is prior to them. And whether the political relations demanded by justice are to be strong or weak depends on the nature of the arbitrariness to be overcome.

Similarly, Sangiovanni's claim that "we owe obligations of egalitarian reciprocity to fellow citizens and residents in the state, who provide us with the basic conditions and guarantees necessary to

---

[43] Nagel, "The Problem of Global Justice," p. 121; see also Blake, "Distributive Justice, State Coercion, and Autonomy."
[44] I develop this argument more fully in Forst, *Normativity and Power*, ch. 10. See also Cohen and Sabel, "Extra Rempublicam Nulla Iustitia."

develop and act on a plan of life, but not to noncitizens, who do not" is too restrictive.[45] It does not sufficiently take into account the many ways in which the welfare of one society (or of parts of one society) often thrives by benefiting from a system of unequal exchange and dominated markets that make it impossible for certain societies to reach a level of cooperation and productivity that Sangiovanni regards as essential for a context of justice to exist. Furthermore, it is true that "the global order does not have the financial, legal, administrative or sociological means to provide and guarantee the goods and services necessary to sustain and reproduce a stable market and legal system";[46] but there is no reason not to regard this as a failure rather than as a normatively relevant fact that constrains duties of justice. Such duties cannot be restricted to the existing frameworks of political life; rather, they call for the establishment of new ones.

A critical theory of (in-)justice needs to avoid such restrictive, positivistic views and locate contexts of injustice wherever forms of rule within a normative order exist or wherever forms of domination within such an order exist, be it an order of the state or of economic exchange. Thus, we need a nuanced view of such normative orders that avoids a non-dialectical opposition between the state, on the one side, and a system of voluntary international cooperation, on the other, such as we also find in Rawls.[47] Relational views should focus exclusively neither on positive relations of cooperation nor on relations of coercion within a state; rather, they must also focus on the negative and structural forms of domination that characterize global and national realities.[48] What we need is a negative version of relationism that can then provide the starting point for a theory of a basic structure of justification to address and overcome relations of domination.

A proper conception of transnational justice tracks forms of rule and domination where they exist. It need not reduce contexts of (in-)justice to contexts of legal coercion, for that criterion tends to be too rigid. To overcome the state-centeredness of such views, Valentini, for example, argues for a notion of systemic coercion designed to capture structural justice-relevant relations beyond the

---

[45] Sangiovanni, "Global Justice, Reciprocity, and the State," p. 20.
[46] Ibid., p. 21.
[47] Rawls, *The Law of Peoples*.
[48] A number of approaches that differ from mine also stress the importance of existing relations of power and domination, for example, Miller, *Globalizing Justice*; Ypi, *Global Justice and Avant-Garde Political Agency*; Nardin, "Realism and Right"; Wenar, *Blood Oil*. Wenar in particular follows the groundbreaking work of Thomas Pogge, *World Poverty and Human Rights*.

state. According to her definition, "a system of rules S is coercive if it foreseeably and avoidably places non-trivial constraints on some agents' freedom, compared to their freedom in the absence of that system."[49] But, take the case of a country that is dependent upon the global market in order to exchange its resources for other goods but is too poor and dependent to alter the rules of that exchange and has to accept its asymmetries, which disproportionately benefit other partners in the exchange. Thus, the country is forced to accept the arrangement in question if it wants to exchange its resources; yet, by doing so, it acquires essential goods and market recognition and thus also achieves greater freedom as compared to the absence of the exchange and its possibility. Thus, the system is one of domination, but not of coercion in Valentini's sense. It is a system of domination that imposes a set of norms that cannot be justified among equals. So, rather than freedom in the absence of a coercive system of rules, the proper baseline for a system of domination is justifiability among equals.

8.7 The nature of injustice

However, the critique of positivistic or coercion-based forms of relationism that do not use a proper conception of domination does not vindicate non-relational accounts of justice. For their basic notion of justice is incompatible with the grammar of justice as shown through the lens of the practice of resistance and the ideas of justice as justifiability and discursive non-domination. According to non-relational views, we ought to focus on the well-being of persons in a cosmopolitan perspective, disregarding more specific contexts of cooperation or domination. These theories start from a normative theory of basic global entitlements of every human being, since, as Caney argues, persons "throughout the world have some common needs, common capacities, and common ends."[50] According to such considerations, persons should be seen on a global scale as "rightful recipients of goods" of a certain kind,[51] and in arguing for a level of entitlement to certain goods, "it is hard to see why economic interaction has any moral relevance from the point of view of distributive justice."[52] To be sure, Caney is right to criticize the priority that

---

[49] Valentini, *Justice in a Globalized World*, p. 137.
[50] Caney, *Justice Beyond Borders*, p. 37.
[51] Ibid., p. 103.
[52] Ibid., p. 111.

some relational accounts of distributive justice give to members of a state or context of cooperation, but his non-contextual view of what justice demands is problematic in a number of ways.[53] First, by denying the positive relevance of particular social relations, Caney also disregards the negative relevance of relations of domination, say, of economic exploitation and political oppression. Thus, the victim of a natural disaster appears to be similar to the victim of exploitation if they lack the same material means. But the difference in question is important from the perspective of justice, and especially from that of struggles for justice. For the social movements Moore and others analyze do not protest against natural or cosmic forces that distributed the "luck" of being born here or there, with these or other resources and talents, in an arbitrary and unequal way and call for compensation for bad luck. Rather, they oppose human-made injustice, that is, particular relations and structures of domination within and/or beyond their society. So, for them, and for the grammar of justice generally, relations and contexts matter: in a structural view, one cannot easily pinpoint concrete responsibilities for generating and reproducing injustice,[54] but one can reconstruct the development of social asymmetries, how they function and who benefits from them in what ways. Otherwise, what is a human structural context of domination gets anonymized and naturalized as something that simply happened as a matter of contingent luck or, in an older language, divine whim. Luck-egalitarian accounts of injustice, in particular, which argue that ambition and desert count as criteria of distribution, but brute luck, whether positive or negative, does not, are out of tune with a practical and emancipatory account of injustice insofar as they reconstruct justice claims as claims for compensation for anonymous bad luck. Such a view turns a narrative of injustice into a narrative of fate, albeit a fate that grounds claims for compensation. The result is a distorted picture of injustice. The struggle against injustice is a struggle against concrete forms of domination, not a struggle against the forces of contingency. Injustice is one thing, fate and fortune another.

Consequentialist accounts of justice thus understood not only provide a misleading picture of injustice but also, secondly, a one-dimensional account of responsibilities for justice. As difficult as an account of structural responsibility is in a postcolonial age,[55]

---

[53] For the following, see my debate with Caney, "Justice and the Basic Right to Justification," in Forst, "Justifying Justification."
[54] Young, *Responsibility for Justice*.
[55] See Lu, *Justice and Reconciliation in World Politics*.

a proper understanding of the history and current system of social and transnational forms of economic, legal or cultural domination (e.g., with respect to race and gender) matters from the perspective of justice. Otherwise, political action lacks orientation. Furthermore, in a dialectic of morality, richer states could offer generous "aid" to poor countries as an act of benevolence, while in reality they owe the latter major structural changes in a global asymmetrical economic system from which they derive unjust benefits. As Kant[56] and, following him, Pogge have argued,[57] one must not mistake duties of justice for duties of benevolence.[58]

This does not mean that there are no general duties of moral solidarity with people in need apart from existing contexts of relational (in-)justice, and it does not mean that duties of justice always take priority over duties of solidarity and assistance, especially in times of grave need and misery, when urgent help is called for. The conceptual distinction between such duties does not accord priority to the one or the other; it just helps us to understand the world we live in and the particular reasons for moral and political action. One owes it to victims of domination not to treat them as "weak" and miserable human beings in need of "help."

The view defended here also does not deny that there is a "natural duty of justice" with respect to victims of domination elsewhere to which, on a counterfactual assumption, one's society has no relevant relation. Every human being has a right to justification and must not be subjected to domination, and every other human being in a position to help has a natural duty to do so – in addition to the more concrete relational duties of those who benefit from or uphold a system of domination – though in complex political structures the conclusion about the right course of action is very difficult to draw and any intervention needs to observe strict criteria of justifiability. Although I cannot go into this here, this natural duty of justice highlights a kind of solidarity based on justice, while the solidarity mentioned above with people in need and misery, even though not victims of domination, also rests on respect for the right to justification, but in a larger moral sense, since nobody has good reasons to deny others in severe need necessary and possible help. The right to justification grounds many moral duties, not just duties of justice, but it is important to sort these duties out, because they all respond

---

[56] Kant, *The Metaphysics of Morals*, VI:454.
[57] Pogge, *World Poverty and Human Rights*.
[58] This is the problem of consequentialist approaches like that of Peter Singer, *One World Now*.

to moral evils of different kinds, and it is required to respond in the right way.

Thirdly, we should also regard those who suffer from injustice as persons whose political agency is being denied; but viewing them primarily as subjects who should receive certain goods does not adequately take this into account. Those who suffer from economic exploitation suffer as much from political exclusion and powerlessness as do those who are oppressed politically, because the key to improving economic conditions of production and distribution is the opportunity to change an economic system by political means. So, the question of social and political power is the first question of justice, whether we are speaking about political *or* distributive justice. There is no distribution machine that would only need to be reprogrammed; there only are normative orders in need of political transformation. Justice is a political construction by way of procedures and practices of justification – a construction by those who are subject to a normative order themselves. Theories that disregard this constructive aspect and leap to conclusions about the right patterns of the distribution of goods ignore this essentially political character of justice. The struggle for effective political agency and for sufficient justification power within a normative order is the first and major struggle for justice. That is also the right way to contextualize claims for justice and not to predetermine what people in societies very different from Western ones "really" want or can justifiably claim.

In sum, a critical theory of justice avoids positivistic and reductive forms of relationism as well as non-contextual non-relationism. It starts from an account of existing structures of rule and/or domination in various normative orders, ranging from the national to the international and the global, and thus develops a critical form of relationism based on a general moral right to justification. In concrete social contexts, this translates into the right to be an equal justificatory authority within the normative orders to which one is subject – either as a subject of justified rule or of domination. Thus, there is a single normative ground of justice but a range of different contexts of justice according to the nature of the subjection in question.[59]

---

[59] This is the essential difference from Mathias Risse, *On Global Justice*, who distinguishes various "grounds" of justice which have distributive relevance, some relational, some non-relational. I think there is only one ground of justice but various contexts of justice marked by different forms of domination. I used that notion of "context" for the first time in Forst, *The Right to Justification*, ch. 12, and it differs from the use I make of the term in Forst, *Contexts of Justice*.

A CRITICAL THEORY OF TRANSNATIONAL (IN-)JUSTICE

In this section, I highlighted the notion of subjection rather than that of being "affected" by certain norms and structures. In contexts of justice, subjection is the proper term, whereas the notion of being affected is too broad.[60] Still, just as different people are differently affected by certain normative structures, so too people are subjected in different ways to certain normative orders – if one compares, for example, the level of subjection to a state with that of subjection to the rules of a global market. So, what we require is a nuanced view of relations of subjection; but at the same time we must resist the tendency to say that tighter, state-like normative orders have priority as contexts of justice over looser, transnational contexts. For the domination exercised, say, in a neo-colonial international relation may be so severe that overcoming it should have priority as a matter of justice. The strength of duties of justice depends on the nature of the domination to be overcome; the more extreme it is, the more stringent are the relevant duties of justice. As I will show in the next section, a critical analysis of contexts of subjection will also take us beyond another overworked distinction, namely that between a cosmopolitan and an international normative order of justice as an alternative. A theory of transnational justice must combine aspects of both.

8.8 Constructing transnational justice

A critical analysis of contexts of subjection shows how intertwined several normative orders are, and how much different dimensions of power intersect. Subnational, national, regional, international, supranational and global contexts of rule and domination overlap, as do economic, racial, gender-based, citizenship-based, religious and other dimensions of domination. I call this the fact of *multiple domination*; as an illustration, think of all the forms of domination to which a low-paid woman from a low social rank in a poor country with authoritarian rule and gendered structures of the division of labor is subjected. We will only find an answer to the question of transnational justice if we address the situation of such persons in the right way.

For that, a critical theory of justice does not start with an internationalist or cosmopolitan thought experiment, but with a realistic view tracking the relevant structures of domination and/or rule and

---

[60] See also Fraser, *Scales of Justice*, ch. 2.

how they interrelate and reinforce each other.[61] The aim of justice is to overcome relations of domination where they exist and to establish structures of justification for that purpose; in contexts of justified rule and government its aim is to prevent structures of rule from degenerating into contexts of domination by strengthening and equalizing relations of justification.

In reconstructing these different contexts as contexts of domination and rule, we have to follow a principle of proportionality, which states that the required structures of justification have to be sufficiently strong to overcome or avoid the kind of arbitrary rule (i.e., domination) that exists or threatens to appear. This must be combined with the main principle of justice as justifiability, namely that the construction of norms of justice has to be a common, autonomous practice of reciprocal and general justification. This means that the first task of justice is to establish basic structures of justification in which the "force toward the better argument" can be generated and exercised by those subject to a normative order – especially those who are in danger of marginalization. I call the establishment of basic structures of justification the achievement of "fundamental justice," while on that basis constructions of "full justice" can be achieved by way of discursive, democratic practice.

I cannot lay out such a theory at this point. Instead, I will sketch a few major lines of argument concerning an account of *fundamental transnational justice*.[62] It aims to create structures of participation and justification that can perform the tasks of opening and critique in various contexts of justice, pointing to structures of asymmetrical rule and exchange, culminating in the justification and adoption of binding national, transnational and international norms. The guiding principle is that of political autonomy and equality, within, between and beyond states, which points to the three main dynamics of domination to be addressed and overcome: domination within states, domination between states and domination beyond states, such as in a global economic order characterized by an unjustifiable distribution of opportunities and benefits with lots of powerful nonstate actors involved.

Realistically and politically speaking, the most important agents in this process are in the first instance democratic states, since these constitute the main normative order capable of generating democratic

---

[61] See, for example, the complex analyses to be found in Avant et al., *Who Governs the Globe?*, as well as Hale et al., *Gridlock*.
[62] For the following, see also Forst, *Normativity and Power*, ch. 10.

power both within their borders and beyond, in international and supranational contexts.[63] A transnational basic structure of justification with sufficient critical force to address current relations of domination will not arise if it is not supported by a relevant number of democratic states. But being aware of the many forms of domination of which states are part, internally and externally, reflexive forms of participation must be found that prevent governments from continuing to dominate parts of their own population or other states or transnational normative orders. Principles of fundamental transnational justice give every political community the right to participate in cross-border normative discourses on an equal footing, and affected parties below the state level simultaneously have the right to demand participation in such discourses – think, again, of issues of class, gender or racial injustice. This means that corresponding forums must be opened up to opposition parties from states, though also to civil society actors as organized, for example, in the World Social Forum.[64] To start with states as the main – but not the only – political units of agency for a politics of transnational justice is not to conserve or strengthen the existing state-centered international system; rather, it is to overcome the latter by generating political power within, between and beyond political communities which understand that globalized forms of politics represent the only way to address and overcome global injustice. But there is a paradox here, as the more powerful states often use their position to prevent the construction of more emancipatory political structures. That is why internal and transnational social movements are essential when it comes to generating the public power required to motivate structural change.[65]

Democracy as the main practice of justice acquires special importance in this context. In the first place, it must be liberated from the narrow choice between a "world state or world of states." It is best understood as a normative order in which those who are subject to rule or norms should also be the normative authority and should exercise it in an active sense within a practice of justification. Thus, the question of the relevant demoi is answered in a non-arbitrary way in terms of the existing structures of rule and/or domination, and the requisite institutional form depends on the degree of subjection. This

---

[63] See also Ypi, *Global Justice and Avant-Garde Political Agency*; Culp, *Global Justice and Development*.
[64] See Zürn and Ecker-Ehrhardt, *Die Politisierung der Weltpolitik*.
[65] On this, see the analysis of transnational politicization in Zürn, "Survey Article: Four Models of a Global Order with Cosmopolitan Intent."

idea of "demoi of subjection" extends the question of democratic rule conceptually beyond national borders, according to the relations of rule or domination in which a state is actively or passively embedded.[66] The principle of political proportionality asserts that structures of justification must be sufficiently open to participation and sufficiently effective to react to a given situation of domination. However, this principle does not predetermine which model of order – ranging from federalist internationalism to global supranationalism – follows. That must be decided with a view to the situation that is supposed to be transformed from an unregulated form of domination into a regulated form of justification or rule; sometimes this can only be done through supranational institutions, sometimes through international contracts.[67] With respect to the global economic order, proportionality calls for relatively strong supranational institutions for regulating production, exchange and distribution. The point of this regulation is not only, as an internationalist neo-republican theory would assert,[68] to protect and enable particular political self-determination within states, important as that is; rather, the main point is to establish distributive justice on a transnational level by political means, because nation-states have lost the capacity to do so in a fundamental, system-transforming way. The same holds for the questions of regulating migration or responding to climate change.

Insofar as democratic justice is understood in processual terms as a practice of justification, it expresses the collective aspiration to subsume the exercise of rule under relations of effective justification and authorization of norms by those who are subjected to them. Justice and democracy are primarily recuperative and processual in nature, because they aim to transform existing forms of rule or domination into structures of justification. Habermas once coined the image of "besiegement" for the exercise of communicative, democratic power: public discourses generate justifying reasons that the political system cannot ignore.[69] The concept of "justificatory power"[70] that takes up these reflections is open when it comes to the question of whether the mode of producing and exercising communicative power is an institutionalized one or not. Democratic justice as

[66] See also Bohman, *Democracy across Borders*.
[67] See, for example, the suggestions by Jürgen Habermas, *The Divided West*, pp. 115–193; Habermas, *The Crisis of the European Union*, pp. 56f.
[68] See Pettit, *Just Freedom*; Laborde and Ronzoni, "What Is a Free State?"
[69] Habermas, *Between Facts and Norms*, pp. 486f.
[70] See my concept of "noumenal power" in Forst, *Normativity and Power*, ch. 2. See also Chapter 9 in this volume.

a practice is always a matter of *democratization*, of expanding and equalizing justificatory power. However, the construction of justice is eventually to become reality within binding institutions of justification, in which those who are subject to rule become the authors of their normative orders – and the first struggle for justice is the struggle for the establishment of such basic structures of justification. Thus, to be theoretically agnostic with respect to the institutional forms that transnational justice should take is not just a reflection of sociological realism; rather, it follows from an understanding of the autonomous and constructive character of a politics of discursive non-domination.

9

STRUCTURAL INJUSTICE WITH A NAME, STRUCTURAL DOMINATION WITHOUT A FACE?*

9.1 An antinomy

The title of this chapter expresses a puzzle that any critical analysis of relations of structural injustice as forms of structural domination must solve. For we encounter an irksome contradiction between these terms in recent discussions. First, regarding injustice, in order to grasp its essence, the corresponding relations between persons or groups should not be misconceived as an anonymous social occurrence without a history, in which no relevant traces of human action and responsibility can be found. Injustice does not simply sweep over societies as a contingent effect of nameless forces; rather, it is something that people *inflict on one another*. This is what lends the critique of injustice its meaning and force – it is an accusation.[1] If we lose sight of this, we will not be able to distinguish clearly

---

* The following reflections are indebted to more discussion contexts and occasions than I can possibly mention here. However, I would like to expressly thank the participants in the discussion of my theory of power at the conference on Philosophy and Social Sciences held in Prague in May 2017, which resulted in the volume *Theorising Noumenal Power*, edited by Mark Haugaard and Matthias Kettner, and previously published as a symposium in the *Journal of Political Power*. I owe further valuable suggestions to a conference on structural domination at the Berlin Social Science Center in November 2018, which I co-organized with Lea Ypi. Finally, the present version was delivered at the conference of the Italian Association for Political Philosophy in Milan in November 2019 and benefited greatly from the discussions there. In Frankfurt, I have discussed these questions over many years with colleagues including Nancy Fraser, Dorothea Gädeke, Tamara Jugov, Christian Schemmel, Miriam Ronzoni, Malte Ibsen, Johannes Schulz, Darrel Moellendorf, Stefan Gosepath and many others to whom I am greatly indebted. In addition, I recall with pleasure, but also sadness, discussions of these issues with Iris Young, who developed theoretically innovative approaches to this topic in her work.

[1] See Moore, *Injustice*; Bloch, *Natural Law and Human Dignity*.

between human-made injustice and, say, natural disasters. In other words, injustice has a *name* that refers to the responsibility of human beings, even if it involves structures that societies have produced over extended periods of time.

From this perspective, it makes sense to regard structural injustice as a form of domination exercised over one collective by another (for example, a class or a colonial power). Domination, contrary to what neo-republican theories propose,[2] means that the dominant group is able to restrict the space of reasons and options for the dominated group in such a way that the latter follow the will of the dominant. The dominated are subjected to a normative order that was not (in fact) justified and could not be (counterfactually) justified to them as equal subjects of justification. This gives rise to an order of structural domination, whereby the relevant structures may be political, economic or legal in nature, or may have some other social and cultural character. In contrast to the normatively neutral concept of "rule," "domination" designates a non-reciprocal relationship between the groups in question that cannot be justified among equals (but which nevertheless raises an ideological claim to be justified).

Especially in complex modern societies, however, structural domination has a specific character that seemingly cannot be traced back to the actions of identifiable individuals, and not to those of collectives such as dominant groups or classes either. As thinkers such as Iris Young and Clarissa Hayward argue,[3] the concrete imputation of responsibility for injustice is difficult when, for example, a single mother and recent immigrant who has no fixed income loses her home and is at risk of becoming homeless. The apartment owner who evicts her, the employers who do not hire her or hire her only for a meager salary, as well as many other individuals and institutions involved, have neither broken laws nor deliberately behaved wrongly or unjustly – and yet they have participated in a social arrangement that produces structural vulnerability, intractable problems and thus social injustice for this person. According to Hayward, such forms and relations of structural power have no face; they are "*de-faced.*" There are subjects who are politically and socially dominated, but there seem to be no identifiable dominators. A "system" has taken shape that creates inclusion and privilege on the one side and exclusion and hopelessness on the other.

---

[2] See Chapter 10 in this volume. On the corresponding understanding of power, see Forst, *Normativity and Power*, ch. 2.

[3] Young, *Responsibility for Justice*; Hayward, *De-Facing Power*.

So, the puzzle is the following: How can it be that *structural injustice* must have a *name* linked to concrete, imputable responsibilities, while the same relations are regarded as anonymous forms of *structural domination* that have *no face*? A critical theory of justice and power must solve this puzzle, for failure to do so results in an antinomy with far-reaching implications – namely, that it is both necessary *and* impossible to analyze structural injustice as structural domination: necessary because the grammar of injustice requires us to identify the names of dominators and dominated, impossible because structural domination does not have a face. This would cast a shadow over the analysis and normative evaluation of social and political conditions, and the concepts we employ would become entangled in contradictions. In what follows, I will outline a way to resolve this antinomy. This calls for a careful consideration of the concepts of justice, power, domination and structure.

9.2 (In-)justice[4]

The virtue of justice requires that human beings should not subject one another to arbitrary decisions and actions, where by "arbitrary" is meant "not justifiable with good reasons between those involved." Therefore, both when it comes to individual acts that claim to be just and to principles of political and social justice, every person has a basic claim or right to be offered adequate reasons for norms of justice as an equal normative authority. In the political and social context, this means that no one should be subjected to a system of institutions, norms and structures that expresses arbitrariness toward them in the sense of not being adequately justified.

Achieving clarity in the face of a multitude of competing determinations of what "adequately justified" means in this context calls for a reflexive turn, a return to the core definition of justice. Since there is no self-evident or natural way of determining what "non-arbitrary" means, the principle of justification acquires central importance for justice, leading to a conception of *justice as justification*. For according to the principle of justification (as a principle of practical justification or practical reason), justifications of social relations and institutions are free from arbitrariness if they can pass the discursive

---

[4] For a more exhaustive discussion, see Forst, *The Right to Justification*, and Forst, *Justification and Critique*, ch. 1, and Chapters 8 and 12 in this volume. A synopsis can also be found in Forst, "Justice."

test of reciprocal–general justification among subjects who enjoy equal normative status. The principle of justification follows from a reflexive and recursive[5] consideration of the validity claims[6] of norms of justice that claim reciprocal and general validity for all members of a normative order. Viewed in this light, the conception of justice as justification is based only on those principles and criteria that are intrinsic to the claim to justification of justice. At the same time, the reflection in question is transcendental in nature, for it reconstructs the conditions of the possibility of rationally justified normative validity.

The criteria of reciprocity and generality, understood discursively, mean that no one may make claims that they deny to others (reciprocity of content), and that the justification of such claims must be made in a language that does not accord priority to one of the perspectives (e.g., a religious one) from the outset or impose a reasonably rejectable interpretation of "true" interests or needs on others (reciprocity of reasons). Generality means that no one who is subjected to a normative order may be excluded from the discourse of justification.

According to the justificatory conception of justice, the key issue is that the real authority of justice resides with the subjects *themselves* who form a normative order; from a normative point of view, they exercise this authority autonomously in establishing a democratic order of justification. Democracy, properly understood, is the political practice of justice. As an empirical matter, those who are subjected to normative orders are hardly justificatory equals, although different regimes exhibit considerable differences in this regard. The primary objective of struggles for justice, therefore, is always to improve the level of justification of an order, both as regards its content and its procedures of justification. The basic claim of justice is that every subject should be legally, politically and socially secured and respected in his or her status as a non-dominated, equal justificatory authority. Safeguarding this status is the task of fundamental justice in a "basic structure of justification."

In this sense, as Barrington Moore has shown, the language of non-domination is, as it were, the natural language of protest against injustice. The sense of justice that motivates people to struggle

---

[5] On the notion of recursive justification, see O'Neill, *Constructions of Reason*, and the Introduction to this volume.

[6] The concept of a validity claim was developed by Jürgen Habermas and Karl-Otto Apel in their discourse ethics. See Habermas, *Moral Consciousness and Communicative Action*.

has many contextual and cultural facets. In essence, however, it is directed at conditions of oppression, be they legal, political, economic or cultural, that deprive certain groups of their voice and of the opportunity to co-determine the general order.[7] It is forms of "not counting," of being a legitimatory "nullity," that prompt the reaction of asserting self-respect by demanding justice. This includes, first of all, recognition as a politically relevant or equal subject of justification, as someone who neither wants to be nor may be dominated. The basic impulse of justice is that of being an equal or, in an abridged form, at least a relevant justificatory authority in the normative order to which one belongs. Therefore, the question of power is the first question of justice.

When analyzing the relevant contexts of justice, a critical theory of justice does not assume a reductionist, positivist conception of belonging.[8] A context of justice exists where people are subject to a normative order and (normatively speaking) can claim their right to achieve a status of non-domination – that is, a status as a justificatory authority – within that order. Relevant orders here may be institutionally thick political orders, but also more diffuse ones such as the global economy. What is decisive is the degree of subjection, especially if it is a form of domination, that is, subordination to an order of action that has not been and cannot be justified toward everyone – in factual–institutional or in counterfactual–normative terms.

It should be noted that the relevant understanding of justice is a relational one, that is, one that looks at relations and relationships between people, also and especially at their structural forms. A critical theory of justice begins with a negative analysis, thus not primarily with positive forms of rule, but with forms of domination. These occur in different, often interrelated varieties, as disenfranchisement, political marginalization and powerlessness, or economic exploitation and cultural devaluation. But social relationships are always involved. For the protest against injustice is not directed against anonymous or cosmic forces that apportion "luck" or "misfortune" as a destiny, but against concrete conditions of domination that are man-made. Accordingly, what is demanded is not "compensation" for nameless relations of inequality, but a change in relations of rule.[9] The grammar of (in-)justice is inseparable from the grammar

---

[7] Moore, *Injustice*, pp. 46 and 90.
[8] For a more detailed account, see Chapter 8 in this volume.
[9] See the more detailed discussion of "luck egalitarianism" in Chapter 12 in this volume.

of the critique of domination. Injustice is not only *lamented*; rather, an *accusation* is made against *someone*. The question of justice ascertains the unjust rule of some people over others and seeks to overcome it.

This is why a justice perspective cannot skate over the problem of accountability. For regardless of the intractability of the question of structural responsibility in a world of multiple political and economic interdependencies,[10] an analysis of existing relations of injustice cannot ignore the requirement to identify the current system of state and transnational economic, political, legal and cultural domination by name. Otherwise, the quest for justice lacks orientation and is in danger, in a bad moral dialectic, of seeking "help" for poorer people or states from those who have contributed to causing their poverty and profit from it.[11]

The key issue is to empower victims of injustice to assert their rights from the outset and not to regard them as "weak" subjects who need assistance, but to understand them as political subjects who are deprived of the status that is due to them – namely, being in a position to co-determine and change the relations to which they are subject. Those who suffer economic exploitation also suffer political powerlessness, and the key to social emancipation lies in establishing political justice – a democracy worthy of the name. As we have seen, the question of social and political power is the key also and especially to social, distributive justice.

9.3 Power, rule and domination[12]

But what is the essence of the phenomenon we call "power"? I propose the following definition: *Power is the capacity of A to motivate B to think or do something that B would otherwise not have thought or done.*[13] Power exists as the capacity or ability to be socially effective in this "cognitive" (*geistig*) way. Correspondingly, it is *exercised* over others with the help of the space of justifications, whereby it remains open whether this is done based on good or bad

---

[10] See Lu, *Justice and Reconciliation in World Politics*.
[11] See Forst, *The Right to Justification*, ch. 11.
[12] On the following, see the more detailed discussion in Forst, *Normativity and Power*, ch. 2.
[13] This definition is based on the "formal definition of power" proposed by Robert Dahl: "*A* has power over *B* to the extent that he can get *B* to do something that *B* would not otherwise do." Dahl, "The Concept of Power," pp. 202–203.

justifications, and whether it is done in accordance with or contrary to B's interests. The proposed basic definition is normatively neutral. The means whereby power is exercised remain indeterminate and can be of very different kinds: a persuasive speech, a piece of good advice, an ideological description of the world, an act of seduction, an order that is accepted or a threat that is taken seriously. All of these are exercises of *noumenal power* that intentionally change the economy of the reasons of those affected. A threat, for example, gives someone who is being threatened a reason to do something; and as long as it is a relationship of power, at least one alternative course of action remains open to the person, even though it may be fraught with risk. Otherwise, she would only be an object at the free disposal of others, like a stone one handles as one likes. Therefore, the case of pure force, in which person A moves person B by physical means alone, such as by handcuffing her or carrying her away, is by definition no longer an exercise of social power, because the person thus treated no longer "does" anything herself, but something is "done" to her. But exercising power means consciously influencing the *actions* of others, not their being in the world in some general sense. In the case mentioned, the relationship between the persons turns into one of pure physical force or violence, and the noumenal character vanishes (which does not mean that such violence cannot intend and have many noumenal effects).

Therefore, the phenomenon of power is noumenal or cognitive in nature: *To have and to wield power means to be able – in a sequence of progressively more extreme forms – to influence, use, determine, occupy or even seal off the space of justifying reasons of other persons*. This can be a matter of a single occurrence, such as an impressive argument or an effective act of deception. But it can also involve a sequence of events that occur within a social structure that makes certain social relations appear justified, whether these relations are subjected to reflexive examination or not. Every social order is in this sense an *order of justification*. Relations and orders of power are relations and orders of justifications. Social power arises and sustains itself where these justifications combine to form accepted, comprehensive *justification narratives*.[14] In the light of such narratives, social relations and institutions, as well as certain ways of thinking and acting, appear as justified and legitimate, perhaps

---

[14] On the concepts of "order of justification" and "justificatory narrative," see Forst and Günther, *Die Herausbildung normativer Ordnungen*, pp. 11–30, and Forst, *Normativity and Power*, ch. 3; as well as Chapter 6 in this volume.

even as natural or willed by God – or at least as unchangeable. The relations in question may be ones of oppression or equality, whether political or personal, and the corresponding justifications may be well grounded, collectively shared, merely "overlapping," or they may be distorted and ideological, meaning that they justify a social relation of asymmetry and subordination on grounds that would not be shared by free and equal, informed subjects of justification in a corresponding undistorted discourse of justification.

How does such a theory explain structural power? The following four aspects must be taken into account in answering this question.

(1) Every social order in general, and every subsystem in particular, is based on a certain understanding of the purpose, goals and rules of this order or system – as orders of justification, therefore, they are normative orders or partial orders. A modern economy, for example, rests on very general notions of value, labor, nature and productivity, as well as on notions of fair exchange, to name only these. Accordingly, it is also vulnerable to criticism concerning how it interprets and realizes these normative conceptions.[15] In this way, we can reconstruct certain justificatory narratives that ground such an order. Here one can think, for instance, of large-scale narratives developed in social theory, such as Max Weber's analysis of the contribution of the Protestant ethic to the formation of the spirit of capitalism. However, a modern economy is not based on only one grand narrative, but on several. And, even though these combine to form an order of justification, their components exhibit various tensions and contradictions, for example between notions of equal opportunity and libertarian conceptions of freedom or the idea of personal merit.[16] Even if a social structure cannot be reduced to its narrative foundations or to a specific justification, as regards its members' self-understanding it is nevertheless based in large part on such foundations, even if these have an ideological character (i.e., justify the unjustifiable).[17]

(2) Structures whose acceptance is based on narratives and justifications of this kind often derive their main support from the idea that, despite internal contradictions and shortcomings, they are without alternative. Not only do these structures rest on certain constellations of noumenal power, therefore, but they also *produce and reproduce* the latter through reinforcement and the suggestion that they are

---

[15] A model of such immanent critique can be found in Honneth, *Freedom's Right*, pt. III, ch. 6.2.
[16] See Boltanski and Thévenot, *On Justification*.
[17] For a similar understanding of ideology, see Piketty, *Capital and Ideology*.

"natural," so that a "second nature" can take shape. By permeating everyday life, these structures limit what can be imagined as possible and acquire a self-evident status in the lifeworld as a conception of how things just are and will remain. These structures reproduce the normative force of the factual. This force is a resource of noumenal power as a mode of justification through everyday practice and socialization, bringing forth a certain mindset.

(3) In this way, structures that rest on and reproduce justifications exercise an *influence* over subjects that appears as a form of power. Within a patriarchal structure, for example, women may continue to follow its rules even when the patriarch grants them freedoms or is absent, or even if he tries to abandon this role. This means that the noumenal power structure persists in the space of justifications that supports the specific power relations, so that a certain order of action is maintained. Here it is more appropriate to speak of "influence" rather than of an exercise of "power," however, since in such situations people do not *intentionally* induce others to think or do something. Structures, unlike persons, do not exercise power; rather, they create opportunities for exercising power and maintain themselves accordingly. They are, so to speak, reified complexes of justifications and thus structure actions and possibilities of action.[18]

(4) This brings us to how power is exercised *within structures*. Since the power potentials of such structures are noumenal in kind and thus shape values, norms, rules and social positions, power structures enable those who possess sufficient *noumenal capital*[19] in the relevant spheres – for example, as a priest, an officer or an employer – to use their social recognition and standing[20] as a *resource* within the structure to wield power over others, who as a result heed an admonition, obey an order, or accept an employment contract and its terms. In this way, structures serve as background resources for exercising power, because within them individuals enjoy a power status that includes and manifests the justifications that define this status and motivate others to act in certain ways. Normative roles, offices and functions are noumenal status positions that facilitate the exercise of power over others by "unburdening" action within such

---

[18] See Giddens, *The Constitution of Society*.
[19] This concept is broader than Bourdieu's related notion of "symbolic capital," because it refers to all means of power, including "material" ones. See Bourdieu, *Practical Reason*.
[20] A discursive conception of *authority* can be developed at this point. To have authority means to have a certain standing within a normative order by means of which one disposes over noumenal capital with regard to certain areas of social life – for example, by exercising the function or role of a teacher or a judge.

contexts of an explicit requirement of justification, because certain justifications are assumed as given with the position. Within structures, we can thus differentiate groups or classes of people according to the noumenal power status they possess. In this sense, social and political structures are *power structures*, because they *structure power* and allocate it as a resource, but without exercising it themselves. They constitute power and powerlessness according to the noumenal position that individuals or groups occupy within them.

The concept of *rule* (*Herrschaft*) refers to a form of power in which the power holders can determine the space of justifications for others, because their power is supported by comprehensive (for instance, historical, religious, metaphysical or moral) justifications that structure the space of reasons within which social and political relations are understood. These relations are thus an enduring and stable social order of action and justification. To reiterate, such rule can be well or poorly founded; it continues to exist as long as its reasons are followed. Democratic rule exists where those who are subjected to a normative order are at the same time the normative authorities who co-determine this order through corresponding justification procedures (including representative institutions).

A situation of *domination* (*Beherrschung*) exists where unjustified asymmetric social relations go hand-in-hand with a closure of the space of justifications, so that these relations appear to be legitimate, natural, divinely ordained or in some other way unalterable (also due to threats of violence) and leave scarcely any alternative possibilities of action open to the subjugated. Such an order is supported by one-sided, hegemonic justifications and deprives those affected of the possibility of – or, normatively speaking, the right to – reciprocal and general justification and criticism. Here, hegemonic justifications dominate the social space of reasons, but they themselves do not "dominate" persons; rather, they *enable* the domination of persons by others. The space of reasons is largely sealed off, either because domination is recognized and accepted as more or less legitimate, or is at least endured, or because effective threats ensure its continued existence. This means that behind domination lurk *coercion* (*Zwang*) and the threat of *violence* (*Gewalt*) – forms of power that rob the subjugated to an even greater extent of their right to normative participation and justification and further restrict the space of reasons.

Unlike the neo-republican conception of (non-)domination, therefore, a discourse-theoretical conception does not primarily emphasize a "robust" safeguarding of spheres of individual freedom of choice;[21] rather, its main point concerns the normative status of persons as equal justificatory authorities within a social and political order. *Political domination* has four essential dimensions that help determine the intensity of domination: first, in purely normative terms, individuals and groups are subjected to norms or institutions that cannot be adequately justified to them; second, these norms and institutions have not been exposed to an appropriate, institutionalized and legitimate (and legitimizing) discourse of justification as a matter of fact either; third, the normative order as a whole exhibits no such institutionalized forums of justification in which reciprocal–general justifications can be generated and false justifications repudiated – thus, it lacks a basic structure of justification (in the sense of fundamental justice); finally, fourth, a structure of domination may be so entrenched and noumenally closed that those who are dominated in this normative order lose any sense that they are normative authorities with a right to justification. In the extreme case, this can lead to "total" domination.[22] I call such a form of self-abnegation "noumenal second-order alienation."[23]

9.4 The faces of structural domination[24]

Structures generate, reproduce, shape – in short, *structure* – social and political power resources and thus constitute power relations; however, they do not themselves *exercise* power, rule or domination. For power, rule or domination are primarily *relational* terms; they designate *intersubjective* relations. Classically speaking, criticism of seemingly anonymous structural power – for example, the critique of the "fetishism of commodities"[25] – exposes the *real* relations of domination as class relations, as relations of *oppression*. Where the human being is, as Marx says, a "contemptible being," they are not

---

[21] See Pettit, *On the People's Terms*, ch. 1. On this, see Forst, "A Kantian Republican Conception of Justice as Non-Domination," and Chapter 10 in this volume. See also Gädeke, *Politik der Beherrschung*.
[22] See Arendt, *Origins of Totalitarianism*, pt. 3.
[23] See Chapter 1 in this volume.
[24] In the following, I refer to critiques of my approach by Lukes, "Noumenal Power: Concept and Explanation," and Hayward, "On Structural Power," to which I have responded in Forst, "Noumenal Power Revisited." In the special issue of the *Journal of Political Power*, I also discuss further issues of structural power with Albena Azmanova, Mark Haugaard and Simon Susen. See Haugaard and Kettner, *Theorising Noumenal Power*.
[25] See my discussion of Marx in Forst, *Normativity and Power*, pp. 46–47.

only structurally dominated, but socially *despised*.[26] The task of a critical theory is to demystify and de-anonymize social structures without reducing them in a simplistic way to a single, all-powerful power center. In order to recognize and critically analyze the different "faces of oppression," to use an expression of Iris Young, one must render their intersubjective quality recognizable.[27] Structures seem to "dominate" people, but what this actually means is that they *enable* and *express* the domination of some by others. This is the normatively relevant truth of a structural analysis that makes criticism in the name of justice and political resistance possible.[28]

I agree with Steven Lukes that explanations of the exercise of power must be "inter-agentive" in the sense that power represents a relationship among free (although not necessarily equally free) agents: however, I add that this view must leave room for collective action, for instance in relation to classes. Otherwise, the concept of "class rule" would lose its meaning. In order to understand such structural forms of rule or domination, one must avoid a dichotomous opposition between intersubjective and structural power. For although it is true that power is exercised between agents, it is nonetheless made possible by structures that, as Hayward stresses, have a noumenal life of their own. "Structural power" is what we call an ensemble of relations, norms and institutions that equip individuals or collectives with varying degrees of noumenal capital enabling them to exercise power over others.

Lukes is also right to stress the connection between the exercise of social and political power and the question of *responsibility*: In complex societies, the questions, "who did it?" or "whom to shoot?" (to use the drastic language from John Steinbeck's *Grapes of Wrath* quoted by Hayward and Lukes)[29] are notoriously difficult to answer, because such social orders are characterized by a diffusion of practical responsibilities. But to speak in an abstract and anonymous sense of structures of injustice having and exercising power over us is to distort the language of (in)justice. Injustice must be attributable to agents, even if they are collectives integrated into structures; and even though tracing back the chain of causes for certain social

---

[26] Marx, "Contribution to the Critique of Hegel's Philosophy of Law," p. 182: "The criticism of religion ends with the teaching that *man is the highest being for man*, hence with the *categorical imperative to overthrow all relations* in which man is a debased, enslaved, forsaken, despicable essence." See my discussion of Marx in Chapter 1 of this volume.
[27] Young, *Justice and the Politics of Difference*, ch. 2.
[28] See also Powers and Faden, *Structural Injustice*.
[29] Hayward and Lukes, "Nobody to Shoot?," pp. 17–18.

relations is often difficult, it is essential for this perspective to ask in a differentiated way who *benefits* from them (and who does not), who plays what role in *reproducing* these relations and who is in a position to *change* them (but does not). These are the three central aspects of an analysis of injustice, especially structural injustice. Otherwise, talk of structural domination would become empty or merely metaphorical. In more complex relationships and situations of structural domination, domination does not have only one face, but many. But these faces exhibit a relevant similarity – that is the decisive point. We must not abandon the language of action in these contexts, whether in the analysis of power or in that of counter-power. No groups of oppressed exist where there are no groups of oppressors, however diverse these relations may be in situations of intersectionality.[30]

Since intersubjective and structural analyses of power must be combined, it is mistaken to assume that one must choose between the two. As Hayward says, we need a conception of justification narratives that legitimize the exercise of power within "inter-agentive relations of domination and subordination."[31] Narratives of this kind "enable and constrain social action by defining relations of power that are structural in form."[32] So far, I agree; and we must differentiate accordingly between individual, collective and structural power. But these are not different forms of the exercise of power, because structural power constitutes the empowering or disempowering background condition for the exercise of the respective power of action.

Hayward believes that my focus on the noumenal and cognitivist dimensions of power cannot fully explain the power of structures that do not operate through cognition but "around" it.[33] In contrast, I believe that power only operates within the space of cognition, even if this space is occupied by ideologies, false beliefs or emotional reactions (which I consider to be part of that space as long as they are no mere impulses). Hayward seeks to contradict my account of how structural normative orders take shape and become stabilized by portraying how racial narratives manifested themselves and became entrenched within U.S. laws and social structures, such as in the form of housing policies and urban development plans. These developed a life of their own, beyond cognitive consent, even after the influence

---

[30] See Castro Varela and Dhawan, *Soziale (Un)Gerechtigkeit*.
[31] Hayward, "On Structural Power," p. 65.
[32] Ibid.
[33] Ibid., p. 57.

of the said narratives waned. I find the story that Hayward tells here (and in her important book *De-Facing Power*)[34] insightful and rich, but I don't think that it contradicts my view. Hayward provides a vivid reconstruction of how the racist narrative led to segregated neighborhoods and schools and combined with economic incentives and price developments of private homes. The policies of the U.S. Federal Housing Administration institutionalized the racial narrative and "insured that public investment would be channeled toward racially exclusive white enclaves";[35] thus, property values mirrored the intentions of these policies. White people who wanted to get a state-backed mortgage were constrained to buy a home "in a racially exclusive white enclave."[36] For Hayward, this shows that such structural power exercises a force of its own, regardless of whether such buyers agreed with racist narratives.

I disagree with the conclusions that Hayward draws from this analysis on several grounds. First, I think the case of structural power she depicts indicates the degree to which, contrary to her thesis, conscious *actions* by an administration play a role in its exercise of racially motivated power. But that is not my main point. For second, rather than separating racist and economic narratives, one should stress how they are connected and overlap, for it is open to question how long such racist policies could survive if they were not shared or at least tolerated by significant portions of the population, quite apart from purely economic motives. Economic incentives have a cultural character and, in this case, it is a racially tinged character. Perhaps it is also a particular ruse of racism to wrap itself in an economic garb. The most important point, however, is a third one, which concerns the people who feel structurally constrained to comply with such policies for social and economic reasons, even though they reject or at least do not support them. Is what is going on here really "extra-discursive," as Hayward argues,[37] that is, a case of structural constraint that has nothing to do with cognitive acceptance? I have my doubts about that, although the key point is to analyze carefully the effects of power at work here. For conforming to a racially motivated policy without sharing the racism (at least explicitly), but only feeling compelled to play along for economic reasons (and for the sake of the children's schooling), presupposes a certain acceptance of the rules of the game. But what kind of acceptance are we dealing with here?

[34] Hayward, *De-Facing Power*, esp. ch. 4.
[35] Hayward, "On Structural Power," p. 61.
[36] Ibid.
[37] Ibid.

A variety of motives may be at work and we cannot rule out that deep-seated racist stereotypes (or "schemas," to use Sally Haslanger's terminology)[38] still play a role in this. In any case, such structures are only accepted and reproduced if those who disagree with their racist point nevertheless regard them – to cite a few possibilities – as (a) unchangeable, (b) based on economic facts and laws and (c) serving their own interest. All of these motivations are cognitive in nature and rest on certain beliefs about how things are, must be or even should be, and in any case must be accepted if you want to promote your own and your family's interests. Would any such structures function if they were not based on and promoted such beliefs? And why shouldn't we call such forms of acceptance "noumenal" and "cognitive" (where "cognitive" does not mean "reflexively examined" or "entirely free of unconscious elements")?

Moreover, those who assume that power operates in non-discursive and non-cognitive ways would have problems explaining why structural power is to be combated in the discursive, cognitive space of the hegemony[39] of justifications, for instance by demystifying and denaturalizing power through genealogical or classical critique of ideology.[40] This only makes sense if power is discursive in nature.

To summarize the foregoing discussion, in a system of structural domination, vulnerable individuals or groups suffer, as Iris Young writes, "systematic threat of domination or deprivation of the means to develop and exercise their capacities."[41] This is the result, to quote Hayward, of "multiple, large-scale social processes, which interact to create patterned inequalities that no identifiable agent directs, controls, or intends."[42] I agree with both claims, but some details need to be added. Young's formulation makes clear that the threat of domination resides in being dominated by *others*, such as the members of a ruling class or of privileged groups. Here domination is conceived in intersubjective terms. If the deprivation of opportunities, which is also mentioned, were a purely social or natural chance occurrence, it could not be described either as domination or as injustice, as Young does. Domination is not an anonymous occurrence, even if the constellation of power within which it occurs was not designed from a center. But someone who is dominated is dominated *by others*. The key issue for the analysis of structural injustice, therefore, is

---

[38] Haslanger, *Resisting Reality*.
[39] See Gramsci, *Prison Notebooks*, vol. 3.
[40] See this discussion in Allen et al., "Power and Reason, Justice and Domination."
[41] Young, *Responsibility for Justice*, p. 52.
[42] Hayward, "On Structural Power," p. 64.

to develop a complete structural and interagentive description of vulnerability, different power potentials and positions, and forms of oppression and domination and not to construct dichotomies according to which structures form anonymous, faceless power complexes – even if they have many different faces. As for Hayward's formulation, while it is certainly true that complex social structures of inequality, for instance, are not produced or controlled by particular individual agents, it does not follow that they are not used by powerful actors for their own purposes and that these actors do not do everything they can to strengthen and maintain these structures in order to continue to enjoy their benefits. The example of housing policies that privilege certain social groups speaks volumes: here, some groups dominate others and various power structures interact in the process; but characteristic of domination and injustice is that the groups involved, the asymmetric structures, their false justifications, etc., remain identifiable in principle. A critique of power that wants to use the grammar of domination and that of injustice must be able to analyze social relations as relations of power – in classical terms, relations of rule. There is no social or political domination without the dominated and those who dominate, no racism without racists, no patriarchy without patriarchs, no capitalism without capitalists, even if these groups are more difficult to define than many a classical theory would have it and structures develop a life of their own that produces noumenal effects. Structural power structures social action, and structures of domination both express and enable the exercise of concrete, dominating power by some over others. If we want to describe this in terms that are relevant for justice and to speak of structural injustice, these structures must be given names *and* faces, from real agents to privileged groups to political parties or leaders. Otherwise, emancipatory practice would have no points of reference and orientation, but would remain in a void of anonymity.

— 10 —

KANTIAN REPUBLICANISM VERSUS THE NEO-REPUBLICAN MACHINE
The Meaning and Practice of Political Autonomy*

10.1 Normative authority

Social and political philosophy reflects on us as social and political beings; but such reflection must include, at a fundamental level, an idea of us as moral beings. More precisely, when dealing with the question of how social or political power should be exercised, we need to develop an understanding of the authority and legitimacy of such exercises, and that leads us to the basic question regarding our nature as normative beings: Who has the justified authority to rule over us?

In his magisterial reconstruction of the history of the idea of recognition, as in his work generally, Axel Honneth shows us that we must turn to the tradition of German Idealism after Kant in order to answer that question. For it was Kant who first formulated the revolutionary idea that in the realm of morality (and hence in other normative realms, especially the political) it is ultimately "we" as human beings, guided by reason, who are the ultimate normative authority. As Honneth shows, there is a complex system of inter-related concepts, such as reason, freedom and mutual recognition, at work here to develop the essential notion of autonomy as crucial to

---

* Earlier versions of this paper were presented at the conference "Kant and Republicanism," which was organized by Peter Niesen and Marcus Willaschek in Hamburg in 2014, and at a panel organized by Volker Gerhardt at the 12th International Kant Congress in Vienna in 2015. I owe special thanks for their commentaries to the colleagues just mentioned, as well as to Pauline Kleingeld, Bernd Ludwig, George Pavlakos, Philip Pettit, Arthur Ripstein and Lea Ypi. Ciaran Cronin kindly corrected my English. My greatest debt, however, is to Axel Honneth. For without his constant reminders of the blind spots in Kant that Hegel saw and our endless discussions of the issues they raise, I would have remained in a dogmatic slumber.

the question of authority; but the basic thought is as simple as it is liberating – namely, that in the normative realm, ideally speaking, we are all equals and ought to follow no other or higher authority than ourselves as equals who construct the moral and political norms that will rule over us together. As Honneth argues, the foundational form of recognition is "a practice in which subjects mutually recognize each other as co-authors of their shared norms."[1] Somewhat contrary to the stark contrast between the French and the German traditions of thought about recognition highlighted by Honneth, I think we should credit Spinoza, and especially Rousseau, when it comes to the genealogy of that notion of autonomy, especially in the political realm.[2] However, I agree with Honneth that the way in which Hegel in particular tried to mediate that notion of autonomy with certain social forms of recognition and institutional forms of life is essential for contextualizing the idea that we are the co-authors of the norms that bind us.[3]

Still, it is I think a Kantian reminder that alerts Honneth to the "blind spot"[4] in Hegel's theory of recognition, one that leads Honneth to interpret a given order of recognition as *constraining* the realm of normative reasons in such a way that certain critical questions regarding its exclusions and asymmetries cannot be asked. In such a situation of constraining noumenal power, as I would call it,[5] in which certain social forms that should in principle be questioned and rejected are accepted as natural, our "nature" as free noumenal equals materializes in the form of critique that is both situated and transcends given orders of recognition. At such moments, the right to and the faculty of justification as a rejection of given forms of justification find expression. And herein lies the *Kantian moment* – in reclaiming one's status as a normative authority equal to all others who should not be dominated by an established but unjustifiable order of recognition and power. That liberating moment consists in breaking up a fixed order of justification and reconstructing it along the lines of normative co-authorship. It is the moral moment of political and social autonomy, a moment of non-domination.

It is in the light of this liberating moment and its political implications that I would like to develop a Kantian form of republicanism

---

[1] Honneth, *Recognition*, p. 151.
[2] On Rousseau and Kant in particular, see Chapter 1 in this volume. For a more general treatment, see Schneewind, *The Invention of Autonomy*.
[3] Honneth, *Freedom's Right*.
[4] Honneth, *Recognition*, p. 167.
[5] Forst, *Normativity and Power*, ch. 2.

and contrast it with contemporary neo-republicanism, especially with Philip Pettit's important theory. Recent interpretations of Kant, such as that of Arthur Ripstein, which focus on the "innate right" to freedom as independence, have injected new life into the debates about Kant's political philosophy, as have neo-republican accounts of non-domination like Pettit's. Like Ripstein, I regard Kant as a theorist of independence as well as of non-domination. But I think that a particular version of Kantian republicanism needs to be added to this conversation because we misunderstand Kant and fail to appreciate what republicanism contributes to contemporary political philosophy if we conceive of the freedom of persons primarily as consisting in "using" or "receiving" legal rights that protect their individual freedom of choice. For we must bear in mind what Honneth's reading brings out, namely that Kant insists on the freedom of persons as *law-givers*, as producers and guarantors of freedom – in short, as politically autonomous citizens. The dignity – to use a recognition-related term that has special importance here – of a free person can never be understood only as that of someone who "enjoys" freedom or certain liberties; it is also always the freedom to give laws to oneself, the freedom of self-determination or autonomy. This is what it means to be a normative authority on an equal footing with others; Kantian dignity is that of equal authors of norms and law-makers. This kind of freedom comes in two modes, one moral and one political–legal; but, despite the difference between them, the basic *modus operandi* is the same in both cases, namely a practice of reciprocal and general justification or a practice of practical reason among normative equals, one moral and one political (but both intertwined). The laws that constitute that practice and those generated within it do not just protect freedom; rather, they *express* it.

In what follows, I will explain the moral grounds of such an approach and its political and legal implications, before I draw a comparison with neo-republicanism. In doing so, I will not dwell too much on "Kant's republicanism" as such but on my own version of "Kantian republicanism," which creates a certain distance to Kant's original account, while remaining true, I think, to the major ideas in his work. Thus, the approach that I suggest is a neo-Kantian one.

10.2 Moral groundwork

Both parts of the *Metaphysics of Morals*, the doctrine of right and the doctrine of virtue, deal with laws of freedom, generally called "moral laws" by Kant.[6] Those that regulate external action are called "juridical," those that are at the same time reason and motive for moral action are called "ethical." Hence, they differ not so much in their content as in their respective modes of law-giving and motivational structures: "The doctrine of right and the doctrine of virtue are therefore distinguished not so much by their different duties as by the difference in their lawgiving, which connects one incentive or the other with the law."[7] Both doctrines explain the relation between freedom, law and reason (the latter being the faculty of justification) in such a way that moral freedom is the freedom determined by practical reason, and legal and political freedom is the freedom within a system of positive law that can be generally and reciprocally justified through an exercise of the public use of reason and with appropriate law-making institutions. Hence at the core of the Kantian view lies this particular connection between freedom, law and the practice of reason-giving, which can best be understood through a reflection on what it means to be an autonomous agent of practical justification in different contexts, one moral and one legal–political.

In order to gain a better understanding of this connection, let us take a closer look at Kant's notion of moral autonomy. Kant's key idea is that the capacity for moral judgment and action must be located exclusively in the faculty of practical reason and that moral action not only presupposes *moral autonomy*, the freedom to determine one's will in accordance with self-imposed laws, but also the *autonomy of morality* from heteronomous determinations of its principle and "incentives," be they doctrines of earthly happiness or heavenly blessedness.[8] A "pure moral philosophy" must be explained in terms of principles of practical reason alone and its imperatives must be justifiable *without exception* because they claim *unconditional* validity for each and every person. Thus, Kant links the question of which actions are morally justifiable with a procedure that tests their universalizability in such a way that no moral person serves "merely as a means" to someone else's end, whatever it might be: each person is and remains a free and equal moral authority in the realm of the justification of moral norms. For, as Kant explains using the example of a false promise, "the one I want to use for my purposes by such a promise cannot possibly

---

[6] Kant, *The Metaphysics of Morals*, VI:214.
[7] Ibid., VI:220.
[8] Forst, *The Right to Justification*, ch. 2.

agree to my way of proceeding with him and thus himself contain the end of this action."[9] Thus, not only must happiness not serve as a motive for acting morally so as not to lead to heteronomous actions, but the happiness of a (responsible adult) person must not be made the end of the action (which affects this person in a relevant way) against his or her will either. Happiness is an object of irresolvable conflicts of opinion, "not an ideal of reason, but of the imagination" and experience, and thus not a reliable guide for moral reflection.[10] Hence, the obligation to promote the happiness of others must take its cue from *their* conception of happiness, even though this need not be accepted as binding or represent the reason for moral action. Neither the imposition of my notions of happiness on them nor, conversely, of theirs on me would be reconcilable with the dignity of a moral person endowed with reason and capable of self-determination. The core of the idea of being an end in itself is that autonomous persons have a "worth" that must not be subsumed under or dominated by other ends, because they are the rational authorities over practical ends in the first place. They are not just end-seekers; they are end-definers and, in this capacity, superior ends in themselves. The only ends worth pursuing are those that such persons adopt and can adopt as justifiable toward others. Justifiability comes first, and with it the person as the highest authority of justification on an equal footing with all others.

The dignity of the person can accordingly be understood in such a way that every moral person has a basic moral *right to reciprocal and general justification* of all action-legitimating norms that claim reciprocal and general validity.[11] In my interpretation, this notion of a basic moral right corresponds to the duty expressed by the categorical imperative, although Kant himself does not use the notion of a moral right in this way, except when he speaks of the "innate" or "original" right to independence or freedom as non-domination (which I discuss below). The decisive point, contrary to a "liberal–ethical" reading, is that the respect for the autonomy of the other person is *not* grounded in the fact that this enables him or her to lead a "good life," for then a specific conception of the good life would once again be guiding. Rather, it consists in respect for the dignity of the other person as a morally self-determining reasonable being and normative authority, who uses, offers and receives reasons, whom

---

[9] Kant, *Groundwork of the Metaphysics of Morals*, IV:429f.
[10] Ibid., IV:418.
[11] For a detailed account see Forst, *The Right to Justification*, pt. I.

one encounters *as an equal* (in that noumenal capacity) and to whom one owes reasons for morally relevant actions. This is the substance of the requirement of respect for maturity [*Mündigkeit*] and the right to make an independent use of one's reason – not just in "religious matters" – which for Kant is the hallmark of an enlightened morality that is not in need of any further ethical or religious grounding. The autonomous person as an agent of justification, and the right to it as an equal normative authority, is the very ground of morality.

The respect that persons owe to each other as autonomous members of a "kingdom of ends," a kingdom in which they mutually recognize and uphold each other's freedom by acting in conformity with laws that they could have given themselves as moral equals, is an unrestricted respect subject to no further qualifications.[12] Hence, the essential point of the Kantian conception of morality is precisely that other persons must be respected unconditionally as moral persons *without* any need of a further reason that refers to one's own well-being, or that of others, or to the will of God, and thereby imports a relativizing element into moral respect. Someone who asks for a further reason of this kind fails to understand the point of morality, according to Kant, as does someone who thinks that moral respect in a Kantian scheme must be proportionate to the cognitive capacities or moral virtue of others. On the contrary, such empirical qualifications deny the noumenal equality between us and commit a category mistake. The Kingdom of Ends contains all human beings independently of their empirical characteristics.

I express the idea of the basic respect for autonomous persons in the language of a moral "right to justification" because, as pointed out above, according to the Kantian conception there is a categorically undeniable subjective claim to be respected as a normative authority who is free and equal to all others – and such a claim I call a moral *right*, one which is binding on every other moral person. It is not a right to some good or a right based on some interest; rather, it is based on being a person as a reason-giving and reason-receiving entity and an authority in the space of reasons.[13] It is therefore the ground of all further claims to moral respect and to the validity of more specific moral norms, which must be justified by appeal to reciprocally and generally non-rejectable reasons. I call this form of justification *moral constructivism*.[14] It is both a discursive and

---

[12] See Kant, *Groundwork of the Metaphysics of Morals*, IV:433f.
[13] For my critique of interest-based notions of rights, see Forst, "The Justification of Basic Rights."
[14] See Forst, *The Right to Justification*, pt. I, and Forst, *Normativity and Power*, ch. 1. See

JUSTICE, RIGHTS AND NON-DOMINATION

a recursive enterprise; discursive, because justification needs to be a practice between free and equal persons, even if it is only counterfactually possible,[15] and recursive, because no content or value is given except that of the agents and criteria of construction.[16] This is what the autonomy of morality really means: its substance is constituted by principles and agents of practical reason. In other words, we can only find out what is morally justified by reconstructing the principles and agents of moral justification and using these principles in the right way.

My discourse-theoretical reconstruction of the moral point of view locates the practice of justification in two worlds, the world of actual and that of possible justification. Moral action here and now needs to take the actual claims of others adequately into account, since this is what moral respect demands. Yet, at the same time, the criteria of generality and reciprocity require us to transcend concrete justification situations and ask a generalized validity question, so that we are not held captive by particular perspectives. The two criteria allow for such a two-world-switch, because my discourse-theoretical view is not based on the idea of consensus but on that of reasonable non-rejectability. Reciprocity means that no one may make a normative claim that he or she denies to others (call that reciprocity of content) and that no one may simply project his or her own perspective, values, interests or needs onto others so that one claims to speak in their "true" interests or in the name of some truth beyond mutual justification (reciprocity of reasons). Generality means that the reasons that are supposed to ground general normative validity have to be shareable by all affected persons, given their (reciprocally) legitimate interests and claims. Thus, even where no consensus – or, classically speaking, "general will" – can be found, these criteria help to filter out reasons that are reciprocally and generally rejectable. In such discourses, the right to justification gives individuals a right to veto rejectable reasons.

10.3 The right to justification in political and legal contexts

It would be mysterious if Kant thought that the moral idea of a kingdom of ends could easily be projected onto legal and political

---

also the Introduction to this volume.
[15] For the idea of discursive justification, see Habermas, "Discourse Ethics."
[16] For the idea of recursive justification, see O'Neill, *Constructions of Reason*.

contexts; but it would be equally mysterious if it had no or very little bearing on it either. Why should the normative order of the law and of the state follow principles and ideas that are completely independent of the notion of autonomy? It is at this point that the *Rechtslehre* comes in. It provides the principles for understanding the justifiable forms of freedom under law as well as the political justification of law that establishes that kind of freedom.

As for Kant's conception of morality, it is essential for his understanding of the moral law that it must remain free from notions of and aspirations to happiness. Kant contrasts law as regards its content with all ethical doctrines of happiness and as regards its form with moral imperatives, because positive law refers only to external actions and not to inner motivation. As I said above, the essential difference between legality and morality resides less in the content of the respective laws than in the "incentives": positive law is external coercive law and constrains freedom of choice, whereas moral laws determine the moral will.[17] Thus, the moral prohibition on unjustifiable restrictions on freedom between autonomous moral persons is enshrined in law in such a way that the supreme principle of law specifies that restrictions on freedom are in need of universal justification: "Right is therefore the sum of the conditions under which the choice of one can be united with the choice of another in accordance with a universal law of freedom."[18] The foundation of this definition of law, according to which all forms of legal coercion are in need of reciprocal and general justification among free and equal persons, is a moral human right to *lawful* freedom prior to any positive law: "*Freedom* (independence from being constrained by another's choice), insofar as it can coexist with the freedom of every other in accordance with a universal law, is the only original right belonging to every man by virtue of his humanity."[19] Note here that in my reading freedom as independence is not the central term – rather, "universal law" is. Kant's "innate right" is the strict implication for law of the (in my terminology) basic moral right to justification, i.e., of the universal right to be respected as an "end in oneself," as a person (representing humanity) whose human dignity is the unconditional basis of morality *and law*. Here once more it becomes apparent that the protection of individual freedom in no way rests on a conception of the good life for which, on a certain liberal

---

[17] Kant, *The Metaphysics of Morals*, VI:220.
[18] Ibid., VI:230.
[19] Ibid., VI:237 (emphasis in original).

conception, legally protected and socially enabled forms of autonomy would be necessary. Kant's conception is rather that it is already the inviolability of the person, that is, his or her dignity, that excludes interference by others – whether this helps the non-"violated" person to achieve a good life is a completely different matter. The barrier posed by the need to justify restrictions on freedom is raised earlier, according to Kant, and it is stricter than that allowed for by such an alternative conception of ethical autonomy:

> But the concept of an external right as such proceeds entirely from the concept of *freedom* in the external relation of people to one another and has nothing at all to do with the end that all of them naturally have (their aim of happiness) and with the prescribing of means for attaining it; hence too the latter absolutely must not intrude in the laws of the former as their determining ground.[20]

Against the background of the original right of human beings and the corresponding definition of law, Kant proceeds to formulate different conceptions of the "person."[21] For, in addition to the autonomous *moral person* who acts in accordance with the categorical imperative and is owed moral respect, Kant distinguishes three "*a priori* principles" in the "civil condition," and correspondingly three further conceptions of the person: namely an ethical, a legal and a political conception. The three principles are as follows: "1. The *freedom* of every member of the society as a human being. 2. His *equality* with every other as a *subject*. 3. The *independence* of every member of a commonwealth as a *citizen*."[22] The first means: "No one can coerce me to be happy in his way (as he thinks of the welfare of other human beings); instead, each may seek his happiness in the way that seems good to him."[23] According to Kant, this excludes a "paternalistic government" in which the subjects are treated as "minor children." The legal autonomy of the person is thus protected from outside interference, and law functions on the inside as a "protective cover" (in my words) for the *ethical person* to live her life in accordance with the conceptions of the good that seem right to her, whatever her reasons may be.[24] Thus, the freedom of the ethical person is secured,

---

[20] Kant, "On the Common Saying," VIII:289 (emphasis in original).
[21] On the following fourfold differentiation of conceptions of the person and conceptions of autonomy, see Forst, *Contexts of Justice*, especially chs. 5.2 and 5.3, and Forst, *The Right to Justification*, ch. 5.
[22] Kant, "On the Common Saying," VIII:290 (emphasis in original); see also Kant, *The Metaphysics of Morals*, VI:314.
[23] Kant, "On the Common Saying," VIII:290.
[24] See my *Contexts of Justice*, ch. 2.

and with it the possibility of living an autonomous and possibly good life, through a law that is agnostic with regard to the good life and is based exclusively on the principle of reciprocal and public justification. Correspondingly, the second principle, equality, signifies that persons as *legal persons*, as "subjects" who are subjected to the law, are bound by laws that hold in the same way for everyone and place the same restrictions on everyone's freedom of choice, regardless of their social status.

Finally, the third principle spells out the role of the person as a citizen, as a "co-legislator."[25] This follows from the fact that, according to the principle of right, only "general laws" can be laws of freedom, and they can be general only if they are in accordance with the "united will of the people."[26] The citizen can be politically autonomous – and here Kant takes up Rousseau's notion of autonomy – only in this role because, as a matter of principle, he obeys only laws that he has given himself, that is, no other law "than that to which he has given his consent"[27] – "for it is only to oneself that one can never do wrong."[28] As an active member of the polity, as a voting citizen, the person is a *citoyen*, not just a *bourgeois* (though Kant, in arguing against feudal privileges, at the same time restricts political rights to men who have a certain economic independence, which servants and laborers, as well as women, lack). The citizen is simultaneously author and addressee of the law. Hence, generally and reciprocally binding law can be legitimate only if it was, or could have been – to add the counterfactual justificatory realm that sheds a critical light on real procedures (and exclusions) – agreed upon in procedures of general and reciprocal justification. The "mere idea of reason," "which, however, has its undoubted practical reality," states that "the touchstone of any public law's conformity with right" is its ability to command general agreement.[29] In short, just as the moral principle that makes it a duty to justify morally relevant actions and norms in a particular way becomes the foundation of the original right to freedom, in the same way it here becomes the foundation of the requirement to justify coercive laws in the medium of "public reason." All forms of coercion are in need of justification before and among those who are subjected to coercion as normative equals, and

---

[25] Kant, "On the Common Saying," VIII:294.
[26] Kant, *The Metaphysics of Morals*, VI:313.
[27] Ibid., VI:314.
[28] Kant, "On the Common Saying," VIII:294f.
[29] Ibid., VIII:297.

it depends on the nature of the norms in question whether the form of justification required is a moral or a political one.

This shows how the right to justification is situated within legal and political contexts. It appears as the "innate right" of human beings who are ends in themselves and have to regard themselves as such, as the first duty of right requires them to. The imperative of *honeste vive* on Kant's interpretation states that every person ought to assert his or her "worth as a human being in relation to others, a duty expressed by the saying, 'Do not make yourself a mere means for others but be at the same time an end for them.'"[30] And he affirms that this is a duty implied by the "right of humanity in our own person," which specifies what kind of freedom free and equal persons can claim from each other (in the strictly relational picture Kant presents), namely only those forms of freedom that can be reciprocally and generally justified between free and equal justificatory beings. If we ignored the nature of persons as justificatory authorities and only focused on the "independence" aspect as one secured by law, we would only get half the picture; for freedom according to the "general law" is as much a part of the first human right as is the right to be the justificatory authority in practically co-determining this general law.

Let us clarify this idea by using a thought-experiment. Imagine a perfect freedom-regulating computing machine that could properly process all justifiable freedom claims and calculate a right, generally justifiable measure that only needed to be secured by law afterwards. Would that be a Kantian regime of freedom? No, it would not, for in such a regime freedom would have come about in a heteronomous way. Legal freedom cannot be thought of or exist without the exercise of political liberty in the form of justificatory autonomy as a co-legislator. The freedom of a subject in the legal state is the freedom "of obeying no other law than that to which he has given his consent."[31] This is the real meaning of legal independence or political–legal non-domination: you are only independent or not dominated if you are at the same time subject *and* author of the law, for otherwise your right to freedom or to justification is only half realized. You might *receive* freedom or some justification, but if you cannot be the *co-author* of the laws of freedom, it is not real freedom that you are being offered, only a dependent or possibly dominated, and in any case heteronomous, scope for action. The laws securing freedom must be reciprocally and generally justifiable; but no one, not

---

[30] Kant, *The Metaphysics of Morals*, VI:236. On this point, see Chapter 1 in this volume.
[31] Kant, *The Metaphysics of Morals*, VI:314.

even a perfect machine, has the authority to fabricate these justifications for you, because you are an autonomous agent of justification.

I consider this to be the essence of Kantian republicanism, in line with Ripstein's interpretation, which stresses independence as a basic moral principle of right for rational, end-setting beings who coexist in social space.[32] It is, in my words, the right to have all other rights (and duties) justified reciprocally and generally, and thus it is the right that grounds all other rights – in a discursive, reflexive way, not by way of a deduction. In the mode of moral constructivism, this leads to a conception of moral rights, and in the mode of *political constructivism*, it leads to a conception of human rights as well as to a conception of democratic political and social justice.[33] Human rights are all the rights that persons who respect each other as free and equal cannot deny each other within a normative order of legal, political and social life.[34] Here again the main point is a reflexive one, namely that no one must be subjected to a normative order that cannot be adequately justified to him or her. This is the basic human right and the basic claim of justice. Thus, basic rights have no other ground than the practice of democracy has, since the aim of basic rights is to secure the status of persons as non-dominated legal, political and social equals.

A comprehensive theory of political and social justice can be constructed on this basis, something at which I can only hint here.[35] First we must make a conceptual distinction between *fundamental (minimal)* and *full (maximal) justice*. Whereas the task of fundamental justice is to construct a *basic structure of justification*, the task of full justice is to construct democratically a *justified basic structure*. The former is necessary in order to pursue the latter, that is, a "putting-into-effect" of justification through constructive, discursive democratic procedures in which the "justificatory power" is distributed as evenly as possible among the citizens. In spite of the appearance of paradox, this means that fundamental justice is a substantive starting point of procedural justice. Based on a moral right to justification, arguments are presented for the basic structure in which those who are part of it have real opportunities to co-determine the institutions of this structure, including economic and social institutions, in a reciprocal and general manner. Fundamental justice guarantees all citizens an effective status "as

---

[32] Ripstein, *Force and Freedom*, pp. 16f. and 371.
[33] See Forst, "The Justification of Basic Rights."
[34] See Chapter 7 in this volume.
[35] For a more detailed discussion, see Forst, *The Right to Justification*.

equals" in this sense. Again, the freedom of being protected in one's liberties and the freedom to co-determine that structure of liberties go hand-in-hand. The democratic institutions of a normative order have to be arranged in such a way that the reasons that guide laws and political decisions are not only publicly justified and justifiable, but that vulnerable minorities have sufficient justificatory power, whether parliamentary, plebiscitary or juridical, to veto unjustifiable majority decisions. Democracy is an arrangement for the public realization of the force "toward the better argument" within a political order.

10.4 Two conceptions of non-domination and the neo-republican machine

The Kantian republican conception I sketched suggests a discourse-theoretical notion of non-domination. Domination in the political sphere has two aspects, namely being subjected to a normative order that cannot be properly justified to you and being subjected to a normative order in which no proper institutions and possibilities of justification are in place to begin with. The second is the more grievous form of domination because it removes the structural possibility of co-determining the normative order.

How does this compare with Philip Pettit's version of neo-republicanism?[36] According to Pettit, republicanism is essentially a theory of legitimate government based on a particular idea of freedom as "non-domination," as "the social status of being relatively proof against arbitrary interference by others, and of being able to enjoy a sense of security and standing among them."[37] In contrast to freedom as mere "non-interference," non-domination is tied to being and seeing oneself as someone who is not at the mercy of others' arbitrary will, even if these others were to leave you alone most of the time. It is the *potential* of arbitrary interference against which the republican notion of self-respect and freedom is directed.[38] Hence the importance of the rule of law and of a legal status protecting persons against social and political vulnerability to the possibility of private or public arbitrary interference. The notion of freedom at work here has as its counterpart the condition of a slave, who represents the extreme case of a dominated person.

---

[36] For a comprehensive discussion, see Forst, "A Kantian Republican Conception of Justice as Nondomination."
[37] Pettit, *Republicanism*, p. vii.
[38] Ibid., pp. 5 and 22f.

Still, even though Pettit is right to stress the difference between freedom as non-interference and freedom as non-domination, a negative conception of liberty remains normatively essential in his view, for the argument for non-domination ultimately serves to secure the realm of freedom of choice of persons against arbitrary interference.[39] This is why I call it *negative republicanism*: the republican infrastructure is mainly a sheltering mechanism for individual liberty thus understood. In his republican theory, citizens are "law-checkers" interested in the security of their freedom of choice, not "law-makers," as on a Rousseauian or Kantian conception.[40] The value of democracy is essentially the instrumental value of a control mechanism to ensure the robust protection of individual freedom of choice.

This seems to establish a huge distance between my Kantian conception of republican justice as non-domination and Pettit's conception of republican freedom as non-domination. However, I would like to propose a reading – or, if you prefer, an immanent critique – of Pettit that brings him closer to the Kantian family. I think that the real force of freedom as non-domination, even in Pettit's view (correctly understood), derives from a notion of justice as justification that both grounds and defines it. Justificatory justice grounds freedom as non-domination because the basic claim of republican citizens is not one for freedom of choice generally, but for freedom from *arbitrary* – i.e., *unjust* and *unjustifiable* – rule, i.e., domination; thus, the claim is ultimately based on one's standing as a free and equal agent of justification, and it is a claim to a kind of liberty (and liberties) defined by what oneself and others can justifiably and justly ask from one another in a basic social structure. Justifiable rule, as Pettit explains in his discussion of Quentin Skinner's view championing non-interference, is *not* seen as domination, which compromises freedom;[41] only *arbitrary* rule is seen as domination, and that means *unjustifiable* rule over others, which denies their standing as free and equal agents with (what I call) a "right to justification." To be denied that right leads to the "grievance [...] of having to live at the mercy of another," which Pettit identifies as the main social and political evil;[42] and, given that interference or rule by others is not seen as an infringement of freedom if it is justifiable between equals, the notion of *justice* referring to the quality of the relations between free and

---

[39] Pettit, "Keeping Republican Freedom Simple," p. 340.
[40] Pettit, *On the People's Terms*, p. 15.
[41] Pettit, "Keeping Republican Freedom Simple."
[42] Pettit, *Republicanism*, pp. 4f.

equal participants in a justifiable political structure is central and *normatively prior* to that of freedom of choice.

Interpreting Pettit in this way might seem to be reading a Kantian notion of freedom into his approach, but only if one overlooks the implications of his distinction between domination, which compromises freedom, and the non-arbitrary rule of law, which does not; rather, that rule is seen as "conditioning" or shaping justifiable forms of freedom, which is close to Kant's view.[43] This shows that the point of republican freedom is the "full standing of a person among persons"[44] and, with explicit reference to Kant, Pettit goes on to explain: "The terrible evil brought about by domination, over and beyond the evil of restricting choice, and inducing a distinctive uncertainty is that it deprives a person of the ability to command attention and respect and so of his or her standing among persons."[45] Pettit not only introduces a Kantian notion of respect here, he also gives it priority over mere freedom of choice, because a "conditioning" of that freedom by reciprocally justifiable laws is not seen as an evil, while a huge space of freedom possibly granted by a mild dictator is. Thus, the main evil, I take it, is that of not being regarded as "a voice worth hearing and an ear worth addressing"[46] – that is, in my words, as a person with a right to justification. As Pettit formulates it: "To be a person is to be a voice that cannot properly be ignored, a voice which speaks to issues raised in common with others and which speaks with a certain authority: enough authority, certainly, for discord with that voice to give others reason to pause and think."[47] Every person is to be respected as such a justificatory authority, and this is the essential meaning of freedom as autonomy: having a *categorical* right not to be subjected to norms that cannot be reciprocally justified and thus having the positive right to co-determine these norms. Contrary to Pettit's view, however, I do not see how that kind of moral–political status can be explained in non-deontological terms. For, can we imagine a value that could trump that kind of right and status? Or a higher value or notion of the good that this status serves?[48]

One might disagree with this interpretation and hold that for Pettit individual freedom of choice, robustly secured, really is the most

---

[43] Pettit, "Keeping Republican Freedom Simple," p. 342.
[44] Ibid., p. 350.
[45] Ibid., p. 351.
[46] Ibid., p. 350.
[47] Pettit, *Republicanism*, p. 91.
[48] I must leave a discussion of the full version of Pettit's moral philosophy aside here, for which see his book *The Robust Demands of the Good*.

important value in political life and that democratic legitimacy and justice only find their place starting from there. So, if – to remind you of my thought-experiment above – there were a perfectly reliable *neo-republican machine* of non-arbitrariness that could compute, determine and robustly secure spaces of reciprocal freedom of choice that pass the "eyeball test," and maybe more determinate tests, would something be missing in a Pettitian scheme? For a Kantian republican there would, and for the Pettit who stresses "voice" and "authority," as in the quotations above, I think there would be, too, but maybe not for the Pettit who emphasizes the supreme importance of the secure private "enjoyment" of freedom of choice. Then it would remain a purely negative form of republicanism, for which political self-determination had a purely instrumental value as long as the perfect machine does not work reliably.

In a recent paper, Pettit responds to this challenge, arguing that such a "robot would have to be installed by will and if this will does not operate under a suitable system of popular control, it is a dominating presence."[49] This seems to leave open the possibility of being ruled by such a machine, provided that its installation and operation can be "suitably" controlled by a public agent, thus denying the value of autonomous agency expressing itself through democratic law-making (since the machine produces the laws). But, if the popular control that is meant here implies that any subjection to such a consequentialist machine producing the right metric of freedom of choice would amount to heteronomous and thus arbitrary rule and domination, then it relies on a notion of non-domination along the Kantian lines I suggest.

In my view and in my preferred Kantian reading of Pettit, we have gone beyond a negative conception of freedom without at the same time adopting a controversial "positive" one based on some notion of the ethical good of leading an autonomous life. Rather, it is freedom as autonomy as a form of freedom *from* unjustifiable subjection or coercion, and freedom *as* a self-determining agent of (moral as well as political) justification, which matters in a Kantian account of non-domination. There is no idea of the good life at work here. Politically speaking, this means freedom within a just(ifiable) regime, and thus it is justice as justifiability that counts – not merely as an idea but as a real practice. Freedom as non-domination is only guaranteed where democratic practices of justification exist that

[49] Pettit, "The General Will, the Common Good, and a Democracy of Standards," p. 30, fn. 18.

prevent some from dominating others. Rather than focusing on the "robust" state of not being dominated in our freedom of choice, we should focus on the *relational* freedom of being a co-determining agent of justification within the normative order that binds you. And we should do so not because the practice of justification is the only valuable practice of freedom, but because it is only through this practice that we can bring about a society in which freedom, equality and justice are autonomously and justly arrived at. Only here are we not at the mercy of masters. This is a society that honors the dignity of its members – or better, that expresses their dignity as law-makers.

10.5 Republicanism and recognition

In a note on his debate with Rawls, Habermas briefly characterizes his own understanding of Kantian republicanism, stressing the central importance of "the collective exercise of giving laws to oneself" (*gemeinsam ausgeübte Selbstgesetzgebung*). For the spheres of liberty to be justly delineated, only the public use of reason in appropriate democratic and discursive institutions is the proper medium: "In an association of free and equal persons, all members must be able to understand themselves as joint authors of laws to which they feel themselves bound individually as addressees." And, a bit more emphatically: "Nobody can be free at the expense of anybody else's freedom."[50] From such a perspective, there is no other just way to determine and realize personal independence or non-domination than through a republican system of law *and* democratic law-making based on the right to justification of agents who have a basic claim to enjoy all the rights that can be mutually and generally justified among themselves, including, first of all, the right to produce, contest and reject normative justifications. In a Kantian scheme, the structure of rights is reflexive and recursive: you have the "innate" right not to be subjected to a normative order of rights and duties that is not justifiable to you as an autonomous person and citizen. It is not that you are only "truly free" if you use that right actively, as older republican theories had it, but that you are only free if you enjoy that right as the right of rights, so to speak. At the social and political level, having that right presupposes not just appropriate collective ways of exercising it, but membership in a community of political respect and equality.

---

[50] Habermas, *The Inclusion of the Other*, p. 101.

It is at this point that Kantian reflections on the deontological nature of "having" basic rights that cannot be reasonably rejected among normative equals need to be combined with Hegelian considerations of the social conditions required to realize such rights. Axel Honneth's work is exemplary for connecting these two dimensions of social and political philosophy, thus remaining true to the legacy of German Idealism as this is continued in a left-Hegelian tradition. In all of his works, he shows that freedom must be realized in *sittliche* ("ethical") social and political forms; but the dynamics of recognition he reconstructs at the core of such forms never accept that a social horizon of recognition limits the possibilities of establishing more egalitarian, more democratic and more culturally sensitive forms of mutual recognition – in short, more justifiable forms of recognition. This is why he argues that "only in the political–democratic sphere does interaction consist in an exchange of arguments, i.e., a reflexive process." And this is why the democratic sphere needs to be enlarged and strengthened as the "sphere of reflexive self-thematization" essential for the autonomous progress of freedom.[51]

In all of this, the main insight interpreted by Habermas in a Kantian way, and by Honneth in a Hegelian way, is that genuine political and social freedom can never be attained at the expense of the other's unfreedom. It can only be realized as a practice of mutual recognition and reciprocal justification, as a practice of autonomy.

---

[51] Honneth, *Freedom's Right*, p. 331.

── Part III ──

DEBATES
Political Liberalism, Luck Egalitarianism, Contractualism and Discourse Ethics

— 11 —

POLITICAL LIBERALISM
A Kantian View*

A political conception of justice is what I call freestanding [...] when it is not presented as derived from, or as part of, any comprehensive doctrine. Such a conception of justice in order to be a moral conception must contain its own intrinsic normative and moral ideal.[1]

11.1 The familiar interpretation of *Political Liberalism*

In the following, I argue against the familiar interpretive story about Rawls's *Political Liberalism*, which asserts that it marks a complete turn away from Kant. If we follow that interpretation, we will not be able to understand Rawls's project, which is to develop a freestanding conception of justice that is justified on the basis of – non-comprehensive – principles and ideas of practical reason alone. It does not depend on any comprehensive doctrine for its validity, and it takes priority over comprehensive views, since it defines autonomously whether they are reasonable or not.

To be sure, the familiar interpretation rightly stresses the differences between Rawls's earlier Kantian theory and the later version of it. As Rawls explained, in his original theory "a moral doctrine of justice general in scope is not distinguished from a strictly political conception of justice."[2] Thus from the perspective of *Political*

---

* I am grateful to the participants of the Rawls Conference at Georgia State University in May 2016 for an extremely helpful discussion of this paper – with special thanks to Andrew Altman for his commentary. I am also indebted to Henry Richardson, Lea Ypi and two reviewers for *Ethics* for their excellent comments and suggestions.
[1] Rawls, *Political Liberalism*, p. xliv.
[2] Ibid., p. xv.

Liberalism, Rawls would no longer regard the original position as "a procedural interpretation of Kant's conception of autonomy and the categorical imperative within the framework of an empirical theory,"[3] as he did in *A Theory of Justice*. Nor would he argue for the motivational "congruence" of political and social justice and individual goodness based on the Kantian idea that "acting justly is something we want to do as free and equal rational beings," so that the "desire to act justly and the desire to express our nature as free moral persons turn out to specify what is practically speaking the same desire."[4] Within such an account of our unified "practical identity," considerations of justice guide the pursuit of all of our practical goals and thus *constitute* rather than simply *constrain* our notion of the good: "What we cannot do is express our nature by following a plan that views the sense of justice as but one desire to be weighed against others. For this sentiment reveals what the person is, and to compromise it is not to achieve for the self free reign but to give way to the contingencies and accidents of the world."[5]

It is not difficult to understand why a reflection on the core aims and history of liberalism, especially when viewed in the light of the question of toleration, as Rawls increasingly did, led him to believe that this Kantian account of the theory was not only "unrealistic"[6] but also contradictory. For it had to be a theory of justice for a *pluralistic* society, and that included, of course, a diversity of religious and philosophical doctrines. And the idea of such a society becoming a society of virtuous Kantians who struggled to liberate themselves from the contingencies of social and ethical life and regarded themselves as noumenal selves who produce values autonomously by following laws of reason seemed to go too far. The theory had to move away from the ground of comprehensive doctrines of this kind and confine itself to "political" conceptions and values that appeared "reasonable" from and "implicit"[7] within the public culture of a democratic modern society. Political liberalism had to apply the principle of toleration to itself and reduce its foundational program to one of reconstructing generally accepted conceptions of social cooperation and democratic citizenship.[8] Or so it seemed.

---

[3] Rawls, *A Theory of Justice*, p. 226.
[4] Ibid., p. 501.
[5] Ibid., p. 503. On "congruence," see especially Freeman, "Congruence and the Good of Justice." See also Weithman, *Why Political Liberalism?*, ch. 7.
[6] Rawls, *Political Liberalism*, p. xvi.
[7] Ibid., p. 13.
[8] Ibid., p. 10.

At the extreme, this alleged turn away from Kant led to interpretations such as that of Rorty, who argued that Rawls's new approach was "thoroughly historicist and antiuniversalist"[9] and simply "a historico-sociological description of the way we live now."[10] In a slightly different version, we find similar thoughts expressed by Burton Dreben, who argued that Rawls gave up all attempts to ground his theory philosophically and simply tried to work out notions implicit in our tradition of democratic thought.[11] And Dreben adds an interesting observation against which I will argue: "Kant's talk about practical reason is useless for understanding Rawls."[12]

11.2 The problem of political liberalism

In my opinion, this familiar interpretive story is wrong. For it overlooks that, as much as Rawls undeniably tried to distance himself from a presentation of his theory of justice in terms of a *comprehensive Kantian moral doctrine*, he did present it as a *non-comprehensive Kantian moral–political doctrine*, one which is compatible with a plurality of comprehensive doctrines *as long as* they share the independently defined and grounded essentials of the doctrine – that is, as long as they are *reasonable*, to use the term that does most of the Kantian work in *Political Liberalism*.[13] In my view, the kinds of conventionalist, historicist and relativistic interpretations cited cannot explain the "as long as" qualifying clause that can be found everywhere in *Political Liberalism*. In other words, they cannot explain the foundational role that a particular conception of practical reason plays in the book. I will explain this in what follows, though not without ultimately criticizing Rawls for not having found the adequate language to describe his new approach.

In order to explain the sense in which Rawls's version of political liberalism is still a Kantian view, I will begin with a brief reflection on

---

[9] Rorty, *Objectivity, Relativism, and Truth*, p. 180.
[10] Ibid., p. 185.
[11] Dreben, "On Rawls and Political Liberalism," p. 323. Another important example of a thoroughly non-foundationalist interpretation is the one presented by Wenar, "*Political Liberalism*."
[12] Ibid., p. 340.
[13] Note that my interpretation does not say that Rawls uses "Kant's ideas of practical reason" in *Political Liberalism*, which Rawls calls a "serious mistake" in his letter to his editor from 1998, reprinted in *Political Liberalism*, p. 438. In the same letter, he affirms the view held in the essay "The Idea of Public Reason Revisited," which exhibits exactly the Kantian structure of argument I highlight. I discuss this essay below.

the central problem that it addresses. As already mentioned, Rawls situates his project firmly within the liberal tradition, and especially within the liberal tradition that deals with the question of toleration. Moreover, he is right to differentiate a form of Enlightenment thought that tries to *replace* the plurality of religions with a new, secular doctrine (or a semi-secular doctrine of reasonable, "natural" religion in a deistic fashion) from other forms of Enlightenment thought, which sought to leave more room for religious diversity and *confined* themselves to political norms that did not conflict with comprehensive doctrines with respect to metaphysical questions or questions of the ultimate values to be realized in life. In my *Toleration in Conflict*,[14] I have reconstructed the discourse of toleration (in the West) and emphasized the difference between these approaches, and Rawls's work can be seen as the most recent expression of one of these strands. In section 11.5, I will show how the seventeenth-century philosopher Pierre Bayle identified the same problem that Rawls addresses and developed a proto-Kantian argument that is close to Rawls's in that it also defends an autonomous notion of reason as the basis for a conception of justice and toleration that binds persons with very different comprehensive views.

In explaining the problem, Rawls stresses from the outset that "political liberalism takes for granted not simply pluralism but the fact of reasonable pluralism."[15] Thus, while he emphasizes that the political doctrine aims to be impartial between the "points of view of reasonable comprehensive doctrines,"[16] he is never for a moment willing to compromise or qualify the meaning of reason or reasonableness with respect to the plurality of existing comprehensive doctrines. The notion of the reasonable is, so to speak, defined *a priori* or, in Rawls's language, in a "freestanding" way, that is, prior to any comprehensive doctrine and it autonomously qualifies which of these doctrines count as reasonable and which do not. It always takes normative priority. That is why at the beginning of the Introduction to *Political Liberalism*, Rawls announces that the first three lectures will "set out the general philosophical background of political liberalism in practical reason."[17] They reconstruct the Kantian program in political–*moral* terms that are *not* comprehensive. As Rawls affirms in many places in the book – and even more so in the added "Introduction to the Paperback Edition" three

[14] Forst, *Toleration in Conflict*.
[15] Rawls, *Political Liberalism*, p. xviii.
[16] Ibid., p. xix.
[17] Ibid., p. xiv.

years later, in which there are abundant passages such as the one cited above as the epigraph – the political conception is, "of course, a moral conception [...] worked out for a specific kind of subject, namely, for political, social, and economic institutions."[18]

Thus, if the question of political liberalism is "How is it possible that there may exist over time a stable and just society of free and equal citizens profoundly divided by reasonable religious, philosophical, and moral doctrines?," then the answer is that this is possible only if the theory gets the notions of reason and of reasonableness right, and, for that purpose, a Kantian (and only a Kantian) would say "that the principles and ideals of the political conception are based on principles of practical reason in union with conceptions of society and person, themselves conceptions of practical reason."[19] In other words, stability "for the right reasons"[20] can only be attained if the right reasons can be identified and vindicated by way of a reconstruction of practical reason. This is the program of political constructivism and, as I will show below, even though it differs in important ways from Kant's moral constructivism, Kantian constructivism is still its model. This is made clear by lecture III of *Political Liberalism* and by a comparison between that lecture and the full reconstruction of Kant in Rawls's text on "Themes in Kant's Moral Philosophy," which shows that the structures are identical despite the differences.[21]

As for any liberal view, the problem was, of course, to explain how the political conception, which provides the "reasonable public basis of justification on fundamental political questions,"[22] was related to the comprehensive doctrines citizens may hold. Rawls often uses the phrase that they are "somehow related"[23] to point to the problem of combining these "two views"[24] – a problem that the notion of reason has to resolve. Reason needs to take priority over comprehensive doctrines in matters of justice, but not in the same way when it comes to metaphysical or ethical matters of the good, and thus both justice and a comprehensive doctrine need to be affirmed by

---

[18] Ibid., p. 11.
[19] Ibid., p. xx.
[20] Ibid., p. xxxvii.
[21] See Rawls, "Themes in Kant's Moral Philosophy," as well as Rawls, *Lectures on the History of Moral Philosophy*, pp. 235–252. I compare the two forms of constructivism more closely in Forst, *Contexts of Justice*, ch. 4.2. See also my Introduction to the present volume and O'Neill, "Constructivism in Rawls and Kant."
[22] Rawls, *Political Liberalism*, p. xix.
[23] Ibid.
[24] Ibid., p. 140.

persons sincerely and "from the inside," so to speak. Reason has to constrain ethical comprehensive doctrines morally when it comes to matters of justice; but, at the same time, it must not colonize them when it comes to the issues that only comprehensive doctrines can answer. When we turn to Bayle, we will see how he tried to solve this problem – and how close his solution is to Rawls's view.

11.3 Kantian constructivism in *Political Liberalism*

Let us take a closer look at the Kantian character of Rawls's enterprise. A first, major issue is the "freestanding" character of the political (and this generally means: moral–political) conception of justice. That a theory of justice ought to be independent with respect to philosophical debates in metaphysics, for example, was a longstanding thesis of Rawls's dating back to the 1970s.[25] In the context of political liberalism this becomes a special, far-reaching kind of independence. Yet there are two ways to look at this. The first, *meliorating* (or accommodating) perspective, is that a freestanding conception of justice that "is neither presented as, nor as derived from"[26] a comprehensive doctrine is not in conflict with such a doctrine, since it avoids rival implications with regard to the truth regime of the doctrine (such as the existence of God, of evil, and so on). So, it is on a peaceful footing with the doctrine and can fit into it as "a module, an essential constituent part."[27] But the other perspective – let us call it the *priority* perspective – is no less, and perhaps even more, relevant. For only an independently grounded conception of norms of justice, i.e., one that is grounded on reason, can generate the normative force to determine which of the comprehensive doctrines is reasonable and which is not; it is the umpire on these questions, the only authority there can be. This is the Kantian aspect, and it is remarkable how many interpreters overlook or play down this aspect – or see it as an aberration.[28] It is the reason why Rawls can rescue his theory from the charge that it is "political in the wrong way,"[29] that it is a mere *modus vivendi* or compromise between comprehensive doctrines, and claim instead that it is a

---

[25] Rawls, "The Independence of Moral Theory." On this, see my "The Method of Insulation."
[26] Rawls, *Political Liberalism*, p. 12.
[27] Ibid.
[28] For the latter, see Wenar, "*Political Liberalism*."
[29] Rawls, *Political Liberalism*, p. 40.

"freestanding view [...] working from the fundamental idea of society as a fair system of cooperation and its companion ideas." And Rawls adds an important statement: "We leave aside comprehensive doctrines that now exist, or that have existed, or that might exist."[30] The priority view is essentially a Kantian view, following Kant in emphasizing that both the categorical imperative and the principle of right had to be grounded completely independently of any doctrine of value leading to the good life (or *Glückseligkeit*) in order to take priority over them.

This aspect of the approach culminates in the thesis of "doctrinal autonomy,"[31] which Rawls states in expounding constructivism in the lecture III, where he connects the notion of "freestanding" with that of autonomy in a Kantian way. He argues that the constructivist program "enables us to state the meaning of an autonomous political doctrine as one that represents, or displays, the political principles of justice [...] as reached by using the principles of practical reason in union with the appropriate conceptions of persons as free and equal and of society as a fair system of cooperation over time. [...] Think of this as doctrinal autonomy."[32] And, in a fashion characteristic of his non-comprehensive, political Kantianism, he adds that the view is autonomous because it is based only on the practical reason of citizens used in grounding and understanding a political conception of justice, and thus "in affirming the political doctrine as a whole we, as citizens, are ourselves autonomous, politically speaking."[33] This is the core of what Rawls calls "full autonomy" in a *political* sense – not an *ethical* conception that guides persons in their personal life choices and considerations of the good life, but nevertheless a *moral* one, because it expresses essential moral duties of citizens when it comes to fundamental questions of justice within the basic structure of the society to which they belong.

The program of an autonomous grounding of a theory of justice is laid out in the lecture on constructivism. The main idea of constructivism is to establish a procedure of construction based on practical reason to generate justifiable norms that no reasonable person can deny.[34] Rawls makes a plausible distinction between a constructivist comprehensive moral doctrine (especially Kant's own) and political constructivism, on the grounds that the latter (a) is not committed

---

[30] Ibid.
[31] Ibid., p. 98.
[32] Ibid.
[33] Ibid.
[34] See ibid., p. 90.

to the metaphysical idea that such construction produces an order of values that did not exist before (instantiating what Rawls calls "constitutive autonomy,"[35] as in Kant) and (b) does not extend to "all of life"[36] but only to political questions of justice within a basic structure. Still, while this characterization excludes metaphysical and ethical constitutivist constructivism, it does not sufficiently stress that the political construction is still a moral one, even though this is Rawls's view.[37] He failed to distinguish, as he should have, between two notions of the moral, one connected to a comprehensive doctrine (which I would prefer to call "ethical") and one connected to the grounds and normative quality of the political conception – though it is obvious that he used "moral" in both of these quite different senses.

Rawls leaves no doubt that the autonomous construction of a political conception of justice relies on a procedure – the original position – that "embodies all the relevant requirements of practical reason and shows how the principles of justice follow from the principles of practical reason in union with conceptions of society and person, themselves ideas of practical reason."[38] Like Kant,[39] Rawls believes that the procedure itself is not constructed, but is instead reconstructed or "assembled"[40] from reflection on our "powers of reason"[41] and is "laid out"[42] in designing the original position – or, in Kant's case, the categorical imperative as a procedure – its basis being "the conception of free and equal persons as reasonable and rational, a conception that is mirrored in the procedure."[43] In explaining political constructivism, Rawls uses exactly the same words as in the original Dewey Lectures, though now redefined with respect to the aim of justifying principles of justice for the basic structure of a pluralistic society, thus relying on "the fundamental idea of a well-ordered society as a fair system of cooperation between reasonable and rational citizens regarded as free and equal."[44] Rawls distinguishes *ideas* of reason such as that of society as a fair

---

[35] See ibid., p. 99.
[36] Ibid., p. 99.
[37] I argue for my own version of non-metaphysical moral or political constructivism, depending on context, in Forst, *The Right to Justification*, pt. I, and in the Introduction to the present volume.
[38] Rawls, *Political Liberalism*, p. 90.
[39] See Rawls, "Themes in Kant's Moral Philosophy," p. 99.
[40] Rawls, *Political Liberalism*, p. 108.
[41] Ibid., p. 96.
[42] Ibid., p. 103.
[43] Ibid.
[44] Ibid.

system of cooperation and that of the person with the two moral powers (explained in lectures I and II) and *principles* of practical reason as principles of using reason as well as rationality, which the original position models in a particular way by imposing reasonable constraints on the rational choice of the parties. The main notion of the reasonable is that of *reciprocity of justification*, which implies that the reasons for organizing the basic structure in a particular way have to be justifiable between free and equal citizens notwithstanding their comprehensive doctrines, solely on the basis of their common practical, public reason. This also becomes the core of the notions of legitimacy and public reason spelled out in the later lectures in the book.[45]

The Kantian character of this approach – despite the reduction to the political – is apparent in many ways, not just if one compares Rawls's analysis of Kant's constructivism[46] in detail with his own approach, where many structural parallels and common thoughts can be found almost verbatim; though I cannot offer such a detailed comparison here. An important point of commonality, despite many differences, is to be found where Rawls rejects Kant's notion of constitutive autonomy but accepts his view that "the principles of practical reason originate [...] in our moral consciousness as informed by practical reason. They derive from nowhere else."[47] Again, the independence of the political conception from comprehensive doctrines does not weaken, but instead *strengthens* its foundations, because reason is autonomous ("self-originating and self-authenticating")[48] and does not need any other normative source to bind moral persons – categorically, we may add, because no other comprehensive system of value can justifiably trump the normativity of reason and its constructions. What often sounds like a modest reduction of justificatory claims for the political conception now appears as what it is: the autonomous rule of reason for autonomous persons in the realm of political and social justice.

---

[45] In the "Introduction to the Paperback Edition," Rawls states that the "criterion of reciprocity" says that "our exercise of political power is proper only when we sincerely believe that the reasons we offer for our political action may reasonably be accepted by other citizens as a justification of those actions" (ibid., p. xlvi) and adds that the duty to follow that criterion "is a duty arising from the idea of reasonableness of persons" (ibid., fn. 14). In my own work, I explain the criterion of reciprocity in justification in a different, but related way, linking it to a categorical duty of justification; see Forst, *Justification and Critique*, chs. 1 and 4, and Forst, *The Right to Justification*, pt. I.

[46] See Rawls, "Themes in Kant's Moral Philosophy" and his *Lectures on the History of Moral Philosophy*, pp. 235–252.

[47] Rawls, *Political Liberalism*, p. 100.

[48] Ibid.

11.4 The impossibility of a practice-dependent hermeneutics

One may wonder how the Kantian character of the theory is compatible with the Rawlsian claim that the political conception relies on "fundamental ideas seen as implicit in the public political culture of a democratic society,"[49] a claim usually cited by conventionalist or historicist interpretations. But, in no way is a conventionalist program of justification lurking here. For Rawls never says that these fundamental ideas are in fact guiding current practice or are widely shared in contemporary democratic societies, nor does he say that the theory of justice uses them *because* they are generally shared or factually present. All that Rawls says is that these are ideas implicit in a democratic society *if* this society can justifiably claim to be democratic at all; and there are a number of passages where – as in his explanation of the original program of reflective equilibrium – he points out that some hard work of abstraction is required to arrive at these ideas, which are presented as ideas of practical reason, reconstructed reflexively and neither arrived at by way of a metaphysical notion of rationality nor interpreted in a conventionalist mode.

When Rawls asks how a shared basis for justifying a conception of justice can be found, he suggests that we "collect"[50] historical and present beliefs conducive to justice, such as the rejection of slavery or religious toleration, as "provisional fixed points that any reasonable conception must account for."[51] The phrase "account for" suggests that the order of justification is not from historical facts or beliefs to the justification of the theory but rather the other way around: the theory has to provide independent normative reasons for such progressive and emancipatory ideas and fit them into a general account of justice. This is the task of reflective equilibrium.[52] Normally, Rawls states, we find the public political culture "of two minds at a very deep level,"[53] and thus the theory has to be based on fundamental ideas that solve such conflicts with an eye to what justice reasonably demands. There can be no purely hermeneutic[54] or "practice-dependent"[55] grounding of principles of justice, especially

---

[49] Ibid., p. 13.
[50] Ibid., p. 8.
[51] Ibid.
[52] Ibid.
[53] Ibid., p. 9.
[54] See Walzer, *Spheres of Justice*.
[55] See Sangiovanni, "Justice and the Priority of Politics to Morality," as well as James, *Fairness in Practice*.

not if the aim is to express the "shared and public political reason"[56] of citizens, because there is no such shared reason as a fact, which historicist readings falsely assume. And, even if there were a strong consensus, that fact would not provide sufficient reason to call the consensus reasonable, since reason must be capable of criticizing any factual normative consensus. Any candidate for such consensus needs to be *argued for* with reasons that are independent of existing comprehensive doctrines and, we may add, of ideological delusions that deny the freedom and equality of persons and are not the result of free public reason guided by reciprocity. Hence, the aim of the construction is to find ideas and principles that democratic citizens "can endorse"[57] if they reason properly. The ideas and conceptions of reason are *shareable* among reasonable persons; they are not called reasonable because many people actually share them. This is where reason acquires its *critical* force, a force that can be directed against ideologies: "The criterion of reciprocity requires that when those terms are proposed as the most reasonable terms of fair cooperation, those proposing them must also think it at least reasonable for others to accept them, as free and equal citizens, and not as dominated or manipulated, or under the pressure of an inferior social position."[58]

Rawls asserts that in "political philosophy the work of abstraction is set in motion by deep political conflicts"[59] and that "we turn to political philosophy when our shared political understandings, as Walzer might say, break down, and equally when we are torn within ourselves."[60] As an example of the reflection he has in mind – and that is, of course, very different from Walzer's own, as Rawls makes clear – he cites "Alexander Stephens rejecting Lincoln's appeal to the abstraction of natural right and replying to him by saying: the North must respect the South's shared political understandings on the slavery question. Surely the reply to this will lead into political philosophy."[61] This is as anti-historicist a statement as you can make, but at the same time it is grounded in a proper historical reflection on the possible ideological use of conventionalism and the need for radical moral argument at a time when the conviction about the abolition of slavery was *not* a shared understanding. And, even

---

[56] Rawls, *Political Liberalism*, p. 9.
[57] Ibid., p. 10.
[58] Rawls, "The Idea of Public Reason Revisited," p. 770. See also *Political Liberalism*, p. xliv.
[59] Rawls, *Political Liberalism*, p. 44.
[60] Ibid.
[61] Ibid., p. 45.

if it had been, we would still need to know why this was right, apart from the fact that it was a shared belief.

Rawls goes on to remind us that "political philosophy cannot coerce our considered judgments any more than the principles of logic can,"[62] which, if you think about it, is not such a weak claim to make about what political philosophy can do.[63] But nowhere did Rawls claim that our societies are already based on ideas leading to a well-ordered society or are, as Rorty thought, to a large extent well-ordered. His exercise was a philosophical one, not a hermeneutic one of bringing out what everyone already knows and thinks. The philosophical exercise is aware that our societies are in deep conflict about justice and that philosophy, insofar as it reconstructs progressive ideas that are implicit in a democratic culture, needs to explain what it would mean to regard society "as a fair system of cooperation over time. Seen in this context, formulating idealized, which is to say abstract, conceptions of society and person connected with those fundamental ideas is essential to finding a reasonable political conception of justice."[64]

11.5 Toleration and reason

It is an important step of critical self-reflection for a liberal doctrine that aims to be compatible with a plurality of notions of the good to consider whether this is indeed the case or whether the theory is based on a doctrine that would exclude religious or metaphysical views which a liberal society should include. So that question for liberalism is far from "new," as Dreben thinks,[65] nor is it true that it had "never been said before in the history of philosophy" that only oppressive power can force a society to unite on one comprehensive doctrine. The history of toleration – not just of liberal views on toleration – abounds with such reflections.[66]

---

[62] Ibid.
[63] Ibid., p. 46. See also Rawls, "Reply to Habermas," p. 138: "No sensible view can possibly get by without the reasonable and rational as I use them. If this argument involves Plato's and Kant's view of reason, so does the simplest bit of logic and mathematics."
[64] The emphasis on the importance of abstraction is also the reason why I disagree with O'Neill's claim that the constructivist approach in *Political Liberalism* is "internal to a bounded society [...] rather than universal or cosmopolitan," i.e., "more Rousseauian than Kantian." O'Neill, "Constructivism in Rawls and Kant," p. 353.
[65] Dreben, "On Rawls and Political Liberalism," pp. 316 and 319.
[66] See my *Toleration in Conflict*, reconstructing such reflections throughout Western history.

The project of *Political Liberalism* begins with two questions which the book unites and seeks to answer. The first is the familiar one which asks what is the best conception of justice "for specifying the fair terms of cooperation between citizens regarded as free and equal."[67] The second asks what are the "grounds of toleration" for a society marked by the "fact of reasonable pluralism."[68] So the second question is not about the possibility of just any kind of toleration, including *modus vivendi* arrangements, *but* about a "ground" of toleration that is strong enough to support a free-standing conception of justice but is nevertheless compatible with a plurality of *reasonable* doctrines. Thus, it applies the principle of toleration to "philosophy itself":[69] a system of norms for social cooperation has to be fair and acceptable to all those comprehensive doctrines that respect all citizens as free and equal and seek productive social cooperation. The conception of justice has to be acceptable to all reasonable doctrines and define independently what "reasonable" means in non-comprehensive terms. Otherwise, the doctrines would quarrel endlessly about the core principles and implications of justice and no public form of reason could ever exist.

In order to understand how much this question aims at the heart of a combination of justice and toleration that has been the focus of centuries of historical struggles, allow me a historical argument that helps to arrive at the correct interpretation of the complex notion of reasonableness in *Political Liberalism*. Rawls was a great interpreter of the history of philosophy and knew Pierre Bayle, whose work is most important in this context, but did not explicitly refer to him in his discussions of toleration.[70] He found other kindred spirits, like the Bodin of the *Colloquium of the Seven*, where Bodin was one of the first to show that there can be a highly reasonable debate between very different religions and metaphysical views without one showing the others to be unreasonable or clearly wrong, judging on the basis of general laws of reason[71] – a good example for what Rawls calls "reasonable disagreement."

But it is Bayle (1647–1706) who presents a theory of toleration that is both proto-Kantian and proto-Rawlsian in important (though

---

[67] Rawls, *Political Liberalism*, p. 47.
[68] Ibid.
[69] Ibid., p. 10.
[70] Teresa Bejan kindly informed me that she has found notes on Bayle in Rawls's papers, which are stored in the Harvard Archives ("Essay and Notes on Toleration," 1950–1955, HUM 48, Box 7, Folder 16). Bejan thinks the notes (which refer to a book by Jean Delvolve on Bayle) have been dated wrongly and stem from the early 1960s.
[71] Rawls, "On My Religion." See also Forst, *Toleration in Conflict*, §12.

not all)[72] respects relevant for our discussion.[73] Bayle, as a Huguenot who suffered persecution in France and an undogmatic thinker who later also became a target of the hostility of his fellow-believers, recognized that a justification of toleration had to include a reciprocal duty of tolerance that needed to be morally justified *independently* of specific articles of religious faith. Otherwise, the endless strife over who was in the right and was allowed to coerce others in the name of the "true religion" could never be resolved. At the same time, however, such a justification should not come at the expense of the convictions of each party to the dispute that they were advocating the true faith; religious skepticism was not a viable solution. Still, it had to be possible to arrive at the shareable moral insight that it is "childish" always to insist only on one's own truth and the authority to suppress others in social conflicts, since that truth is precisely what is in dispute.[74] There had to be a form of practical reason that made it clear that, without independent and shared principles, any act of violence could be deemed godly.

Bayle develops these ideas in detail in his *Commentaire philosophique* (1685). There he argues that the "natural light" of reason, which God has implanted in all human beings independently of their religion, reveals the "most general and infallible principles" of morality: "But since passions and prejudices only too often obscure the ideas of natural equity, I would advise a person who intends to know them well to consider these ideas in general and as abstracted from all private interest and from the customs of his country."[75] One should then ask oneself whether a certain practice could meet with universal agreement: "Is such a practice just in itself? If it were a question of introducing it in a country where it would not be in use and where he would be free to take it up or not, would one see, upon examining it impartially that it is reasonable enough to merit being adopted?"[76]

Bayle argued that proponents of forced conversions and persecution were inverting the requirements of morality and turned virtues into vices. The mistake was the presumption that one has the right to

---

[72] One important difference is that Bayle did not develop a liberal political theory, as he thought that only a strong sovereign like Henri IV could provide a safe framework for social toleration.

[73] For the following, see Forst, *Toleration in Conflict*, §18. I discuss Bayle and Kant in Forst, "Religion, Reason and Toleration."

[74] Bayle, *Philosophical Commentary*, pp. 13f. For the French version, see Bayle, "Commentaire Philosophique."

[75] Ibid., p. 31.

[76] Ibid., p. 30.

impose the true religion by force, so that violence suddenly becomes "good" or "salutary." According to Bayle, this is "the most abominable doctrine that has ever been imagined."[77] With this argument, anyone could turn any position on its head:

> If one would say, 'it is very true, Jesus Christ has commanded His Disciples to persecute, but that is none of your business, you who are heretics. Executing this commandment belongs only to us who are the true Church,' they would answer that they are agreed on the principle but not in the application and that they alone have the right to persecute since truth is on their side. [...] When one reflects on all this impartially, one is reduced necessarily to this rare principle, I have truth on my side, therefore my violences are good works. So and so errs: therefore his violences are criminal. To what purpose, pray, are all these reasonings? Do they heal the evils which persecutors commit, or are they capable of making them reconsider? Is it not absolutely necessary in order to cure the furor of a zealot who ravages a whole country or to make him comprehend his doings, to draw him out of his particular controversies and remind him of principles which are common to both parties such as the maxims of morality, the precepts of the Decalogue, of Jesus Christ and of His Apostles, concerning justice, charity, abstinence from theft, murder, injuries to our neighbour, etc.?[78]

There are two key components of Bayle's argument for toleration: the *normative* component of the morality of reciprocity and the *epistemological* component of the non-demonstrability of the undeniably true faith by means of reason alone. For violence on "natural" moral concepts remains mere violence, and the claim to speak for the unquestionably true religion cannot be redeemed by "natural" reason on grounds that *cannot be reasonably rejected*. According to Bayle, it is not just a matter of appealing to an independent, rational sense of morality that is free from fanatical distortions and is shared by all human beings, in order to be able to differentiate moral from religious truths. It is also a matter of undercutting religious disputes by showing that, although they are not pointless, they cannot be resolved here on earth by rational means alone. This calls for a conception of the *finitude of reason*, which states that disagreements among finite rational beings in questions of faith are unavoidable.

Bayle defends a conception of finite practical and theoretical reason whose guiding assumption is that reason must recognize its own limits regarding "speculative truths." This opens up the space for metaphysical or religious conflict between positions that can be

---

[77] Ibid., p. 47.
[78] Ibid., pp. 84f.

reasonably held, but can also be *reasonably rejected*. The reason is that "evidence is a relative quality" especially in religious matters.[79] Habit, training, or other factors mean that rational individuals arrive at very different evaluations and judgments. A reasonable person is aware, we might say here, of the "burdens of reason" (or "judgment"), to use Rawls's phrase, and, according to Bayle, knows that "difference in opinion [is] man's inherent infelicity, as long as his understanding is so limited and his heart so inordinate."[80] Therefore, the desire that all human beings should unite in one religion will remain unfulfilled, and the reasonable response is to espouse toleration. Rational human beings recognize that their reason is finite and that religious differences are rationally unresolvable.

This is the central theme of Bayle's *Dictionnaire historique et critique* (1696).[81] His main concern in this work is to create room for religious answers to metaphysical questions by placing limits on the force of reason. This cuts the ground out from under dogmatic disputes about and alleged proofs of the "true faith," without faith, which remains within the boundaries of what can be rationally debated, becoming empty or irrational as a result. Both sides, reason and faith, must heed their respective limits: reason recognizes its limitations in speculative matters to which faith alone can provide further answers; and faith does not try to present and impose its "truths" as conclusive matters that are beyond reasonable dispute. Reasonable faith knows that it is a *faith*; it is aware that "the mysteries of the Gospels are above reason [*au-dessus de la Raison*]." That is an insight, Bayle continues, into the "limits" of reason which "can never attain to what is above it."[82]

11.6 Relating the political conception and comprehensive doctrines in the right way

If we take the two main – normative and epistemological – aspects of Bayle's theory of toleration based on reason into account, it becomes apparent how they help us to understand the two aspects of the reasonable in Rawls's account in Lecture Two of *Political Liberalism*. Like Bayle, Rawls distinguishes between a normative

---

[79] Ibid., p. 93.
[80] Ibid., p. 141.
[81] Bayle, *Historical and Critical Dictionary*, p. 409. For the French version, see Bayle, "Choix d'articles tirés du Dictionnaire historique et critique."
[82] Ibid., pp. 410f.

and an epistemological aspect of the reasonable, with the first being accorded priority (given the priority of practical reason).[83] The first aspect says that persons are reasonable "when, among equals say, they are ready to propose principles and standards as fair terms of cooperation and to abide by them willingly, given the assurance that others will likewise do so."[84] The second aspect is "the willingness to recognize the burdens of judgment and to accept their consequences for the use of public reason in directing the legitimate exercise of political power in a constitutional regime."[85] These are precisely the two aspects of reason that Bayle thought were necessary to establish, in Rawlsian language, a "public and shared basis of justification"[86] for the normative basic structure of a pluralistic society and to explain how reasonable citizens can respect each other as reasonable and politically autonomous and cooperative agents, even though they differ deeply in their comprehensive doctrines. Insofar as we are reasonable, we recognize in particular "that our own [comprehensive] doctrine has, and can have, for people generally, no special claims on them beyond their own view of its merits. Others who affirm doctrines different from ours are, we grant, reasonable also, and certainly not unreasonable."[87]

This is the same lesson that Bayle's reflection on the difference between reason and faith was intended to teach, and both Bayle and Rawls extend this to other metaphysical disputes about, say, the sources of evil or the ultimate meaning of life. Reason has a stake in these debates, insofar as it tries to draw the line between reasonable forms of faith and unreasonable, that is, immoral and irrational (superstitious) ones; but by its own powers it cannot resolve these debates – it can neither prove nor finally reject any of the reasonable doctrines. But reason remains aware of its own powers when it comes to matters of morality – and, in Rawls's case, we should say, to matters of political morality, which is one of the differences from Bayle, who had a more expansive conception of the realm of morality. So, my point is not to deny that Bayle, both in this expansion and in his own seventeenth-century rationalistic view of the sources of reason, was also defending a "comprehensive" doctrine in some way. My point is that, in an early form, he saw exactly the problems of

---

[83] This is why Rawls, *Political Liberalism*, p. 62, says that being reasonable "is not an epistemological idea (though it has epistemological elements)."
[84] Ibid., p. 49.
[85] Ibid., p. 54.
[86] Ibid., p. 61.
[87] Ibid., p. 60.

grounding a scheme of justice and toleration on a doctrine that rivals with religious ones on the same level.

It is striking how close Rawls's explanation of the "burdens of judgment" is to Bayle's explanation of the fact of a reasonable plurality of religious and metaphysical views, by reminding us of relative evidence, habit, different upbringing, and so on. Rawls lists exactly the same difficulties in assessing evidence, difference in evaluations, indeterminacy in hard cases, the influence of biographical experience and socialization on our judgments, when he lists the limits "to the theoretical uses of our reason."[88] Reflection on the limits of reason in metaphysical and religious matters already makes one aware that "reasonable disagreement" is a normal condition of life, especially in a pluralistic society, but reciprocity of justification does not automatically follow from this. For this, the first aspect of practical reason is essential. Here are the Baylean conclusions drawn by Rawls:

> [T]hose who insist, when fundamental political questions are at stake, on what they take as true but others do not, seem to others simply to insist on their own beliefs when they have the political power to do so. Of course, those who do insist on their beliefs also insist that their beliefs alone are true: they impose their beliefs because, they say, their beliefs are true and not because they are their beliefs. But this is a claim all equally could make; it is also a claim that cannot be made good by anyone to citizens generally. [...] It is unreasonable for us to use political power, should we possess it, [...] to repress comprehensive views that are not unreasonable.[89]

Rawls has often been criticized for the seeming "schizophrenia"[90] of his idea that citizens regard other views they find wrong (insofar as they consider the comprehensive doctrine they themselves hold to be true) nevertheless to be reasonable in practical and theoretical terms. Others have described this view – and the reduction of the truth claims of the political conception – as one of "epistemic abstinence," which mistakes political philosophy for some kind of accommodating politics.[91] But there is nothing contradictory or empty here;

---

[88] Ibid., p. 56.
[89] Ibid., p. 61. It is interesting that Rawls, directly after the remark about claims to religious dominance and before the (thoroughly Baylean) reciprocity counter-argument, inserts a footnote citing Bishop Bossuet defending Catholic persecution by appealing to religious truth after the Edict of Nantes had been revoked in 1685 – the same Bossuet whom Bayle attacked in his *Commentaire* written in the same year, a famous speech by the bishop having provided Bayle with the reason to begin the book.
[90] Mulhall and Swift, *Liberals and Communitarians*, p. 178.
[91] Raz, "Facing Diversity."

Rawls simply explains, as any liberal should, how a devout Catholic can respect a Muslim as an equal and reasonable citizen, while still rejecting Islamic faith as false. He shows precisely the possibility of what Brian Barry doubted, namely that "certainty from the inside about some view can coherently be combined with the line that it is reasonable for others to reject that same view."[92] As Bayle and Rawls argue, the kind of toleration that goes along with this is not doomed to skepticism, as you retain your belief in the truth of your doctrine if you respect others as not unreasonable.[93] But if it is a religious doctrine and you think that it is demonstrably the *only* one reasonable persons can hold with good, rational reasons, you are being dogmatic and have not understood the nature of religious faith and disagreement as viewed from a reasonable perspective. Rawls provides an insight into the core of the connection between reason, justice and toleration, and it in no way diminishes either the truth claims of religions (as some worry) or the independent grounding of his own conception (as others worry). But this becomes apparent only if one understands the notion of the reasonable in all of its facets and strengths. This is what Bayle and Rawls share with Kant, whose philosophy brings out the autonomy of reason in all its clarity.[94]

Arguing that there is nothing schizophrenic about relating the "two views"[95] of citizens, as Rawls expresses it, does not mean that there is an easy explanation of how this is achieved within the perspective of one and the same person. Rawls addresses this issue in terms of the notion of an "overlapping consensus," which plays an important role in explaining the stability of a well-ordered pluralistic society after the foundations in practical reason have been laid out. But the account of stability generated by an overlapping consensus has often been misunderstood, as though the only grounds for accepting the political conception were those from within the comprehensive doctrine, leaving no shared moral substance to the conception of justice.[96] For, from the start, we speak only of a "reasonable overlapping

---

[92] Barry, *Justice as Impartiality*, p. 179.
[93] The burdens of judgment do not deny, as Wenar, "*Political Liberalism*," p. 46, believes, that religious truth is "accessible to all clear minds and open hearts." They only imply that religious faith requires "a religious assent of the soul" (ibid., p. 45, citing the Catholic teaching of *Lumen gentium* from 1964) that reason alone cannot produce, as it requires belief in divine revelation.
[94] I won't discuss Kant's view of toleration at this point, but see Forst, *Toleration in Conflict*, §21.
[95] Rawls, *Political Liberalism*, p. 140.
[96] Among many others, see Weithman, *Why Political Liberalism?*, p. 308.

consensus,"[97] which neither is a *modus vivendi* compromise nor comes about by "striking a balance" between existing comprehensive doctrines; rather, according to Rawls, "we formulate a freestanding political conception having its own intrinsic (moral) political ideal expressed by the criterion of reciprocity."[98] Rawls considers the "values of the special domain of the political" as a "subdomain of the realm of all values"[99] and leaves the latter to be comprehensively determined by the various ethical doctrines; but as reasonable doctrines they all accept that the political values "normally outweigh whatever values may conflict with them."[100] This is because the "values of the political are very great values and hence not easily overridden":[101] they constitute the shared framework of political and social life for citizens, and reasonable citizens know that they *owe* each other the duty to establish and preserve justice when it comes to this framework. This is what their sense of justice, as an essential characteristic of citizens, tells them. So it is not correct to say that the overlapping consensus is the only answer to the question of stability that Rawls addresses in the second part of *Political Liberalism*, for in this context he also reminds us of the independent normative quality of the "ideal of citizenship"[102] and its motivating force: "[C]itizens in a well-ordered society acquire a normally sufficient sense of justice so that they comply with its just arrangements."[103] Hence just as the "principles of justice are not affected in any way by the particular comprehensive doctrines that may exist in society,"[104] so too citizens are autonomously motivated to accept these principles. This is the meaning of "full autonomy" discussed above.

Thus, when Rawls explains the different comprehensive grounds – some religious, some based on moral doctrines – and shows how reasonable citizens affirm the political conception from within their own view, he is not saying that these are the *only* grounds on which they do so. For, insofar as they are reasonable, they always recognize their duties of justice, and they accept the political conception as a "moral conception."[105] In a crucial passage, where Rawls argues (again) against the *modus vivendi* interpretation, he adds that the

---

[97] Rawls, *Political Liberalism*, p. xlvii.
[98] Ibid.
[99] Ibid., p. 139.
[100] Ibid.
[101] Ibid.
[102] Ibid., p. 84.
[103] Ibid., p. 141.
[104] Ibid.
[105] Ibid., p. 147.

political conception as a moral conception "is affirmed on moral grounds, that is, it includes conceptions of society and of citizens as persons, as well as principles of justice, and an account of the political virtues through which those principles are embodied in human character and expressed in public life."[106] It is with these grounds in place that citizens also draw on their comprehensive doctrines when they affirm the political conception, and Rawls says that this "does not make their affirming it any less religious, philosophical or moral,"[107] which follows from a successful integration of the political conception into a comprehensive doctrine as a "module, an essential constituent part"[108] of that doctrine. But that does not mean that by doing so persons are no longer aware of the political values and the moral character of the conception as binding on reasonable citizens generally: there is no *gestalt shift* in the reasons from the moral–political conception to the comprehensive doctrine; rather, the comprehensive doctrine shows its reasonableness by *integrating* and at the same time *preserving* the binding force of the conception of justice. This is why, as Rawls goes on to say, "those who affirm the various views supporting the political conception will not withdraw their support from it should the relative strength of their view in society increase and eventually become dominant."[109] Hence, they will accord justice priority over the good, even if their religion tells them something different, since they know that it would be unreasonable and unjust to do otherwise. That priority could not be upheld and affirmed if the political conception was no longer an independent moral force. Another passage makes this clear: "Thus the political conception can be seen as part of a comprehensive doctrine but it is *not a consequence of that doctrine's nonpolitical values*. Nevertheless, its political values normally outweigh whatever other values oppose them, at least under the reasonably favorable conditions that make a constitutional democracy possible."[110] So, we must not misunderstand what it means to "apply the principles of toleration to philosophy itself":[111] it means to seek moral grounds for a political conception of justice that citizens cannot reasonably reject (to use Scanlon's phrase) and that leave room for all of the religious or ethical or metaphysical answers to questions that point beyond

---

[106] Ibid.
[107] Ibid., pp. 148f.
[108] Ibid., p. 12.
[109] Ibid., p. 148.
[110] Ibid., p. 155 (emphasis R.F.).
[111] Ibid., p. 154.

the realm of the reasonably non-rejectable without thereby being unreasonable.[112] "Thus, the values that conflict with the political conception of justice and its sustaining virtues may be normally outweighed because they come into conflict with the very conditions that make fair social cooperation possible on a footing of mutual respect."[113] Only a Kantian reading, I believe, can make sense of the meaning and priority of "mutual respect" mentioned here.

In his "Reply to Habermas,"[114] Rawls also asserts that there is an independent *pro tanto* justification of the political conception of justice "without looking to, or trying to fit, or even knowing what are, the existing comprehensive doctrines."[115] In "full justification," that conception gets "embedded" into the comprehensive doctrines of persons individually, and that responds to the task of relating political and non-political values in the right way, for which, Rawls affirms, the political conception gives no ethical or comprehensive guidance. Reason, however, which defines a reasonable comprehensive doctrine, does provide such guidance: it integrates the political conception and the other comprehensive aspects of the doctrine in the proper way, because the doctrine is reasonable not just from the perspective of an outside observer's description but also, so to speak, "from the inside," as a personal–political, reflexive point of view. This is why "public justification" can take place on a third level of justification, where citizens debate issues of justice and where "the shared political conception is the common ground."[116] And, indeed, we should ask: how would that kind of public justification, or what Rawls calls the exercise of "public reason," be possible if the political conception did not serve as such a common ground, constraining other aspects of the comprehensive doctrines?

Rawls's view of public reason changed over time as regards the question of how permissive it could be of reasons that stem from comprehensive doctrines and that are not based on political values of the political conception alone (when it comes to essential questions of justice).[117] But, be that as it may, the whole approach presupposes an "ideal of citizenship"[118] where citizens give strict priority to political values and reasons and accept – as the liberal principle of legitimacy

---

[112] I present my own theory of toleration as a "tolerant" one in my *Toleration in Conflict*, pt. II.
[113] Rawls, *Political Liberalism*, p. 157.
[114] I discuss the debate between the two in detail in Forst, *The Right to Justification*, ch. 3.
[115] Rawls, "Reply to Habermas," p. 145.
[116] Ibid., p. 144.
[117] I discuss this in Forst, *Contexts of Justice*, ch. 3.1.
[118] Rawls, *Political Liberalism*, p. 213.

asserts – that "our exercise of political power is proper and hence justifiable only when it is exercised in accordance with a constitution the essentials of which all citizens may reasonably be expected to endorse in the light of principles and ideals acceptable to them as reasonable and rational."[119] Here we see that the justification of the political conception in the constructivist procedure also grounds the very possibility of political legitimacy and justification. For, if citizens were completely caught up in their comprehensive doctrines as their only view, the exercise of public justification would be a burden they could not shoulder; in fact, they would lack the perspective on which it relies, the perspective of a shared conception of justice. So, they accept the "duty of civility" to act in accordance with the principle of legitimacy as "a moral, not a legal, duty."[120] And, even in the "wide" view of public reason that Rawls later espoused,[121] citizens have the duty and ability to distinguish between comprehensive and public reasoning, and comprehensive views may only be introduced in public reasoning "provided that in due course public reasons, given by a reasonable political conception, are presented sufficient to support whatever the comprehensive doctrines are introduced to support."[122] Again, it is not conceivable that persons could be held to this duty if they did not have an independent and effective understanding and sense of justice based on practical reason – a capacity all citizens are seen as sharing. Otherwise, as Bayle, Kant and Rawls fear, a public conception of justice would not develop; rather, questions of justice would be the subject of constant conflicts between comprehensive doctrines. Justice may be, to use a metaphor, a diamond that shines in different colors depending on the plurality of comprehensive views directed at it, but its intrinsic worth does not depend on the light shone on it by the comprehensive views.

11.7 Ambiguities

In conclusion, I would like – making a long story very short – to remark on a fundamental ambiguity in Rawls's theory at which I already hinted.[123] I hope to have shown that *Political Liberalism*

---

[119] Ibid., p. 217.
[120] Ibid.
[121] See Rawls, "The Idea of Public Reason Revisited," and Rawls, *Political Liberalism*, p. l.
[122] Rawls, *Political Liberalism*, pp. xlix–l.
[123] For my earlier critique of this, see Forst, "Review of John Rawls' *Political Liberalism*," and Forst, *Contexts of Justice*, ch. 4.2. A similar ambiguity, though not criticized

is best read as a Kantian view; that is, as one that conceptualizes a non-comprehensive, autonomous, morally grounded theory of political and social justice for a pluralistic society. It is non-comprehensive in that it neither rests on some metaphysical notion of human nature nor seeks to give guidance on questions of the good life. It is autonomous in that it is based on practical reason as the capacity of autonomous citizens who respect each other as free and equal to reciprocally and generally justify and accept principles of justice. And it is moral insofar as it has an independent normative force that is strong enough to outweigh other, competing values.

The problem, however, is that Rawls did not fully develop the conceptual tools he required for this project. Most importantly, he did not distinguish between Kantian constructivism in moral theory all the way down (e.g., as denying moral realism, for example) and Kantian constructivism in political theory as a matter of avoiding metaphysical claims as well as norms governing life as a whole. But above all, Rawls did not find a terminology for distinguishing between the notion of morality he required and used for the political conception and the notion of morality that was part of a comprehensive view. One could follow Habermas and others like Dworkin or Williams and use "moral" – or better: moral–political – for the first and "ethical" for the second, or phrase this in some other way. There are different ways to conceptualize this terminologically, but to avoid ambiguities a distinction needs to be made. For as much as Rawls stressed that the political conception is a "moral" conception that contains "its own intrinsic normative and moral ideal,"[124] he also emphasized that the political conception is affirmed on "moral" grounds stemming from the comprehensive doctrines of persons.[125] Of course, both can be the case, depending on how one looks at it, since from a personal perspective a conception of justice can be affirmed on more than one ground as long as there is the required "common ground" between citizens; but, by not making the difference more explicit, Rawls did not distinguish clearly between these different meanings of the word "moral." Thus, at times his Kantianism is more veiled than outspoken.

Still, the justification, design and implications of the theory are best explained by regarding it as having a non-comprehensive Kantian character. One may think, as I do, that such an approach

---

from a Kantian perspective, is pointed out by Larmore, *The Morals of Modernity*, pp. 149–152.
[124] Rawls, *Political Liberalism*, p. xliv.
[125] See ibid., p. 148.

is the most promising one for theorizing political and social justice, and one may think, as I also do, that Rawls's approach exhibits a number of problems we ought to avoid.[126] But he was right that any such approach needs to apply the principle of toleration to itself in the right way, responding to (reasonable) ethical pluralism, while still holding onto a moral–political conception of justice based on practical reason. For what better ground can a theory of justice have than that one?

---

[126] I discuss these in Forst, *Contexts of Justice*, chs. 3 and 4, as well as in Forst, *The Right to Justification*, ch. 3. See also my "The Method of Insulation."

— 12 —

THE POINT OF JUSTICE
On the Paradigmatic Incompatibility Between Rawlsian "Justice as Fairness" and Luck Egalitarianism*

John Rawls famously claimed that we need to look for a "conception of justice that nullifies the accidents of natural endowment and the contingencies of social circumstance as counters in quest for social and economic advantage," as these aspects are "arbitrary from a moral point of view."[1] Luck egalitarians believe that a conception of justice that eliminates the effects of circumstance but not of choice or, in Ronald Dworkin's words, that is "endowment-insensitive" and "ambition-sensitive,"[2] captures that intuition better than Rawls's own principles of justice. G. A. Cohen even went so far as to say that Rawls "was not (really) investigating the nature of justice as such"[3] when he stopped pursuing his luck egalitarian intuition and went into the business of constructing "rules of social regulation,"[4] which took many other things into account besides pure justice.[5]

In what follows, I argue that the opposite is the case. As I show in section 12.1, we can learn from Rawls that one cannot overcome moral arbitrariness in social life by using or implementing a morally arbitrary distinction between choice and circumstance or between ambition and endowment, which is why he never made use of such a distinction in his conception of justice. Rather, Rawls argued that principles of justice should be *chosen* (or constructed) in an

---

* I am grateful to Sarah Roberts-Cady, Jon Mandle, Amadeus Ulrich, Felix Kämper and Ciaran Cronin for their helpful comments and questions.
[1] Rawls, *A Theory of Justice*, p. 15. In this chapter, references will be to the original edition of *A Theory of Justice*, as this was the version to which the debates I discuss refer.
[2] Dworkin, *Sovereign Virtue*, p. 89.
[3] Cohen, *Rescuing Justice and Equality*, p. 301.
[4] Ibid., p. 285.
[5] See also Kymlicka, *Contemporary Political Philosophy*, ch. 3.1.

"original position" that "ensures that no one is advantaged or disadvantaged in the choice of principles by the outcomes of natural chance or the contingency of social circumstances."[6] That does not mean that these principles eradicate such chances or circumstances or compensate persons for "brute luck" and honor their "option luck";[7] rather, it means that the chosen principles deny that persons have any prerogative in virtue of "natural" or "social" luck, *whatever* such luck is based on, whether it be chance or choice.

In section 12.2, I argue that the incompatibility between these two approaches points to a deeper difference between a deontological and a teleological paradigm that is relevant for the debate between relational and non-relational notions of political and social justice.

12.1 The impossibility of overcoming moral arbitrariness in a morally arbitrary way

One of the major points of Rawls's theory is that there are no valid claims of justice *before* a properly constructed conception of justice is in place that is justifiable between persons without regard to natural luck or social contingency. This is what libertarian critics like Robert Nozick[8] took issue with, especially with Rawls's claim "to regard the distribution of natural talents as a common asset and to share in the benefits of this distribution whatever it turns out to be. Those who have been favored by nature, whoever they are, may gain from their good fortune only on terms that improve the situation of those who have lost out."[9] In the eyes of these critics, this would amount to expropriating individuals and would turn them into the servants of society. And, indeed, for Rawls there is no pre-social ground – or, better, no ground prior to the construction of a suitable conception of justice – for any claim to what is justly "yours" or what you deserve. According to Rawls, "no one deserves his greater natural capacity nor merits a more favorable starting place in society. But it does not follow that one should eliminate these distinctions. There is another way to deal with them."[10] This "other way" is the way of justice, and Rawls does not argue for this way as a practical concession to

---

[6] Rawls, *A Theory of Justice*, p. 12
[7] Dworkin, *Sovereign Virtue*, p. 73.
[8] Nozick, *Anarchy, State, and Utopia*.
[9] Rawls, *A Theory of Justice*, p. 101. On this point, see also his more extensive discussion in Rawls, *Justice as Fairness*, pp. 75–78.
[10] Rawls, *A Theory of Justice*, p. 102.

what is feasible in human society; rather, his idea is to construct a system of social cooperation in which talents can develop and claims of entitlement can be raised, but only on the basis of a conception of justice that follows a strict imperative of reciprocal and general justification between moral and political equals.

So luck egalitarianism, as seen from a Rawlsian perspective, commits a number of errors.

12.1.1 Against pre-social considerations of (in-)justice

First, it starts either from a pre-social notion of "brute bad luck" that serves as a basis for claims to compensation or from a pre-social notion of "ambition" that serves as a ground of justice claims. But that runs counter to Rawls's essentially social perspective on both phenomena. He argues that the "natural distribution is neither just nor unjust; nor is it unjust that persons are born into society at some particular position. These are simply natural facts. What is just and unjust is the way that institutions deal with these facts."[11] There are no "natural" justice claims – neither for compensation nor that ambition or choice should be honored. Will Kymlicka, for example, argues that people with "natural handicaps," similar to people born into a "disadvantaged class or race,"[12] should be compensated for their disadvantage. But there is nothing "natural" about handicaps when it comes to matters of justice. A just society does not compensate persons for a natural injustice; rather, it removes the socially established barriers and (ideally) the assumptions that put people in a descriptive box of the "handicapped." "Natural" differences are an issue for justice because society turns them into social disadvantages; but then the persons affected are not owed compensation for "natural" bad luck but are instead owed the means to be a participating member of society to the greatest extent possible.[13]

The other side of the coin of the pre-social and pre-political view of the grounds of justice claims found in luck egalitarianism is the idea that the choices or ambitions of individuals should be sufficiently honored, assuming that there is some objective measure of "sufficiently." Kymlicka, for example, raises the issue that the difference principle, which states that all inequalities must be justifiable to the

---

[11] Ibid.
[12] Kymlicka, *Contemporary Political Philosophy*, pp. 72f.
[13] This does not imply that the way Rawls dealt with disabilities was adequate; for a critique, see Nussbaum, *Frontiers of Justice*.

worst off as contributions to their greatest benefit, does not take into account the claim of a person who says: "What if I was not born into a privileged social group, and was not born with any special talents, and yet by my own choices and effort have managed to secure a larger income than others?"[14] According to an "ambition-sensitive" luck egalitarianism, this larger income is justified. But, according to Rawls it is not, because the claim this person makes falls under the verdict of the moral arbitrariness of any desert or entitlement claim that is raised outside the context of a system of fair social cooperation.

Luck egalitarians try to adopt and use a libertarian argument for egalitarian purposes[15] – but, in fact, they fall prey to a libertarian idea that gives a prerogative to individual claims as naturalized asocial claims to be rewarded for one's own efforts unaided by circumstance. In Rawls's view, this is a natural desert claim that has no status as a justice claim – not only because there are no "natural" justice claims of such a kind but also because the distinction between "pure" effort (and choice) and the benefit from personal or social advantage (as circumstance) is, to use Samuel Scheffler's apt phrase, "philosophically dubious and morally implausible."[16] Which brings me to the next point: the distinction is morally arbitrary in Rawls's sense.

12.1.2 Choice or circumstance?

Luck egalitarian writers such as Dworkin are well aware of the difficulties in distinguishing between "choice" and "circumstance." Choices, Dworkin argues, reflect a person's ambition and character: the ambitions "include all his tastes, preferences and convictions as well as his overall plan of life,"[17] while someone's character includes personality traits, such as "energy, industry, doggedness, and ability to work now for distant rewards,"[18] that affect the pursuit of ambitions. Someone's circumstances, on the other hand, "consist of his personal and his impersonal resources" such as, among the personal ones, "physical and mental health and ability – his general fitness and capacities, including his wealth-talent, that is, his innate

---

[14] Kymlicka, *Contemporary Political Philosophy*, p. 58.
[15] Cohen, *On the Currency of Egalitarian Justice and Other Essays in Political Philosophy*, p. 32.
[16] Scheffler, *Equality and Tradition*, p. 187.
[17] Dworkin, *Sovereign Virtue*, p. 322.
[18] Ibid.

capacity to produce goods or services that others will pay to have."[19] According to Dworkin, persons are responsible for their choices as well as for their character traits, but not for their circumstances. And he adds that there are often "formidable difficulties in deciding whether someone's failure to find employment at a decent wage is a consequence of his lack of wealth-talent or his lack of industry and application, for example."[20]

This raises a number of questions. The most important is: Can one ever reliably make such distinctions? How have my tastes, preferences and convictions been formed, and are they really not just grounds of my choices but *chosen* grounds of my choices, such that I am responsible for these choices and the character traits on which they are based? And is talent an "innate" force within me, such that the way it has been formed and developed is pure circumstance and not part of my character, reflecting certain choices? If one traces decisions as choices back to their sources, will one not find many circumstances, and if one traces someone's circumstances, will one not find many choices? And the more one traces both, the more the line between them gets blurred to the point of becoming effaced altogether. And the more one tries to draw the distinction in spite of the never-ending mixtures of the two, the more arbitrary it becomes. Since the distinction does a lot of work in moral and political assessments, its application becomes morally arbitrary in Rawls's sense by attaching moral value to a distinction that arbitrarily carves out a space of "pure" choice within an inextricable genealogical combination of personality and social context in a given case. According to Rawls, "character depends in large part upon fortunate family and social circumstances for which [one] can claim no credit."[21] There is no place in Rawls's theory for the idea of pure choice or ambition or character for which one is solely responsible, "since the initial endowment of natural assets and the contingencies of their growth and nurture in early life are arbitrary from a moral point of view. [...] Once again [...], it seems clear that the effort a person is willing to make is influenced by his natural abilities and skills and the alternatives open to him."[22] Thus, the distinction between "energy" or "industry" as choice-related character traits and endowment or talent as circumstance breaks down, because persons are not "unencumbered" agents of free choice.

[19] Ibid., pp. 322f.
[20] Ibid., p. 324.
[21] Rawls, *A Theory of Justice*, p. 104.
[22] Ibid., pp. 311f.

This does not mean that Rawls did not hold persons responsible for their choices, since he stresses the autonomy of persons as having two moral powers, namely the capacity for a conception of the good and the capacity for a sense of justice. But Rawls was aware that ascribing responsibility is a matter of a practical attitude of respect toward the other as an equal moral agent, and that this normally means not considering whether a person is guided in her acts by choice or circumstance but assuming that she takes responsibility for her ends, whether chosen or inherited, as in cases of what has been called "expensive tastes": "That we can take responsibility for our ends is part of what free citizens may expect of one another. Taking responsibility for our tastes and preferences, whether or not they have arisen from our actual choices, is a special case of that responsibility."[23]

12.1.3 A dystopia of control

Following Elizabeth Anderson and Jonathan Wolff,[24] I also think that it would be disrespectful, and to some extent unjust, to establish a social order on the distinction between choice and circumstance if – on a counterfactual assumption – we could make it.

A luck egalitarian society could be a veritable dystopia of control and mistrust involving the administration of harsh sanctions or broad compensation schemes. All of this violates basic norms of equal respect. First, think of the level and degree of information needed to discover whether some action with consequences relevant for social justice was due to choice or circumstance. That would entail "insulting levels of scrutiny," as Wolff argues,[25] since it would require a panopticon-like institution of social analysis that tracked the actions of persons as regards their motives and deeper causes. The state might have to enforce a daily protocol on persons to list their reasons for doing this and that and the risks as they saw them, but these protocols would have to be checked by authorities with profound knowledge of the person, the situation, and so on. Such a state would be authoritarian in two respects – on the one hand, because of the intrusion into people's lives, and on the other hand

---

[23] Rawls, *Political Liberalism*, p. 185.
[24] Anderson, "What Is the Point of Equality?," and Wolff, "Fairness, Respect, and the Egalitarian Ethos."
[25] Ibid., p. 112.

because of the sanctioning and punitive implication with which this was being done.

This leads to the second reason why such a system would be far from establishing justice as based on mutual respect. If the disciplining administration found out that you were reckless or careless in your actions and, as a result, had an accident that, for example, caused you severe health damage, the luck egalitarian system would regard this as a consequence of your choices, provided that you could not show why your decision really had deeper causes you could not control, such as a bad upbringing or a risk gene. The state would have to differentiate, as Anderson criticizes,[26] between cases of people with severe health problems according to their responsibility for those problems, so that an active smoker would be treated differently from a passive smoker if they both developed lung diseases. Society would turn into a system of blame or excuse, guilt or innocence, with respect to every relevant instance of distribution. For the blameworthy, this would be a very bad combination of an authoritarian and a libertarian state.

That has an implication for the rewarding side of a libertarian-plus-luck-egalitarian system. If persons are successful in their economic activities without being aided by circumstance (another huge counterfactual), as in Kymlicka's aforementioned example, then, according to the luck egalitarian view, they deserve their special gains as claims of justice. But that could establish social reward systems and hierarchies that are not acceptable from a Rawlsian perspective, because they honor desert claims of dubious justifiability.

A third reason for why such a system would fail to show appropriate respect for individuals as autonomous sources of claims is that it turns claims of justice into claims for compensation, either for the lack of certain personal endowment or for social circumstances that had negative consequences. As Anderson convincingly shows,[27] state agencies explaining to persons why they should be compensated for being physically disabled, less intelligent or less beautiful than dictated by social norms would be demeaning and reproduce exclusive stereotypes. With respect to the negative effects of social circumstances, the language of compensation is also the wrong language, because it turns social mechanisms like class or racial domination into cases of "bad luck," thereby anonymizing structures of domination and exploitation as if they were mere contingencies whose results need to

---

[26] Anderson, "What Is the Point of Equality?," p. 296.
[27] Ibid., p. 305.

be corrected, as is especially apparent in the welfare-oriented versions of luck egalitarianism.[28]

12.1.4 Procedural distributive justice

At this point, luck egalitarians might be inclined to have recourse to Rawls's discussion of what he calls the "principle of redress."[29] The principle states that "undeserved inequalities call for redress; and since inequalities of birth and natural endowment are undeserved, these inequalities are to be somehow compensated for."[30] Rawls regards this as a plausible "prima facie principle."[31] But he argues that better than to try to "eliminate"[32] these personal differences is to use the difference principle, which "is not of course the principle of redress. It does not require trying to even out handicaps as if all were to compete on a fair basis in the same race."[33] Rather, it allows all persons to enjoy their benefits only on the condition that the principles of justice are met, that is, that the principle of equal opportunity and the difference principle especially are satisfied.

The structuring idea behind this notion of social cooperation is that of *reciprocity*.[34] It implies that the "social order can be justified to everyone, and in particular to those who are least favored; and in this sense it is egalitarian."[35] This is connected to a particular aspect of Rawls's theory that luck egalitarianism neglects, namely the idea of what he calls "pure procedural justice." The conception of democratic equality Rawls favors implies that the combination of equal opportunity and the difference principle establishes a basic structure of institutions guided by public rules such that "pure procedural justice" exists, that is, a kind of justice for which no independent criterion for just results exists apart from a notion of just procedures. "The intuitive idea is to design the social system so that the outcome is just whatever it happens to be."[36] The basic structure is one of procedural and reciprocal justice if it is set up in such a way that it establishes a form of social cooperation based on the two principles

---

[28] See, for example, Arneson, "Luck Egalitarianism Interpreted and Defended."
[29] See Lippert-Rasmussen, "Rawls and Luck Egalitarianism."
[30] Rawls, *A Theory of Justice*, p. 100.
[31] Ibid., p. 101.
[32] Ibid., p. 102.
[33] Ibid., p. 101.
[34] Ibid., p. 102.
[35] Ibid., p. 103.
[36] Ibid., p. 85.

of justice; and if that is the case, distributive justice is realized in comparison with what Rawls calls "allocative justice." The latter abstracts from "what individuals have done in good faith in the light of established expectations" and asks "whether one distribution of a given stock of things to definite individuals with known desires and preferences is better than another."[37] In the case of justice as fairness, by contrast, "the great practical advantage of pure procedural justice is that it is no longer necessary in meeting the demands of justice to keep track of the endless variety of circumstances and the changing relative positions of particular persons. One avoids the problem of defining principles to cope with the enormous complexities which would arise if such details were relevant."[38]

Rawls's argument here is not just a practical one, as luck egalitarians tend to think. Rather, it is based on a certain idea of cooperation as reciprocity within a system of institutionalized public rules that makes it unnecessary to establish individual protocols of transactions and desert or ambition or failure. According to Rawls, it is a mistake to aim at such protocols, for only the general features of the basic structure ought to be judged according to principles of justice, but not the situation that individuals occupy within it as a result of chance or choice. Again, we see an important incompatibility between Rawlsian and luck egalitarian accounts of justice, incompatibilities that, I think, point to a deeper disagreement about the point of justice.

12.2 Two paradigms of justice

12.2.1 Agents vs. recipients of justice

There is a fundamental difference between two paradigmatic ways of thinking about political and social justice.[39] The first – and in my view a deficient one – is the result of a particular interpretation of the ancient principle *suum cuique*, which is taken to mean that the primary issue of justice is what goods individuals justly receive or deserve – in other words, who "gets" what. This then leads either to comparisons between people's sets of goods, and thus to relative conclusions, or to the question of whether individuals have "enough"

---

[37] Ibid., p. 88.
[38] Ibid., p. 87.
[39] In the following, I adapt some sections of my "Two Pictures of Justice"; see Forst, *Justification and Critique*, ch. 1.

of the essential goods, regardless of comparative considerations. Such goods- and distribution-centered, *recipient-oriented* points of view have their merits, for distributive justice is, of course, concerned with the goods individuals can appropriately claim.

Nevertheless, this paradigm obscures essential aspects of justice. In the first place, the question of how the goods to be distributed come into existence is neglected in a purely goods-focused view; hence issues of production and its just organization are largely ignored.[40] Furthermore, there is the second problem that the *political* question of who determines the structures of production and distribution and in what ways is disregarded, as though a great distribution machine – a neutral "distributor"[41] – could exist that only needs to be programmed correctly using the right "metric" of justice.[42] But, according to a more thoroughly political understanding of justice, it is not only essential that there should not be such a machine, because this would mean that justice would no longer be understood as a political accomplishment of the subjects themselves but would turn them into passive recipients of goods – but not of justice. This is a point where the often-made distinction between "pure" distributive and political justice[43] has to be problematized, for, according to the second paradigm of justice, social justice can only come about through political institutions that are politically just. A benevolent distributive dictator in this view could not establish distributive justice, even if he or she used the right metric, for justice is about the standing you enjoy within the institutional scheme to which you are subject – which necessarily includes your standing as a politically autonomous member who co-determines the basic structure.

The goods-oriented view also neglects, thirdly, the fact that justified claims to goods do not simply "exist" but can be arrived at only through discourse in the context of corresponding procedures of justification, in which – and this is the fundamental requirement of political as well as social justice – all can in principle participate as free and equal individuals.

Finally, in the fourth place, the goods-fixated view of justice largely leaves the question of injustice out of account; for, by concentrating on overcoming deficiencies in the distribution of goods, it deems someone

---

[40] Not all luck-egalitarian theories are guilty of that charge; G. A. Cohen, for example, in a number of his writings, addresses questions of the organization of production. See his *On the Currency of Egalitarian Justice and Other Essays in Political Philosophy*, ch. 7.
[41] In a telling phrase from Cohen, ibid., p. 61.
[42] For the first two points, see esp. Young, *Justice and the Politics of Difference*.
[43] For this see Caney, "Justice and the Basic Right to Justification."

who suffers want as a result of a natural catastrophe to be equivalent to someone who suffers want as a result of economic or political exploitation. Although it is correct that assistance is required in both cases, according to my understanding of the grammar of justice it is required in the one case as an act of *moral solidarity*, but in the other as an act of *justice* conditioned by the nature of one's involvement in relations of exploitation and injustice and of the specific wrong in question.[44] Hence there are different grounds for action as well as different kinds of action that are required. Ignoring this difference can lead to a situation in which – in a dialectic of morality, as it were[45] – what is actually a requirement of justice is seen instead as an act of generous assistance or "aid," thus adding insult to injury.

For these reasons, it is especially important when dealing with questions of *distributive* justice to recognize the *political* point of justice and to liberate oneself from a one-sided and truncated notion fixated on quantities of goods (or on a measure of well-being to be produced by them). On a second, fuller and more apt paradigm, by contrast, justice must be geared to *intersubjective structural relations*, not to *subjective* or *putatively objective states* of the provision of goods or of well-being. Only in this way, by taking into consideration the first question of justice – namely, the question of the justifiability of social relations and, correspondingly, how much "justification power" individuals or groups have in a political context – can a critical conception of justice be developed, one that gets to the roots of relations of injustice. In short, the basic question of justice is not *what you have* but *how you are treated*.[46] Thus, we see that the real difference between the two paradigms of justice is one of teleology versus deontology.

12.2.2 Justice as justification

When it comes to how to decide between the two rivaling paradigms, we need to consider the concept of justice itself. This concept possesses

---

[44] Here a whole series of cases would have to be distinguished: direct participation in or (joint) causation of injustice; indirect participation in injustice by profiting from it without oneself actively contributing to relations of exploitation; and the ("natural") duty to put an end to unjust relations, even if one does not benefit from them but possesses the means to overcome them.

[45] See Forst, *The Right to Justification*, ch. 11.

[46] Derek Parfit's distinction between a "telic" and a "deontic" egalitarian view captures important aspects of these different ways of thinking about justice, and it is interesting to note that – without commenting explicitly on this – he uses the term justice only in connection with the deontic view. See Parfit, "Equality or Priority?," p. 90.

THE POINT OF JUSTICE

a core meaning to which the essential contrasting concept, as Rawls argued,[47] is that of *arbitrariness*. The second paradigm understands arbitrariness in a social and political sense – that is, as assuming the form of arbitrary rule by individuals or by a part of the community (for example, a class) over others, or of the acceptance of social contingencies that lead to social subordination and domination. A metaphysical conception of arbitrariness in the context of social justice would go further, as luck egalitarianism does, and aim to eradicate or compensate for all differences between persons that give some an advantage over others due to brute luck, regardless of whether the differences in question lead to social domination.

The term "domination" is important in this context, because it signifies the arbitrary rule of some over others – that is, rule without proper reasons and justifications and (as a higher-order form of domination) without proper structures of justification existing in the first place.[48] When people engage in struggles against injustice, they are combating forms of domination of this kind. The basic impulse that opposes injustice, according to the second paradigm, is not primarily one of wanting something, but is instead that of not wanting to be dominated or overruled in one's claim to a *basic right to justification*.[49] This moral right of persons as equal normative authorities expresses the demand that no political or social–economic relations should exist that cannot be adequately justified toward those involved. This constitutes the profoundly *political* essence of justice, which is not captured, but rather is suppressed, by the recipient-focused interpretations of the principle *suum cuique*, whether of a luck egalitarian or sufficientarian kind.

12.2.3 Constructive autonomy

Since Nozick's influential critique, Rawls's theory has often been interpreted as belonging to the first, allocative-distributive and recipient-oriented paradigm of justice. Nozick criticizes Rawls's

---

[47] See Rawls's definition in *A Theory of Justice*, p. 5: "Those who hold different conceptions of justice can, then, still agree that institutions are just when no arbitrary distinctions are made between persons in the assigning of basic rights and duties and when the rules determine a proper balance between competing claims to the advantages of social life."
[48] I explain the difference between such a discourse–theoretical understanding of domination and a neo-republican one based on freedom of choice in Forst, *Normativity and Power*, ch. 10, and in Chapter 10 in this volume.
[49] I explain this more fully in Forst, *The Right to Justification*.

principles of justice as "end-state principles" that correspond to pre-given patterns that illegitimately constrain the liberty of market participants.[50] Even Thomas Pogge regards Rawls's as a "purely recipient-oriented approach," because it concentrates on comparisons between distributive results as regards basic goods.[51] This assessment has a certain justification, given the importance of primary goods in Rawls's theory. Nevertheless, Rawls does not share the first but rather the second paradigm of justice, the one that accords priority to social structures and relations, and the social status of the individual within such a scheme of cooperation. The main reason for this is the Kantian character of his theory, based on the idea that persons are equal normative authorities when it comes to the construction of principles for a basic structure of society.

In the first place, the Kantian character of Rawls's theory implies that the autonomy of free and equal persons, which is at the normative heart of the approach, is not the autonomy of individuals who are primarily conceived as recipients of goods that they would need in order to lead a "good life." It is rather the *constructive autonomy* of free and equal subjects of justification that manifests itself in the fact that individuals are able to regard the principles of justice as morally self-given; hence, the citizens view the social basic structure as the social expression of their self-determination.[52] The relevant conception of autonomy is that of the autonomy to actively determine the basic structure, not that of the autonomy to enjoy its goods. The emphasis on public reason in the later works underscores this, because public reason represents the medium of discursive justification in which an autonomous conception of justice that all can accept as free and equal individuals is grounded: "In affirming the political doctrine as a whole we, as citizens, are ourselves autonomous, politically speaking."[53]

An important aspect of the Kantian background of the theory consists in the aim of excluding the aspects of the social world that seem "arbitrary from a moral point of view," both in justifying the principles and in the institutions of the basic structure, as shown previously. In this way differences in natural endowments and social inequalities should not lead to advantages that cannot be legitimized,

[50] Nozick, *Anarchy, State, and Utopia*, pp. 149ff. Young, *Justice and the Politics of Difference*, p. 28, agrees with Nozick in criticizing end-state theories (to which in her view the Rawlsian belongs).
[51] Pogge, "The Incoherence between Rawls's Theories of Justice," p. 1739.
[52] Rawls, *A Theory of Justice*, §40.
[53] Rawls, *Political Liberalism*, p. 98.

especially toward the worst off. This is a criterion for social relations between citizens of a "well-ordered society," not primarily a criterion for determining the amounts of goods to which everyone can lay claim as an independent metric of justice.[54]

With this we arrive at the most important concept as regards the Kantian character of the theory, namely that of social cooperation as a system of reciprocity. As we saw in the context of the discussion of the principle of redress, Rawls's conception of "procedural justice" is geared to social relations and structures. It leads to a system of social cooperation that expresses the "sociability of human beings" in such a way that they complement each other in productive ways and participate in a context of cooperation that includes all as politically and socially autonomous members – think of the picture of the orchestra employed by Rawls as an ideal of social cooperation.[55] In the *Restatement* of his theory, he comes back to the contrast between his conception of justice as fairness and a conception of "allocative justice":

> The problem of distributive justice in justice as fairness is always this: how are the institutions of the basic structure to be regulated as one unified scheme of institutions so that a fair, efficient, and productive system of social cooperation can be maintained over time, from one generation to the next? Contrast this with the very different problem of how a given bundle of commodities is to be distributed, or allocated, among various individuals whose particular needs, desires, and preferences are known to us, and who have not cooperated in any way to produce those commodities. This second problem is that of allocative justice [...]. We reject the idea of allocative justice as incompatible with the fundamental idea by which justice as fairness is organized [...]. In a well-ordered society [...], the distribution of income and wealth illustrates what we may call pure background procedural justice. The basic structure is arranged so that when everyone follows the publicly recognized rules of cooperation, and honors the claims the rules specify, the particular distributions of goods that result are acceptable as just [...] whatever these distributions turn out to be.[56]

The overriding issue within such a context of production and distribution is who the individuals "are," and not primarily what they receive according to an independent yardstick that theories such as luck egalitarian ones provide. The point is that the institutions function in accordance with justified principles, such as the difference

---

[54] See also Scheffler, *Equality and Tradition*, pp. 195f.
[55] Rawls, *A Theory of Justice*, §79.
[56] Rawls, *Justice as Fairness*, p. 50.

principle, and do not involve any social privileges, and that they do not lead to the creation and cementing of groups that are excluded from the system of cooperation and permanently depend on allocative transfers of goods. This is also what underlies Rawls's criticism of the capitalist welfare state model, because this, in contrast to a "property-owning democracy," does not ensure that the ownership of wealth and capital is sufficiently dispersed and as a result cannot prevent "a small part of society from controlling the economy, and indirectly, political life as well."[57]

12.2.4 Going further

At this point, however, we can ask whether Rawls's theory sufficiently accommodates the principle that social asymmetries are in need of justification and provides for corresponding institutional practices of justification. I have my doubts about that and would argue for a discourse-theoretical conception of justice that differs from Rawls's theory in central aspects, while nevertheless remaining true to its deontological spirit. However, I will have to leave this argument for another occasion.[58]

---

[57] Ibid., p. 139.
[58] See especially my *Right to Justification* and *Justification and Critique* as well as Part II of this volume.

— 13 —

JUSTIFICATION FUNDAMENTALISM
A Discourse-Theoretical Interpretation of Scanlon's Contractualism*

In my brief remarks, I develop a particular, discourse–theoretical reading of Thomas Scanlon's theory of contractualism with respect to moral justification and then suggest a conception of political justification as following from it. The latter provides the core for a conception of political and social justice that I find close to Scanlon's own views. So, what I present here is less of a critique than it is an invitation. But Scanlon may not enthusiastically welcome that invitation, as it makes him appear more of a *justification fundamentalist* rather than a reasons fundamentalist and, in addition, his theory moves closer to a certain version of Kantianism. Which is, as I think, where it belongs.

13.1 Moral justification

I would like to start my reflections with a quote from an interview of Scanlon with Alex Voorhoeve, where he says that the very structure of the contractualist test of reasonable rejectability is "already a moral principle" – such "that everybody counts – that we should be able to justify our norms to everyone. The reason is that we are all reasonable creatures, to whom it makes sense to want to justify our

---

* Thanks to the participants of the Lauener Symposium on Thomas Scanlon's work in Bern in September 2016 for a productive discussion, especially to Tim Scanlon for his reply; see Scanlon, "Responses to Forst, Mantel, Nagel, Olsaretti, Parfit, and Stemplowska." I also owe thanks to Felmon Davis and Isaac Taylor for their helpful remarks on an earlier version of this text. On the occasion of Scanlon receiving the Lauener Award, I also presented the laudation; see my "Deontological Communitarianism."

norms to everyone."[1] I agree with this, and also with Scanlon when he continues by saying "I find it hard to accept a notion of wrongness that is prior to or independent of justification [...]."[2] He furthermore suggests the contractualist test of the generalizability of moral norms as an alternative to Kant's test of contradiction in conception or in will and emphasizes the relational, intersubjective character of this test, which involves regarding every person as an equal author(ity) on moral claims and justifications, i.e., as in that sense an autonomous member of a universal moral community of respect and mutual justification.

In light of that, I would call his approach "justification fundamentalism" rather than "reasons fundamentalism," the term that Scanlon chooses in *Being Realistic About Reasons*.[3] I think he is a justification fundamentalist in not accepting any notion of wrongness or rightness prior to a certain form and procedure of intersubjective justification; thus he takes, as he says in *What We Owe to Each Other*, "the idea of justifiability to others [...] to be basic"[4] since it is these others to whom one primarily owes appropriate, mutually justifiable moral reasons. So they are equal justificatory authorities when it comes to evaluating good moral reasons. Yet at the same time, the demand of *reasonable* rejectability or justification implies another authority to be in play here, namely that of reason as a faculty that we exercise *together* when we determine which reasons are good ones and which are not.

According to Scanlon's contractualism, moral persons have a basic moral claim to be respected as equal justificatory authorities, and this kind of respect requires such persons to follow the reason-based contractualist test of justification to determine moral rightness or wrongness. There are two main components of this view – to regard persons as equal moral authorities, and to regard a certain procedure of justification (or of reasonable rejectability) as required to exercise that authority. Both are components, I think, of what I call "justification fundamentalism": First, the main point – and ground – of morality (in the narrow meaning of what we owe to each other) is to respect others as moral equals to whom I owe a proper justification for my moral actions; and second, the proper justification is to be found by way of a certain procedure of intersubjective (or discursive), reasonable justification.

---

[1] Scanlon, "The Kingdom of Ends on the Cheap," p. 182.
[2] Ibid., p. 185.
[3] Scanlon, *Being Realistic About Reasons*, lecture I.
[4] Scanlon, *What We Owe to Each Other*, p. 5.

These are very Kantian formulations, but I think they are in line with Scanlon's views – at least as long as we do not imply some kind of transcendental rational agency in a Korsgaardian fashion to explain the ground of the moral ought here.[5] For I agree with Scanlon that it is not the constitution of our rational agency that grounds morality but a reflection on us as equal justificatory authorities who have a basic moral responsibility to exercise the faculty of justification in a respectful way, i.e., to respect every other human being as a moral equal. That kind of respect – or the "idea of justifiability to others"[6] – is the "motivational basis" and normative core of contractualism and, if we understand Kant's moral philosophy as not primarily a philosophy of rational action but as one of morally *responsible* – i.e., justifiable – and in that sense *autonomous* and reason-guided action, the same idea lies at the core of Kant's project.[7]

I would therefore *not* call the basic kind of contractualist respect, as Scanlon does, "avowedly heteronomous,"[8] though it is based on an ideal of certain social relations with others. Yet these relations are always mediated by reasonable justification, and thus they are themselves based on the proper exercise of practical reason-seeking principles that "govern" our social relations morally. Here is a Kantian-sounding quote by Scanlon, expressing what I have in mind:

> [R]especting the value of human (rational) life requires us to treat rational creatures only in ways that would be allowed by principles that they could not reasonably reject insofar as they, too, were seeking principles of mutual governance which other rational creatures could not reasonably reject.[9]

That social version of the "kingdom of ends," as I would call it, expresses not just a social ideal of mutual recognition, but beyond that an ideal of mutual justification guided by principles relating to the use of reason – which is what Kantians call an "ideal of practical reason": practical as it applies to norms of action, reason as these norms have to go through a process of mutual justifiability guided by rational criteria, ideal as it spells out a way of relating to oneself and others as justificatory equals. I will come back to this point below.

---

[5] Korsgaard, *Self-Constitution*. See Scanlon's critique of her approach in his "How I Am Not a Kantian."
[6] Scanlon, "How I Am Not a Kantian," p. 139.
[7] See my *Right to Justification*, chs. 1 and 2, and the Introduction and Part II of this volume.
[8] Scanlon, *What We Owe to Each Other*, p. 6.
[9] Ibid., p. 106.

I stress *justifiability*, as, like Scanlon, I do not think that an actual or some imagined hypothetical consent can deliver the moral justification we are seeking but that a judgment based on the best reasons is needed. This is why Scanlon thinks reasons, rather than imperatives of rationality, are fundamental. But what makes these reasons justifiable, I take it, is the proper exercise of practical reason respecting every moral person as an equal moral authority deserving proper reasons and (in the standard case) being able to respond with reasons. So the alternative between a view based on *reasons* and one based on *reason* seems to disappear: reason operates through reasons, but it is not guided by them; rather, reason is the faculty used to test reasons, question them and evaluate them in the light of *principles* suitable to determine justifiable reasons in the various domains of justification – which is how I interpret the notion of "domains."[10] Otherwise, such domains would have no unity, and we would not know how to use reason to distinguish better from worse reasons within such contexts. Reasoning guided by principles of reasoning determines good reasons, not the other way around. Thus, if the contractualist test is one of reasonable justification, it expresses principles and criteria of practical reason, which *constitute* good reasons. And that is why reasons fundamentalism has to give way to justification fundamentalism; in other words, if the contractualist test tests something, it is reasons of rightness or wrongness – and thus it cannot be guided by such reasons. A justification fundamentalist does indeed believe that reasons can be explained in terms of something more fundamental: principles of reasoning, i.e., of justification.

Why would Scanlon disagree? He defines a reason as "a consideration that counts in favor of"[11] something, and the faculty for arriving at such considerations is that of reflective judgment as guided by "standards" of rationality.[12] Similarly, he describes the process of arriving at truths about reasons as a process of "thinking carefully about what seem to us to be reasons, considering what general principles about reasons would explain them, what implications these would have, and considering the plausibility of the implications of these principles."[13] Across various domains, some general

---

[10] Scanlon, *Being Realistic About Reasons*, pp. 19–26.
[11] Scanlon, *What We Owe to Each Other*, p. 17.
[12] "[I]n order for judgments about reasons to be taken to be about some subject matter independent of us in the sense required for it to be possible for us to be mistaken about them, what is necessary is for there to be standards for arriving at conclusions about reasons." Ibid., p. 63.
[13] Scanlon, *Being Realistic About Reasons*, p. 102.

principles like those of logic apply, but there are domain-specific principles of judging reasons – yet all of these have to be principles of reasonable justification. They constitute good reasons.

It might be helpful at this point to mention briefly my particular rendering of what mutual justifiability means. I suggest to interpret "reasonable rejectability" as "reciprocal and general rejectability," assuming, as contractualism does, that the realm of what people can reciprocally and generally accept may be broader than what they can reciprocally and generally reject – and that the latter realm thus circumscribes the narrow realm of morality. The first criterion implies that one must not make normative claims one denies to others (reciprocity of claims) or impose one's own interests or particular views on others who could reject them as partial (reciprocity of reasons), while the second implies that one must not exclude others from the moral justification community (generality). To reject a norm or a principle by showing that it violates reciprocity or generality is a *reasonable rejection* (while one could also accept it as an act of supererogation). Thus, it is not consensus that determines moral rightness but the quality of the reasons given – yet that quality is determined by the discursive use of the two criteria, in practice as well as in one's judgment.[14] These two criteria constitute non-rejectable reasons.

It would be a mistake to read the word "constitute" in metaphysical terms and to think that this is the terrain in which the debate between realism and constructivism takes place.[15] For a justification fundamentalist can remain agnostic about the question of whether contractualist justification discovers "real" moral truths or produces them in any way that would be inconsistent with such a form of realism.[16] The view that a justification procedure generates good reasons by way of certain criteria of justification need not take a stance on that issue. All that matters is that the normative criteria of reason are decisive for us to be able epistemically to distinguish good from bad reasons. Whether these reasons are "created" or "discovered" in a metaphysical or ontological sense is a question that does not matter from a moral or from an epistemic point of

---

[14] I take this to be in line with Scanlon when he writes: "When we think of those to whom justification is owed, we naturally think first of the specific individuals who are affected by specific actions. But when we are deciding whether a given principle is one that could reasonably be rejected we must take a broader and more abstract perspective." *What We Owe to Each Other*, p. 202.

[15] See, for example, Enoch, "Can There Be a Global, Interesting, Coherent Constructivism About Practical Reason?"

[16] Scanlon, *Being Realistic About Reasons*, lecture II.

view. I call such a version of constructivism *pragmatic* rather than metaphysical.[17]

At least with respect to the domain of morality narrowly understood, pragmatic constructivism suggests itself as the proper view. And, indeed, when it comes to questions of social and political justice and to individual morality, Scanlon thinks a constructivist account of objectivity – i.e., judgment- and choice-independence as he defines them[18] – has "considerable plausibility,"[19] as judgments about rightness or wrongness depend on certain procedures of justification properly performed.

The reason why Scanlon does not accept constructivism all the way down is that he believes that it cannot deliver a general account of reasons for action. A Kantian view, for example, cannot explain why certain ends should be valuable only if I have chosen them autonomously according to the categorical imperative.[20] This objection is correct if, for example, we think of many values and ideals about which persons care deeply, apart from the (narrow) moral realm, such as religious values or particular conceptions of the good. Such (in my terminology)[21] "ethical" ends are seen as valuable for particular reasons, but they are not made valuable through adopting them autonomously. But Scanlon does not just criticize such an overstretch of Kantian accounts of morality into the realm of the ethical; rather, with respect to morality narrowly understood, his view is that while all the moral reasons that go through the contractualist test can be seen as constructed by that test, the very reason to engage in the test in the first place cannot be constructed in that way. There has to be an independently valid reason to accept the contractualist moral principle which cannot be reduced to reasons of rational agency.[22]

This problem is notorious for a constructivist view, as no constructivist theory can deliver the basic reason to be moral (and to use a certain justification procedure expressing equal respect) in a purely constructivist fashion. A constructivist view (of justice or morality) entails two different kinds of normative arguments, or two kinds of normativity: *first*, the normativity of the principles and ideas of practical reason, as Rawls phrases it in his version of constructivism[23]

---

[17] Forst, *The Right to Justification*, p. 50.
[18] Scanlon, *Being Realistic About Reasons*, pp. 93f.
[19] Ibid., p. 98.
[20] Ibid., pp. 98–100.
[21] Forst, *The Right to Justification*, ch. 3.
[22] Scanlon, *Being Realistic About Reasons*, p. 100.
[23] See Rawls, "Kantian Constructivism in Moral Theory," and Rawls, *Political Liberalism*,

– or, on Scanlon's account, the principle of reasonable rejectability and the substantive claim that every moral person owes following this principle to every other moral person, or, in my view, the principle of reciprocal and general justification and the moral notion of free and equal persons as equal normative authorities with a right to justification. Then there is, *second*, the normativity of the norms (or "laws") generated by the constructivist, contractualist or discursive procedure, be it the categorical imperative, the contractualist test or a notion of free and equal discourse. In a Kantian view, it is essential that practical reason (on my understanding, justificatory reason) provides the basis for the principles and ideas used, where practical reason is understood as a rational and, at the same time, *moral* capacity, that is, not just as a matter of knowing *how* to justify norms, but also of knowing *that* one is under a *duty* to do so.

One cannot infer, however, that since the second kind of normativity is based on the first, which is not constructivist in the same way as the second, that constructivism fails. All one needs to say is that the moral ground of the constructivist procedure is a substantive moral ground, but not one that is separate from a reflection on us as reasonable justificatory beings who have a moral duty to respect others as justificatory equals by using the faculty of justification in the right way. Thus, while I think, as I tried to explain above, that the notion of "reasons fundamentalism" does not do justice to the priority of justification and the criteria of justification that the contractualist test implies, I also think, as I briefly suggested, that the "ideal of justifiability to others"[24] that contractualism is based on is indeed an *ideal of reason* insofar as its ideal of moral community is one of a community ruled by reasonable norms of "mutual governance" – and thus also of moral autonomy in a Kantian sense of the term. And the idea of moral persons as having a right to and a duty of justification seems to be a good way of expressing the basic imperative of moral respect that contractualism emphasizes: "Human beings are capable of assessing reasons and justifications, and proper respect for their distinctive value involves treating them only in ways that they could, by proper exercise of this capacity, recognize as justifiable."[25]

Thus, I think that Scanlon is right to say that a constructivist account of morality is based on a substantive answer to what grounds the moral duty of justification, but I think that it is not correct to say

---

ch. 3. For a Kantian interpretation of Rawls's constructivism, see the Introduction and Chapter 11 in this volume.

[24] Scanlon, *What We Owe to Each Other*, p. 155.
[25] Ibid., p. 169.

that this is independent of our faculty of practical reason. For the moral duty of justification is a moral duty that reflects our status as moral authorities in the space of justifications who are equal to all other humans, and it further entails that the way to exercise that duty is through a proper procedure of justification respecting us and others as equals. This is still justification fundamentalism, but in a different key: the basic contractualist ideal of justifiability to others is not just one normative ideal among others that we have good reason to accept. Unlike other ethical or religious ideals, it is an *ideal of reason*, as it expresses what it means to be (noumenally, in traditional terms) part of and to help create in practice a "kingdom of ends," or a moral community of mutual respect and *reasonable* justifiability. Reason is a faculty that binds us in this sense; it contains a categorical imperative to use it in the morally right way.

13.2 Political justification

According to my discourse-theoretical, Kantian interpretation of contractualism, human beings have a basic moral right to justification, which is so to speak a veto right against reciprocally and generally non-justifiable normative claims. To respect that right means to respect others as ends in themselves, to use Kant's term and give it a (hopefully) more precise meaning. I think this accords with Scanlon's way of understanding and respecting the moral value of human persons as the individuals they are and as moral equals at the same time.

Like Scanlon and Rawls, I believe that our basic moral standing as equals travels from the moral realm to that of political and social justice, i.e., to that of our basic standing as members of a legal and political normative order who justifiably demand legal, political and social justice. From that perspective, I see many parallels with Scanlon's arguments about human rights, toleration and equality. But, in the realm of justice, I think the part of the contractualist formula that requires norms to be a "basis for informed, unforced general agreement"[26] becomes more relevant for a conception of reciprocal and general justification as a social *practice* of justice – the practice of a society whose members have a basic standing as justificatory equals such that they are not subjected to a normative order (of institutions and laws) that cannot be justified to them in a practice we

[26] Ibid., p. 153.

call *democracy* (in the ideal sense of the term). Here, the ideal of justifiability toward others has a concrete, institutional meaning calling, among other things, for a legally, politically and socially secure status of non-domination, i.e., of not being subject to a normative order without proper justification and, especially, of not being subjected to a normative order without proper procedures and institutions of justification in place. To have such a status of non-domination or, positively speaking, of being a legally, politically and socially equal authority of justification, is the basic demand of justice, and thus it is the task of what I call *fundamental justice* to secure this status – with the help of basic rights, democratic procedures and powers which enable all members to use their rights and avoid being forced to accept social structures and relations of domination.[27]

On my discourse-theoretical understanding (which differs substantially from neo-republican versions),[28] domination does not primarily mean being denied equal status in the sense of no longer enjoying personal freedom of choice protected from arbitrary interference; rather, it means in a more basic sense being disrespected in one's basic claim to be a free and equal *normative authority* within the order to which one is subject. This implies the basic right to co-determine the structure of that society. Basic rights are not just rights to be protected in one's status as a legally, politically and socially non-dominated person; they are, in a reflexive sense, also rights to determine the rights and duties that define this status.[29] Thus, the authority to determine your rights must reside in a discursive procedure of reciprocal and general justification in which all participants are justificatory equals. This is what justification fundamentalism means in the political realm.

I think this is not just a notion of justice close to Scanlon's views; it is also the best extension of moral contractualism to the realm of social and political life. Let me explain. In my view, following Rawls's and close to Scanlon's, I believe, the concept of justice possesses a core meaning whose essential contrasting concept is that of *arbitrariness*.[30] Arbitrariness can assume the form of direct arbitrary rule over others by individuals or by a part of the community (for

---

[27] See Forst, *The Right to Justification*, pt. II, and *Justification and Critique*, esp. ch. 1.
[28] See Chapter 10 in this volume.
[29] See Forst, "The Justification of Basic Rights."
[30] Rawls, *A Theory of Justice*, p. 5: "Those who hold different conceptions of justice can, then, still agree that institutions are just when no arbitrary distinctions are made between persons in the assigning of basic rights and duties and when the rules determine a proper balance between competing claims to the advantages of social life."

example, by a class), or it can involve the acceptance of social contingencies that lead to asymmetrical social positions and relations of domination as if they were unalterable or beyond justification, even though they are nothing of the sort. Arbitrary rule is the rule of some people over others without legitimate reason, and where social struggles are conducted against injustice, they are directed against forms of domination of this kind. The underlying impulse that opposes injustice is not primarily that of wanting something or more of something, but of no longer wanting to be dominated, harassed or overruled in one's claim and basic right to justification. Herein resides the profoundly *political* essence of justice that a purely goods- or recipient-oriented view fails to grasp: justice concerns *who determines who receives what* and not only or primarily who should receive what.

That is also why a well-meaning authoritarian regime that provides its citizens with a decent package of basic goods of housing, health and income does a lot to improve its citizens' lives – but serves no justice. Those who dissect justice into social or distributive justice as a matter of the provision of goods, whether sufficientarian or egalitarian, on the one hand, and political justice or legitimacy, on the other, would disagree. But I think that is a mistake: if there were an ideal Cohenite "egalitarian distributor,"[31] who had figured out the right metric of justice and instantiated it by authoritarian rule, justice would not have been done, *neither* politically *nor* socially. People would just be better off but still dominated and not treated as *autonomous* subjects of justice because that autonomy implies that *they* determine the metric of justice (in a procedure on the basis of fundamental justice).

It is on this basis that we can construct a comprehensive theory of political and social justice, though in the present context I can only hint at what such a theory would entail. First, we must distinguish between *fundamental* and *full* justice. Whereas the task of fundamental justice is to construct a *basic structure of justification*, the task of full justice is to construct a *fully justified basic structure*. In order to pursue the latter, the former is necessary, that is, a "putting-into-effect" of justification through constructive, discursive democratic procedures in which justificatory power is distributed as evenly as possible among the citizens. Fundamental justice guarantees all citizens an effective status as justificatory equals. This would still fall short of guaranteeing "informed, unforced general agreement," as

---

[31] Cohen, "Afterword to Chapters One and Two," p. 61.

the political contractualist would wish for, but it would still aim at establishing a basic structure in which asymmetries of justificatory power that keep reproducing themselves can be overcome.

I think that such a conception of fundamental justice is much in accord with Scanlonian contractualism. Let me first point out the parallels and then also reflect on the reasons why Scanlon still might not follow me on this path. To start with, a conception of basic rights as expressing respect for others as justificatory equals in legal, political and social life is in line with contractualism going political, but it differs from Scanlon's conception of rights, which is closer to an interest theory, arguing that rights protect (or promote) central valuable interests of human beings.[32] According to the notion of basic rights I have in mind, these rights are status- rather than interest-based, i.e., they are justified by a consideration of a secure status of non-domination and an inquiry into the relevant contexts of such non-domination and the possibilities of being a justificatory subject that is able to co-determine the normative order to which he or she is subject.[33] Sure, we can say that basic interests in non-domination are protected by this, but this is not our main argument, for the status of being a justificatory equal carries the justificatory weight, not the idea of certain interests, whether real, ideal or objective (and Scanlon taught us a lot about the problems in defining such interests). Such a conception of basic rights explains best, I think, why human rights are a "neutral concern,"[34] as Scanlon argues, and how a core of them remains firm while interpretations of that core may differ among societies and cultural contexts.

That political justice demands a secure status of being a justificatory equal also fits with Scanlon's important reflections on toleration. For he rightly argues that toleration "involves 'accepting as equals' those who differ from us"[35] and who are nevertheless equally entitled to co-determine social life. I may reject their views but have to accept other persons as equal members, as long as they do not deny my standing of an equal or that of others. So, my *ethical* objection to their, say, religious views is reasonable but need not be shared by all such that it can ground a *moral* rejection; if it grounds such a rejection, toleration is out of place.[36] Tolerated beliefs and practices are reasonable to hold and reasonable to reject as a general

---

[32] Scanlon, "Rights, Goals, and Fairness."
[33] See my "Justification of Basic Rights."
[34] Scanlon, "Human Rights as a Neutral Concern."
[35] Scanlon, "The Difficulty of Tolerance," p. 190.
[36] See my *Toleration in Conflict*.

norm (a case of what Rawls called "reasonable disagreement"); and intolerable beliefs and practices are those that violate reciprocally and generally non-rejectable norms.

Finally, I think that the notion of equal respect and of standing as non-dominated justificatory equals in legal, political and social contexts is very close to the important reasons that Scanlon isolates for equality, especially the three reasons he mentions of preventing the stigma of inferiority, avoiding domination and preserving procedural fairness.[37] My justification fundamentalist reconstruction of contractualism can show, I think, that these three powerful considerations have a *common source*, i.e., our status as justificatory equals with a right to justification. I think that this notion of moral equality *is* the core of any justified claim to legal, political and social equality, and that greater equality of outcomes or strict equality of social standing and resources is only justified if it can be justified on these grounds of justificatory equality. This establishes a normative order among the equality considerations that Scanlon distinguishes, something missing in his account (so far).

All of these reflections about rights, about toleration and about equality presuppose, in my view, the notion of the authority of persons to co-determine the structure of their normative order as *democratic* justificatory equals. And that is no add-on or separate consideration of political justice; rather, it lies at the heart of a just regime. So, I wonder why democracy as the practice of political justification plays no bigger role in Scanlon's political philosophy. I don't want to speculate about this, but it might have something to do with certain aspects of his thought that are less justification fundamentalist and more reasons fundamentalist. It may be a remnant of a value-based approach to political philosophy, where it is not through justificatory discourse that autonomous members of a normative order determine their society, but where they are called upon to order and arrange their society according to an order of values they can find through impersonal reflection. That, however, is an approach that I find hard to square with the interpretation of contractualism I laid out.

---

[37] Scanlon, "The Diversity of Objections to Inequality." See also his *Why Does Inequality Matter?*

14

THE AUTONOMY OF AUTONOMY
On Jürgen Habermas's *Auch eine Geschichte der Philosophie**

14.1 Redemptive translation

Major books like *Auch eine Geschichte der Philosophie*[1] start from and develop a single (although complex) idea. This idea has been present in Habermas's work for some time. It can be traced back to the core project of the Frankfurt School, in the tradition of Horkheimer and Adorno's *Dialectic of Enlightenment* and Horkheimer's *Critique of Instrumental Reason* (*Eclipse of Reason*), of reconstructing the genesis of and criticizing one-sided forms of rationality that lead to positivism, scientism and other reductionist accounts of morality and social life.[2] The critique of naturalism that Habermas developed over the past twenty years and that leads to *Auch eine Geschichte*

---

* This text represents a further stage in a dialogue that I have had the privilege of conducting since my student days with Jürgen Habermas and over the course of which I have learned a great deal and continue to do so. Our dialogue has repeatedly brought some differences between us to the surface, one of which concerns our respective understandings of a cognitivist, deontological conception of morality. This played a certain role in our frequent discussions during the writing of *Also a History of Philosophy*, and, in what follows, I try to articulate my reservations. I had the opportunity to develop and present these reflections before a larger audience at our major conference in Frankfurt on the occasion of Jürgen Habermas's ninetieth birthday in June 2019, on a panel at the annual meeting of the American Political Science Association in September 2020, and at a workshop in Bad Homburg in November 2020. I benefited greatly from these discussions; Jürgen Habermas was present on the first and third occasions, and I thank him for his responses. The text is part of a symposium on his work that appeared in *Constellations* in March 2021, and in his "Reply," which also appeared there, he responds at length to my critique and clarifies his position. The discussion went to a next stage with my "Die Welten der Rechtfertigung," to which Habermas replied again in his "Antworten."
[1] Translations from the German have kindly been provided by Ciaran Cronin to whom I also owe many thanks for checking my English.
[2] For a comprehensive analysis of this theme, see Jay, *Reason After Its Eclipse*.

der Philosophie marks the most recent development of this theme; however, it has been a life-long preoccupation, if one thinks, for example, of *Technik und Wissenschaft als "Ideologie"* from 1968.

When it comes to reflecting on modernity, or what Habermas now calls *"entgleisende Moderne"* (derailed modernity), discussions of religion have not been absent from his work either, if one thinks, for example, of some of his reflections on Bloch, Scholem, Benjamin, Horkheimer and Adorno. Take, for example, his analysis of Benjamin's alternative to ideology critique, namely *"rettende Kritik"* (redemptive or salvaging critique), which tries to hold onto the moments of the past that had the – to a certain extent messianic – potential to save us from a path of historical catastrophe.[3] Furthermore, in dialogues with theologians he developed the idea of a "transcendence from within,"[4] which he still upholds.

Although *Auch eine Geschichte der Philosophie* is part of this long series of reflections, it has, as far as I can see, a more determinate occasion and starting point. It dates back to the period around 2000 when Habermas combined his reflections on the work of John Rawls – and the idea (which we shared) that religious views had to "translate"[5] their arguments into a secular language of public reason – with his critique of liberal eugenics. At the end of his book on *The Future of Human Nature* (German original 2001)[6] as well as in his *Peace Prize Speech* from the same year,[7] he asks whether we have – or could have – a good secular translation within the limits of a rational morality (*Vernunftmoral*) of the religious idea that we are not authorized to "play God" and determine the nature and fate of human beings by means of biogenetic engineering. In this context, he formed the idea of a *twofold* or reciprocal translation process, such that not only religious views have to engage in a work of secular translation, but secular views also have a duty to learn from and try to understand and translate religious insights:

> But only if the secular side, too, remains sensitive to the force of articulation inherent in religious languages will the search for reasons that aim at universal acceptability not lead to an unfair exclusion of religions from the public sphere, nor sever secular society from

---

[3] Habermas, "Walter Benjamin."
[4] Habermas, "Transcendence from Within, Transcendence in This World."
[5] For a use of this term in this context, see my discussion of Rawls in Forst, *Contexts of Justice*, pp. 98f. Habermas shares this meaning of the term in his essay "'Reasonable' versus 'True' or the Morality of Worldviews," and in "Religion in the Public Sphere."
[6] Habermas, *The Future of Human Nature*.
[7] Habermas, "Faith and Knowledge."

important resources of meaning. In any event, the boundaries between secular and religious reasons are fluid. Determining these disputed boundaries should therefore be seen as a cooperative task, which requires *both* sides to take on the perspective of the other side.[8]

This idea of a *reciprocal duty of translation* was also one of the main points in his dialogue with Joseph Ratzinger (2004), then Cardinal, and soon to become Pope, in which Habermas speaks about the need for an "appropriation of genuine Christian contents" (*Aneignung genuin christlicher Gehalte*) in a secular language without deflating them:

> One such translation which salvages the substance of a term is the translation of the concept of 'man in the image of God' into that of the identical dignity of all men that deserves unconditional respect.[9]

Seen in this light, *Auch eine Geschichte der Philosophie* is the grand reconstruction of such forms of "*rettende Übersetzung*" as a historical learning process, reaching back to the important historical juncture of the Axial Age. The point remains to be aware of the importance of such "redemptive or salvaging translations" and view that process as open-ended, so that postmetaphysical thought is both the product of such cognitive progress and at the same time remains sensitive to the still existing normative potential of religious thought and "open to further learning in a dialogical attitude."[10]

This major project determines the structure and tone of the book. For, on the one hand, the narrative is one of secularization, and that of course includes the critique and overcoming of religious forms of thought in a process of emancipatory progress, leaving the confines of religion when it comes to developing the autonomy of reason and human agency.[11] According to Habermas's primarily vindicative genealogy, reason is not simply the *product* of contingent historical processes; rather, it remains the critical *authority* when it comes to evaluating what counts as generally justifiable.[12] *Genese* (genesis) and *Geltung* (validity) remain distinct. Yet, on the other hand, the narrative is one of dialogue involving a certain esteem for elaborate religious and theological theories and arguments; hence, the learning involves

---

[8] Ibid., p. 109 (emphasis in original).
[9] Habermas, Ratzinger, *The Dialectics of Secularization*, p. 45.
[10] Habermas, *Auch eine Geschichte der Philosophie*, vol. 1, p. 79: "*eine lernbereit dialogische Einstellung zu religiösen Überlieferungen [...]*."
[11] In this respect, there are important parallels between his project and mine in Forst, *Toleration in Conflict*.
[12] Habermas, *Auch eine Geschichte der Philosophie*, vol. 1, pp. 71, 111.

critique as well as appreciation, a *dialectical* learning in the Hegelian sense of the term. That also justifies the adaptation of Herder's title for the book, because Herder tries to do justice to different cultural historical forms (although his developmental narrative is weaker than Habermas's).[13] After all, according to Habermas, postmetaphysical thinking after Kant remains true to a form of philosophical thought that does not reduce philosophy to a scientistic-naturalistic enterprise, but upholds the perspective on our understanding of ourselves and the world (*Selbst- und Weltverständnis*)[14] as a whole, continuing to pose Kant's four questions. That is why, in the last paragraph of the book, Habermas affirms that a notion of reason that had no way of transcending the given world would wither away (*"verkümmern"*)[15] – and that this is where postmetaphysical thinking and religious consciousness still meet. The main point of the book, however, is not primarily to highlight the need for an ongoing constructive dialogue between philosophy and religion (or theology), but instead to make an argument for a nonreductive form of postmetaphysical philosophy.[16]

14.2 Moral autonomy and the autonomy of morality

Despite Habermas's intentional avoidance of a narrative of decline (*Verfallsgeschichte*), as highlighted in the first chapter of *Auch eine Geschichte der Philosophie*, there are important aspects of the narrative where the translation from religious to secular language involves both *progress and loss*, and this, let us say, negative-dialectical twist is what I want to focus on. I will concentrate on the formation of the concept of moral autonomy that culminates in Kant, is transformed, following Peirce, into a notion of discursive autonomy in Habermas's discourse ethics, and forms the core of the central notion of reasonable freedom (*vernünftige Freiheit*) elaborated in the second volume of the book. Yet, according to Habermas, something gets lost in the process of transforming a religious form of morality into a secular and postmetaphysical one – namely, a certain sense of "unconditional" (*unbedingtes*) and "absolute ought"

---

[13] See my brief discussion of Herder in Forst, *Toleration in Conflict*, §23.
[14] Habermas, *Auch eine Geschichte der Philosophie*, vol. 1, p. 12.
[15] Ibid., vol. 2, p. 807.
[16] He highlights this in the opening text of a symposium on the book in *Constellations*: Habermas, "An Author's Retrospective View."

(*absolutes Sollen*), leaving a systematic "gap" (*Lücke*)[17] that cannot be fully closed. As a result, *vernünftige Freiheit* suffers from a core weakness – and the autonomy of autonomy, so to speak, is placed in question, because it needs constant motivational support from other sources (though not from religious ones, because that would be a form of regression).

In what follows, I will briefly reconstruct that argument and highlight (even more briefly) why I have qualms about it.

On the one hand, Habermas regards Kantian and post-Kantian conceptions of autonomy – of moral autonomy and the autonomy of morality – as the major achievement of modern philosophy.[18] In his critique of Rawls, for example, he affirms the priority of autonomous reason and morality[19] and argues that justice has to rest on its own foundation of reasonable justification.[20] On the other hand, the postmetaphysical conception of reason is a *secular*, but not a *secularistic* one,[21] so that it is not only aware of its religious past but is also conscious of its own limits.

One of these limits resides in what might be called a *semi-translation* of the Christian notion of the two kingdoms and of the divine authority of universal morality into a postmetaphysical conception, which occurred between Luther and Kant, following a tradition that began with Augustine.[22] Although Kant saved the "deontological substance of a morality of reason and of rational natural law,"[23] he had to make a clear separation between the religious conception of "redemptive justice" (*rettende Gerechtigkeit*) and deontological morality, shifting from divine to self-given, rational moral law. But that leaves a "gap" between moral duty and the attraction of a larger (religious) notion of the good that Kant could not fill (though he tried to narrow it in his philosophy of religion) – and which Hegel attempted to close with the notion of *Sittlichkeit* (ethical life), with only limited success (a point to which I will return).

Habermas elaborates on this in the crucial chapter on Hume and Kant and the very last chapter, together with the Postscript

---

[17] Habermas, *Auch eine Geschichte der Philosophie*, vol. 1, pp. 166f.
[18] Ibid., vol. 2, pp. 209, 562.
[19] Ibid., vol. 1, p. 98.
[20] Ibid., p. 131: "*selbsttragende 'vernünftige' Rechtfertigung*." See also my critique of Rawls since *Contexts of Justice*, ch. 4.2; *The Right to Justification*, ch. 4; and Chapter 11 in this volume.
[21] Habermas, *Auch eine Geschichte der Philosophie*, vol. 1, p. 133.
[22] Ibid., p. 164.
[23] Habermas, *Auch eine Geschichte der Philosophie*, vol. 1, pp. 166f.: "*deontologische Substanz von Vernunftmoral und Vernunftrecht*."

and subsequent texts.[24] He stresses the innovative character of the conception of moral autonomy as self-legislation grounded in reason, especially in connection with the idea of emancipatory social and political practice in Kant, Hegel and, in particular, the young Hegelians leading up to Marx. Yet at the same time that notion of moral freedom can only ground moral duty in a "need" or an "interest" of reason basically in itself, as affirming its own legislative power.[25] The result is a "motivational deficit of a reason-based morality conceptualized in cognitivist terms, which [...] intrinsically lacks the motivational force of the religious promise of salvation [...]."[26] Or, in a later passage: "After the critique of metaphysics had decoupled faith and knowledge, what could replace the authority of the divine will and its laws as a justification of the *binding force* of moral norms?"[27] The result is a profound "embarrassment of secular postmetaphysical thinking at being unable to find a rational explanation for the normative binding forces originally nourished by the sacred complex."[28]

I am skeptical about this argument for two reasons. First, I think Habermas's reading of Kant is one-sided, because it does not sufficiently stress the *social*–practical, *moral* character of reason in Kant. The categorical imperative is a principle of rational self-legislation, yet it is grounded in the moral – and not "just" rational – idea that we are all (equal) members of the kingdom of ends, who are responsible to and for each other. Thus, a notion of *moral community* and moral responsibility is built into the very conception of reasonable autonomy in addition to the assumption that we are bound by rational principles. Reflecting on our status as moral law-givers also means reflecting on our membership in a social community of equals and the responsibilities that flow from that – at least that is how I read Kant.[29]

---

[24] See especially his Frankfurt lecture on his 90th birthday, "Noch einmal."
[25] Habermas, *Auch eine Geschichte der Philosophie*, vol. 2, pp. 308, 319.
[26] Ibid., p. 332: "*Motivationsschwäche einer vernünftigen, also kognitivistisch begriffenen Moral, der [...] von Haus aus die Antriebskraft des religiösen Heilsversprechens fehlt [...].*"
[27] Ibid., p. 344 (emphasis in original): "*Was konnte, nach der metaphysikkritischen Entkoppelung des Wissens vom Glauben, an die Stelle der Autorität des göttlichen Willens und seiner Gesetze treten, um die* Bindungskraft *moralischer Normen zu begründen?*"
[28] Ibid., p. 347: "*Verlegenheit des säkularen nachmetaphysischen Denkens, eine vernünftige Erklärung für normative Bindungskräfte zu finden, die ursprünglich vom sakralen Komplex gezehrt hatten.*"
[29] I elaborate on this in Forst, *The Right to Justification*, chs. 1 and 2, and in the Introduction and Chapter 1 of this volume. For an interpretation of Kant's ethics that

Second, the idea of the justificatory or motivational gap (Habermas uses both terms, as seen above, with special emphasis on the motivational aspect), the notion that the categorical imperative has only "weak" motivational force, and the charge that it lacks full moral authority give too much credit to a religiously grounded morality – which is thereby almost posited as an ideal. For, from the perspective of postmetaphysical morality, such a religious morality is highly *deficient*, as critics such as Castellio, Bayle and Kant (and, to some extent, Habermas himself)[30] have pointed out (and as I try to show in the narrative of my *Toleration in Conflict*), for a number of reasons. First, it is not really a form of intersubjective morality, because the main reason for seeing oneself as being bound to obey the moral law is love or fear of God – not respect for the other as a human being. But, whether the resulting kind of behavior is based on love or fear of God, it is not morally motivated in the full sense; hence, it is a form of heteronomy. Second, such a notion of morality is authoritarian, because it regards the law as being imposed by a higher authority outside the moral subject itself. Third, if an essential reason for being moral is the hope of becoming worthy of grace and salvation, then the resulting action is not really moral either but (in Habermas's words) "ethically" – that is, hypothetically, in Kant's sense of the term – motivated, and hence, again, a form of heteronomy. Fourth, such a notion of morality is extremely limited and is not truly universal, because from that perspective one cannot fully trust nonbelievers to be morally responsible persons, because they have no way of seeing the point of morality – and can at best be only "anonymous" moral persons. And, finally, within a religious framework such as the Christian or Muslim one, moral norms can be trumped by other imperatives in order to defend the honor of God – against blasphemy, for example, as the long history of religious intolerance demonstrates.[31]

For all of these reasons, a morality based on the autonomy of practical reason – as the imperative to respect others as equal justificatory authorities, to put it in my terms – is not a weaker form of morality, neither with respect to motive, foundation, nor content, but a *stronger* one as compared to a religiously based one. Overcoming

---

stresses its social, intersubjective character, see also Herman, *The Practice of Moral Judgment*.

[30] See Habermas, *Auch eine Geschichte der Philosophie*, vol. 2, pp. 219f. I discuss this in my essay "Religion and Toleration from the Enlightenment to the Post-Secular Era: Bayle, Kant and Habermas," ch. 5 of *Normativity and Power*.

[31] See on these various points Forst, *Toleration in Conflict*, §§5, 9, 18, 21, 29–32.

heteronomous aspects of morality means strengthening it, not reducing it to a weaker form of motivation. Autonomous morality, after all, also proved to be strong enough, historically speaking, to challenge and overcome religious restrictions of morality, allowing the learning process of modernity to unfold historically, the very process that Habermas stresses. This may not count as a form of historical proof in a strong sense of the term but, like Habermas, I consider the advances during the period of modernity as important stages of progress, and overcoming the restrictions of religious morality was essential for that process to unfold.[32]

In light of this, I agree with Habermas that it is a highly relevant question whether and in what way "the motivating force of good reasons can replace the sacred binding force of divine commands";[33] however, from the perspective outlined above, I see the replacement of divine authority by the authority of reason not as an enduring *problem* for postmetaphysical thought but as a major *advantage*. Morality ought not to be thought of as an authoritarian and alien, divine force but as an at once liberating and binding force in our rational life, in the sense of our *autonomous* responsibility toward others (and not, or at least not primarily, toward God).

I also agree fully with Habermas's claim that the "detranscendentalizing" move beyond Kant toward a discursive conception of morality (which was possible after Peirce) represented a further progressive step; but I would distinguish between a "detranscending" move away from religious to autonomous morality and a "detranscendentalizing" step, which is quite a different matter. And the latter move has to be limited, for, despite the corresponding transformation of philosophy (as Apel called it), we remain citizens of *two worlds*. As Peirce's (and Habermas's) stress on the unlimited community of discourse (and justification) shows, there can be no meaningful normative notion of the "counterfactual" transcending what is empirically given without the transcendental idea that we are always members of a discursive or communicative kingdom of ends in which we are ideally truly equals, even when as an empirical matter we are treated as low, undeserving, worthless, and are silenced.[34] That is the truth of the doctrine of two worlds that remains even after all secular translations. The "counterfactual element" is essential for any thought of *vernünftige Freiheit* and true emancipation: "Only a form of freedom about which we

---

[32] Habermas, *Auch eine Geschichte der Philosophie*, vol. 2, pp. 215–217.
[33] Ibid., p. 370: "*die motivierende Kraft guter Gründe die sakrale Bindungskraft göttlicher Gebote ersetzen kann.*"
[34] See also Habermas, "An Author's Retrospective View," sec. 4.

know *that nobody is truly free until everyone is* satisfies the concept of autonomy."[35] If we are to have this kind of *Wissen*, then a *detranscendentalization* (*Detranszendentalisierung*) cannot be a complete *elimination of the transcendental* (*Enttranszendentalisierung*). That is how the "transcending force of validity claims"[36] becomes part of the lifeworld and at the same time transcends it – from "within," as it were.[37] This means that we cannot and must not look for a notion of "unconditional" (*unbedingte*) or "absolute" duty or binding force that is structured like a religious one.[38] Rather, for postmetaphysical thought it means that reason accepts *no* higher authority than itself and ought not to do so in order to avoid regression. To look for an equivalent of religious authority that could "anchor" reason would be to look for something that should not and cannot exist. This is also Habermas's view.

In my view, the noumenal power of religious authority could also only be based on reasons, "good" reasons, as religious believers assumed. And I do not see why the moral reason that you owe all others respect as equal members of the community of justification of all humans who are bound together by the capacity for justification, responsiveness and responsibility would be "weaker" because it is "only" based on reason.[39] Would that imply that cognitivistic morality is weaker because it lacks – what exactly? Emotional depth, ethical aspirations, love or fear of God? But these are all *extra-moral* motives from a Kantian or post-Kantian viewpoint, and thus we would declare only those moralities to be "strong" that go beyond moral motives and leave autonomy behind, because they require an anchor external to morality. That would amount to a contradiction, because "strong" morality would no longer be morality properly speaking. It is part of the very definition of a deontological notion of morality that its justification and its motivation are inseparable, and that is why I disagree with Habermas's claim that post-Kantian morality can only rely on a "weak motivational force of good reasons" in need of further support.[40] There is no stronger force

---

[35] Habermas, *Auch eine Geschichte der Philosophie*, vol. 2, p. 552 (emphasis in original): "*Nur die Freiheit erfüllt den Begriff der Autonomie, von der wir wissen*, dass niemand wirklich frei ist, bevor es nicht alle sind." See Habermas, "An Author's Retrospective View," sec. 5.
[36] Habermas, *Auch eine Geschichte der Philosophie*, vol. 2, p. 584: "*transzendierende Kraft von Geltungsansprüchen*"; see also pp. 596f. on Apel.
[37] Ibid., pp. 752–754.
[38] Ibid., pp. 588f.
[39] Ibid., p. 761.
[40] Ibid., p. 804. See Habermas, "An Author's Retrospective View," sec. 5 in very clear

from the perspective of morality than good moral reasons. To search for other, additional motivational reasons would lead us back to – Hume.

To put it in a nutshell, it seems that, on the one hand, Habermas does not go far enough in *detranscending* morality, so that it could be regarded as fully autonomous and binding, whereas, on the other hand, he goes too far in *detranscendentalizing* morality, explicitly questioning what he must implicitly assume, namely, the binding force of the socially relevant, transcendental-moral idea that we are members in a kingdom of ends.

14.3 Moral "encouragement" after Kierkegaard and the Young Hegelians

In the Postscript (and in his Frankfurt lecture on *Moralität und Sittlichkeit*),[41] Habermas returns to this central issue around which the whole book revolves. With Hegel, and following up on his earlier writings on discourse ethics, he once again addresses the "embarrassment that the abstract ought lacks a motivational embedding," and reminds us of an "excess" (*Überschuss*) of unconditional obligation and absolute duty that stems from religious background assumptions.[42] Because these assumptions are no longer tenable from the perspective of postmetaphysical reason, Habermas reinterprets the point of the Kantian conception of freedom as expressing the "*self-understanding* of humans as *autonomous beings of reason*,"[43] such that there are a number of reasons (some of them historical) to accept such a self-understanding; but ultimately it remains dependent on – shall we say, an *ethical* – decision in the sense of *fides qua*,[44] an act (or perhaps a leap?) of faith. If we read this in a post-Kierkegaardian way, a non-moral, heteronomous, namely, ethical (in Habermas's sense of the term) consideration or identity came to motivate moral action.[45] And moral autonomy withered away, because merely ethical

---

terms. My disagreement, I admit, is a long-standing one. See, for example, Forst, *The Right to Justification*, chs. 3 and 4. And, more recently, Forst, *Normativity and Power*, ch. 5. We continue this discussion in Forst, "Die Welten der Rechtfertigung," and the reply in Habermas, "Antworten."
[41] Habermas, "Noch einmal."
[42] Habermas, *Auch eine Geschichte der Philosophie*, vol. 2, p. 804.
[43] Ibid., p. 805 (emphasis in original): "Selbstverständnis *des Menschen als eines autonomen Vernunftwesens*."
[44] Ibid., p. 805.
[45] See also Habermas, "An Author's Retrospective View," p. 9 (emphasis in original):

"oughts" are, in Kantian terms, hypothetical and not categorical.[46] Ethical values attract us in guiding our lives, whereas moral norms bind us as reasonable and responsible persons.

In modernity, however, such an act of ethical–moral faith is not the heroic or decisionistic act of a single individual, as Habermas explains using a Hegelian thought. As I mentioned above, Habermas is highly critical of Hegel's attempt to include, modify and preserve (*aufheben*) Kantian morality in the *Sittlichkeit* of the state. This is because it cannot do justice to the transcending power of the *unconditional* moral ought that remains a "thorn in the flesh of ethical life,"[47] both in the sense that *individual* moral actions go beyond conventional norms and *collective* democratic action transcends the given normative order.[48] Hegel's notion of "objective spirit" does not leave sufficient room for reasonable freedom to radically transcend what is normatively given toward further emancipation, individually and socially. This latter point was stressed especially by the young Hegelians and Marx.

Still, with regard to the period after the detranscendentalization of the Kantian notion of autonomy, following the path prepared by the young Hegelians, Habermas is convinced that successful historical struggles to achieve democratic political orders and institutionalize human rights *create* political–moral forms of life that not only *encourage collectives* to aim for further democratic and moral progress, but also *nourish* the motivation of *individuals* to act according to the moral law[49] and develop the self-understanding mentioned above. In democracies, Kantian morality acquires empirical political and legal reality,[50] and moral, discursive reason not only becomes situated in legal and political institutions and social life-worlds, but is also supported by a practice of reason-giving that aims to make these practices more democratic and egalitarian:

> Without the task of justifying *standards* of political justice in discourse, which originated in natural and rational law but has now been assigned to the respective historical participants in a historical constituent assembly themselves, it would not have been possible to convince entire

---

"*such a* self-understanding *can also provide a motivational reason for us to strive* to be moral."
[46] See my critique in Forst, *The Right to Justification*, ch. 3.
[47] Habermas, *Auch eine Geschichte der Philosophie*, vol. 2, p. 550: "Stachel im Fleisch der Sittlichkeit."
[48] Ibid., p. 535. See especially Habermas, "An Author's Retrospective View," sec. 4.
[49] Habermas, *Auch eine Geschichte der Philosophie*, vol. 2, pp. 550–552.
[50] Ibid., pp. 553.

populations with arguments that there is a *secular equivalent* for the religious legitimization of the exercise of political rule.[51]

In this way, Habermas combines a post-Kierkegaardian ethic with a post-Hegelian idea of *sittlicher* progress in the form of learning processes "that do not, as Kant thought, only take place in the heads of the individual subjects, but that also do not simply progress above the heads of communicatively socialized subjects."[52]

The Postscript summarizes this thought as follows, combining the two, in my terms, (post-)Kierkegaardian and the (post-)Hegelian aspects:

> The individual's self-understanding as an autonomous rational being can find encouragement above all in the historical traces of those moral–practical learning processes which are embodied in the increase in institutionalized freedoms and, today especially, in the practices and legal guarantees of democratic constitutional states. These empirical reasons can reinforce the fragile trust in one's own powers.[53]

Habermas suggests a complex, post-Hegelian notion of moral–political *Aufhebung*: While the young Hegelians developed a radical notion of rational freedom to transcend conventional forms of *Sittlichkeit*,[54] modern forms of democratic *Sittlichkeit* contain that moment of transcendence *within themselves*, so to speak, an *inherent transcendence*: they institutionalize a form of legal and political order that reflexively generates the duty to improve on itself, procedurally and substantively, by establishing superior forms of democratic organization, of securing and interpreting human rights, and by aiming at transnational forms of democratic cooperation. It is thus a *Sittlichkeit* that is *present and at the same time yet to come*; it generates the empirical motivational force to act morally through forms of socialization and learning that aim at further social and political progress.

This way of combining *Moralität und Sittlichkeit*, which Habermas also summarizes and develops further in his Frankfurt lecture,[55] is unique, and it marks the culmination of the argument of the book – and, needless to say, constitutes the core of his view of the

---

[51] Ibid., p. 554 (emphasis in original).
[52] Ibid., p. 555: "*die sich zwar nicht mehr wie bei Kant im Kopf des einzelnen Subjekts vollziehen, die sich aber ebenso wenig objektiv über die Köpfe der kommunikativ vergesellschafteten Subjekte hinweg durchsetzen.*"
[53] Ibid., p. 806: "*Diese empirischen Gründe können das fragile Vertrauen in die eigenen Kräfte stützen.*"
[54] Ibid., p. 597.
[55] See Habermas, "Noch einmal."

relationship between reason, progress, democracy and morality (which was also laid out in *Between Facts and Norms*). It is very much informed by the philosophy of Kant, who saw progressive "historical sign[s]"[56] (*Geschichtszeichen*) such as the enthusiasm about the French Revolution as indications of the moral and progressive nature of human beings that encourage them to believe in and act toward social and political improvement.

Still, the argument cannot fully succeed, because it leans toward an excessively empirical (almost empiricist) interpretation of motivation. For the radical demand (Habermas speaks of a "*Zumutung*")[57] of the unconditional moral ought could not have been salvaged into modernity and postmetaphysical thinking if its motivational force were empirically dependent on the individual *ethical* will to be moral that is *encouraged* by social and political institutions and established norms. In that case, neither could we hold onto the moral *duty* to be such a person as a duty that is, as Habermas affirms, *independently* "distinguished as right"[58] and can be used to criticize the self-understanding of persons; rather, we would have to translate that duty into an ethical consideration. Nor could we motivationally hold onto the moral *imperative* of rational freedom, individually and collectively, independently of social progress or regress. We would be bereft of the moral force of the duty to aim at emancipation for the sake of justice if that force depended on historical success. Rather, the situation is the other way around: the duty remains an autonomous one and increases in importance in times of despair and political regress. In addition, if morality did not transcend every form of *Sittlichkeit*, we could not even identify progress or regress, whether times were good or ill.[59] This is why Habermas, at the end of his Frankfurt lecture, speaks of reason as a mole who stubbornly works toward its realization, citing Kant: "Kant inculcated this mentality in us [...]."[60] This means that the work of rational freedom is aided by an "empirical" support, but its normative bindingness and validity remains *independent* of this; and, if that is the case, its motivational force cannot depend on nonmoral motives, on *ethical* decisions or on *established* institutional forms. If reason did not motivate the mole to work tirelessly, even if the ground gets very hard, it would

---

[56] Kant, *The Conflict of the Faculties*, VII:84.
[57] Habermas, *Auch eine Geschichte der Philosophie*, vol. 2, p. 805.
[58] Ibid.: "*als richtig ausgezeichnete.*"
[59] See Chapters 2 and 3 in this volume.
[60] Habermas, "Noch einmal," p. 41: "*Diese Gesinnung hat uns Kant [...] eingeprägt.*"

not fully understand itself as being both historical and progressive, transcending the given.

In other words, the transcendental – that is, our membership in a kingdom of ends that transcends every given community generating an imperative of progressive realization, despite the odds – has to remain the "thorn in the flesh" of every ethical or *sittliche* form of life in order to guide *and* motivate human action in secular modernity. And, likewise, it remains a thorn in the flesh of every religious body of faith that could only express the point of morality in a mediated, limited form (as argued above). The "excess" of the moral ought is not homeless in the postmetaphysical age, and hence it is not in need of empirical, ethical–political shelter or guidance; rather, it is on its way to itself as a demand of reason and (rational) hope, even in times of despair. If we had to translate moral reasons back into ethical and *sittliche* reasons, we would practice a form of *reverse translation* – quite against the spirit of his book and Habermas's general enterprise.

BIBLIOGRAPHY

Adorno, T. W., *Aspects of the New Right-Wing Extremism*, trans. W. Hoban. Cambridge: Polity, 2020.
—, *Negative Dialectics*, trans. E. B. Ashton. New York: Continuum, 1973/1966.
Adorno, T. W., Albert, H., Dahrendorf, R., Habermas, J., Pilot, H. and Popper, K. R., *The Positivist Dispute in German Sociology*, trans. G. Adey and D. Frisby. London: Heinemann Education Publishers, 1976.
Ahlhaus, S. and Niesen, P., "Regressionen des Mitgliedschaftsrechts: Für einen Kosmopolitismus von innen." In U. Bohmann and P. Sörensen (eds.), *Kritische Theorie der Politik*. Berlin: Suhrkamp, 2019, pp. 608–631.
Alexy, R., *A Theory of Constitutional Rights*, trans. J. Rivers. Oxford: Oxford University Press, 2010.
Allen, A., "Progress, Normativity, and Universality: Reply to Forst." In A. Allen and E. Mendieta (eds.), *Justification and Emancipation: The Critical Theory of Rainer Forst*. Pennsylvania: The Pennsylvania State University Press, 2019, pp. 145–156.
—, *The End of Progress: Decolonizing the Normative Foundations of Critical Theory*. New York: Columbia University Press, 2016.
—, "The Power of Justification." In R. Forst, *Justice, Democracy and the Right to Justification: Rainer Forst in Dialogue*. London: Bloomsbury, 2014, pp. 65–86.
Allen, A., Forst, R. and Haugaard, M., "Power and Reason, Justice and Domination: A Conversation." *Journal of Political Power* 7: 1, 2014, 7–33.
Allen, A. and Mendieta, E. (eds.), *Justification and Emancipation: The Critical Theory of Rainer Forst*. Pennsylvania: The Pennsylvania State University Press, 2019.
Anderson, B., *Imagined Communities: Reflections on the Origin and Spread of Nationalism*. London: Verso, 2016.
Anderson, E. S., "What Is the Point of Equality?" *Ethics* 109: 2, 1999, 287–337.
Apel, K.-O., "The Apriori of the Communication Community and the Foundations of Ethics." In *Towards a Transformation of Philosophy*, trans. G. Adey and D. Fisby. Milwaukee: Marquette University Press, 1998, pp. 225–300.
Arant, R., Dragolov, G. and Boehnke, K., *Radar gesellschaftlicher Zusammenhalt: Sozialer Zusammenhalt in Deutschland 2017*. Gütersloh: Bertelsmann Stiftung, 2017.

Arato, A. and Cohen, J. L., *Populism and Civil Society: The Challenge to Constitutional Democracy*. Oxford: Oxford University Press, 2021.

Arendt, H., "On Violence." In *Crisis of the Republic*. San Diego: Harvest, 1972, pp. 103–184.

—, *Origins of Totalitarianism*. New York: Harcourt, Brace and Co., 1951.

—, "Philosophy and Politics." *Social Research* 71: 3, 2004/1990, 427–454.

Arneson, R., "Luck Egalitarianism Interpreted and Defended." *Philosophical Topics* 32: 1/2, 2004, 1–20.

Avant, D. D., Finnemore, M. and Sell, S. K. (eds.), *Who Governs the Globe?* Cambridge: Cambridge University Press, 2010.

Bajaj, S. and Rossi, E., "Noumenal Power, Reasons, and Justification: A Critique of Forst." In E. Herlin-Karnell and M. Klatt (eds.), *Constitutionalism Justified: Rainer Forst in Discourse*. Oxford: Oxford University Press, 2019, pp. 117–131.

Banai, A., Ronzoni, M. and Schemmel, C. (eds.), *Social Justice, Global Dynamics: Theoretical and Empirical Perspectives*. London: Routledge, 2011.

Banting, K. and Kymlicka, W. (eds.), *The Strains of Commitment: The Political Sources of Solidarity in Diverse Societies*. Oxford: Oxford University Press, 2017.

Barry, B., *Justice as Impartiality*. Oxford: Clarendon Press, 1995.

Bayertz, K. (ed.), "Four Uses of 'Solidarity.'" In *Solidarity*. Dordrecht: Kluwer Academic Publishers, 1999, pp. 3–28.

—, *Solidarity*. Dordrecht: Kluwer Academic Publishers, 1999.

Bayle, P., "Choix d'articles tirés du Dictionnaire historique et critique." In E. Labrousse (ed.), *Œuvres Diverses*, supplementary volume. Hildesheim: Georg Olms, 1982.

—, "Commentaire Philosophique sur ces paroles de Jesus-Christ 'Contrain-les d'entrer.'" In E. Labrousse (ed.), *Œuvres Diverses*, vol. 2. Hildesheim: Georg Olms, 1965.

—, *Historical and Critical Dictionary: Selections*, ed. and trans. R. H. Popkin. Indianapolis: Hackett, 1991.

—, *Philosophical Commentary on These Words of Jesus Christ, Compel Them To Come In*, ed. and trans. A. Godman Tannenbaum. New York: Peter Lang, 1987.

Beitz, C. R., "Human Dignity in the Theory of Human Rights: Nothing But a Phrase?" *Philosophy & Public Affairs* 41: 3, 2013, 259–290.

—, *The Idea of Human Rights*. Oxford: Oxford University Press, 2009.

Benhabib, S., *Dignity in Adversity: Human Rights in Troubled Times*. Cambridge: Polity, 2011.

—, "On Reconciliation and Respect, Justice and the Good Life: Response to Herta Nagl-Docekal and Rainer Forst." *Philosophy & Social Criticism* 23: 5, 1997, 97–114.

—, *Situating the Self: Gender, Community and Postmodernism in Contemporary Ethics*. New York: Routledge, 1992.

—, *The Reluctant Modernism of Hannah Arendt*. London: Sage, 1996.

—, *The Rights of Others: Aliens, Residents, and Citizens*. Cambridge: Cambridge University Press, 2004.

—, "The Uses and Abuses of Kantian Rigorism: On Rainer Forst's Moral and Political Philosophy." *Political Theory* 43: 6, 2015, 777–792.

Besson, S., "Human Rights and Constitutional Law: Patterns of Mutual Validation and Legitimation." In R. Cruft, M. Liao and M. Renzo (eds.),

Philosophical Foundations of Human Rights. Oxford: Oxford University Press, 2015, pp. 279–299.
Blake, M., "Distributive Justice, State Coercion, and Autonomy." *Philosophy & Public Affairs* 30: 3, 2001, 257–296.
Bloch, E., *Natural Law and Human Dignity*, trans. D. F. Schmidt. Cambridge, MA: MIT Press, 1986.
Boltanski, L. and Thévenot, L., *On Justification: Economies of Worth*, trans. C. Porter. Princeton: Princeton University Press, 2006.
Bourdieu, P., *Practical Reason: On the Theory of Action*, trans. R. Johnson. Stanford: Stanford University Press, 1998.
Buchanan, A., "Exploitation, Alienation, and Injustice." *Canadian Journal of Philosophy* 9: 1, 1979, 121–139.
—, *The Heart of Human Rights*. Oxford: Oxford University Press, 2013.
Buchanan, A. and Powell, R., *The Evolution of Moral Progress: A Biocultural Theory*. Oxford: Oxford University Press, 2018.
Bohman, J., *Democracy across Borders: From Dêmos to Dêmoi*. Cambridge, MA: MIT Press, 2007.
Brown, W., "Neoliberalism's Frankenstein: Authoritarian Freedom in Twenty-First Century 'Democracies.'" In W. Brown, P. Gordon and M. Pensky (eds.), *Authoritarianism: Three Inquiries in Critical Theory*. Chicago: The University of Chicago Press, 2018, pp. 7–43.
—, *Undoing the Demos: Neoliberalism's Stealth Revolution*. Princeton: Princeton University Press, 2015.
Brunkhorst, H., *Solidarität unter Fremden*. Frankfurt/Main: Fischer, 2017.
—, *Solidarity: From Civic Friendship to A Global Legal Community*. Cambridge, MA: MIT Press, 2015.
Caney, S., "Justice and the Basic Right to Justification." In R. Forst, *Justice, Democracy and the Right to Justification: Rainer Forst in Dialogue*. London: Bloomsbury, 2014, pp. 147–166.
—, *Justice Beyond Borders: A Global Political Theory*. Oxford: Oxford University Press, 2005.
Castro Varela, M. d. M. and Dhawan, N. (eds.), *Soziale (Un)Gerechtigkeit: Kritische Perspektiven auf Diversität, Intersektionalität und Antidiskriminierung*. Münster: LIT Verlag, 2011.
Chan, J., To, H.-P. and Chan, E., "Reconsidering Social Cohesion: Developing a Definition and Analytical Framework for Empirical Research." *Social Indicators Research* 75, 2006, 273–302.
Celikates, R. and Jaeggi, R., *Sozialphilosophie: Eine Einführung*. München: C. H. Beck, 2017.
Chakrabarty, D., *Provincializing Europe: Postcolonial Thought and Historical Difference*. Princeton: Princeton University Press, 2000.
Ci, J., *Moral China in the Age of Reform*. Cambridge: Cambridge University Press, 2014.
Cohen, G. A., "Afterword to Chapters One and Two." In *On the Currency of Egalitarian Justice, and Other Essays in Political Philosophy*. Princeton: Princeton University Press, 2011, pp. 61–72.
—, *On the Currency of Egalitarian Justice, and Other Essays in Political Philosophy*. Princeton: Princeton University Press, 2011.
—, *Rescuing Justice and Equality*. Cambridge, MA: Harvard University Press, 2008.

—, *Why Not Socialism?* Princeton: Princeton University Press, 2009.
Cohen, J., *Rousseau: A Free Community of Equals*. Oxford: Oxford University Press, 2010.
Cohen, J. and Sabel, C., "Extra Rempublicam Nulla Iustitia." *Philosophy & Public Affairs* 34: 2, 2006, 147–175.
Culp, J., *Global Justice and Development*. New York: Palgrave Macmillan, 2014.
Dahl, R. A., "The Concept of Power." *Behavioral Science* 2: 3, 1957, 201–215.
Darwall, S. L., *The Second-Person Standpoint: Morality, Respect, and Accountability*. Cambridge, MA: Harvard University Press, 2006.
Denninger, E., "Constitutional Law and Solidarity." In K. Bayertz (ed.), *Solidarity*. Dordrecht: Kluwer Academic Publishers, 1999, pp. 223–242.
Derpmann, S., *Gründe der Solidarität*. Münster: Mentis, 2013.
De Wilde, P., Koopmans, R., Merkel, W., Strijbis, O. and Zürn, M. (eds.), *The Struggle Over Borders: Cosmopolitanism and Communitarianism*. Cambridge: Cambridge University Press, 2019.
Dragolov, G., Ignácz, Z., Lorenz, J., Delhey, J. and Boehnke, K., *Radar gesellschaftlicher Zusammenhalt: Gesellschaftlicher Zusammenhalt im internationalen Vergleich*. Gütersloh: Bertelsmann Stiftung, 2013.
Dreben, B., "On Rawls and Political Liberalism." In S. Freeman (ed.), *The Cambridge Companion to Rawls*. Cambridge: Cambridge University Press, 2003, pp. 316–346.
Dübgen, F., *Was ist gerecht? Kennzeichen einer transnationalen solidarischen Politik*. Frankfurt/Main: Campus, 2014.
Durkheim, É., *The Division of Labour in Society*, trans. W. D. Halls. London: Palgrave Macmillan, 1984/1893.
Dworkin, R., *Sovereign Virtue: The Theory and Practice of Equality*. Cambridge, MA: Harvard University Press, 2002.
Eberl, O., *Naturzustand und Barbarei: Begründung und Kritik staatlicher Ordnung im Zeichen des Kolonialismus*. Hamburg: Hamburger Edition, 2021.
Enoch, D., "Agency, Shmagency: Why Normativity Won't Come From What Is Constitutive of Action." *The Philosophical Review* 115: 2, 2006, 169–198.
—, "Can There Be a Global, Interesting, Coherent Constructivism About Practical Reason?" *Philosophical Explorations* 12: 3, 2009, 319–339.
Erman, E. and Möller, N., *The Practical Turn in Political Theory*. Edinburgh: Edinburgh University Press, 2018.
Esping-Andersen, G., *Social Foundations of Postindustrial Economies*. Oxford: Oxford University Press, 1999.
Estlund, D., *Utopophobia: On the Limits (If Any) Of Political Philosophy*. Princeton: Princeton University Press, 2020.
Fanon, F., *The Wretched of the Earth*, trans. C. Farrington. New York: Grove Press, 2004.
Ferrara, A., *Modernity and Authenticity: A Study in the Social and Ethical Thought of Jean-Jacques Rousseau*. Albany: State University of New York Press, 1993.
—, *Reflective Authenticity: Rethinking the Project of Modernity*. London: Routledge, 1998.
Flikschuh, K., "Human Rights in Kantian Mode: A Sketch." In R. Cruft, M. Liao and M. Renzo (eds.), *Philosophical Foundations of Human Rights*. Oxford: Oxford University Press, 2015, pp. 653–670.

Flikschuh, K. and Ypi, L. (eds.), *Kant and Colonialism: Historical and Critical Perspectives*. Oxford: Oxford University Press, 2014.

Frankfurt, H., *Necessity, Volition, and Love*. Cambridge: Cambridge University Press, 1999.

—, *The Importance of What We Care About*. Cambridge: Cambridge University Press, 1988.

Forst, R., "A Critical Theory of Politics: Grounds, Method and Aims – Reply to Simone Chambers, Stephen White and Lea Ypi." *Philosophy & Social Criticism* 41: 3, 2015, 225–234.

—, "A Kantian Republican Conception of Justice as Nondomination." In A. Niederberger and P. Schink (eds.), *Republican Democracy: Liberty, Law and Politics*. Edinburgh: Edinburgh University Press, 2013, pp. 154–168.

—, *Contexts of Justice: Political Philosophy Beyond Liberalism and Communitarianism*, trans. J. M. M. Farrell. Berkeley: University of California Press, 2002.

—, "Das Recht der Negativität." T. Khurana, D. Quadflieg, F. Raimondi, J. Rebentisch and D. Setton (eds.), *Negativität: Kunst, Recht, Politik*. Berlin: Suhrkamp, 2018, pp. 196–206.

—, "Deontological Communitarianism. Laudation for Thomas M. Scanlon." In M. Stepanians and M. Frauchiger (eds.), *Reason, Justification, and Contractualism: Themes from Scanlon*. Berlin: De Gruyter, 2021, pp. 11–16.

—, *Die noumenale Republik: Kritischer Konstruktivismus nach Kant*. Berlin: Suhrkamp, 2021.

—, "Die Welten der Rechtfertigung: Die Diskursethik als kantischer Konstruktivismus" In S. Müller-Doohm, S. Rapic and T. Wesche (eds.), *Vernünftige Freiheit und öffentliche Vernunft: Beiträge zum Spätwerk von Jürgen Habermas*. Berlin: Suhrkamp, 2024, pp. 238–259.

—, "Freiheiten, Risiken und Rechtfertigungen: Eine deontologisch-demokratische Perspektive auf die Bekämpfung der Pandemie." In K. Günter and U. Volkmann (eds.), *Freiheit oder Leben? Das Abwägungsproblem der Zukunft*. Berlin: Suhrkamp, 2022, pp. 312–325.

—, "Human Rights in Context: A Comment on Sangiovanni." In A. Etinson (ed.), *Human Rights: Moral or Political?* Oxford: Oxford University Press, 2016, pp. 200–208.

—, *Justice, Democracy and the Right to Justification: Rainer Forst in Dialogue*. London: Bloomsbury, 2014.

—, "Justice: Procedural and Substantive." In R. Bellamy and J. King (eds.), *The Cambridge Handbook of Constitutional Theory*. Cambridge: Cambridge University Press, forthcoming.

—, *Justification and Critique: Towards a Critical Theory of Politics*, trans. C. Cronin. Cambridge: Polity, 2014.

—, "Justifying Justification: Reply to my Critics." In R. Forst, *Justice, Democracy and the Right to Justification: Rainer Forst in Dialogue*. London: Bloomsbury, 2014, pp. 169–216.

—, "Letzte Gründe: Karl-Otto Apel zum Gedenken – persönliche und philosophische Bemerkungen." *Topologik* 26, 2019, 60–65.

—, "Might and Right: Ripstein, Kant and the Paradox of Peace." In E. Herlin-Karnell and E. Rossi (eds.), *The Public Uses of Coercion and Force: From Constitutionalism to War*. Oxford: Oxford University Press, 2021, pp. 32–42.

—, "Navigating a World of Conflict and Power: Reply to Critics." In A. Allen and E. Mendieta (eds.), *Justification and Emancipation: The Critical Theory of Rainer Forst*. Pennsylvania: The Pennsylvania State University Press, 2019, pp. 157–188.

—, *Normativity and Power: Analyzing Social Orders of Justification*, trans. C. Cronin. Oxford: Oxford University Press, 2017.

—, "Noumenal Power Revisited: Reply to Critics." *Journal of Political Power* 11: 3, 2018, 294–321.

—, "Religion, Reason and Toleration: Bayle, Kant – and Us." In C. Laborde and A. Bardon (eds.), *Religion in Liberal Political Philosophy*. Oxford: Oxford University Press, 2017, pp. 249–261.

—, "Review of John Rawls' *Political Liberalism*." *Constellations* 1: 1, 1994, 163–171.

—, "Situations of the Self: Reflections on Seyla Benhabib's Version of Critical Theory." *Philosophy & Social Criticism* 23: 5, 1997, 79–96.

—, "The Constitution of Justification: Replies and Comments." In E. Herlin-Karnell and M. Klatt (eds.), *Constitutionalism Justified: Rainer Forst in Discourse*. Oxford: Oxford University Press, 2019, pp. 295–346.

—, "The Dialectics of Toleration and the Power of Reason(s): Reply to My Critics," trans. C. Cronin. In R. Forst, *Toleration, Power and the Right to Justification: Rainer Forst in Dialogue*. Manchester: Manchester University Press, 2020, pp. 167–220.

—, "The Grounds of Institutional Moral Theory: On the Political Philosophy of Allen Buchanan." *Danish Yearbook of Philosophy* 55: 1, 2020, 7–18.

—, "The Justification of Basic Rights: A Discourse–Theoretical Approach." *The Netherlands Journal of Legal Philosophy* 45: 3, 2016, 7–28.

— "The Justification of Trust in Conflict: Conceptual and Normative Groundwork." *ConTrust Working Paper* 2, Frankfurt/Main: ConTrust – Trust in Conflict, 2022, https://contrust.uni-frankfurt.de/files/2022/10/ConTrust-WorkingPaper-No2_Forst.pdf.

—, "The Meaning(s) of Solidarity." In A. Sangiovanni, *Solidarity: Nature, Grounds, and Value. Andrea Sangiovanni in Dialogue*. Manchester: Manchester University Press, forthcoming.

—, "The Method of Insulation: On the Development of Rawls's Thought after *A Theory of Justice*." In P. Weithman (ed.), *Rawls's A Theory of Justice at 50*. Cambridge: Cambridge University Press, 2023, pp. 140–150.

—, "The Neglect of Democracy." *Los Angeles Review of Books Blog*. 2020, December 1, https://blog.lareviewofbooks.org/55-voices/55-voices-democracy-neglect-democracy-rainer-forst/.

—, *The Right to Justification: Elements of a Constructivist Theory of Justice*, trans. J. Flynn. New York: Columbia University Press, 2012.

—, "The Right to Justification: Moral and Political, Transcendental and Historical – Reply to Seyla Benhabib, Jeff Flynn and Matthias Fritsch." *Political Theory* 43: 6, 2015, 822–837.

—, *Toleration in Conflict: Past and Present*, trans. C. Cronin. Cambridge: Cambridge University Press, 2013.

—, *Toleration, Power and the Right to Justification: Rainer Forst in Dialogue*. Manchester: Manchester University Press, 2020.

—, "Two Bad Halves Don't Make a Whole: On the Crisis of Democracy." *Constellations* 26: 3, 2019, 378–383.

—, "What Does It Mean to Justify Basic Rights? Reply to Düwell, Newey,

Rummens and Valentini." *Netherlands Journal of Legal Philosophy* 45: 3, 2016, 76–90.

—, "What's Critical About a Critical Theory of Justice?" In B. Bargu und C. Bottici (eds.), *Feminism, Capitalism, and Critique: Essays in Honor of Nancy Fraser*. Basingstoke: Palgrave Macmillan, 2017, pp. 225–242.

Forst, R. and Günther, K. (eds.), *Die Herausbildung normativer Ordnungen: Interdisziplinäre Perspektiven*. Frankfurt/Main: Campus, 2011.

—, *Normative Ordnungen*. Berlin: Suhrkamp, 2021.

Foucault, M., *The Politics of Truth*, ed. S. Lotringer and trans. L. Hochroth and C. Porter. Los Angeles: Semiotexte, 2007.

—, "What Is Enlightenment?" In P. Rabinow (ed.), *The Foucault Reader*, trans. C. Porter et al. New York: Pantheon Books, 1984, pp. 32–50.

Frankfurt, H., *The Importance of What We Care About*. Cambridge: Cambridge University Press, 1988.

Fraser, N., *Scales of Justice: Reimagining Political Space in a Globalizing World*. New York: Columbia University Press, 2009.

Freeman, S., "Congruence and the Good of Justice." In S. Freeman (ed.), *The Cambridge Companion to Rawls*. Cambridge: Cambridge University Press, 2003, pp. 277–315.

Gädeke, D., *Politik der Beherrschung: Eine kritische Theorie externer Demokratieförderung*. Berlin: Suhrkamp, 2017.

Gauchet, M., *La Révolution des droits de l'homme*, Paris: Gallimard, 1989.

Gallie, W. B., "Essentially Contested Concepts." *Proceedings of the Aristotelian Society* 56, 1956, 167–198.

Gearty, C., "Human Rights: The Necessary Quest for Foundations." In C. Douzinas and C. Gearty (eds.), *The Meanings of Rights: The Philosophy and Social Theory of Human Rights*. Cambridge: Cambridge University Press, 2014, pp. 21–38.

Geiselberger, H. (ed), *Die große Regression: Eine internationale Debatte über die geistige Situation der Zeit*. Berlin: Suhrkamp, 2017.

Gethmann, C. F., "Universelle praktische Geltungsansprüche: Zur philosophischen Bedeutung der kulturellen Genese moralischer Überzeugungen." In P. Janisch (ed.), *Entwicklungen der methodischen Philosophie*. Frankfurt/Main: Suhrkamp, 1991, pp. 148–175.

Geuss, R., *Philosophy and Real Politics*. Princeton: Princeton University Press, 2008.

Giddens, A., *The Constitution of Society: Outline of the Theory of Structuration*. Berkeley: University of California Press, 1984.

Gilabert, P., "Kantian Dignity and Marxian Socialism." *Kantian Review* 22: 4, 2017, 553–577.

Goethe, J. W., *Maximen und Reflexionen*. In *Werke in sechs Bänden*, vol. 6. Frankfurt/Main: Insel, 1981.

Gordon, P. E., "The Authoritarian Personality Revisited: Reading Adorno in the Age of Trump." In W. Brown, P. E. Gordon and M. Pensky (eds.), *Authoritarianism: Three Inquiries in Critical Theory*. Chicago: The University of Chicago Press, 2018, pp. 45–84.

Gould, C. C., "Transnational Solidarities." *Journal of Social Philosophy* 38: 1, 2007, 148–164.

Gramsci, A., *Prison Notebooks*, vol. 2, trans. J. A. Buttigieg. New York: Columbia University Press, 1996/1930.

Griffin, J., *On Human Rights*. Oxford: Oxford University Press, 2008.

Günther, K., "Menschenrechte zwischen Staaten und Dritten." In N. Deitelhoff and J. Steffek (eds.), *Was bleibt vom Staat? Demokratie, Recht und Verfassung im globalen Zeitalter*. Frankfurt/Main: Campus, 2009, pp. 259–280.
Habermas, J., "A Positivistically Bisected Rationalism." In T. W. Adorno, H. Albert, R. Dahrendorf, J. Habermas, H. Pilot and K. R. Popper (eds.), *The Positivist Dispute in German Sociology*, trans. G. Adey and D. Frisby. London: Heinemann, 1976, pp. 198–225.
—, "An Author's Retrospective View." *Constellations* 28: 1, 2021, 5–10.
—, "Antworten." In S. Müller-Doohm, S. Rapic and T. Wesche (eds.), *Vernünftige Freiheit und öffentliche Vernunft: Beiträge zum Spätwerk von Jürgen Habermas*. Berlin: Suhrkamp, 2024, pp. 357–422.
—, *Auch eine Geschichte der Philosophie*. Berlin: Suhrkamp, 2019.
—, *Between Facts and Norms: Contributions to a Discourse Theory of Law and Democracy*, trans. W. Rehg. Cambridge, MA: MIT Press, 1996.
—, "Discourse Ethics: Notes on a Program of Philosophical Justification." In *Moral Consciousness and Communicative Action*. Cambridge, MA: MIT Press, 1990, pp. 43–115.
—, "Faith and Knowledge." In *The Future of Human Nature*, trans. H. Beister et al. Cambridge: Polity, 2003, pp. 101–115.
—, *Im Sog der Technokratie*. Berlin: Suhrkamp, 2013.
—, "Justice and Solidarity: On the Discussion Concerning 'Stage 6.'" *Philosophical Forum* 21: 1, 1989, 32–52.
—, *Moral Consciousness and Communicative Action*, trans. C. Lenhardt and S. W. Nicholsen. Cambridge: Polity, 1990.
—, "Noch einmal: Zum Verhältnis von Moralität und Sittlichkeit – Vortrag an der Universität Frankfurt, 19. Juni 2019." In R. Forst and K. Günther (eds.), *Normative Ordnungen*. Berlin: Suhrkamp, 2021, pp. 25–41.
—, "On Social Identity." *Telos* 19, 1974, 91–103.
—, "'Reasonable' versus 'True' or the Morality of Worldviews." In *The Inclusion of the Other: Studies in Political Theory*, trans. C. Cronin. Cambridge, MA: MIT Press, 1998, pp. 75–101.
—, "Religion in the Public Sphere: Cognitive Presuppositions for the 'Public Use of Reason' by Religious and Secular Citizens." In *Between Naturalism and Religion: Philosophical Essays*, trans. C. Cronin. Cambridge: Polity, 2008, pp. 114–147.
—, "Reply." *Constellations* 28: 1, 2021, 67–78.
—, "The Concept of Human Dignity and the Realistic Utopia of Human Rights." *Metaphilosophy* 41: 4, 2010, 464–480.
—, *The Crisis of the European Union: A Response*, trans. C. Cronin. Cambridge: Polity, 2012.
—, *The Divided West*, trans. C. Cronin. Cambridge: Polity, 2006.
—, *The Future of Human Nature*, trans. H. Beister et al. Cambridge: Polity, 2003.
—, *The Inclusion of the Other: Studies in Political Theory*. Cambridge, MA: MIT Press, 1998.
—, *The Theory of Communicative Action*, trans. T. McCarthy. Boston: Beacon Press, 1984/87.
—, *Theory and Practice*, trans. J. Viertel. Boston: Beacon Press, 1973.
—, "Towards a Reconstruction of Historical Materialism." *Theory and Society* 2: 3, 1975, 287–300.
—, "Transcendence from Within, Transcendence in this World." In *Religion*

and Rationality: Essays on Reason, God and Modernity, ed. E. Mendieta and trans. C. Cronin et al. Cambridge, MA: MIT Press, 2002, pp. 67–94.
—, *Truth and Justification*, ed. and trans. B. Fultner. Cambridge, MA: MIT Press, 2003.
—, "Walter Benjamin: Consciousness-Raising or Rescuing Critique." In *Philosophical-Political Profiles*, trans. F. G. Lawrence. Cambridge, MA: MIT Press, 1983, pp. 131–165.
—, *Zur Logik der Sozialwissenschaften*. Frankfurt/Main: Suhrkamp, 1982.
Habermas, J. and Ratzinger, J., *The Dialectics of Secularization: On Reason and Religion*, ed. F. Schuller and trans. B. McNeil. San Francisco: Ignatius Press, 2006.
Hale, T., Held, D. and Young, K., *Gridlock: Why Global Cooperation Is Failing Us When We Need It Most*. Cambridge: Polity, 2013.
Hartmann, M. and Offe, C. (eds.), *Vertrauen: Die Grundlage des sozialen Zusammenhalts*. Frankfurt/Main: Campus, 2001.
Haslanger, S., *Resisting Reality: Social Construction and Social Critique*. Oxford: Oxford University Press, 2012.
Haugaard, M. and Kettner, M. (eds.), *Theorising Noumenal Power: Rainer Forst and his Critics*. London: Routledge, 2020.
Hayward, C. R., *De-Facing Power*. Cambridge: Cambridge University Press, 2000.
—, "On Structural Power." *Journal of Political Power* 11: 1, 2018, 56–67.
Hayward, C. R. and Lukes, S., "Nobody to Shoot? Power, Structure, and Agency: A Dialogue." *Journal of Power* 1: 1, 2008, 5–20.
Heidegger, M., *Being and Time*, trans. J. Macquarrie and E. Robinson. Oxford: Blackwell, 1962/1927.
Herlin-Karnell, E. and Klatt, M. (eds.), *Constitutionalism Justified: Rainer Forst in Discourse*. Oxford: Oxford University Press, 2019.
Herman, B., *Moral Literacy*. Cambridge, MA: Harvard University Press, 2008.
—, *The Practice of Moral Judgment*. Cambridge, MA: Harvard University Press, 1993.
Hinshelwood, A., "The Relation between Agency, Identification, and Alienation." *Philosophical Explorations* 16: 3, 2013, 243–258.
Honneth, A., *Disrespect: The Normative Foundations of Critical Theory*, trans. J. Ganahl et al. Cambridge: Polity, 2007.
—, *Freedom's Right: The Social Foundations of Democratic Life*, trans. J. Ganahl. New York: Columbia University Press, 2014.
—, *Pathologies of Reason: On the Legacy of Critical Theory*, trans. J. Ingram. New York: Columbia University Press, 2009.
—, "Pathologies of the Social: The Past and Present of Social Philosophy," trans. S. Swindal. In D. M. Rasmussen (ed.), *Handbook of Critical Theory*. Oxford: Blackwell, 1996, pp. 369–398.
—, *Recognition: A Chapter in the History of European Ideas*, trans. J. Ganahl. Cambridge: Cambridge University Press, 2021.
—, *Reification: A New Look at an Old Idea*. Oxford: Oxford University Press, 2008.
—, *The Struggle for Recognition: The Moral Grammar of Social Conflicts*, trans. J. Anderson. Cambridge, MA: MIT Press, 1996.
Horkheimer, M. and Adorno, T. W., *Dialectic of Enlightenment: Philosophical Fragments*, trans. E. Jephcott. Stanford: Stanford University Press, 2002/1944.
Howard, D., "From Marx to Kant: The Return of the Political." *Thesis Eleven* 8: 1, 1984, 77–91.
Hunt, L., *Inventing Human Rights: A History*. New York: Norton, 2008.

Ignatieff, M., *Human Rights as Politics and Idolatry*. Princeton: Princeton University Press, 2001.
Iser, M., *Empörung und Fortschritt: Grundlagen einer kritischen Theorie der Gesellschaft*. Frankfurt/Main: Campus, 2008.
Jaeggi, R., *Alienation*, trans. F. Neuhouser and A. E. Smith. New York: Columbia University Press, 2014.
—, *Critique of Forms of Life*. Cambridge, MA: Harvard University Press, 2018.
—, "Solidarity and Indifference." In R. ter Meulen, W. Arts and R. Muffels (eds.), *Solidarity in Health and Social Care in Europe*. Dordrecht: Kluwer Academic Publishers, 2001, pp. 287–308.
—, "Vorne: Die Fortschrittsidee in Zeiten der Regression." In Heinrich Böll Foundation (ed.), *Stichworte zur Zeit: Ein Glossar*. Bielefeld: Transcript, 2020, pp. 279–292.
James, A., *Fairness in Practice: A Social Contract for a Global Economy*. New York: Oxford University Press, 2012.
Jay, M., *Reason After Its Eclipse: On Late Critical Theory*. Madison: University of Wisconsin Press, 2016.
Jellinek, G., *System der subjektiven öffentlichen Rechte*. Tübingen: Mohr Siebeck, 2011/1892.
Kant, I., "An Answer to the Question: 'What Is Enlightenment?'" In Kant, *Practical Philosophy*, ed. and trans. M. J. Gregor, 1996/1784, pp. 16–22.
—, "Anthropology From a Pragmatic Point of View," trans. R. Louden. In G. Zöller and R. Louden (eds.), *Immanuel Kant: Anthropology, History, and Education*. Cambridge: Cambridge University Press, 2007/1798, pp. 227–429.
—, *Critique of Practical Reason*, ed. and trans. M. J. Gregor. Revised Edition. Cambridge: Cambridge University Press, 2015/1788.
—, *Critique of Pure Reason*, ed. and trans. P. Guyer and A. Wood. Cambridge: Cambridge University Press, 1998/1781.
—, *Groundwork of the Metaphysics of Morals*, ed. and trans. M. J. Gregor and J. Timmermann. Revised Edition. Cambridge: Cambridge University Press, 2012/1785.
—, "On the Common Saying: 'This May Be Correct in Theory, but It Is of No Use in Practice'." In Kant, *Practical Philosophy*, ed. and trans. M. J. Gregor. Cambridge: Cambridge University Press 1996/1793, pp. 273–309.
—, *The Conflict of the Faculties*. In Kant, *Religion and Rational Theology*, ed. and trans. A. Wood and G. di Giovanni. Cambridge: Cambridge University Press, 1996/1798, pp. 233–328.
—, *The Metaphysics of Morals*. In Kant, *Practical Philosophy*, ed. and trans. M. J. Gregor. Cambridge: Cambridge University Press, 1996/1797, pp. 353–603.
Kateb, G., *Human Dignity*. Cambridge, MA: Harvard University Press, 2011.
King, P., *Toleration*. London: Frank Cass Publishers, 1998.
King, V., "Autoritarismus als Regression." *Westend. Neue Zeitschrift für Sozialforschung* 1, 2021, 87–102.
—, "Psyche and Society in Critical Theory and Contemporary Social Research: With Special Reference to Horkheimer/Adorno and Bourdieu." *Azimuth. International Journal of Philosophy* 16: II, 2020, 15–33.
King, V. and Sutterlüty, F., (eds.), "Destruktivität und Regression im Rechtspopulismus." *Westend. Neue Zeitschrift für Sozialforschung* 1, 2021.
Khalil, K., *Messages from Tahrir: Signs from Egypt's Revolution*. Cairo: American University in Cairo Press, 2011.

Kleingeld, P., "Kant's Second Thoughts on Colonialism." In K. Flikschuh and L. Ypi (eds.), *Kant and Colonialism: Historical and Critical Perspectives*. Oxford: Oxford University Press, 2014, pp. 43–67.

—, "Kant's Second Thoughts on Race." *The Philosophical Quarterly* 57: 229, 2007, 573–593.

Kojève, A., *Introduction to the Reading of Hegel: Lectures on the Phenomenology of Spirit*, ed. Allan Bloom and trans. J. H. Nichols. Ithaca: Cornell University Press, 1980/1947.

Kolers, A., *A Moral Theory of Solidarity*. Oxford: Oxford University Press, 2016.

Korsgaard, C., *Self-Constitution: Agency, Identity, and Integrity*. Oxford: Oxford University Press, 2009.

—, *The Sources of Normativity*. Cambridge: Cambridge University Press, 1996.

Koschorke, A., "Öffnen und Schließen: Modellierungen von Zukunft im Kampf der politischen Narrative." Lecture at the University of Essen, November 2017.

—, "Twitter, Trump und die (Ent-)Demokratisierung der Demokratie." *Merkur* 74: 856, 2020, 5–15.

Kymlicka, W., *Contemporary Political Philosophy: An Introduction*. Oxford: Clarendon Press, 1997.

Laborde, C. and Ronzoni, M., "What Is a Free State? Republican Internationalism and Globalization." *Political Studies* 64: 2, 2016, 279–296.

Laden, A., "The Practice of Equality." In R. Forst, *Justice, Democracy and the Right to Justification: Rainer Forst in Dialogue*. London: Bloomsbury, 2014, pp. 103–126.

Lafont, C., *Democracy without Shortcuts: A Participatory Conception of Deliberative Democracy*. Oxford: Oxford University Press, 2020.

Larmore, C., *Morality and Metaphysics*. Cambridge: Cambridge University Press, 2021.

—, *The Morals of Modernity*. Cambridge: Cambridge University Press, 1996.

—, *What Is Political Philosophy?* Princeton: Princeton University Press, 2020.

Lear, J., *Radical Hope: Ethics in the Face of Cultural Devastation*. Cambridge, MA: Harvard University Press, 2008.

Lefort, C. and Gauchet, M., "Sur la démocratie: Le politique et l'institution du social." *Textures* 2–3, 1976, 7–78.

Leibniz, G. W., "Öffentliche Assekuranzen." In *Sämtliche Schriften und Briefe*, Reihe 4, Band 3. Berlin: Akademie, 1986/1680, pp. 421–432.

Leipold, B., "Marx's Social Republic: Radical Republicanism and the Political Institutions of Socialism." In K. Nabulsi, S. White and B. Leipold (eds.), *Radical Republicanism: Recovering the Tradition's Popular Heritage*. Oxford: Oxford University Press, 2020, pp. 172–194.

Lessenich, S., "Doppelmoral hält besser: Die Politik mit der Solidarität in der Externalisierungsgesellschaft." *Berliner Journal für Soziologie* 30, 2020, 113–130.

Lippert-Rasmussen, K., "Rawls and Luck Egalitarianism." In J. Mandle and S. Roberts-Cady (eds.), *John Rawls: Debating the Major Questions*. New York: Oxford University Press, 2020, pp. 133–147.

Lorenzen, P., *Normative Logic and Ethics*. Mannheim: Bibliogprahisches Institut, 1969.

Lu, C., *Justice and Reconciliation in World Politics*. Cambridge: Cambridge University Press, 2017.

—, "The Right to Justification and the Good of Nonalienation." In A. Allen

and E. Mendieta (eds.), *Justification and Emancipation: The Critical Theory of Rainer Forst*. Pennsylvania: The Pennsylvania State University Press, 2019, pp. 76–92.
Lukes, S., "Noumenal Power: Concept and Explanation." *Journal of Political Power* 11: 1, 2018, 46–55.
Manow, P., *(Ent-)Demokratisierung der Demokratie: Ein Essay*. Berlin: Suhrkamp, 2020.
Marshall, T. H., *Citizenship and Social Class and Other Essays*. Cambridge: Cambridge University Press, 1950.
Marx, K., *Capital,* vol. 1. In *Karl Marx, Frederick Engels: Collected Works*, vol. 35, trans. S. Moore and E. Aveling. New York: International Publishers, 1996/1867.
—, *Capital*, vol. 3. In *Karl Marx, Frederick Engels: Collected Works*, vol. 35, trans. S. Moore and E. Aveling. New York: International Publishers, 1998/1867.
—, "Contribution to the Critique of Hegel's Philosophy of Law: Introduction." In *Karl Marx, Frederick Engels: Collected Works*, vol. 3, trans. J. Cohen et al. New York: International Publishers, 2005/1844, pp. 175–187.
—, "Economic and Philosophic Manuscripts of 1844." In *Karl Marx, Frederick Engels: Collected Works*, vol. 3, trans. J. Cohen et al. New York: International Publishers, 2005/1844, pp. 229–346.
—, "Letters from the Deutsch-Französische Jahrbücher." In *Karl Marx, Frederick Engels: Collected Works*, vol. 3, trans. J. Cohen et al. New York: International Publishers, 2005/1843, pp. 133–145.
—, "Letter to Ruge, September 1843." In Q. Hoare (ed.), *Karl Marx: Early Writings*, trans. R. Livingstone and G. Benton. New York: Vintage Books, 1975/1843, pp. 206–209.
—, "On the Jewish Question." In *Karl Marx, Frederick Engels: Collected Works*, vol. 3, trans. J. Cohen et al. New York: International Publishers, 2005/1844, pp. 146–174.
—, "The Holy Family, or Critique of Critical Criticism: Against Bruno Bauer and Company." In *Karl Marx, Frederick Engels: Collected Works*, vol. 4, trans. C. Dutt et al. New York: International Publishers, 1975/1844, pp. 5–211.
—, "Theses on Feuerbach." In *Karl Marx, Frederick Engels: Collected Works*, vol. 5, trans. C. Dutt et al. New York: International Publishers, 1976/1845, pp. 3–5.
—, "Zur Kritik der Hegelschen Rechtsphilosophie: Einleitung." In *Karl Marx, Friedrich Engels: Werke (MEW)*, vol. 1. Berlin: Dietz, 1976/1844, pp. 378–390.
Maus, I., *Zur Aufklärung der Demokratietheorie: Rechts- und demokratietheoretische Überlegungen im Anschluß an Kant*. Frankfurt/Main: Suhrkamp, 1994.
May, L. *The Socially Responsive Self: Social Theory and Professional Ethics*. Chicago: The University of Chicago Press, 1996.
Mbembe, A., *Critique of Black Reason*. Durham: Duke University Press, 2017.
McCarthy, T., *Race, Empire, and the Idea of Human Development*. Cambridge: Cambridge University Press, 2009.
McCormick, J. P., "'A Certain Relation in the Space of Justifications': Intentions, Lateral Effects and Rainer Forst's Concept of Noumenal Power." In A. Allen and E. Mendieta (eds.), *Justification and Emancipation: The Critical Theory of Rainer Forst*. Pennsylvania: The Pennsylvania State University Press, 2019, pp. 93–106.

McCrudden, C. (ed.), *Understanding Human Dignity*. Oxford: Oxford University Press, 2013.
McNay, L., "The Limits of Justification: Critique, Disclosure, and Reflexivity." In E. Herlin-Karnell and M. Klatt (eds.), *Constitutionalism Justified: Rainer Forst in Discourse*. Oxford: Oxford University Press, 2019, pp. 131–156.
Metz, K. H., "Solidarity and History: Institutions and Social Concepts of Solidarity in 19th Century Western Europe." In K. Bayertz (ed.), *Solidarity*. Dordrecht: Kluwer Academic Publishers, 1999, pp. 191–207.
Miller, R. W., *Globalizing Justice: The Ethics of Poverty and Power*. Oxford: Oxford University Press, 2010.
Moellendorf, D., *Cosmopolitan Justice*. Boulder: Westview Press, 2002.
Moore, B., *Injustice: The Social Bases of Obedience and Revolt*. White Plains: M. E. Sharpe, 1978.
Moran, R., *Authority and Estrangement: An Essay on Self-Knowledge*. Princeton: Princeton University Press, 2001.
Mounk, Y., *The People vs. Democracy: Why Our Freedom Is in Danger and How to Save It*. Cambridge, MA: Harvard University Press, 2018.
Mousnier, R., *The Assassination of Henry IV: The Tyrannicide Problem and the Consolidation of the French Absolute Monarchy in the Early Seventeenth Century*. London: Faber and Faber, 1973.
Moyn, S., *The Last Utopia: Human Rights in History*. Cambridge, MA: Harvard University Press, 2012.
Mulhall, S. and Swift, A., *Liberals and Communitarians*. Oxford: Blackwell, 1992.
Müller, J.-W., *Democracy Rules*. London: Penguin Books, 2021.
—, *What Is Populism?* Pennsylvania: The University of Pennsylvania Press, 2016.
Munoz-Dardé, V., "Fraternity and Justice." In K. Bayertz (ed.), *Solidarity*. Dordrecht: Kluwer Academic Publishers, 1999, pp. 81–97.
Nagel, T., "The Problem of Global Justice." *Philosophy & Public Affairs* 33: 2, 2005, 113–147.
—, *The View From Nowhere*. Oxford: Oxford University Press, 1986.
Nandy, A., "Fortschritt." In H. Joas (ed.), *Vielfalt der Moderne: Ansichten der Moderne*. Frankfurt/Main: Fischer, 2012, pp. 53–66.
Narayan, U., "Essence of Culture and a Sense of History: A Feminist Critique of Cultural Essentialism." *Hypatia* 13: 2, 1998, 86–106.
Nardin, T., "Realism and Right: Sketch for a Theory of Global Justice." In C. Navari (ed.), *Ethical Reasoning in International Affairs: Arguments from the Middle Ground*. London: Palgrave Macmillan, 2013, pp. 43–63.
Nassehi, A., "Inklusion, Exklusion, Zusammenhalt: Soziologische Perspektiven auf eine allzu erwartbare Diagnose." In M. Reder, H. Pfeifer and M.-D. Cojocaru (eds.), *Was hält Gesellschaften zusammen? Der gefährdete Umgang mit Pluralität*. Stuttgart: Kohlhammer, 2013.
Neuhouser, F., "Rousseau: Freedom, Dependence, and the General Will." In *Foundations of Hegel's Social Theory: Actualizing Freedom*. Cambridge, MA: Harvard University Press, 2000, pp. 55–81.
—, *Rousseau's Theodicy of Self-Love: Evil, Rationality, and the Drive for Recognition*. Oxford: Oxford University Press, 2008.
Nietzsche, F., *Nachgelassene Fragmente 1885–1887*. In *Sämtliche Werke: Kritische Studienausgabe in 15 Bänden*, vol. 12. München: Deutscher Taschenbuch Verlag, 1988.

Nozick, R., *Anarchy, State, and Utopia*. New York: Basic Books, 1974.
Nullmeier, F., "Eigenverantwortung, Gerechtigkeit und Solidarität: Konkurrierende Prinzipien der Konstruktion moderner Wohlfahrtsstaaten?" *WSI Mitteilungen* 59: 4, 2006, 175–180.
Nussbaum, M., *Frontiers of Justice: Disability, Nationality, Species Membership*. Cambridge, MA: Harvard University Press, 2006.
Owen, D., "Power, Justification and Vindication." In R. Forst, *Toleration, Power and the Right to Justification: Rainer Forst in Dialogue*. Manchester: Manchester University Press, 2020, pp. 150–164.
—, *What Do We Owe to Refugees?* Cambridge: Polity, 2020.
O'Neill, O., *Constructing Authorities: Reason, Politics and Interpretation in Kant's Philosophy*. Cambridge: Cambridge University Press, 2015.
—, *Constructions of Reason: Explorations of Kant's Practical Philosophy*. Cambridge: Cambridge University Press, 1989.
—, "Constructivism in Rawls and Kant." In S. Freeman (ed.), *The Cambridge Companion to Rawls*. Cambridge: Cambridge University Press, 2003, pp. 347–367.
—, *Towards Justice and Virtue: A Constructive Account of Practical Reasoning*. Cambridge: Cambridge University Press, 1996.
Parfit, D., "Equality or Priority?" In M. Clayton and A. Williams (eds.), *The Ideal of Equality*. Basingstoke: Palgrave Macmillan, 2002, pp. 81–125.
Pettit, P., *Just Freedom: A Moral Compass for a Complex World*. New York: W. W. Norton, 2014.
—, "Keeping Republican Freedom Simple: On a Difference with Quentin Skinner." *Political Theory* 30: 3, 2002, 339–356.
—, *On the People's Terms: A Republican Theory and Model of Democracy*. Cambridge: Cambridge University Press, 2012.
—, *Republicanism: A Theory of Freedom and Government*. Oxford: Oxford University Press, 1997.
—, "The General Will, the Common Good, and a Democracy of Standards." In Y. Elazar and G. Rousselière (eds.), *Republicanism and the Future of Democracy*. Cambridge: Cambridge University Press, 2019, pp. 13–40.
—, *The Robust Demands of the Good: Ethics with Attachment, Virtue, and Respect*. Oxford: Oxford University Press, 2015.
Piketty, T., *Capital and Ideology*, trans. A. Goldhammer. Cambridge, MA: Harvard University Press, 2020.
Plato, *The Republic*, trans. T. Griffith. Cambridge: Cambridge University Press, 2001.
Pogge, T., "The Incoherence between Rawls's Theories of Justice." *Fordham Law Review* 72, 2004, 1739–1759.
—, *World Poverty and Human Rights*. Cambridge: Polity, 2002.
Powers, M. and Faden, R., *Structural Injustice: Power, Injustice, and Human Rights*. New York: Oxford University Press, 2019.
Preuß, U. K., "National, Supranational, and International Solidarity." In K. Bayertz (ed.), *Solidarity*. Dordrecht: Kluwer Academic Publishers, 1999, pp. 281–289.
Priester, K., *Rechter und linker Populismus: Annäherung an ein Chamäleon*. Frankfurt/Main: Campus, 2012.
Prichard, H. A., "Does Moral Philosophy Rest on a Mistake?" *Mind* 21: 81, 1912, 21–37.
Putnam, R. D., *Bowling Alone: The Collapse and Revival of American Community*. New York: Simon & Schuster, 2000.

Quante, M., "Das gegenständliche Gattungswesen: Bemerkungen zum intrinsischen Wert menschlicher Dependenz." In R. Jaeggi and D. Loick (eds.), *Nach Marx: Philosophie, Kritik, Praxis*. Berlin: Suhrkamp, 2013, pp. 69–87.

Ramose, M., *African Philosophy Through Ubuntu*, trans. L. Dubois. Harare: Mond Books, 2005.

Ratner, S., *The Thin Justice of International Law: A Moral Reckoning of the Law of Nations*. Oxford: Oxford University Press, 2015.

Rasmussen, D. M., "The Symbolism of Marx: From Alienation to Fetishism." *Cultural Hermeneutics* 3: 1, 1975, 41–55.

Rawls, J., *A Theory of Justice*. Original Edition. Cambridge, MA: Harvard University Press, 1971.

—, *A Theory of Justice*. Revised Edition. Cambridge, MA: Harvard University Press, 1999.

—, *Justice as Fairness: A Restatement*. Cambridge, MA: Harvard University Press, 2001.

—, "Kantian Constructivism in Moral Theory." *Journal of Philosophy* 77: 9, 1980, 515–572.

—, *Lectures on the History of Moral Philosophy*, ed. B. Herman. Cambridge, MA: Harvard University Press, 2000.

—, "On My Religion." In T. Nagel (ed.), *John Rawls: A Brief Inquiry into the Meaning of Sin and Faith With "On My Religion."* Cambridge, MA: Harvard University Press, 2009, pp. 266–269.

—, *Political Liberalism*. Expanded Edition. New York: Columbia University Press, 2005.

—, "Reply to Habermas." *Journal of Philosophy* 92, 1995, 132–180.

—, "The Idea of Public Reason Revisited." *The University of Chicago Law Review* 64: 3, 1997, 765–807.

—, "The Independence of Moral Theory." *Proceedings and Addresses of the American Philosophical Association* 48, 1974, 5–22.

—, *The Law of Peoples*. Cambridge, MA: Harvard University Press, 1999.

—, "Themes in Kant's Moral Philosophy." In E. Förster (ed.), *Kant's Transcendental Deductions: The Three Critiques and the Opus Postumum*. Stanford: Stanford University Press, 1989, pp. 81–113.

Raz, J., "Facing Diversity: The Case of Epistemic Abstinence." *Philosophy & Public Affairs* 19: 1, 1990, 3–46.

—, "Human Rights in the Emerging World Order." In R. Cruft, M. Liao and M. Renzo (eds.), *Philosophical Foundations of Human Rights*. Oxford: Oxford University Press, 2015, pp. 217–231.

—, *The Morality of Freedom*. Oxford: Clarendon Press, 1986.

Ripstein, A., *Force and Freedom: Kant's Legal and Political Philosophy*. Cambridge, MA: Harvard University Press, 2009.

—, "From Constitutionalism to War – and Back Again: A Reply." In E. Herlin-Karnell and E. Rossi (eds.), *The Public Uses of Coercion and Force: From Constitutionalism to War*. Oxford: Oxford University Press, 2021, pp. 229–333.

—, "Rationality and Alienation." *Canadian Journal of Philosophy* 19: Supplementary Volume 15, 1989, 449–466.

—, "The Innate Right of Humanity and the Right to Justification." In E. Herlin-Karnell and M. Klatt (eds.), *Constitutionalism Justified: Rainer Forst in Discourse*. Oxford: Oxford University Press, 2019, pp. 3–32.

Risse, M., *On Global Justice*. Princeton: Princeton University Press, 2012.

Rorty, R., *Contingency, Irony, and Solidarity*. Cambridge: Cambridge University Press, 1989.
—, *Objectivity, Relativism, and Truth: Philosophical Papers*. Cambridge: Cambridge University Press, 1991.
Rosa, H., *Resonance: A Sociology of Our Relationship to the World*, trans. J. C. Wagner. Cambridge: Polity, 2019.
Rosen, M., *Dignity: Its History and Meaning*. Cambridge, MA: Harvard University Press, 2012.
Rossi, E. and Sleat, M., "Realism in Normative Political Theory." *Philosophy Compass* 9: 10, 2014, 689–701.
Rousseau, J.-J., "Discourse on the Origin and Foundations of Inequality among Men *or* Second Discourse." In V. Gourevitch (ed.), *Rousseau: 'The Discourses' and Other Early Political Writings*. Cambridge: Cambridge University Press, 1997/1755, pp. 113–231.
—, "Discourse on the Sciences and Arts *or* First Discourse." In V. Gourevitch (ed.), *Rousseau: 'The Discourses' and Other Early Political Writings*. Cambridge: Cambridge University Press, 1997/1750, pp. 1–110.
—, "Of the Social Contract." In V. Gourevitch (ed.), *Rousseau: 'The Social Contract' and Other Later Political Writings*. Cambridge: Cambridge University Press, 1997/1762, pp. 39–152.
Said, E., *Orientalism*. London: Penguin Books, 2003/1978.
Sangiovanni, A., "Beyond the Political–Orthodox Divide: The Broad View." In A. Etinson (ed.), *Human Rights: Moral or Political?* Oxford: Oxford University Press, 2016, pp. 174–199.
—, "Global Justice, Reciprocity, and the State." *Philosophy & Public Affairs* 35: 1, 2007, 3–39.
—, "How Practices Matter." *Journal of Political Philosophy* 24: 1, 2016, 3–23.
—, *Humanity without Dignity: Moral Equality, Respect, and Human Rights*. Cambridge, MA: Harvard University Press, 2017.
—, "Justice and the Priority of Politics to Morality." *Journal of Political Philosophy* 16: 2, 2008, 137–164.
—, "Response to Critics." In *Solidarity: Nature, Grounds, and Value. Andrea Sangiovanni in Dialogue*. Manchester: Manchester University Press, forthcoming.
—, "Scottish Constructivism and the Right to Justification." In R. Forst, *Justice, Democracy and the Right to Justification: Rainer Forst in Dialogue*. London: Bloomsbury, 2014, pp. 29–64.
—, "Solidarity as Joint Action." *Journal of Applied Philosophy* 32: 4, 2015, 340–359.
—, *Solidarity: Nature, Grounds, and Value. Andrea Sangiovanni in Dialogue*. Manchester: Manchester University Press, forthcoming.
—, "Why There Cannot Be a Truly Kantian Theory of Human Rights." In R. Cruft, M. Liao and M. Renzo (eds.), *Philosophical Foundations of Human Rights*. Oxford: Oxford University Press, 2015, pp. 671–690.
Sartre, J.-P., *Anti-Semite and Jew: An Exploration of the Etiology of Hate*, trans. G. J. Becker. New York: Schocken, 1948.
Satz, D., *Why Some Things Should Not Be for Sale: The Moral Limits of Markets*. Oxford: Oxford University Press, 2010.
Scanlon, T. M., *Being Realistic About Reasons*. Oxford: Oxford University Press, 2014.

—, "Contractualism and Utilitarianism." In A. Sen and B. Williams (eds.), *Utilitarianism and Beyond*. Cambridge: Cambridge University Press, 1982, pp. 103–128.
—, "How I Am Not a Kantian." In D. Parfit, *On What Matters*, vol. 2. Oxford: Oxford University Press, 2011, pp. 116–139.
—, "Human Rights as a Neutral Concern." In P. Brown and D. Maclean (eds.), *Human Rights and U.S. Foreign Policy*. Lexington: Lexington Books, 1979, pp. 83–92.
—, "Responses to Forst, Mantel, Nagel, Olsaretti, Parfit and Stemplowska." In M. Stepanians and M. Frauchiger (eds.), *Reason, Justification, and Contractualism: Themes from Scanlon*. Berlin: De Gruyter, 2021, pp. 131–153.
—, "Rights, Goals, and Fairness." In S. Hampshire (ed.), *Public and Private Morality*. Cambridge: Cambridge University Press, 1978, pp. 93–125.
—, "The Difficulty of Tolerance." In *The Difficulty of Tolerance: Essays in Political Philosophy*. Cambridge: Cambridge University Press, 2003, pp. 187–201.
—, "The Diversity of Objections to Inequality." In *The Difficulty of Tolerance: Essays in Political Philosophy*. Cambridge: Cambridge University Press, 2003, pp. 202–218.
—, "The Kingdom of Ends on the Cheap." In A. Voorhoeve, *Conversations in Ethics*. Oxford: Oxford University Press, 2009, pp. 179–194.
—, *What We Owe to Each Other*. Cambridge, MA: Harvard University Press, 1998.
—, *Why Does Inequality Matter?* Oxford: Oxford University Press, 2018.
Schäfer, A. and Zürn, M., *Die demokratische Regression: Die politischen Ursachen des autoritären Populismus*. Berlin: Suhrkamp, 2021.
Scheffler, S., *Equality and Tradition: Questions of Value in Moral and Political Theory*. New York: Oxford University Press, 2010.
Schiefer, D., van der Noll, J., Delhey, J. and Boehnke, K., *Kohäsionsradar: Gesellschaftlicher Zusammenhalt in Deutschland – ein erster Überblick*. Gütersloh: Bertelsmann Stiftung, 2012.
Schidel, R., *Relationalität der Menschenwürde: Zum gerechtigkeitstheoretischen Status von Menschen mit kognitiven Beeinträchtigungen*. Frankfurt/Main: Campus, 2023.
Schimank, U., *Differenzierung und Integration der modernen Gesellschaft: Beiträge zur akteurzentrierten Differenzierungstheorie 1*. Wiesbaden: VS Verlag für Sozialwissenschaften, 2005.
Schleiermacher, F. D. E., "Über die Religion: Reden an die Gebildeten unter ihren Verächtern." In G. Meckenstock (ed.), *Schleiermacher: Kritische Gesamtausgabe*, I. sec., vol. 2: *Schriften aus der Berliner Zeit 1796–1799*. Berlin: De Gruyter, 1984/1799, pp. 185–326.
Schmitz-Berning, C., *Vokabular des Nationalsozialismus*. Berlin: De Gruyter, 2007.
Schneewind, J. B., *The Invention of Autonomy: A History of Modern Moral Philosophy*. Cambridge: Cambridge University Press, 1998.
Scholz, S. J., *Political Solidarity*. Pennsylvania: The Pennsylvania State University Press, 2008.
Schroeder, T. and Arpaly, N., "Alienation and Externality." *Canadian Journal of Philosophy* 29: 3, 1999, 371–387.
Sen, A., *Development as Freedom*. Oxford: Oxford University Press, 2001.

—, *The Idea of Justice.* Cambridge, MA: Harvard University Press, 2011.
Shelby, T., *We Who Are Dark: The Philosophical Foundations of Black Solidarity.* Cambridge, MA: Harvard University Press, 2005.
Shell, S. M., *The Rights of Reason: A Study of Kant's Philosophy and Politics.* Toronto: University of Toronto Press, 1980.
Singer, P., *One World Now: The Ethics of Globalization.* New Haven: Yale University Press, 2002.
Sleat, M. (ed.), *Politics Recovered: Realist Thought in Theory and Practice.* New York: Columbia University Press, 2018.
Spivak, G. C., *A Critique of Postcolonial Reason: Toward a History of the Vanishing Present.* Cambridge, MA: Harvard University Press, 2000.
Stjernø, S., *Solidarity in Europe: The History of an Idea.* Cambridge: Cambridge University Press, 2005.
Strauss, L., *Persecution and the Art of Writing.* Chicago: The University of Chicago Press, 1988.
Talbott, W., *Human Rights and Human Well-Being.* Oxford: Oxford University Press, 2010.
—, *Which Rights Should Be Universal?* Oxford: Oxford University Press, 2005.
Taylor, A. E., "Solidarity: Obligations and Expressions." *Journal of Political Philosophy* 23: 2, 2015, 128–145.
Taylor, C., "Conditions of an Unforced Consensus on Human Rights." In J. R. Bauer and D. A. Bell (eds.), *The East Asian Challenge for Human Rights.* Cambridge: Cambridge University Press, 1999, pp. 124–144.
—, *Human Agency and Language.* Cambridge: Cambridge University Press, 1985.
Teufel, E. (ed.), *Was hält die moderne Gesellschaft zusammen?* Frankfurt/Main: Suhrkamp, 1996.
Tilly, C., *Why? What Happens When People Give Reasons ... and Why.* Princeton: Princeton University Press, 2006.
Tully, J., "On Law, Democracy and Imperialism." In *Public Philosophy in a New Key*, vol. 2. Cambridge: Cambridge University Press, 2008, pp. 127–165.
—, "Two Traditions of Human Rights." In M. Lutz-Bachmann and A. Nascimento (eds.), *Human Rights, Human Dignity, and Cosmopolitan Ideals: Essays on Critical Theory and Human Rights.* London: Ashgate, 2014, pp. 139–158.
Unseld, S. (ed.), *Politik ohne Projekt? Nachdenken über Deutschland.* Frankfurt/Main: Suhrkamp, 1993.
Urbinati, N., *Me the People: How Populism Transforms Democracy.* Cambridge, MA: Harvard University Press, 2019.
Valdez, I., *Transnational Cosmopolitanism: Kant, Du Bois, and Justice as a Political Craft.* Cambridge: Cambridge University Press, 2019.
Valentini, L., *Justice in a Globalized World: A Normative Framework.* Oxford: Oxford University Press, 2011.
van der Linden, H., *Kantian Ethics and Socialism.* Indianapolis: Hackett Publishing, 1988.
Walzer, M., "Philosophy and Democracy." *Political Theory* 9: 3, 1981, 379–399.
—, *Spheres of Justice: A Defense of Pluralism and Equality.* New York: Basic Books, 1983.
Waldron, J., *Dignity, Rank, and Rights.* Oxford: Oxford University Press, 2012.
—, "Is Dignity a Foundation of Human Rights?" In R. Cruft, M. Liao and M. Renzo (eds.), *Philosophical Foundations of Human Rights.* Oxford: Oxford University Press, 2015, pp. 117–137.

Weber, M., *The Vocation Lectures*, trans. R. Livingstone. Indianapolis: Hackett Publishing Company, 2004/1919.
Weithman, P., *Why Political Liberalism? On John Rawls's Political Turn*. New York: Oxford University Press, 2011.
Wenar, L., *Blood Oil: Tyrants, Violence, and the Rules that Run the World*. Oxford: Oxford University Press, 2016.
—, "*Political Liberalism*: An Internal Critique." *Ethics* 106: 1, 1995, 32–62.
White, S., "Does Critical Theory Need Strong Foundations?" *Philosophy & Social Criticism* 41: 3, 2015, 207–211.
Wildt, A., "Solidarität." In J. Ritter, K. Gründer and G. Gabriel (eds.), *Historisches Wörterbuch der Philosophie*. Basel: Schwabe, 1995, pp. 1004–1015.
—, "Solidarity: Its History and Contemporary Definition." In K. Bayertz (ed.), *Solidarity*. Dordrecht: Kluwer Academic Publishers, 1999, pp. 209–220.
Williams, B., *In the Beginning Was the Deed: Realism and Moralism in Political Argument*. Princeton: Princeton University Press, 2005.
Williams, H., "The Political Philosophies of Kant and Marx." *Kantian Review* 22: 4, 2017, 619–640.
Wingert, L., *Gemeinsinn und Moral: Grundzüge einer intersubjektivistischen Moralkonzeption*. Frankfurt/Main: Suhrkamp, 1993.
Wittgenstein, L., *Philosophical Investigations*, trans. G. E. M. Anscombe. Oxford: Basil Blackwell, 1968/1953.
Wolin, S. S., *Politics and Vision: Continuity and Innovation in Western Political Thought*. Boston: Little, Brown and Company, 1960.
Wolff, J., "Fairness, Respect, and the Egalitarian Ethos." *Philosophy & Public Affairs* 27: 2, 1998, 97–122.
Wood, A. W., *Kant's Ethical Thought*. Cambridge: Cambridge University Press, 1999.
Ypi, L., "From Revelation to Revolution: The Critique of Religion in Kant and Marx." *Kantian Review* 22: 4, 2017, 661–681.
—, *Global Justice and Avant-Garde Political Agency*. Oxford: Oxford University Press, 2012.
—, "On Revolution in Kant and Marx." *Political Theory* 42: 3, 2014, 262–287.
—, "What's Wrong with Colonialism?" *Philosophy & Public Affairs* 41: 2, 2013, 158–191.
Young, I. M., *Justice and the Politics of Difference*. Princeton: Princeton University Press, 1990.
—, *Responsibility for Justice*. Oxford: Oxford University Press, 2011.
Zürn, M., "Survey Article: Four Models of a Global Order with Cosmopolitan Intent – An Empirical Assessment." *Journal of Political Philosophy* 24: 1, 2016, 88–119.
Zürn, M. and Ecker-Ehrhardt, M. (eds.), *Die Politisierung der Weltpolitik: Umkämpfte internationale Institutionen*. Berlin: Suhrkamp, 2013.
Zwierlein, C., *Prometheus Tamed: Fire, Security, and Modernities, 1400 to 1900*. Leiden: Brill, 2021.

INDEX

active status: political imaginary of
    human rights 137–139
  passive status and 133
Adorno, T. W. 52, 67, 74, 76, 81, 113,
    267, 268
  and Horkheimer, M. 74, 76, 267
agency, exercise of 35
agents vs. recipients of justice 248–250
Ahlhaus, S. and Niesen, P. 75
Alexy, R. 133
alienation
  "double alienation" 75
  first and second order 27, 34, 35, 36,
    41, 45, 48, 49–50, 84
  and normative authority (Kant)
    33–43
  and the inalienable 25–28, 50–53
  see also Marx, K.; Rousseau, J.-J.
Allen, A. 20, 21, 55, 60, 61, 62, 63, 64
  and Mendieta, E. 20
Anderson, B. 95
Anderson, E. S. 245–246
Apel, K.-O. viii, 6, 7, 274
  and Habermas, J. 159, 181
"Arab Spring", Egypt 137–138
Arant et al., R. 103
Arato, A. and Cohen, J. L. 81
arbitrariness 157–158, 161, 167, 180,
    207, 251, 263–264
  justice as fairness vs. luck
    egalitarianism 241–248
Arendt, H. 118, 120, 188
Arneson, R. 247
authoritarian populism 81, 83
authority of justice 161

autonomy
  constructive 251–254
  and freedom 201–205
  moral authority as 37–38
  of autonomy 267–280
  political see Kantian republicanism vs.
    neo-republican machine; political
    autonomy
  resistance and demand for 163
  Rousseau's notion of 38–40, 195, 203
  see also dignity; moral autonomy;
    normative authority
Avant, D. D. et al. 174
Azmanova, A. 20

Bajaj, S. and Rossi, E. 21, 123
Banting, K. and Kymlicka, W. 85
Barry, B. 233
Bayertz, K. 85, 86
Bayle, P. 68, 69, 218, 227–233
Beitz, C. 134, 143
Bejan, T. 21, 227
Benhabib, S. 20, 67, 99, 119–120, 125,
    128, 129
Benjamin, W. 268
Berlin, I. 86
Bertelsmann Foundation: cohesion study
    102–103
Blake, M. 167
Bloch, E. 136, 178
Bodin, J. 227
Bohman, J. 176
Boltanski, L. and Thévenot, L. 130, 185
Bourdieu, P. 186
Brown, W. 74, 95

300

INDEX

Brunkhorst, H. 85, 94
Buchanan, A. 19, 135
  and Powell, R. 57

Caney, S. 20, 154, 169–170, 249
capitalism 67, 79–80, 110
  and alienation 46–48
Castro Varela, M. d. M. and Dhawan, N. 190
categorical imperative 7, 33
  and alienation 34, 45
  and human rights 142, 145
causal–normative fallacy 80–81
cave paradox (Plato) 117–118, 120–121
Celikates, R. and Jaeggi, R. 15
Chakrabarty, D. 155
Chambers, S. 20
Chan, J. et al. 103
China 58
Christman, J. 21
choice vs. circumstance 243–245
Ci, J. 42
Cohen, G. A. 96, 240, 249, 264
Cohen, H. 50
Cohen, J. 32
  and Sabel, C. 167
colonialism
  colonial domination 55, 62, 154–155, 163
  Kant and colonialism 14, 37, 42, 55
common bond, solidarity as 87, 89, 93
common good: social cohesion orientation 103
congealed and solidified justifications, human rights as 147
consequentialist accounts of injustice 170–171
conservation and production of normativity, principle of 146
constructivism
  and human rights 148–152
  basis not constructed 7, 10
  Kantian 1–14, 220–226, 238
  moral constructivism 10, 199–200, 205
  political constructivism 11, 205, 219
  practical, not metaphysical 6, 222, 259–260
  Rawls's 7–8, 219–226, 238, 260–261
contextualism 64, 65
contractualism 255
  moral justification 255–262
  political justification 262–266
Corradetti, C. 21

Covid-19 pandemic 83, 102, 113
crises
  of democracy see democracy
  of justification 131
  social projects and social cohesion 112–113
critical constructivism (overview) 1–14
critical and realistic theory of politics see normativity and reality and see realism
critical theory 17, 65–66, 69–71, 110, 129–130, 155–180, 182, 189, 267–270
  critical theory principle 68, 126, 161, 165
  of normativity 10, 13–14, 117–131
  of transnational justice 71, 153–177
Culp, J. 153, 175
cultural positivism and parochialism, avoiding 154–155, 164

Dahl, R. A. 121–122, 183
Daly, E. 21
Darwall, S. L. 3, 37
democracy
  conceptual reduction of 78–80
  crises
    and concept of regression 73–75
    and paradox of regression 82–84
  as form of rational rule 78
  guiding culture and permission conception of tolerance 108–109
  as major practice of overcoming alienation 28
  misclassification critiques of 80–82
  normative notion and "democratic iterations" 128–129
  and political justification 262–263
  as practice of justice 5, 79, 128–129, 175, 181, 262
  status quo (ante) fallacy 75–78
  and structural injustice 181
  and transnational justice 174–177
Denninger, E. 93
Derpmann, S. 85
development perspective see progress
dialectics of progress 54–56
difference principle 96, 247
dignity 34–35, 37, 43, 127, 166, 196, 198–199
  and human rights 135–136, 141–143
  see also autonomy; normative authority

301

discursive and reflexive conception of justice 157–161
distributive justice 169–170, 172, 183
procedural 247–248
doctrine of right and doctrine of virtue 196–197
domination 17–18, 29–32, 36, 39, 44–48, 53–55, 59–61, 64–65, 70–72, 77–79, 123, 128, 135–139, 148, 152, 157, 160, 163–177, 178–193, 206–209, 251, 263
and rule, coercion, violence 123, 168–169, 183–187
economic and social 45–48
multiple 173
structural 179–193
see also non-domination; structural analysis
Dragolov, G. et al. 101
Dreben, B. 217, 226
Durkheim, É. 93, 101
Dübgen, F. 61, 163
Düwell, M. 20
Dworkin, R. 238, 240, 243–244
dystopia of control 245–247

Eberl, O. 14
ecological crisis 83
economic exploitation and political exclusion 172, 183
economic globalization 70–71
economic policies and structural racism 191
economic and social alienation 45–48
Edict of Nantes (1598) 107, 232
emancipation 72, 139, 160–163, 183, 279
categorical imperative of 45
and regression 78
reverse orientalism and foundationalism 59–65
Enlightenment
postcolonial critiques of 63, 64–65, 74, 164–165
and toleration 218
Enoch, D. 9, 259
equality 128, 265–266
see also dignity; human rights; normative authority
Erman, E. 20
and Möller, N. 160
Esping-Andersen, G. 93
Estlund, D. 119

ethical contexts of solidarity 92–93
ethical–political form of solidarity 95

fairness *see* justice as fairness vs. luck egalitarianism
Fanon, F. 163
feminist perspective, postcolonial 64–65, 164
Ferrara, A. 26, 29
financial crisis (2008) 82
Flikschuh, K. 144
and Ypi, L. 14, 42, 55
Flynn, J. 20
Foucault, M. 64–65, 162–165
foundationalism 63
Frankfurt, H. 26, 37–38, 93
Fraser, N. 19, 173
freedom 31, 41, 60, 66
and autonomy 163, 201–205, 208–209
and equal normative authority 187–188, 263 *see also* normative authority
law and reason 197, 201–203 *see* law
as non-domination 135, 206–210
noumenal freedom 33–34
reasonable freedom 270, 277
right to freedom 144, 148
true freedom 40, 43–44
Fritsch, M. 20
fundamental and full justice distinction 11, 205–206, 264
fundamental transnational justice 174–175

Gädeke, D. 56, 163, 188
Gallie, W. B. 91
Gauchet, M. 136
and Lefort, C. 49
Gearty, C. 137
Geiselberger, H. 73
gender: postcolonial feminist perspective 64–65, 164
genealogy, vindicative 269
general and reciprocal justification 5–6, 10, 12, 37, 66–69, 131, 145, 152, 158–160, 166, 174, 180–181, 187, 196, 198, 200, 261–263 *see* justification
and human rights 145, 148, 149
and transnational (in-)justice 158–159, 160–161, 167–168, 174
German Research Institute Social Cohesion (RISC) 103–104
Gethmann, C. F. 65

Geuss, R. 120, 160, 161
Giddens, A. 186
Gilabert, P. 20, 50
global migration crisis 83
globalization as economic domination 70–71
Goethe, J. W. 107
Gordon, P. 76
Gould, C. C. 89
Gramsci, A. 74, 192
Griffin, J. 146
Günther, K. 139
  and Forst, R. 120, 184

Habermas, J. 20, 31, 56, 60, 74, 96, 210, 211, 236
  and Apel, K.-O. 159, 181
  autonomy of autonomy 267–280
  normativity and reality 120, 126, 129
  transnational (in-)justice 161, 165, 176
Hale, T. et al. 57, 174
happiness 38, 198
Harel, A. 21
Hartmann, M. and Offe, C. 101
Haslanger, S. 192
Haugaard, M. and Kettner, M. 20, 122, 188
Hayward, C. R. 179, 189, 190–191, 192, 193
  and Lukes, S. 189
Hegel, G. W. F. 25, 26, 27, 66, 68, 93, 101, 195, 272, 277
  and young Hegelians 276–280
Heidegger, M. 66
Herder, J. G. 270
Herlin-Karnell, E. 21
  and Klatt, M. 20
Herman, B. 9, 99, 273
Hiebaum, C. 21
Hinshelwood, A. 38
historicism, subaltern reason and critique of 65–70
Hobbes, T. 28–29
Honneth, A. 2, 36, 65–66, 194–195, 196, 211
Horkheimer, M. 267
  and Adorno, T. W. 74, 76, 267
Horton, J. 21
Howard, D. 49
human rights 132–136
  constructing 148–152
  grounds of 140–148
  point of 136–140

Hume, D. 99, 271–272, 276
Hunt, L. 136

ideology
  as justifying the unjustifiable 3, 78, 185
  Marx on ideology 43–44
  and narratives of justification 124–126
  and power 122, 192
Ignatieff, M. 133
"immanent" critique 66–67, 159–160
individual alienation and political solution 28–33
inequality 2, 30, 182
innate right to independence 141–142, 143–145, 148, 204, 210
instrumentalization and lack of control 43–50
intellectual–noumenal and empirical dualism 1–14
international legal rights, human rights as 134–135
Iser, M. 21, 27, 64

Jaeggi, R. 26, 77, 86
  and Celikates, R. 15
James, A. 224
Jay, M. 267
Jellinek, G. 133
justice as fairness vs. luck egalitarianism 240–241
  constructive autonomy 251–254
  moral arbitrariness 241–248
  two paradigms 248–254
justice as justification 59, 129, 153, 158–160, 180–181, 207, 250–251
  basic structure of justification 11
  fundamental and full justice 11, 205–206, 264
  see also democracy; general and reciprocal justification; right to justification
justice and solidarity 96–98
justification see also general and reciprocal justification
  concept of social cohesion 110–112
  contested and contestable 156
  critical and realistic theory of politics see normativity and reality
  modernization perspective see progress
justification fundamentalism see contractualism

Kant, I. 33–39, 48–54, 107, 194–204, 215–223, 233, 257, 270–272
Kantian constructivism 1–14, 220–226, 238
Kantian republicanism vs. neo-republican machine
　moral groundwork 196–200
　normative authority 194–196
　republicanism and recognition 210–211
　right to justification in political and legal contexts 200–206
　two conceptions of non-domination and neo-republican machine 206–210
　see also non-domination
Kateb, G. 142
Kettner, M. and Haugaard, M. 20, 122, 188
Khalil, K. 137
Kierkegaard, S. 276
King, P. 106
King, V. 74, 84
　and Sutterlüty, F. 73
kingdom of ends 4, 34–35, 36, 142, 143–144, 199, 200–201, 257, 262, 274, 280
Klatt, M. 21
　and Herlin-Karnell, E. 20
Kleingeld, P. 37
Kojève, A. 27
Kolers, A. 85
Korsgaard, C. 9, 34, 37, 257
Koschorke, A. 81, 110
Kukathas, C. 21
Kymlicka, W. 242–243, 246

Laborde, C. and Ronzoni, M. 176
Laden, A. S. 20, 68
Lafont, C. 80
Larmore, C. 6, 9, 118, 160, 238
Law
　and human rights 143–144, 148–149
　laws of freedom (Kant) 196–201
　persons as law-givers and subjects of the law 34, 127–128, 141, 152, 196, 272
　reciprocally and generally justifiable 32, 144
　rule of law 119, 208
　and solidarity 87, 93–95
　U.S. laws and social structures 190
Lear, J. 42

Lefort, C. and Gauchet, M. 49
legal contexts
　of right to justification 200–206
　of solidarity 93–95
Legitimacy 44, 67,123, 223
　and democracy 82
　justified authority to rule 194
　as normatively dependent 91
　Rawls's liberal principle of legitimacy 236–237
Leibniz, G. W. 93
Leipold, B. 48
Lessenich, S. 97
Linden, van der M. 50
Lippert-Rasmussen, K. 247
Lorenzen, P. 6
Lu, C. 21, 42, 170, 183
luck egalitarianism
　accounts of injustice 170
　see also justice as fairness vs. luck egalitarianism
Lukes, S. 20, 122
　and Hayward, C. R. 189
Luther, M. 67, 271

Mann, T. 76
Manow, P. 81
Markell, P. 21
Marshall, T. H. 94
Marx, K. 157, 160–161, 188–189, 272, 277
　alienation
　　comparative view 25–28, 50–53
　　instrumentalization and lack of control 43–50
Maus, I. 32
May, L. 85
Mbembe, A. 71, 72
McCarthy, T. 55
McCormick, J. 21, 122
McCrudden, C. 141
McNay, L. 21, 123
Menke, C. 19
Metz, K. H. 93
Miller, R.W. 168
Miller, S. C. 21
modernization perspective *see* progress
modus vivendi 220, 227, 234
Moellendorf, D. vii, 156, 178
Möller, N. and Erman, E. 160
Montaigne, M. de 37
Moore, B. 170, 181–182
"pan-human sense of injustice" 162

INDEX

moral authority, autonomy as 37–38
moral autonomy 13, 38, 143, 197, 270–277
  and autonomy of morality 197–198, 270–276
  and political autonomy 31, 32–33
moral constructivism 10, 199–200, 205
moral contexts of solidarity 98–99
moral "encouragement" 276–280
moral groundwork 196–200
morality and the good 9, 13, 27, 38, 146, 198,
  distinction between questions of the good and the just 15, 219–220, 235
  Plato's metaphysics 117
moral and political alienation 27
moral status and social and political status 166–167
moral–political context of conceptions of human rights 149–151
moral–political progress 56–57
Moran, R. 38
Mounk, Y. 80, 125
Mousnier, R. 107
Moyn, S. 136
Mulhall, S. and Swift, A. 232
Müller, J.-W. 80, 125
multiple domination 173
Munoz-Dardé, V. 98
mysticism 44, 46, 50
  see also religion

Nagel, T. 118, 167
Nandy, A. 54
Narayan, U. 64, 164–165
Nardin, T. 168
narratives
  structures and reality 124–125
  U.S. racial 190–191
Nassehi, A. 105
nationalism 89, 90, 95, 113
negative republicanism 207
neo-republicanism 18, 163, 176, 187–188, 194–211, 263
Neuhouser, F. 29, 32
Nietzsche, F. 52, 105
non-domination 18, 32–33, 41, 45, 55, 59–60, 128, 133, 136, 144, 163, 169, 182, 195–196, 204, 206–210, 263
  two conceptions of 206–210
normative authority 194–196, 263

and alienation 33–43
equal 5–6, 12, 31, 97–98, 127, 128, 251
  see also dignity; human rights
normative dependency and solidarity 89–99
normativity and reality
  critique of relations of justification 129–130
  justification as mediating term 119–121
  loss of shared language in political science 118–119
  narratives, structures and reality 124–125
  power of justifications 121–124
  realistic normative view 126–127
  strong normative program 127–129
  summary and conclusion 130–131
  see cave paradox (Plato)
noumenal alienation 27, 34–36, 43–53, 84
  see also alienation
noumenal capital 124, 186, 189
noumenal power 4, 51, 71, 121–123, 184–188
Nozick, R. 241, 251–252
Nullmeier, F. 93
Nussbaum, M. 154, 242

O'Neill, O. 3, 6, 140, 158, 219, 226
Olson, K. 20
oppression 72, 79, 112, 182, 188
  call for democracy as an instrument of oppression 83
  dialectic of liberation and oppression 138
  political and legal 46
  and sense of justice 181–182
  sexual 63
orders of justification 3, 156, 185
  see also normativity and reality
orientalism 60–62
  and Other 64–65, 154–155, 164–165
  reverse 63–64
  subaltern reason and critique of historicism 65–70
other-directedness: slave metaphor 29
others: moral contexts of solidarity 98–99
Owen, D. 21, 98, 123

Parfit, D. 250

parochialism and cultural positivism, avoiding 154–155, 164
permission conception of tolerance 107, 108
person, conceptions of 202–203
patriarchy 186
Peirce, C. S. 274
Pettit, P. 133, 176, 188 206–210
philistines 43–44
Piketty, T. 185
pluralism 154–155, 163, 218, 227
Pogge, T. 168, 171, 252
point of justice *see* justice as fairness vs. luck egalitarianism
political autonomy 39–40
  and moral autonomy 31, 32–33
  and social autonomy 48–49
  see also Kantian republicanism vs. neo-republican machine
political constructivism 205
political contexts
  construction of conception of human rights 150–151
  right to justification 200–206
  of solidarity 95–98
political domination, dimensions of 188
political exclusion and economic exploitation 172, 183
political liberalism
  ambiguities 237–239
  familiar interpretation of 215–217
  impossibility of practice-dependent hermeneutics 224–226
  problem of 217–220
  relating political conception and comprehensive doctrines in right way 230–237
  toleration and reason 226–230
political science, loss of shared language in 118–119
political–social form of solidarity 95–96
positivism
  cultural 154–155, 164
  practice 155–157
  resistance 157
postcolonial perspective 63, 64–65, 74, 164–165
  subaltern reason and critique of historicism 65–70
power *see* noumenal power
power, rule and domination 123, 183–188
power of justifications 121–124

power struggles 125–126, 131
Powers, M. and Faden, R. 189
practical attitude, solidarity as 87, 89
practical reason, principle of 160
practice positivism, avoiding 155–157
pre-social considerations of (in-)justice 242–243
Preuß, U. K. 93
Prichard, H. A. 13
Priester, K. 81
procedural distributive justice 247–248
progress
  conception of 77–78
  dialectics of 54–56
  emancipation, reverse orientalism and foundationalism 59–65
  moral–political 56–57
  self-determined 57–59
  subaltern reason and critique of historicism 65–70
proportionality principle 174, 176
Putnam, R. D. 101

Quante, M. 46

racial narratives, U.S. 190–192
Ramose, M. 70, 72
Rasmussen, D. M. 48
Ratner, S. 136
Ratzinger, J. 269
Rawls, J. 7–8, 86, 96, 103, 145, 210, 227, 230, 263–264, 268
  transnational (in)justice 154, 157–158, 168
  see also justice as fairness vs. luck egalitarianism; political liberalism
Raz, J. 146, 232
realism 9, 17, 118, 259
  critical realism 153–154
reality and normativity *see* normativity and reality
reason
  practical 5, 7–14, 12, 14, 19, 61, 143, 145, 148, 160, 180, 197, 200, 218–224, 257–262
  right to 70–72
  subaltern 65–70
  toleration and 226–230
reasonable pluralism 218, 227
reciprocity
  procedural and reciprocal justice 247–248
  and solidarity 88, 96

INDEX

see also general and reciprocal justification
recognition 194–195, 210–211
reflective equilibrium 86–87, 224
reflexive approach to human rights 135, 140–141, 144–145, 150, 151, 152
reflexive and discursive conception of justice 157–161
reflexive universalism 165
rejectability 19, 250, 255–256, 259
relational view
  structural domination 188–193
  vs. non-relational view in transnational (in)justice 165–166, 168, 169–170, 171–172
relations of justification, critique of 130
religion
  and alienation 44–45
  secular and postmetaphysical morality 270–276
  secular translation of 268–270
  toleration and reason 226–230
republican account of alienation 38–39, 48–49
republican and non-republican order 41–42
resistance *see* active status: political imaginary of human rights; transnational (in-)justice
respect conception of tolerance 107–108
responsibility 189–190
reverse orientalism 63–64
right, doctrine of 196–197
right to justification 5, 8, 10, 13, 27, 41, 59, 61, 68, 80, 127, 140–148, 152, 160–163, 171–172, 199–204, 207, 251
  and democracy 80, 82, 84
  and duty of 144–146
  human rights 140–148
  and normativity 127–128, 145–147
  in political and legal contexts 200–206
  and progress 59, 61–62, 63, 64, 65, 67–68
  transnational (in-)justice 162–163, 166, 171–172
  see also justice as justification
Ripstein, A. 21, 40–41, 144, 196, 205
Risse, M. 172
Rorty, R. 65, 217, 226
Rosa, H. 26
Rosen, M. 141

Rossi, E.
  and Bajaj, S. 21, 123
  and Sleat, M. 160
Rostbøll, C. 21
Rousseau, J.-J.
  alienation
    comparative view 25–28, 50–53
    individual, and political solution 28–33
  notion of autonomy 38–40, 195, 203
  romanticism 52
Rummens, S. 20
rule, concept of 123, 187

Said, E. 62, 154–155
Sangiovanni, A. 19, 20, 21, 166, 167–168, 224
Sartre, J.-P. 27
Satz, D. 52
Scanlon, T. M. 10, 235, 255–266
Schäfer, A. and Zürn, M. 73, 75
Scheffler, S. 243
Shelby, T. 85
Shell, S. M. 32
Schidel, R. 14
Schiefer, D. et al. 103
Schimank, U. 101
Schleiermacher, F. D. E. 74
Schlink, B. 21
Schmitz-Berning, C. 89
Schneewind, J. B. 3, 195
Scholz, S. J. 85
Schroeder, T. and Arpaly, N. 26
self and social alienation *see* first and second order alienation
self-determination *see* autonomy
self-determined progress 57–59
Sen, A. 58, 154
shared identity, solidarity as 87, 89
shared language in political science, loss of 118–119
Singer, P. 171
Skinner, Q. 207
slave metaphor of alienation 29–32, 36–37, 43–44
Sleat, M. 118, 160
social cohesion 101–102
  justification narratives and justice 110–112
  levels of 104
  neutral core definition 102–105
  social projects and crises 112–113
  tolerance and solidarity 105–110

social contract
  and alienation 31, 32
  see also contractualism
social justice movements 96
social and political autonomy 48–49
solidarity
  concept of 87–89
  contested and elusive concept of 85–87
  and normative dependency 89–99
  and social cohesion 109
  summary and conclusion 99–100
Spivak, G. C. 61, 71
status quo (ante) fallacy 75–78
Stjernø, S. 85
Strauss, L. 118
strong normative program 127–129
structural analysis
  antinomy 178–180
  domination 179–193
  (in-)justice 180–183
  power, rule and domination 183–188
subaltern reason and critique of historicism 65–70
subjection 172–173, 175–176, 182
Susen, S. 20, 188
suum cuique (to each his own) 248–251

Talbott, W. 133, 146
Taylor, A. E. 89, 93
Taylor, C. 125, 154
technological and social progress 56, 57–58, 59
Tilly, C. 125
tolerance/toleration
  and contractualism 265–266
  and reason 226–230
  and solidarity 105–110
  two conceptions 107–108
transcendental
  and context-immanent theorizing 159–160
  membership of kingdom of ends 280
  reflection 4–5, 140, 152, 159–160, 181, 274–276, 280
transnational crises 83–84
transnational "democratic iterations" 128–129
transnational (in-)justice 71–72
  avoiding parochialism and cultural positivism 154–155, 164
  avoiding practice positivism 155–157
  constructing 173–177
  contexts of (in-)justice 165–169

critical realism 153–154
nature of (in-)justice 169–173
reflexive and discursive conception of justice 157–161
struggles for justice 162–165
trust
  and loss of stability 42
  mistrust in a luck egalitarian society 245
  and related normatively dependent concepts 52, 105, 111
Tully, J. 56, 139

Universal Declaration of Human Rights (1948) 136–137, 141
universality, transnational (in-)justice and problem of 162–165
Urbinati, N. 81

Valdez, I. 55
Valentini, L. 20, 168–169
value theory of rights 146–147
virtue, doctrine of 196–197
Voorhoeve, A. 255

Waldron, J. 142, 143
Walzer, M. 118, 256, 225
Weber, M. 118, 185
Weinstock, D. 21
Weithman, P. 215
Wenar, L. 168, 217, 223, 233
White, S. 20, 67
Wilde, P. de et al. 112
Wildt, A. 87, 93
Williams, B. 60, 126, 161, 238
Williams, H. 49
Williams, M. 21
Wingert, L. 9, 99
Wittgenstein, L. 86, 157
Wolff, J. 245
Wolin, S. S. 118
Wood, A. 36, 39
World Social Forum 175

Yates, M. 21
Young, I. 179, 189, 192
Ypi, L. 20, 39, 44, 49, 137, 163, 168
  and Flikschuh, K. 14, 42, 55

Zürn, M. 73–76, 81, 175
  and Ecker-Ehrhardt, M. 175
  and Schäfer, A. 73, 75
Zwierlein, C. 93